Praise for *Urban Operations:*
War, Crime, and Conflict

Edited by John P. Sullivan, Nathan P. Jones, and Daniel Weisz Argomedo

The editors of *Urban Operations: War, Crime, and Conflict* have assembled a stellar group of scholars and professionals contributing to this extremely important work. The sixteen chapters address critical contemporary themes including those of the impacts of organized crime and terrorism, artificial intelligence, subterranean operations, and civil protection on the urban conflict environment.
— *Dr. Robert J. Bunker, Director of Research and Analysis, C/O Futures, LLC*

A critical book on a crucial topic: This volume is timely, comprehensive, and remarkably balanced across topics, vantage points, and methods. From proactive intelligence topost-war recovery, from crime to large-scale conflict, the powerhouse and prescient contributions will enable scholars to better understand this complex subject and practitioners to better execute urban security operations.
— *Dr. Kerry Chávez, Assistant Professor, Military & Strategic Studies, United States Air Force Academy and Nonresident Research Fellow, Modern War Institute at West Point*

Urban Operations: War, Crime, and Conflict is a vital exploration into the many facets of urban safety and conflict. This compelling anthology, edited by John P. Sullivan, Nathan P. Jones, and Daniel Weisz Argomedo brings together a diverse collection of case studies and scholarly analyses that span historical events, modern crises, and futuristic hybrid warfare scenarios. From the strategic operations in Antwerp during World War II to recent urban siege tactics in Culiacán, each chapter delves into the critical challenges and strategies of managing security in densely populated areas. This book is essential reading for understanding how urban environments influence security dynamics, the duality of technology in enhancing or

undermining safety, and the continuous evolution of threats within cities. It's a scholarly resource that addresses the past, present, and emerging issues critical for academics, policy makers, and security professionals alike.
— *Sean Costigan, PhD, Professor, Transnational Security Studies, George C. Marshall European Center for Security Studies*

An excellent, wide-ranging survey of many of the complex challenges posed by warfare and violence in a dense urban environment written by the top experts in the field. Required reading for all those interested in understanding the dominant military environment of the twenty-first century!
— *Louis A. DiMarco, PhD, Professor, Department of Military History, USA Command and Staff College*

Over the past two and half decades, cities have become the fulcrum of violent struggle by insurgents, terrorists, and criminal groups. Great power competition reinforces the centrality of cities in yet another type of war. Sullivan, Jones, and Weisz Argomedo and the experts they bring together analyze many dimensions of battles over cities and produce a most timely and valuable repository of knowledge about urban warfare.
— *Vanda Felbab-Brown, PhD, Director, Initiative on Nonstate Armed Actors; Co-Director, Africa Security Initiative; Senior Fellow, Foreign Policy; The Brookings Institution*

Urban Operations: War, Crime and Conflict illustrates the many challenges security forces, police and military, face in urban warfare – from criminal gangs to large scale combat operations. This is a must read for professionals and all those interested in the modern face of war.
— *Professor Michael A. Hennessy, PhD, Head, Defence Studies, Canadian Forces [Higher Command] College*

This informative book could not be more timely. The bloody battles of Stalingrad, Budapest, Manila, Hue, Beirut, Fallujah, Mosul, and Idlib teach us that militaryoperations in urban areas are difficult, deadly, and destructive. But that is just onedimension of a bigger story. This volume reaches beyond the subject of combat in citiesto address a broader constellation of issues-- urban surveillance, high intensity andorganized crime, terrorism, tunnel warfare, civilian protection, safeguarding criticalinfrastructure, civil affairs, post-war urban recovery. These are the complex challengesseen today in Ukraine, Haiti, Venezuela, Gaza, and in places that will feature intomorrow's headlines.
— *Brian M. Jenkins, Senior Adviser to the President of the RAND Corporation*

This book preeminently captures the critically important topic of conflict in the urban littoral regions, a key component of our current reality and preeminent feature of future warfare, and the growing haven of hybrid threat actors. The wars in Ukraine and Israel immediately saw fierce urban littoral battlefields erupt in Mariupol and Gaza City, and this shift in the venue of armed conflict is going to become more profound throughout the 21st Century. Having known and worked with Dr. John Sullivan for a quarter century, there is no one better qualified to compile a work of this stunning magnitude.
— *Hal Kempfer, CEO Global Risk Intelligence & Planning (GRIP), Inc. and Retired Intelligence Officer (LtCol), USMCR*

Urban Operations: War Crime and Conflict offers an unparalleled exploration of modern urban warfare, blending historical insights with cutting-edge analyses. This comprehensive volume, enriched by top scholars and practitioners, is essential reading for understanding the complexities and future trends of urban security and conflict management.
— *Dr. Jorge Lasmer, Professor of International Relations, The Pontifical Catholic University of Minas Gerais (PUC Minas), Brazil*

The United States' law enforcement has protocols that are increasingly sophisticated in the use of intelligence, sector analysis, levels of lethality, and the development of appropriate legal authorities. The US military has not adequately defined the "surfaces and gaps" required for effective urban operations. International law enforcement reflects an Infinity Puzzle: no fixed shape, no starting point, and no edges. Sullivan is one of the few people who has studied and worked in all three sectors.
— *Pauletta Otis, PhD, Professor, USMC Command and Staff College*

John Sullivan, Nathan Jones, and Dan Weisz Argomedo provide a timely and welcomed contribution to the growing literature on the importance of urban operations, and the implications for future warfare. Through an impressive array of case studies and strategic environments, this volume delves into the complexities in dealing with contemporary threats, implications for human security, and what this means for urban recovery—a must read for scholars with a keen interest in irregular warfare.
— *Dr. Alexandra Phelan, Lecturer in Politics and International Relations, Monash University and author of The Combination of All Forms of Struggle: Insurgent Legitimation and State Response to FARC (Columbia University Press)*

In an increasingly urbanised world, densely constructed and populated spaces not only represent one of the most challenging operating environments for military forces but also represent an increasingly common operational reality. This timely volume addresses some of the most pressing contemporary issues around urban warfare operations today. From criminal governance to the role of AI in surveillance, critical case studies and lightening rod issues such as the imperative to protect civilians in urban warfare operations, this excellent collection builds knowledge in a key area and will be of great value and interest to both academics and practitioners in the field.
— *Dr. Rashmi Singh, Professor of International Relations, The Pontifical Catholic University of Minas Gerais (PUC Minas), Brazil and Associate Editor, Perspectives on Terrorism*

Urban Operations: War Crime and Conflict is insightful. Drawing lessons from past urban operations, understanding current challenges to policymakers, warfighters, police, and civilians, and taking a look into the future. Urban warfare is here to stay!
— ***Professor Todor Tagarev, former Minister of Defense, Republic of Bulgaria***

Urban Operations is an essential resource for military leaders and national security professionals. Its detailed analysis of urban conflict, from historical battles to contemporary hybrid challenges, provides strategic lessons and actionable insights. It is an invaluable guide for practitioners seeking to enhance their operational effectiveness in dense urban environments.
— ***BG Rob Wooldridge, Deputy Commanding General for Operations, 40th Infantry Division, California Army National Guard***

URBAN OPERATIONS

War, Crime, and Conflict

EDITED BY
John P. Sullivan, Nathan P. Jones, & Daniel Weisz Argomedo

PREFACE BY Jayson Geroux and John Spencer
POSTSCRIPT BY David Kilcullen

KEYPOINTPRESS
BOULDER, COLORADO

An AUSA Book

Copyright © 2024 by Dr. Nathan P. Jones, Dr. John P. Sullivan, Dr. Daniel Weisz Argomedo (Editors), David J.H. Burden, Michael L. Burgoyne, Fausto Carbajal-Glass, Alex Case, Andrew Craig, Dr. José de Arimatéia da Cruz, Dr. Magdalena Denham, Dr. James M. Duggan, Amos Fox, Major Jayson Geroux, Dr. Russell W. Glenn, Dr. Anthony King, Dr. David Kilcullen, Dr. Jorge Mantilla, Dr. Nadav Morag, Sahr Muhammedally, Dinesh Napal, Gordon Pendleton, Carolina Andrade Quevedo, John Spencer, Dr. Jacob Stoil, Dr. Louise Tumchewics, María Fe Vallejo, (Contributors).

All rights reserved. No portion of this book may be reproduced in any form without written permission from the publisher or author, except as permitted by US copyright law.

KeyPoint Press
Boulder, Colorado
keypointpress.com

Cover design and interior design: Andy Meaden meadencreative.com

ISBN 979-8-9909158-8-6 (hardback)
ISBN 979-8-9909158-3-1 (paperback)
ISBN 979-8-9909158-2-4 (ebook)

www.urbanoperationsbook.com

Cover Images

Front cover: West Mosul, Nineveh, or Ninawa Province, Iraq. Large parts of West Mosul are still in hands of ISIS that is surrounded in the old city. Destruction and fighting in or near the frontline. Iraqi soldiers, along them some members from the elite Iraqi unit called the Emergency Response Division (ERD) using a kitchen ladder to go from house to house and to get closer to the front lines. © Teun Voeten, 18 April 2017.

Back cover: West Mosul, Nineveh or Ninawa Province, Iraq. Large parts of West Mosul are still in hands of ISIS that is surrounded in the old city; Destruction and fighting in or near the frontline. Soldiers from an elite Iraqi unit called the Emergency Response Division (ERD). © Teun Voeten, 18 April 2017.

Dedications

John P. Sullivan:
For Annie

Nathan P. Jones:
For Sofía, Ethan, and Sean

Dan Weisz Argomedo:
For Ashlee, Leo, Patricia and Gabriel,
Thank you for all your love and support

Contents

Abstracts   1

Preface – The Battles of the Past Shape the Wars of Tomorrow
Jayson Geroux and John Spencer   11

Introduction – Urban Operations: War, Crime, and Conflict
John P. Sullivan, Nathan P. Jones, and Daniel Weisz Argomedo   17

CHAPTER 1
Urban Security: From High-Intensity Crime to Large-Scale Combat Operations and Everything in Between
John P. Sullivan, Nathan P. Jones, and Daniel Weisz Argomedo   23

CHAPTER 2
Civil Affairs in Antwerp 1944-1945: Critical Infrastructure and Civil Defense
Louise Tumchewics   35

CHAPTER 3
Urban Disaster Wrought by Man: The Battle for Manila, 1945
Russell W. Glenn   55

CHAPTER 4
Virtual Urban Siege: Modern Urban Siege and Swarming in Culiacán 2019 & 2023
Daniel Weisz Argomedo, Nathan P. Jones, and John P. Sullivan   69

CHAPTER 5
Implementing NIMS: Lessons Learned from the Boston Marathon Bombing
James M. Duggan, John Petrozzelli, and Jay Slattery   97

CHAPTER 6
Urban Warfare: The Recent Israeli Experience
Nadav Morag   125

CHAPTER 7
Artificial Intelligence and Urban Operations
Anthony King   151

CHAPTER 8
Wide Area Motion Imagery and the Colonial Antecedents of Surveillance
Dinesh Napal   169

CHAPTER 9 The Battles of Hue: Understanding Urban Conflicts through Wargaming
David J.H. Burden — 183

CHAPTER 10 Why Cities Fail: The Urban Security Crisis in Ecuador
Jorge Mantilla, Carolina Andrade, and Maria Fe Vallejo — 207

CHAPTER 11 The Political Trajectory of Urban Violence: Organized Crime in Michoacán's Apatzingán
Fausto Carbajal — 233

CHAPTER 12 NATO's path to addressing Urban and Urban Littoral Operations
Alex Case and Gordon Pendleton — 259

CHAPTER 13 Subterranean Operations
Andrew Craig — 277

CHAPTER 14 Creating Light at Tunnel's End: Ukraine's Post-war Urban Recovery
Russell W. Glenn — 303

CHAPTER 15 Black Shabbat: Learning Lessons from the Urban Battles of October 7th
Jacob Stoil — 319

CHAPTER 16 Civilian Protection in Urban Operations: Legal and Policy Approaches
Sahr Muhammedally — 333

Postscript – The Future of Urban Operations in Context
David Kilcullen — 345

Appendices — 359

Appendix One: Book Reviews — 359

Appendix Two: Book Review Essay — 370

Appendix Three: Acronyms — 391

Biographies — 397

Abstracts

Preface: The battles of the past shape the wars of tomorrow
Jayson Geroux and John Spencer

Two urban warfare scholars and practitioners set the stage for this edited collection. They note that the collection provides a diverse and balanced presentation of the scope of issues involved in contemporary urban operations in a range of settings. As a result, the text is a foundational resource that will help shape an understanding of the urban battles to come.

Urban Security: From High-Intensity Crime to Large-Scale Combat Operations and Everything in Between
This was the introduction to the Urban Security issue special issue of the Journal of Strategic Security in the Fall 2023. It provides an overview of the 10 peer reviewed articles submitted for this special issue by 15 authors. It surveys the literature on urban operations and identifies key trends leading to increases in urban security issues including, but not limited to, trends toward megacities, the growth of cities in coastal environments in an era of climate change, and international humanitarian law related to urban warfare. It surveys key urban operations concepts presented in the literature such as feral cities, which are utilized by authors in this volume.

Civil Affairs in Antwerp 1944-1945: Critical Infrastructure and Civil Defense
Louise Tumchewics

In the autumn of 1944, as the Allies moved through France and towards Germany, the city of Antwerp became a key logistics hub owing to its large and, for the time, modern port facilities. Owing to its strategic significance, it became a prime target for German V-1 and V-2 rocket strikes. In order to keep the population in the bombarded city, 1st Canadian Army Civil Affairs took on the challenge of Civil Defense to keep the population safe and the port operational.

Urban Disaster Wrought by Man: The Battle for Manila, 1945
Russell W. Glenn

Urban warfare tends to be intimate. If soldiers do not see the faces of those they kill—and they frequently will—those men and women will hear the screams or muffled groans of the wounded. US forces waging the battle to recapture Manila in 1945 experienced these horrors. Yet it was the noncombatants who suffered far more; 100,000—approximately one of every ten Manileños at the time—died during the fighting. Thousands more suffered wounds, disease or struggled with hunger and malnutrition. Recent fighting in Syria, Ukraine, Khartoum, and elsewhere tells us that too little has changed three-quarters of a century later. Though urban warfare is a special case of disaster, its lessons are relevant when floods, earthquakes, typhoons, or other forms of crisis strike a city. This chapter goes beyond confrontations between enemies and the resultant civilian suffering to identify the challenges inherent in preserving noncombatant life during and in the aftermath of these clashes. *What* is targeted will impact both immediate and longer-term recovery, just as will decisions regarding *how* a force inflicts destruction. The lessons of 1945 have much to tell today's and future leaders preparing for, responding to, and guiding recovery from combat and other forms of urban catastrophe.

Virtual Urban Siege: Modern Urban Siege and Swarming in Culiacán 2019 & 2023
Daniel Weisz Argomedo, Nathan P. Jones, and John P. Sullivan

Modern urban siege is a metaphor for evolved urban campaigns. The template for such attacks draws from the tactics seen in the 26/11 Mumbai attack in 2008 and continued with the 2013 Westgate Mall attack in Kenya, the January 2015 Charlie Hebdo and Hyper Cacher attacks in Paris, and the November 2015 attacks against the Stade de France and Bataclan. These virtual sieges employ swarming tactics, techniques, and procedures (TTPs) to provide a template for urban strife and insecurity. This chapter provides an overview of terrorist swarming tactics, expanding the aperture to review the use of similar TTPs by criminal gangs in Brazil in the Novo Cangaço style high-intensity robberies and raids. The chapter then reviews the October 2019 Battle of Culiacán or Culiacanazo, where elements of the Cártel de Sinaloa (CDS) employed urban siege TTPs to counter the arrest of cartel leaders by state security forces. The second incident occurred in January 2023 when the CDS again employed swarming TTPs in an unsuccessful attempt to thwart the arrest of Ovidio Guzmán.

Implementing NIMS: Lessons Learned from the Boston Marathon Bombing
James M. Duggan, John Petrozzelli, and Jay Slattery

Many opportunities to learn from the 2013 Boston Marathon bombing have not been capitalized on. The terrorist attack was launched in the heart of Boston, a densely populated urban area with a population of approximately 670,000. Those numbers are amplified by the hundreds of thousands of spectators that line the streets along the Marathon route, with most at the finish line on Boylston Street. Two pressure cooker bombs were detonated in the finish line area, killing three and injuring 264. Among the injured were 16 who suffered traumatic amputations. Numerous reviews of the response and investigation identified positive aspects to be expanded upon and others needing improvement. This monograph presents lessons learned within the context of the National Incident Management System. Individuals who responded to and investigated the attack provided insights into what went well and, more importantly, what didn't in the days and weeks following the attack. How would the proper implementation of Unified Command have improved outcomes? Find out from those who were there, have separated from service, and are now free to speak. The lessons presented provide critical guidance for the proper preparation for and response to terrorist attacks in urban environments.

Urban Warfare: The Recent Israeli Experience
Nadav Morag

This chapter analyzes the evolution of urban warfare tactics, technologies, and approaches in Israel. The authors briefly address the nature and constraints of modern urban warfare, examine Israel's early experience with urban warfare during the 1982 Lebanon War, and then describe and assess the development of Israeli urban warfare in a range of wars and operations, starting with Defensive Shield in the West Bank, then moving to the Second Lebanon War, and then addressing a number of conflicts between Israel and Hamas in the Gaza Strip between 2007 and 2021. This chapter will also identify a few overarching trends in the evolution of Israeli urban warfare.

Artificial Intelligence and Urban Operations
Anthony King

It is widely believed that artificial intelligence (AI) is about to revolutionize military operations. Many scholars have claimed that AI-enabled lethal autonomous weapons, especially drone swarms, are about to take over the battlefield. This chapter assesses the merits of those claims in relation to urban operations. Examining the cases of the Joint Special Operations Command in Baghdad in 2004-08 and the IDF's Operation Guardian of the Walls in 2021, it argues that AI will primarily be for military intelligence and targeting rather than lethal autonomy.

Wide Area Motion Imagery and the Colonial Antecedents of Surveillance
Dinesh Napal

Wide area motion imagery (WAMI) technologies are procured by federal and state security institutions across the United States due to their capacity to surveil at an extraordinary scale. Innovation in WAMI development seeks to make them more compact or convenient to use and employ in a variety of situations. The increased use of WAMI, particularly through uncrewed aerial combat vehicle (UCAV) systems and operations, is able to render visible people, communities, and behaviors at an unprecedented level. This has implications for individuals' and communities' perception of surveillance and the ontology of security. The experience of being secured or kept safe is brought about through the surveillance apparatus, which imposes an unending gaze upon the secured population. This chapter argues that WAMI technology replicates the totalizing gaze of colonial surveillance architecture, and its deployment in areas such as Baltimore, Maryland and Dayton, Ohio, reifies disciplinary boundaries around legitimate behavior in law enforcement and warfare.

The Battles of Hue: Understanding Urban Conflicts through Wargaming
David J.H. Burden

Recent years have seen increased interest in the professional use of wargames, and wargames are a potential tool to enable a better understanding of past urban conflicts and to plan for future urban security. While access to professional wargames is limited, hobby wargames have been identified as useful and closely related areas to study. Previous work has identified around 214 manual hobby wargames that deal with urban conflict, but only 5 battles are covered by 5 or more wargames, so provide a reasonable sample for comparative reviews. The Battle of Hue battle had many of the hallmarks of a modern urban battle, with both symmetric and asymmetric opposition, combined arms, a civilian and media presence, and the use of innovative technology. This chapter examines how 6 different wargame designers have approached the Battle of Hue and how their design choices relate to the key characteristics of the Battle of Hue. The chapter also identifies where the principal deficiencies are. The chapter concludes by considering the issues highlighted by these games that wargaming has in representing urban conflict, and how these could be addressed in order to make wargaming a more useful tool to model urban conflict and security.

Why Cities Fail: The Urban Security Crisis in Ecuador
Jorge Mantilla, Carolina Andrade, and Maria Fe Vallejo

Compared to other countries in Latin America, Ecuador was traditionally considered a peaceful territory. However, 2022 was the most violent year in the history of Ecuador, with a homicide rate of 25.6. In particular, the littoral city of Guayaquil (46.6) poses extraordinary challenges to Ecuadorian security agencies, while criminal governance and firepower of criminal armed groups have increased steadily in the past four years. This chapter explores the relationship between ports, violence, and governance in the context of criminal wars. Through a process-tracing method, it studies the path through which Guayaquil ended up in a security crisis between 2018 and 2022. Using in-depth interviews, criminal justice data, and direct observations, the authors argue that the relations between states and communities can dramatically change under the perception of state weakness despite the implementation of iron fist approaches as exceptional public safety measures.

The Political Trajectory of Urban Violence: Organized Crime in Michoacán's Apatzingán
Fausto Carbajal

Contrary to the "narco-centric" explanation of homicidal violence in Mexico, this chapter proposes "the political trajectory of urban violence" (PTUV) as an additional analytical category to nuance the developmental process of today´s large-scale violence in Mexican urban enclaves. Building on previous research, this chapter argues that organized crime-related violence in Mexican cities today has unveiled and exacerbated intricate power tensions among private actors—both illegal and, perhaps more importantly, legal ones—which need to be explored by considering the historical evolution of these political processes within a given urban context. The PTUV, then, regards recent organized crime-related violence as part of a continuum of the socio-political complex in urban environments and not only due to criminal conduct or activity per se. Because a concrete case study is central to advancing this research agenda, the chapter posits that repeated outbreaks of homicidal violence in the city of Apatzingán, Michoacán, Mexico, have been the result of a rooted local conflict over land access, economic hegemony, political dominance, and increased urbanization.

NATO's path to addressing Urban and Urban Littoral Operations
Alex Case and Gordon Pendleton

It is widely assumed that NATO has doctrine and operational capabilities for the urban environment. In fact, NATO's urban doctrine had mainly been at the tactical level and was insufficient for large-scale operations in cities or urban littorals. It has, however, invested significant resources to address this over the last decade through its conceptual study and strategic and operational concept development work. These efforts have been well researched, contributed to widely by the Allied Nations and have been rigorously tested and validated through a series of operational wargames.

Subterranean Operations
Andrew Craig

Underground warfare has been around for as long as war itself and remains a complex and wicked problem. Contemporary adversaries have already demonstrated proficiency at maneuvering multi-dimensionally throughout the urban environment, and with the decisive battles of the future likely to be urban, there will be the inevitable need to consider joint and combined subterranean operations. Depending on the underlying geology and history, the urban environment may comprise a complex and interlaced system of natural, historical, and modern-day subterranean networks, features, and facilities. Those using such spaces range from combat forces to insurgents and terrorists, to civilians and organized criminals. Commanders will be heavily reliant on a range of specialist advisors to help facilitate the detection and understanding of subterranea prior to adopting an appropriate military effect and the means with which to neutralize the risk it makes to combatants and civilians. Western military doctrine largely focuses on countering the threat posed by subterranea, but efforts must be taken to look more proactively at how to better utilize this environment for our own means. An urban battle at any scale will necessitate the use of generalist capabilities and the UK military's Defence Lines of Development are used as a logical framework to follow on how to acquire and sustain this. This is appropriate on the assumption that special forces will be reserved as a matter of last resort or for high-value targets. Despite ongoing research and development activity, a strategic, coordinated, and cooperative approach must be shaped as part of international efforts to embrace the subterranean environment. This must now happen at pace.

Creating Light at Tunnel's End: Ukraine's Post-war Urban Recovery
Russell W. Glenn

The US response to Iraq's recovery in the aftermath of 2003 Operation Iraqi Freedom suffered from an initial conclusion that it was the country's petroleum infrastructure rather than its electrical networks that were in greater need of recovery resources. The resulting misallocation of resources delayed power restoration to much of the country and frustrated those in affected regions. Whether the cause is war or a catastrophe sparked by Mother Nature, accurately identifying and correctly prioritizing post-disaster requirements is fundamental to an effective and efficient response. Ukraine has demonstrated a commendable ability to repair war damage even as conflict continues, but ground operations in Bakhmut and elsewhere and continued aerial strikes nationwide mean much will remain to be done once hostilities cease. How best to accomplish that desirable response—one sure to involve hundreds of millions of donor dollars—will be a herculean task, a task greatly complicated by the number of donors, consequent challenges to their effective management, and—sadly—Ukraine's legacy of corruption. History has much to offer in the way of how to address these challenges. Now is the time to draw on its lessons and initiate the process of determining Ukrainian urban areas' post-war needs.

Black Shabbat: Learning Lessons from the Urban Battles of October 7th
Jacob Stoil

On the 7th of October 2023, members of Hamas and its allied forces attacked out of an urban area under their governance known as the Gaza Strip, across a border and into the State of Israel. In places, their attempts to carry out massacres and atrocities resulted in urban combat as the citizens, police, security forces, and military of Israel opposed them. Although there has been much attention given to the Israeli counterattack into Gaza and the urban battles that occurred there starting weeks after the initial Hamas attack, the battles of the 7th have faded into the background. Yet, there is much to learn from the combat of that terrible day. It offers numerous lessons on the defense of cities in friendly territory and the nature of urban security and urban combat. This chapter examines two battles in particular—those in the cities of Ofakim and Sderot. It provides a chronology of some of the key events during the operation but, more importantly, draws some critical lessons for students and practitioners of urban security.

Civilian Protection in Urban Operations: Legal and Policy Approaches
Sahr Muhammedally

The humanitarian consequences of urban warfare—as seen in Aleppo, Gaza, Kyiv, Khartoum, Marawi, Mosul, and Raqqa—demand an improved approach to warfighting. The complexity of the urban battle, with its terrain, population, and infrastructure, creates unique problems for commanders to select appropriate means and methods of warfare, enable mission success, protect their forces, operate within the rules of international humanitarian law (IHL), and integrate civilian protection as a strategic requirement. This chapter provides an overview of core IHL rules and cites new strategic and policy approaches to civilian protection undertaken by some militaries that, if implemented, can reduce civilian harm.

Future Urban Operations in Context
David Kilcullen

Urban conflict forms part of a complex adaptive system and is shaped by demographic, economic, technological, and organizational changes, which can be studied to predict general future trends. The author notes the books' ability to expose current urban conflict types, including organized crime, guerrilla warfare, and large-scale combat, to hypothesize about future urban operations. Kilcullen summarizes the main hypotheses in the book, which include the acceleration of state-on-state high-intensity urban conflict, the increasing importance of interior and subterranean spaces for maneuver, the impact of space as a warfighting domain, the rise of info-kinetic operations, weaponization of urban environments, expanded use of robotics and AI, and the trend towards remote, collaborative engagement by small, distributed teams. The concept of a combat fitness landscape is used to analyze how adaptive traits proliferate, and maladaptive ones diminish, influencing future urban conflict. The author concludes that by examining today's traits and behaviors, it is possible to identify elements of future urban warfare that are already emerging. Continuous monitoring of these hypotheses through observable indicators will help validate these predictions and guide strategic planning for the future.

Preface

The Battles of the Past Shape the Wars of Tomorrow

Jayson Geroux and John Spencer

Operations within the urban environment have prevailed throughout human history due to the fact that people have been fighting each other for thousands of years and have built and lived in cities for almost just as long. However, the recognition of these two factors repeatedly colliding in the past, how urban operations have become more frequent as the world continues to rapidly urbanize in the present, and the opinion that all of these factors will lead to even more conflict in cities for the foreseeable future, is only just becoming the more dominant thought in a number of circles—government, military, policing, media, and academic.

Although society has awakened to the reality that there will be continued and growing urban conflicts, the focus of this particular topic tends to drift toward the military context. Military history in and of itself has always tended to draw its fair share of interest. However, the larger study of military history in general has within it the subject of urban warfare history in particular, and when one mentions the latter subject, it often has both military and civilian personnel raising an eyebrow due to curious interest. At its simplest and most cliché, it is merely seen as soldiers clearing rooms and incurring an alarming number of casualties. Then, if one's interest becomes more investigative, the challenges of conducting combat operations in the urban environment become more apparent and even overwhelming. After more serious study, it then elicits one of two common reactions from both military and civilian alike—either complete revulsion due to those complexities and the number of military and civilian casualties created, which in turn drives people away from wanting to know more about it; or continued inquisitive interest in those same complexities to understand how urban warfare battles were and continue to be fought.

As a result of the latter, modern urban warfare—generally recognized as those battles in which conventional, modern militaries fought either symmetric or asymmetric threats in the urban environment from the Battle of Stalingrad (23 August 1942-02 February 1943) to the current Russo-Ukrainian War (24 February 2022-Present) and the Israeli-Hamas War (07 October 2023-Present)—has been a growing emphasis in documentaries, podcasts, media and social media, journal articles and books for the past eighty years.

Within the late 20th and early 21st centuries and reflecting this concern about how to conduct urban operations properly, Western militaries have slowly implemented more and more urban operations training into their courses and exercises, while military alliances are having more conferences with the subject included. Militaries are updating their doctrinal publications on urban operations due to the new (and old but still relevant) lessons learned from the number of urban battles that have occurred just in the first two decades of the 21st century. Both military and civilian historians, academics, journalists, and research centers are producing more podcasts, articles, and books on the topic. Journalists flock by the hundreds to wars in general and cities in particular when the bullets and rockets strike buildings, and the tank treads roll over asphalt, willing to brave the dangers in what for them might be only a once-in-a-lifetime opportunity to establish their careers and reputations. Hopefully, while speaking into that camera or having their photo taken, there will be, in the background, people firing automatic weapons from building rooftops and/or big explosions with black smoke and concrete dust filling the air.

Yet, this growing popularity to understand urban conflict in just the military context is arguably erroneous. History has its many fields of study, and within military history there are many topics to research and discuss. Like a city made up of many suburbs and neighborhoods, urban conflict also has many different subjects within it that must be explored in order to understand the urban environment in its completeness. To merely focus on what soldiers, sailors, and aviators (and if a country has them, Marines) do when they are fighting in a city is to only understand a few pieces of the urban puzzle. Those who become invested in understanding the urban environment and the conflict that occurs within it must be prepared to explore the myriad of other important factors that pertain to it. Due to the complexity of the topic, this in itself is quite an overwhelming task to take on, yet if urban conflict is becoming more prevalent in the present and will only dominate in the future, it is nevertheless necessary.

Thus, the importance of this book produced by Drs. Sullivan, Jones, and Weisz Argomedo. The authors whose works have been accumulated and discussed on these pages allow the reader—regardless of whether they are new students to the topic or have been studying it for years—to become immersed in the variety of urban conflict's different fields. Certainly, military urban operations are included: the importance of civil affairs and infrastructure and the difficulties in its maintenance during times of peer-on-peer conflict; the brutality of modern urban conventional combat against an entire, dense city; and the challenges of fighting asymmetric urban enemies over decades in an area of the world which has witnessed reciprocating violence for centuries. However, there are also articles on a nation's internal urban challenges in the form of domestic terrorism, organized crime, and cartels, the techniques these groups use, and the lessons learned from those experiences—good when these parties are defeated; bad when there are no controls in place to limit their actions and an entire city succumbs to their despicable methods.

The consistent and always evolving technological developments that make our lives both easier when used for good and more challenging when used for nefarious purposes also apply to urban conflict, with artificial intelligence and wide area motion imagery now being used in cities. Wargaming has been a popular pastime for several decades. Its appeal in the 21st century has skyrocketed, and its popularity has and continues to entice thousands of more people—both military and civilian—who have become quickly addicted to both its educational and entertainment values. Not surprisingly, independent creators have quickly realized the advantage of creating urban wargames to satisfy the needs of those who are interested in this type of warfare, using their initiative to produce basic games focused on small unit tactics or investing considerable historical research and creating substantially larger games simulating the complex operational and strategic battles that occurred at Huê, South Vietnam (30 January-02 March 1968) and Mosul, Iraq (16 October 2016-20 July 2017).

Given the wide variety of topics within urban conflict, it should not come as a surprise that a number of books have been produced on the subject. With that comes the necessary book reviews by military and academic scholars, and the editors of this volume have wisely ensured to include those as well in order to demonstrate urban conflict's depth and breadth. Interestingly, the background of these books' writers, their contributors and their reviewers are just as varied as the urban topics they discuss, a further demonstration that the subject's growing interest is not reserved for just those in the military—soldiers (active, retired and from various branches/trades), historians, police officers, political scientists, economists, mathematicians, diplomats, scientists, educators, engineers, security specialists, computer scientists, geography specialists, and sociologists have tackled the subject with their unique backgrounds and methodologies. These book reviews discuss their authors' prophetic and modern theories that determine why cities will become more prominent as battlefields, the rising number and challenges of megacities throughout the world, and discussions on understanding a city's complexities complemented with historical military case studies to reinforce those complications.

Of course, to produce a book on urban conflict that covers every single one of its challenges and mitigations would be a fairly sizeable undertaking, and it would result in a rather massive body of work that would require years upon years to research and write, be expensive to produce and time-consuming to read, and only the most dedicated student of the topic would be keen to pull it from the local bookstore's shelf and transfer it to their own bookshelf at home; we will arguably suggest that no author(s) or publisher(s) will ever create the urban conflict equivalent of William Shirer's well-known magnum opus on Nazi Germany. Nevertheless, the growing popularity of the subject due to its past history, present trends, and future commonality requires a multifaceted book that serves as the subject's "start state," with the additional hope that it will serve as the template for many more works to come. We believe the book that you currently have in your possession is that comprehensive foundational work.

Introduction

Urban Operations: War, Crime, and Conflict

John P. Sullivan, Nathan P. Jones, and Daniel Weisz Argomedo

This volume, *Urban Operations: War, Crime and Conflict* started as a special issue on Urban Security at the *Journal of Strategic Security*, Vol. 16, No., 3 (2023). It brings together new contributions from top scholars and practitioners to augment the content of the special issue and provide a comprehensive look at modern and historic urban security operations. It is difficult to imagine a timelier contribution to the academic and practitioner literature on urban security. Global news has been rife with urban security issues, with the top headlines covering the Gaza war in response to the Hamas terrorist attack of October 7th and Russia's February 2022 invasion of Ukraine, which in its initial phase tried and failed to take the urban center Kyiv.

The world has watched Israeli military forces grapple with thorny urban operations that have resulted in what is likely more than ten thousand civilian losses. As the reader will find, this volume speaks directly to the vexing underlying features of urban operations that lead to these phenomena. Beyond terror/insurgent networks, this volume also provides insight into new trends in urban security, like criminal governance in the urban environ (Chapters 4, 10, 11), and new trends in urban operations such as surveillance (Chapter 8), "Artificial Intelligence and Urban Operations" by Anthony King (Chapter 7), underground warfare (Chapter 13), Urban Littoral Operations (Chapter 12), urban post-war recovery operations (Chapter 14), and finally the ever-present imperative of protecting civilians in urban operations (Chapter 16).

This introduction will not recapitulate the special issue introduction entitled "Urban Security: From High-Intensity Crime to Large-Scale Combat Operations and Everything in Between" (reproduced here as Chapter 1), which discusses the content of Chapters 1-11 and Appendices 1-2. Instead, here we will focus on the new contributions from top scholars and practitioners on urban security and operations in the preface by Jason Geroux and John Spencer, postscript by David Kilcullen, and the addition of Chapters 12–16, which were not included in the original *Journal of Strategic Security* special issue.

Preface

Jason Geroux and John Spencer, widely considered some of the top urban security specialists, wrote a masterful preface notable for describing the reactions of policymakers, scholars, and practitioners to the complexity of urban security. They also point to an unfair and undesirable tendency to militarize the subject, a tendency that misses the proverbial boat by leaving out important factors.

Urban Littoral Operations

Alex Case and Gordon Pendleton, authors of NATO's Path to Addressing Urban and Urban Littoral Operations (Chapter 12), cover the important nexus for future conflict of coastal littoral zones and urban operations. The authors were part of the original NATO Strategic Foresight Analysis in 2013, which identified the rising prevalence of urban littoral operations given key world demographic trends. They clearly recapitulate NATO's strategic level thinking on why urban littoral operations will become increasingly important such as coastal population growth and the value of ports. Thus, Alex Case and Gordon Pendleton's chapter on urban littoral ops is an important analysis for near future conflict and describes the development of a NATO urban littoral operation war game set in Naples, Italy in a "futuristic environment called 'Archaria'" (Chapter 16). This chapter provides the reader with an insider's view of NATO's strategic thinking, planning, and thoughtful wargaming development process.

The Gaza War and Subterranean Ops

We write this introduction at a time of difficult urban operations. The Israeli war in Gaza following the horrific terrorist attack by Hamas on October 7, 2023, has led to urban fighting against an entrenched terror network replete with tunnels. It has proved the importance of urban warfare and the difficulties of protecting civilians in the context of well-entrenched non-state actors using tunnels and civilians to shield their positions.

"Black Shabbat: Learning Lessons from the Urban Battles of October 7th" (Chapter 15) by Jacob Stoil covers the urban operations of Israel in response to the "Black Shabbat" attacks of October 7, 2023. He begins with a sobering description of the security failure of the IDF to protect Israel from a dense urban environment in Gaza. Stoil focuses his chapter on incidents of urban fighting on October 7th. The battles of Ofakim and Sderot overwhelmed the Israeli counterterror capacities, which had been based on a response to a 2008 Mumbai-style attack. He found key issues such as situational awareness difficulty in the urban environ and a lack of planning of defensive rather than offensive counter terror ops. Stoil provides important tidbits such as response being complicated when emergency call centers were overwhelmed and calls were rerouted to different intake centers with no ground knowledge. In one case, the mother of a police officer was able to call her son with real-time intel on the location of Hamas commandos from civilian surveillance cameras. He also covers the difficult choices made by advancing scratch forces, which at times halted to care for wounded civilians. The chapter is an incredibly thoughtful and well-written empirical contribution that grounds the reader in the operations of that fateful day.

"Underground Warfare (Subterranean Operations)" (Chapter 13) by Andrew Craig also directly speaks to the war in Gaza, but begins with a historical overview of subterranean military operations. While he points out that subterranean ops are the past of warfare being used for more than 4 millennia in human warfare, subterranean operations are also its future. Most analysts see underground facilities (UGF) as an important future trend driven to some degree by the advent of 20th-century airpower. Craig offers a useful way to categorize underground facilities such as Category 1 natural, Category 2, modern-day urban systems for water and power, and Category 3 UGFs specifically designed for concealment and protection. He goes on to provide an overview of counter-subterranean operations like denial via tactics such as flooding, among others.

Post-War Urban Recovery and Civilian Protection

The war in Ukraine has, from its inception, in February 2022, an urban component. While Russian forces failed in their objective to take the capital city of Kyiv and pivoted to taking areas in the Donbas, and many of their operations are rural-urban areas that have long been strategic targets. The recovery of these urban areas is the subject of a winter 2023 article in the *Journal of Strategic Security* (Vol. 16, No. 4) that appears here as Chapter 14, "Creating Light at Tunnel's End: Ukraine's Post-war Urban Recovery" by Russell W. Glenn. Glenn assesses the lessons of post-urban warfare recovery from Japan and Germany, seeking lessons for Ukraine's post-war future, which fortunately will not be as dire. He points to important lessons learned from Japan and Germany that could apply to Ukraine like a large-scale migration to the capital city.

"Civilian Protection in Urban Operations: Legal and Policy Approaches" (Chapter 16) by Sahr Muhammedally covers the perennial issue of protecting civilians in urban warfare from legal and policy perspectives. It argues that International Humanitarian Law (IHL) and the Law of Armed Conflict (LOAC) and their requirements to protect civilians must be incorporated into all stages of planning and implementation of urban operations. Importantly, this chapter covers the rights of civilians in besieged areas, a particularly relevant subject given the Gaza war and its tactics. Muhammedally also points to the military importance of protecting civilians in urban ops as it benefits the legitimacy of the military mission. Muhammedally concludes with a call for more analysis of IHL priorities in urban operations at the planning phases and "integrat[ing] civilian protection as a strategic requirement."

Postscript

We are honored to have David Kilcullen provide the postscript to this text. Kilcullen is the author of *Out of the Mountains: The Coming Age of the Urban Guerrilla* (New York: Oxford University Press, 2015), which served as one of the key pieces of literature inspiring the *Journal of Strategic Security* special issue on urban security, which is the foundation of this volume. Those articles are reproduced here in Chapters 1–11.

In his postscript looking at the present and future of urban warfare, he describes urban warfare as a complex adaptive system that is difficult to predict. Based on his analyses of the chapters he posits hypotheses about the near future of urban conflict including (1) the return of large scale state on state urban combat; (2) increased importance of interior space both aerial and underground; (3) "space as a warfighting domain" will make urban ops more "legible," "limiting" maneuver at scale; (4) the rise of info-kinetic operations; (5) varied actors will use the city environ and "subsystems" as "tools for combat;" (6) robotic autonomous systems (RAS) "will replace humans for high risk tasks;" and (7) remote engagement "by distributed small teams" will be a "common response" to the complexities of the urban combat environment.

Beyond his hypotheses, Kilcullen's postscript is rich with useful concepts like the fitness landscape, acephalous swarms, and peri-urban zones. As always, Kilcullen is thought-provoking and has established new lines of debate in the urban security agenda with this postscript.

The Purpose of this Volume

This edited volume will provide readers with a comprehensive overview of the key issues related to urban security. Beyond that, it will further provide the reader with a glimpse of the future of urban operations in the context of artificial intelligence, surveillance, post-urban warfare recovery, and the critical issues of the protection of civilians through international humanitarian law application in the planning phases of urban operations. For scholars, it will give a window into the practitioner's understanding of urban operations, and for practitioners, it will provide a wide-ranging conceptual scholarly foundation for understanding urban operations. We are confident that this volume will become a seminal reading for all those interested in urban security, be it urban warfare, criminal governance, responses to non-state actors, technology, and humanitarian protection.

CHAPTER 1
Urban Security: From High-Intensity Crime to Large-Scale Combat Operations and Everything in Between

John P. Sullivan, Nathan P. Jones, and Daniel Weisz Argomedo

Introduction to the Special Issue (2023): Urban Security

Fifteen authors across ten articles in this special issue explore key events that shape our understanding of urban security and provide valuable strategic lessons to better prepare for the growing threat of conflict in urban areas. This volume seeks to compile cases of urban warfare throughout different regions and decades to expose the ever-increasing trends of urban conflict and expose the complexities of urban combat in an increasingly urbanized world. It also provides lessons learned and makes theoretical contributions in areas such as urban warfare, urban conflict and non-state actors, emergency response to urban terror, artificial intelligence (AI) and data processing, and urban security. Battle in urban areas continues to develop with state and non-state actors, so it is crucial to understand the tactics and strategies that have succeeded and failed to continue to create a successful system for urban warfare.

Urbanization has increased substantially over time. The *UN World Cities Report 2022* states that half of the world's population will live in cities in 2020 and that by 2070, 60 percent of the world's population will live in cities.[1] The increase in urbanization will likely produce megacities and mega slums that interact with one another and comprise entire theaters of operation for those seeking to control them.[2] Mike Davis exposed how since the 1970s, slums have outpaced urbanization in the global south, with places like São Paulo's slums representing 1.2 percent of the total population in 1973 and exploding to 19.8 percent by 1993.[3] Cities continue to gain importance as they become critical for the global economy as they produce, manufacture, and connect cities transnationally.[4] Under this new demographic reality, security experts must renew their focus on urban warfare and its emerging challenges. Then Army Chief of Staff, who later served as Chairman of the United States Joint Chiefs of Staff, General Mark Milley, acknowledged that "the Army has been designed, manned, trained and equipped for the last 241 years to operate primarily in rural areas."[5] Milley recognizes the army's need to reorganize to fight successfully in urban areas.[6] As the armed forces adapt their strategies to fight in urban settings, new planes of the battlefield have emerged.

Urban operations include a range of activities spanning urban security for high-intensity crime through riots and disorder, terrorism, conventional and criminal insurgencies, hybrid warfare, and large-scale combat operations (LSCO). Indeed, these varieties of crime and conflict often interact and provide layers (or strata) of complexity and competition for power and profit. John P. Sullivan and Adam Elkus note the strategic importance of urban security and urban operations. The authors explain how urbanization has led most people to live within cities that are fundamentally contested as they have become "commons of political, economic, and thus strategic importance."[7] Contested cities will erode distinctions between national and domestic policing strategies complicating issues of jurisdiction and making urban policy part of a grand strategic policy as cities become critical for national prosperity.[8] The growth in size and importance of contested cities requires new policies and approaches to provide security to these urban centers and to combat globalized gangs that have made crime endemic in many parts of the developing (and developed) world.[9]

At a recent Security Council meeting, UN Secretary-General António Guterres noted that "90% of those affected when combatants use explosive weapons in cities are civilians" and that "50 million people currently face the dire consequences of urban warfare."[10] Despite the historical importance of urban insurgency in the 20th century, as evidenced by the Tupamaros and Marighella cases, insurgency and counterinsurgency (COIN) researchers with a concentration on the rural environment have minimized the importance of urban warfare.[11] The US experience in Vietnam and Afghanistan, Mao's ascendancy in China and its ramifications, and demographic trends of the 20th century may have all contributed to this overemphasis on rural COIN.[12] Conventional and unconventional warfare will increase in urban spaces as the world's cities and population grow.

Scholar-practitioners, including David Kilcullen, Anthony King, Jamison Medby, and Russell Glenn, have identified megatrends that raise the possibility of increased urban violence in the future.[13] These megatrends include population growth, rising urbanization, the expansion of coastal cities, and the benefits of connection found in metropolitan contexts. Kilcullen notes how several growing cities are also at risk because of climate change's sea-level effects. In many urban environments,

"ungoverned spaces" should be understood as places with contested or alternative authority under weak sovereignty.[14] Various actors such as warlords, insurgencies, militias, pirates, or nefarious organizations rule over these urban environments and are only interested in making money.[15] The security community has also come to understand that mega-cities, which are cities with a population of more than 10 million, are much likelier to experience urban conflict.[16]

According to scholars like Medby and Glenn (2002), urban intelligence plays a crucial role in conflict. "Intelligence preparation of the battlefield" (IPB) is an analytical strategy that aims to comprehend how an enemy in an urban environment might respond in eclectic circumstances given terrain and other contingent factors.[17] Several researchers have recently published numerous anthologies, edited volumes, and collections on urban security, exposing the field's expanding popularity. For instance, researchers, including Glass, Seybolt, and Williams (2022), wrote their edited book on the significance of urban violence resilience in the global south.[18] Another example is *Blood and Concrete*, a recent anthology collection on urban combat and its effects from the *Small Wars Journal*, anthologizing many paramount pieces from its website.[19]

The atrocities of urban warfare have become more evident thanks to the crisis in Ukraine. Urban warfare will play a role in the resurgence of great power conflict, whether from nations seeking to recover lost territory or status like Russia and China or democratic countries in the West like Ukraine defending their national sovereignty. Urban defenders in Ukraine's most recent urban warfare received guidelines and handbooks on urban warfare published by academic practitioners like John Spencer. His *Mini-Manual for the Urban Defender* is available on his website in both English and Ukrainian.[20] The dissemination of the handbook from a personal computer located in the United States to social media and then the battlefield illustrates the practical ramifications of scholar-practitioner activity in urban security. This special issue for the *Journal of Strategic Security* seeks to contribute to the critical body of research on urban security. The following discussion recaps the articles featured in this special issue.

Urban Warfare

David J.H. Burden explores the value of wargames for planning and understanding urban warfare and security. The article takes a comparative case-study approach by analyzing the Battle of Hue, an urban battle fought during the Vietnam War, and the wargames produced about it. The author concludes that no single game model can capture urban conflict, but each contains important complexities of the information that can be aggregated. Burden asserts that nested wargaming techniques can help flesh out an approach that uses different critical lessons to help understand the battle of Hue and plan better for future urban conflict.

In their respective articles, Russell Glenn and Louise Tumchewics explore urban warfare conducted during World War II to extract essential lessons on urban warfare that scholars and practitioners can apply to today's Russian-Ukrainian war. Glenn focuses on the battle for Manila in 1945, one of the world's most populated cities. The author details the process of liberating Manila from the Japanese, who had set mines and booby traps and faced off with Americans in close combat. Glenn goes beyond the strategic lessons learned by the US Army to minimize casualties during the battle but goes beyond as he points to the complexities of urban architecture in which a clear recovery plan must accompany destruction.

Louise Tumchewics also looks at conflict within World War II but focuses attention on Antwerp, Belgium, as a vital logistics center. The author follows the Canadian Army Civil Affairs unit responsible for revitalizing Antwerp's civil defense and essential services. The author notes that although V-1 and V-2 rockets were essentially impossible to stop, the Civil Affairs unit still managed to provide the city with essential services and governance. The well-organized Civil Affairs unit also set up a vital civil defense organization and offered valuable insights into maintaining critical national logistics infrastructure despite heavy bombardment. These insights benefit the Ukrainian conflict but may also provide useful insights for urban warfare, including non-state actors seeking control over urban populations.

Urban Conflict and Violent Non-State Actors (VNSAs)

Daniel Weisz Argomedo, Nathan P. Jones, and John P. Sullivan focus primarily on urban warfare against violent non-state actors (VNSAs) in

México. The authors focus on the two military operations conducted to capture Ovidio Guzmán in Culiacán (son of El Chapo) and the valuable insights from the first and second attempts. The authors compare both military operations and discuss the broader risks and implications of modern urban sieges and swarming. In the first operation in October 2019 in Culiacán, the arrest of Ovidio Guzmán led to an urban siege of the city by the Sinaloa Cartel, which ultimately forced his release because of the extreme threats to civilians. The second operation, conducted in January 2023, succeeded in capturing him, in part because of the rapid aerial exfiltration, a generally less urban environment, and a casualty-acceptant Mexican security force strategy. It is notable that as this issue goes to press, the Mexican government extradited Ovidio Guzmán to Chicago in record time.[21]

On the other hand, Fausto Carbajal focuses on Michoacán's Apatzingán, uncovering urban violence's historical and political trajectory. The author reveals how organized crime is not solely responsible for violence experienced in Apatzingán. Instead, the author argues that the instability is caused by the reconfiguration of political-economic-criminal factions fighting over political and economic power.

México is an interesting case study for urban warfare as it faces increasingly sophisticated organized crime groups (OCGs), which are also more recently called Criminal Armed Groups (CAGs) in the urban security literature. These CAGs have led to heavy urban fighting nationwide.

Jorge Mantilla, Carolina Andrade and María Fe Vallejo trace the increase in violence in Ecuador, particularly in the city of Guayaquil, which saw an uptick in homicide rates from 2018 to 2022. The authors argue that hardline policies, in combination with a fragmented criminal justice institution, only exacerbate urban violence. The authors note the importance of the prisons in Guayaquil as they govern criminals in the streets and are empowered by corruption and limited law enforcement. Mantilla, Andrade, and Vallejo urge policymakers to consider spatial connections between prisons, violent slums, and illicit economic circuits and to reinstall institutional infrastructures that help prevent and control crime.

Urban Terrorism and Emergency Response

Nadav Morag traces the development of tactics and technologies designed for urban counter-terrorism developed by the Israel Defense Forces. The author traces the evolution of tactics spanning from ground operations in urban settings to focusing mostly on aerial operations. Several overarching trends from Israel's approach to urban warfare in the last few decades have been identified. There is a greater focus on accurate battlefield intelligence, the use of more accurate offensive and defensive weapons, and more focus on air defense systems. There is also a greater willingness to use reservists for ground operations, increased use of combined arms, and a willingness to ensure operations respect laws of war and other legal conventions. The author concludes that Israel will have to continue to adapt as its enemies evolve and present it with new challenges that may require it to continue to evolve its operational doctrine.

James Duggan, John Petrozzelli, and Jay Slattery provide valuable firsthand accounts of the implementation of the incident command during the Boston Marathon bombing. Duggan, Petrozzelli, and Slattery explain how the terrorists selected the Boston bombing partly because of the televised nature of such a large event in a densely populated area. The authors unearth several essential lessons from the attack to better respond to these types of attacks. They find that communication was a fundamental problem both immediately after the bombing, as well as before, given that several officers present at the marathon had no knowledge of radio channels made available to them for the day of the marathon. Other communication issues spanned from the need for a liaison officer to facilitate interagency intelligence to leaks to the media that caused the suspects to go on the offensive. As intelligence and communication can be designed to better respond to attacks, other authors in this special issue have pointed out the dangers of surveillance as a rebirth of past colonial surveillance systems.

Urban Security and Surveillance

Dinesh Napal looks at the issues of surveillance in urban contexts. Napal argues that wide area motion imagery (WAMI) is a new surveillance technology that repeats mechanisms of dehumanization and disposability inherent to imperial and colonial endeavors. Napal shows the links between the colonial surveillance imposed on Mauritius from India with the surveillance provided by WAMI. The author argues that such surveillance does not follow a logic of justice and fairness but seeks to maintain discipline and control over the population. Napal notes the problematic ways WAMI has been applied to specific neighborhoods that perpetuate narratives around "suspect" individuals and communities.

Anthony King also looks at surveillance issues as he explores the importance of artificial intelligence (AI) for urban operations. King asserts that the true potential for AI on the battlefield is not in lethal autonomy. The author uncovers that the true value of AI for urban operations lies in its ability to process data and support intelligence and targeting. Several cases are presented by the author to illustrate the importance of AI for data dissemination and targeting, including the Ukrainian attacks on Russian command posts and logistical hubs.

The Book Reviews

The special issue includes three book reviews and one book review essay all of which review seminal works in urban security over the last two decades. First, Dr. Magdalena Denham masterfully reviews Russell Glenn's *Hell or High Fever*.[22] This comprehensive work touches upon emergency management issues in urban security, conflict, and pandemics.

Second, Amos Fox reviews the seminal *Understanding Urban Warfare* (2022) by Liam Collins and John Spencer. Collin's and especially John Spencer's work has become critically important in the zeitgeist around urban security, especially vis-à-vis Russia's invasion of Ukraine and its urban security implications.

Third, Mike Burgoyne writes an important review in the *Small Wars Journal* anthology *Blood and Concrete*. *Blood and Concrete* is a collection of important essays on urban security covering issues like urban terrorism, urban (COIN) counterinsurgency, and urban insurgency, as well as the tactical and operational issues related to complex urban operations.

Finally, José de Arimatéia da Cruz writes a masterful review essay of four seminal works in urban security. These include Kilcullen's *Out of the Mountains*, an edited volume by Mary Kaldor and Saskia Sassen *Cities at War*, *Blood and Concrete,* edited by Dave Dillege, Robert J. Bunker, John P. Sullivan, and Alma Keshavarz. It also reviews and synthesizes the most recent work of Anthony King a seminal author in urban security studies. King's *Urban Warfare in the Twenty-First Century* is usefully contrasted with Kilcullen's *Out of the Mountains*.[23] These reviews and review essays represent a useful starting point for any scholar or practitioner beginning their urban security journey and looking for seminal works.

Conclusions

Richard J. Norton describes a feral city as a Metropolis with a population of more than a million people in a state where the government has lost the ability to maintain the rule of law within the city's boundaries yet remains a functioning actor in the greater international system.[24]

He asserts that these feral cities can provide safe havens for armed resistance groups that can then contest the power of the state.[25] Robert J. Bunker and John P. Sullivan note the potential rise of a globalized network among feral cities that flourish in the global illicit economy as criminal enterprises compete for a stake in the licit and illicit global economies.[26] The authors warn that the flourishing of feral cities and mega slums is forming a confederation of illicit non-state actors linked globally that challenges states and their structure of governance, security, and economic power.[27]

Overall, this peer-reviewed special issue presents useful case studies regarding urban warfare and security that help develop a more complex understanding of the phenomenon. The cases spanned various locations, actors, and periods, but they all help inform one another and build a practical list of recommendations for current or future urban warfare.

Several authors present vital strategic solutions and lessons learned from these operations. Others focus more on the mechanisms that lead to urban violence, and some offer a cautionary tale for using WAMI surveillance. All authors agree that urban warfare is a growing challenge that requires further research to develop better combat strategies in urban settings.

Endnotes

1. Neil Khor, Ben Arimah, Raymond Otieno Otieno, Matthijs van Oostrum, Mary Mutinda, and Judith Oginga Martins, *World Cities Report 2022: Envisaging the Future of Cities* (Nairobi: United Nations Human Settlements Programme, 2022), https://unhabitat.org/sites/default/files/2022/06/wcr_2022.pdf.
2. John P. Sullivan and Adam Elkus, "Command of the Cities: Towards a Theory of Urban Strategy," *Small Wars Journal*, (September 26, 2011), https://smallwarsjournal.com/jrnl/art/command-cities-towards-theory-urban- strategy.
3. Mike Davis, *Planet of Slums*, (New York: Verso, 2006).
4. Saskia Sassen, *The Global City* and *Cities in a World Economy*, (London: Pine Forge Press, 1994).
5. Tan, Michelle. "Army Chief: Soldiers Must Be Ready To Fight in 'Megacities.'" *Defense News*, October 5, 2016. https://www.defensenews.com/digital-show-dailies/ausa/2016/10/05/army-chief-soldiers-must-be-ready-to-fight-in-megacities/.
6. Tan, "Army Chief: Soldiers Must Be Ready."
7. Sullivan and Elkus, "Command of the Cities."
8. Sullivan and Elkus, "Command of the Cities."
9. John P. Sullivan and Adam Elkus, "Global Cities – global gangs," *Open Democracy*, (December 2, 2009), https://www.opendemocracy.net/en/opensecurity/global-cities-global-gangs/.
10. "Urban Warfare Devastates 50 Million People Worldwide, Speakers Tell Security Council, Calling for Effective Tools to End Impunity, Improve Humanitarian Response," (Security Council, January 25, 2022), https://www.un.org/press/en/2022/sc14775.doc.htm.
11. John P. Sullivan and Nathan P. Jones, "Bandits, Urban Guerrillas, and Criminal Insurgents: Crime and Resistance in Latin America," in *The Routledge Handbook of Latin America and the Caribbean (Twentieth and Twenty-First Century)* Pablo Baisotti, ed., (New York: Routledge, 2021).

12. David Kilcullen, *Out of the Mountains: The Coming Age of the Urban Guerrilla* (New York: Oxford University Press, 2015); Mao Tse-tung, *Mao Tse-Tung on Guerrilla Warfare*, trans. Samuel B. Griffith, FMFRP 12-18 (Washington, DC: US Marine Corps, 1989), https://www.marines.mil/Portals/1/Publications/FMFRP%2012- 18%20%20Mao%20Tse-tung%20on%20Guerrilla%20Warfare.pdf.
13. Kilcullen, Out of the Mountains: The Coming Age of the Urban Guerrilla; Anthony King, Urban Warfare in the Twenty-First Century (Medford: Polity, 2021); Jamison Jo. Medby and Russell W. Glenn, Street Smart: Intelligence Preparation of the Battlefield for Urban Operations (Santa Monica, CA: RAND, 2002), https://apps.dtic.mil/sti/pdfs/ADA411686.pdf.
14. Anne L. Clunan and Harold A. Trinkunas, *Ungoverned Spaces: Alternatives to State Authority in an Era of Softened Sovereignty* (Stanford: Stanford University Press, 2010), 19.
15. Howard Campbell, "Downtown Juárez," in *Downtown Juárez: Underworlds of Violence and Abuse* (Austin: University of Texas Press, 2022), 19.
16. Dave Dillege, Robert J. Bunker, John P. Sullivan, and Anna Keshavarz., eds., *Blood and Concrete: 21st Century Conflict in Urban Centers and Megacities*, A Small Wars Journal Anthology (Bloomington, IN: Xlibris, 2019), https://www.amazon.com/Blood- Concrete-Conflict-Megacities-Anthology/dp/1984573756.
17. Jamison Jo. Medby and Russell W. Glenn, *Street Smart: Intelligence Preparation of the Battlefield for Urban Operations* (Santa Monica, CA: RAND, 2002), https://apps.dtic.mil/sti/pdfs/ADA411686.pdf.
18. Michael R. Glass, Taylor B. Seybolt, and Phil Williams, "Introduction to Urban Violence, Resilience and Security," in *Urban Violence, Resilience and Security: Governance Responses in the Global South* (Cheltenham: Edward Elgar Publishing, 2022).
19. Dave Dillege, Robert J. Bunker, John P. Sullivan, and Anna Keshavarz., eds., Blood and Concrete.
20. John Spencer, The Mini-Manual for the Urban Defender: A Guide to Strategies and Tactics for Defending a City, Fourth Version, April 3, 2022, https://static1.squarespace.com/static/622cbafd4ab19b7c0966d469/t/624b0fcc746c1e4ec5984cd6/1649086413544/Mini_Manual_Spencerv4_English_03APR22v2.pdf; John Spencer, "John Spencer Online," Professional, John Spencer, 2022, https://www.johnspenceronline.com/urban-warfare.
21. Dave Graham, "Mexican Capo Ovidio Guzman Extradited to US in Win on Fentanyl War," Reuters, September 16, 2023, https://www.reuters.com/world/americas/mexican-kingpin-ovidio-guzmanextradited-us-source-says-2023-09-16/.
22. Russell W Glenn, Come Hell or High Fever: Readying the World's Megacities for Disaster (Canberra: ANU Press, 2023).
23. David Kilcullen, Out of the Mountains: The Coming Age of the Urban Guerrilla (New York: Oxford University Press, 2015); Anthony King, Urban Warfare in the TwentyFirst Century (Medford: Polity, 2021).
24. Richard J. Norton, "Feral Cities," Naval War College Review 56, no. 4, (2003), https://digital-commons.usnwc.edu/nwc-review/vol56/iss4/8.
25. Norton, "Feral Cities."

26. Robert J. Bunker and John P. Sullivan, "Integrating feral cities and third phase cartels/third generation gangs research: the rise of criminal (narco) city networks and BlackFor," Small Wars & Insurgencies 22, no. 5, (November 2011): 765-787, https://doi.org/10.1080/09592318.2011.620804.
27. Bunker and Sullivan, "Integrating feral cities."

CHAPTER 2
Civil Affairs in Antwerp 1944-1945: Critical Infrastructure and Civil Defense

Louise Tumchewics

Introduction

Antwerp, Belgium was a vital logistics center as the Allies advanced towards Germany in 1944-1945. Antwerp offered proximity to Germany and a vast cargo capacity, reducing the pressures on the Allies' long supply lines from France. As a major port under Allied control, Antwerp was a prime target for German V-1 and V-2 rocket strikes, and German forces bombed the city daily for over five months. As the bombardment intensified, Allied leadership feared the relentless bombardment would drive the civilian workforce to seek safety outside of the city, reducing the port's capacity.

Preventing a mass exodus of the civilian population fell to 1st Canadian Army Civil Affairs. In a matter of months, a small detachment of Civil Affairs staff officers supporting Belgian authorities revitalized Antwerp's civil defense and essential services. The story of Antwerp offers a case study of preserving critical national infrastructure and logistics capability through protecting a city's population and systems, despite intense air strikes.

Literature Review

Antwerp's experience of V-1 and V-2 rockets is addressed in several studies of these weapons, including Michael Neufeld's *The Rocket and the Reich*.[1] The bombardment of the port is analyzed in detail by Ben King in a study for the United States Army Transportation Corps.[2] The air defense of Antwerp and the Scheldt was the subject of a thesis by Lieutenant Colonel Richard Backus.[3] Medical reports on the psychological effects of the V-weapons on the combatants in Antwerp.[4] The city's losses during the bombardment are the subject of several popular commemorative historical websites and museum collections in Canada and the United Kingdom.[5]

Canadian Army Civil Affairs is a relatively obscure aspect of the Allied liberation of Northwest Europe, largely overshadowed by the military aspects of the campaign. While there is no official history of Canadian Army Civil Affairs, there are official histories of British and American Civil Affairs that make limited mention of their Canadian counterparts but provide information on the operational challenges and policy direction of Civil Affairs in Europe.[6] War diaries, military records, and other surviving documentation from Canadian Army Civil Affairs held at national archives in the United Kingdom and Canada provide a rich source of detailed information on civil affairs operations. These sources offer insight into events, the multifaceted challenges presented by liberation, and an understanding of the context in which Civil Affairs officers operated.

Civil Affairs' role in the liberation and governance of specific occupied countries has been the subject of several valuable studies by Canadian scholars. Terry Copp and Michelle Fowler explored 21st Army Group Civil Affairs in Caen and Northwest France.[7] Matthew Wiseman has detailed the role of civil affairs in the urban operation for the city of Groningen, exploring Civil Affairs' role in managing a complex humanitarian operation amidst significant urban combat.[8] Kirk Goodlet has examined the role of Civil Affairs in the reconstruction of the agrarian province Zeeland, largely flooded in the liberation of the Netherlands.[9] Canadian historian David Borys has written the first comprehensive history of Canadian Army Civil Affairs across Northwest Europe, looking at Civil Affairs operations in France, Belgium, the Netherlands, and Germany, as well as the historical origins of Civil Affairs and the institutional changes and political developments during the war.[10] Borys devotes a chapter of his study to Civil Affairs efforts in Antwerp and throughout Belgium. He approaches the bombardment of Antwerp from the perspective of protecting civilian morale in the city and surrounding suburbs. Studies of Civil Affairs acknowledge the importance of logistics yet focus instead on other aspects of Civil Affairs' diverse and complex roles and responsibilities. Using archival sources and building on existing scholarship, this article assesses Civil Affairs' role in maintaining critical national logistics infrastructure through its support for the civilian population in a city subject to widespread bombardment.

Canadian Army Civil Affairs

Prior to the invasion of Sicily in 1943, the Allies were aware that, once in Europe, their troops would encounter a continent of civilians trying to flee the battlespace and suffering from the deprivation brought by years of Nazi occupation. They anticipated there would be a need to prevent populations from impeding military objectives and a requirement to restore functioning national governments and local authorities as soon as possible. Allied governments had to develop doctrine for managing the civil-military relationship in liberated and occupied countries.

The legal basis for operations in liberated countries was the formal agreement or invitation by the accredited government of that country. In liberated countries, Civil Affairs worked to reconcile the needs of the population with practical military requirements. Civil Affairs' mission was twofold: Assisting the military commander's plans by liaising with civil authorities and controlling to prevent "disorganization, disease, or unrest from hampering the activities of fighting troops activities."[11] Second, Civil Affairs exercised administrative control and supervision, where needed, to preserve law and order. Its mission was not to win hearts and minds but to help rebuild local and national administrative capacity so critical population needs did not interfere with or overwhelm military objectives.

Training and Selection

Civil Affairs training was delivered at Southwolds House in Wimbledon, Southwest London.[12] Over six weeks, prospective Civil Affairs officers received instruction in military organization and staff officer responsibilities, as well as the history, government structure, and administrative system of France, Belgium, the Netherlands, Denmark, and Norway.[13] After qualifying, newly minted Civil Affairs officers received additional instruction on a specialized area, such as international law, finance, fire, and civil defense, public safety, or relief, and then were sent to the front.[14]

Not everyone was eligible to become a Civil Affairs officer. Candidates for Civil Affairs roles required second language proficiency and experience in either law, finance, engineering, trade, and industry, or civil defense. These criteria meant for most, joining the army had interrupted a well-established civilian career, and many were above the age of the average combat soldier or officer. Their life experience, skills, and greater maturity assisted with the many and varied challenges that arose and the diplomacy and judgment required in building relationships with local governments, businesses, and individuals.[15]

Structure and Deployment

The liberation of Belgium was the responsibility of British 21st Army Group, a multinational formation including 1st Canadian Army and 2nd British Army, as well as Polish I Corps, and smaller Dutch, Belgian, Czechoslovak, and American units. Within First Canadian Army, Major General Kirby led the Directorate of Civil Affairs, (DCA) supported by a small staff. The DCA provided the overall direction of Civil Affairs, as well as liaising with government bodies. The DCA worked in an advisory capacity to Supreme Headquarters Allied Expeditionary Force (SHAEF) and G-5 SHAEF issued orders to all Allied Civil Affairs in Europe.[16]

Civil Affairs units integrated into the headquarters of military formations, organized by pools, groups, and detachments, at Army, Corps, and Division levels, respectively. A detachment comprised one Senior Civil Affairs Officer and a small supporting staff of administrative and public safety officers and other ranks attached to the division headquarters to ensure communication and coordination with combat formations.[17] As required, their numbers would be supplemented by specialist officers providing expertise in law, labor relations, public health, relief, logistics, transport, and engineering.[18]

There were two types of Civil Affairs detachment: Spearhead and static. As the name suggests, spearhead detachments moved alongside their assigned combat division, rapidly assessing the civilian situation in newly liberated areas and providing immediate and short-term relief for the most acute problems. Spearheads moved quickly, identifying key local authorities, influential figures, and known collaborators. Spearhead detachments then handed over responsibility to static detachments, who established a base of operations in major towns and cities and made a much longer-term commitment to relief and rehabilitation needs.[19] Both spearhead and static detachments had to be flexible to handle the wide range of tasks they encountered.

The Liberation of Antwerp and The Battle of the Scheldt

Throughout the late summer and early autumn of 1944, the Allies pushed onward through France and into Belgium. The United States First Army liberated the south of the country, while 1st Canadian Armored Division and 1st Polish Armored Division captured Bruges and Ghent to the northwest, and British 2nd Army took Brussels and then Antwerp on September 4, 1944.[20] The breakout from Normandy had moved the frontline forward at great speed, leading Allied planners to anticipate, perhaps with a degree of hubris, that the war could end by late 1944.[21] The advance, however, outpaced the capacity of overstretched Allied supply lines.

The liberation of Antwerp, therefore, represented a major strategic success for the Allies. Antwerp was a vast deep-water port with greater capacity to receive Allied shipping than the ports on the Pas de Calais. Antwerp had modern berthing facilities, 592 cranes, dry docks, and storage capacity for 120 million gallons of fuel.[22] Though Eisenhower and Montgomery differed in their respective strategies for defeating Germany, both recognized the crucial importance of the city and its port to ensure the Allied advance proceeded.[23] Supply lines from the French ports were over-extended, and Antwerp offered a large logistics hub closer to the front lines. Eisenhower underscored the importance of Antwerp in a note to General George Marshall on October 23, 1944, writing, "the logistical problem had become so acute that all plans had made Antwerp a *sine qua non* to the waging of the final all-out battle."[24]

The port of Antwerp had suffered limited damage during the war and the battle for liberation, and port installations were largely intact, unlike Brest and Cherbourg, which had been heavily damaged. However, Antwerp lay at the end of the heavily fortified 80-kilometer long Scheldt estuary. Though the Allies had liberated Antwerp city itself, if the Germans controlled the banks of the river and their mines remained embedded in the estuary and the harbor, the port was off limits to the Allies.

Field Marshal Montgomery, commander of 21st Army Group, proposed to focus efforts on establishing his narrow thrust into the Ruhr in Operation Market Garden. The objective was to seize the bridges over Lower Rhine river in the Netherlands to ensure a swift Allied advance into the German industrial heartland, thereby accelerating the end of the war. The operation ultimately failed but, crucially, drew attention, effort, and resources away from the clearance of the Scheldt estuary.

The focus on Market Garden, rather than prioritizing the clearance of the Scheldt, prolonged the end of the war by delaying the opening of a major

Allied logistics port.[25] However, given the strategic significance of Antwerp, it was likely to have been a target for V-weapons once under Allied control, regardless of the date the liberation of the city occurred. In mid-September 1944, Montgomery ordered First Canadian Army to secure the Scheldt estuary and opened access to Antwerp.

Commander of First Canadian Army, Lieutenant General Guy Simonds, planned three advances to capture the Scheldt Estuary, and break through the German defenses on the Beveland Isthmus to the north, the Breskens Pocket to the south, and Walcheren Island at the mouth of the estuary. The fighting for the estuary was tough and intense.[26] with First Canadian Army troops bogged down by thick mud in the low-lying polder fields. Progress was slow, and casualties were heavy.[27]

German forces finally surrendered on November 2, 1944. The Canadian operations to open the estuary to Antwerp had taken much longer than anticipated, at a cost of 13,000 casualties to First Canadian Army.[28] For three weeks following the German surrender, ten flotillas of minesweepers worked to clear the river of mines. After nearly three months of effort, the first Allied ships docked at Antwerp on November 28.[29]

Physical access and control of the estuary and the port were important, but only one part of the port's functionality. November 1944 was still two decades before the advent of container shipping, and with breakbulk cargo still the norm, thousands of dockers were needed to unload Allied cargo ships. Once a ship docked, dockers used shipboard derricks or shore-based cranes to lift heavy goods off the ship. Other items would be carried off the ship by hand and organized into warehouses for shortage or immediate onward overland shipping. [30] Loading and unloading cargo was hugely labor- and time-intensive work, and in Antwerp, it was an essential part of keeping Allied supplies moving. It was expected that the port would handle 40,000 tons of cargo per day.[31]

While 1st Canadian Army engaged in clearing the Scheldt estuary, the city of Antwerp became the target for German V-1 and V-2 rocket attacks. Though v-weapons' gyroscopic guidance systems were too rudimentary to deliver any kind of precision strike, they packed considerable destructive punch with payloads of 1,000 kg or (2,000lbs) of explosives.[32] In the absence of a credible bomber force, V-weapons offered a means for the Germans to strike back at the Allied advance and attempt to thwart progress through northwest Europe by targeting logistical centers like Antwerp. They were also vengeance weapons, intended to spread fear and wear down civilian morale. Even if they could not hit a precise target, V-1 and V-2 rockets were devastating area weapons, especially for urban centers.

Initially, Allied leadership expected V-weapons to be a mere nuisance because of the rockets' inaccuracy, and effects on the port would be minimal.[33] As attacks intensified, Allied leadership feared the bombardments would drive dock workers to leave their jobs and seek refuge in the comparative safety of the countryside. This situation had already occurred in London, where factory production dipped as workers fled to the countryside to avoid v-weapon bombardment.[34] Antwerp's operations could not support a similar decline in productivity or Allies' supply needs would suffer.

Though the port was largely intact and the city secured, it was critical that the 13,000 Belgian civilian dockers who lived in the city and its suburbs continued to go the docks.[35] Without these men (and dockers were overwhelmingly male), Allied ships could not be unloaded. The Allies did not have 13,000 replacement dock workers available, and the steady flow of supplies from Antwerp, across the Netherlands, and into Germany was essential for the last winter of the war. It was important, therefore, that daily life in Antwerp proceeded as normal and that people felt sufficiently safe to go to work. Keeping the city stable and secure would be the mission of 1st Canadian Army Civil Affairs.

Civil Affairs in Antwerp

Unlike the Scheldt estuary, Allied troops liberated Antwerp speedily, with minimal damage to the port installations. During the Nazis' four-year occupation of the country, Belgium suffered far less material damage than other parts of France and the Netherlands.[36] There was not the same urgent hunger crisis that Civil Affairs officers would see in the Netherlands, nor the widespread destruction and civilian dislocation that characterized northern

France.[37] However, the civil affairs situation in Belgium was neither easy nor straightforward.

Though a small country, Belgium presented a complex cultural and socio-economic picture. Historic distinctions between the French and Flemish, Walloons and Flemings, rural and urban, and rivalries amongst the industrialized cities of Ghent, Bruges, Brussels, and Antwerp divided the small country's population. The Nazi occupation added to these divisions by creating another fault line between those who collaborated with the occupiers and those who did not.[38] Even the resistance was highly factionalized: A wide range of groups were drawn from differing political convictions. Many resistance groups pursued vigilante justice, punishing suspected collaborators, settling personal and political scores, and participating in a range of criminal activities, including theft, arson, and murder.[39]

Belgians had little in the way of central authority to promote unity in the country. At the start of the war, the Belgian King, Leopold II, had surrendered to the Nazis and remained in the country throughout the occupation. The government, led by Walloon Hubert Pierlot, had fled into exile in London. After the liberation, the government was slow to return to the country and even slower to reassert its authority. The Belgian government was ineffective, unwilling, or unable to assert control and provide clear administrative direction, out of step with the population, and uncertain of its course. Provincial authorities were reluctant to act without consultation with the national government, adding to uncertainty and lack of decision-making.[40] Civil Affairs thus took on a much larger administrative role, becoming heavily involved in long-term commitments, especially as Belgium became an increasingly important rear area for the Allies in the late autumn and winter.[41]

Bombardment

Against a backdrop of division and discord, Civil Affairs officers faced the challenge of establishing the civil defense and emergency response infrastructure needed to manage the threat of the V-1 and V-2 rocket attacks. Antwerp had not experienced as much bomb damage as other major European cities had in the past four years. Compared to port cities like Rotterdam, Liverpool, and London, it was relatively unscathed. The bombardment of V-1 and v-2 rockets was the first sustained bombing campaign the city had experienced. The First V-2 rocket hit the city on October 7, 1944, and for 175 consecutive days, the bombing and V rocket attacks continued, with an average of 35 strikes per day. The bombing campaign killed 8,333 civilians, and 5,960 bombs and rockets hit the 900 square kilometers (347 square miles) of greater Antwerp.[42]

An estimated 150 V-1s and 152 V-2s fell inside the dock area. Another 47 V-1s and 31 V-2s fell north of the dock area between the docks and the city limits. The rocket strikes on the dock area killed 53 military personnel and 131 civilians and injured a further 174 military and 380 civilians.[43] V-weapons destroyed two warehouses, sunk a 150-ton floating crane, and sunk or damaged 150 ships.[44]

Even before the port was fully operational, SHAEF expressed concerns about transporting ammunition into a port subject to bombardment. A rocket strike on a port full of ammunition and fuel would be disastrous. Allied naval command and British 21st Army Group determined ammunition ships could be brought into the port only if their numbers were strictly limited to operational requirements, docked in an isolated part of the port, and additional firefighting preparations were made.[45]

As well as limiting damage to physical installations at the port, it was vital to keep the port operational by maintaining the workforce. Antwerp municipal authorities offered a 25 percent pay differential for dockers to encourage them to stay in their jobs. The additional pay incentivized workers, but it also led to disagreements because it was paid only for those working in the immediate dock area, and the V-weapons were so inaccurate that many fell outside the designated danger zones of the port, leading other workers in the city to demand higher pay rates for their increased risk too.[46]

A pay increase did not relieve the danger of the V-weapons and the chronic, persistent worry these weapons created. There was widespread anxiety in Antwerp as people, both soldiers and civilians, feared when the next attack might occur and what could happen to them, their families, and their property.[47] There was limited protection from V-weapons. Allied antiaircraft batteries stationed around Antwerp attempted to provide air defense but had limited range due to were hampered by the number of airfields surrounding Antwerp. To add further challenge, V-weapons' steel fuselage and aerodynamic shape meant a direct hit was required to bring a rocket down.[48] The city was highly vulnerable, and there was little in the way of public services to respond effectively to incidents and maintain public confidence.

There was virtually no functioning civil defense infrastructure in the city. The civil defense organization, the Passive Air Defense (*Passive Lucht Beschering*, or PLB), slipped into decline during the Nazi occupation. The organization suffered from insufficient personnel, inadequate training, transportation, and equipment, a lack of centralized operational control, poor incident response management, and little in the way of working relationships with the fire brigade, police, and medical aid agencies. Compounding these problems was an absence of leadership, with the former chief of the PLB suspended for collaboration and his deputy under investigation for the same charge.[49]

Without a local authority directing the *Passive Lucht Beschering* (PLB), it was the task of Senior Civil Affairs Officer Henry Barnes and Detachment 325 to create a functional PLB for Antwerp and its surrounding suburbs.[50] The PLB and attendant services needed to respond swiftly to attacks, manage incidents, provide emergency medical and relief assistance, and return the scene to normalcy as soon as possible. A functioning and responsive Civil Defense organization would, in turn, boost public confidence and keep workers in the city.

Forming such an entity was not a straightforward task. Antwerp city authorities and the leadership of surrounding suburbs and villages did not cooperate with each other. The Nazi occupation forcibly amalgamated municipal administrations, and after the liberation, these organizations withdrew to traditional pre-war parochial structures. They were reluctant to relinquish control once again over their respective jurisdictions. Civil Affairs officers had to effectively re-merge these entities, impressing upon Belgian representatives that the Allies wanted a centralized Civil Defense organization in Antwerp and its environs.[51]

Once established, local Belgian officials, including the head of the fire service, formally led the PLB committee. Although local officials assumed leadership positions, Barnes remained part of the committee for the rest of the war, providing direction, support, and liaison with military leadership. The organizational scheme of the PLB included Canadian Civil Affairs officers alongside police, fire service, relief agencies, gendarmerie, the police, the Belgian Red Cross, and the Flemish Red Cross.[52]

As Barnes and his detachment were trying to rally the cooperation of local authorities, Antwerp suffered some of its most serious rocket attacks, underscoring the need for a functioning civil defense entity. In October 1944, a rocket struck Bontemantelstraat in Central Antwerp, destroying 40 buildings and killing 71 people.[53] In November, a V-2 rocket struck the city's busiest intersection at noon, killing 200 people and breaking the water mains.[54] These devastating incidents emphasized the need for a coordinated civil defense and emergency response capability.

With leadership and organizational structure established, it was time to improve the physical resources of the PLB. The PLB headquarters received additional telephone lines, additional phone lines, incident boards, and city maps. Necessary equipment, such as trucks, bicycles, heavy rescue equipment, and petrol, were gathered from Canadian Army stores or local contractors.[55] An additional 1400 PLB staff were recruited to provide a 24-hour emergency response service, including women who hitherto could not serve in the PLB.[56]

It was difficult to attract staff to the PLB. The work was dangerous, and compared to the PLB, the port authority and other military works projects offered higher wages. It was difficult to stop workers from switching from PLB roles to more competitively paid opportunities elsewhere in the city. To resolve this, the PLB, with Barnes' support and the Ministry of Labor, agreed the port authority would not hire workers who had left roles at the PLB. PLB workers, still dissatisfied with their wages, went on strike twice. Eventually, to improve the pay offer, the PLB awarded workers hourly incident pay on top of their monthly wage.[57]

Two Civil Affairs officers developed and implemented the PLB training program, providing instruction on all aspects of disaster response to new PLB recruits and members of ancillary services: The police, fire service, and aid agencies. Rocket attacks frequently interrupted training, although these incidents provided experiential learning opportunities for new recruits. Civil Affairs alone could not manage the instructional needs of the rapidly growing organization. In time, additional Belgian trainers who had received instruction in the United Kingdom., relieved some of the training burden.[58]

Rocket strikes escalated throughout the winter, reaching their peak in December 1944. That month, a strike on the Cinema Rex killed 519 people and injured 291, half of whom were civilians, the other half off-duty military personnel.[59] After this attack, on Lieutenant Colonel Barnes' advice, municipal leadership forbade gatherings of over 100 people to prevent further mass casualty events. All cinemas and theaters closed to prevent a similar event.[60]

Mass casualty incidents highlighted the need for medical services to be centralized. Much as municipal authorities had been, local hospitals operated as individual entities, with no coordination amongst medical services. Some hospitals received overwhelming numbers of casualties after air strikes, while others had empty beds.[61] By centralizing the administration of medical services, hospitals reported on the numbers of casualties and beds available, so ambulances could distribute casualties more evenly and hospitals could attend to casualties more rapidly.

As late as the winter of 1944, as bombings escalated, there was no single organization for the welfare of people bombed out of their homes. Without centralized support, civilians made homeless by bombings had to visit separate offices for clothing, food, money, and temporary accommodation assistance. Major J.J. Opray, detachment 325 relief officer, and Captain J. Patterson, SHAEF's post-air raid advisor, encouraged the Belgian government to centralize responsibility for relief and rehabilitation. Civil Affairs officers helped expand the number of rest centers from 3 to 23, requisitioning schools and organizing staff to provide hot food, clothing, and safe temporary shelter.[62] A single point of support and shelter prevented disorganized flight to the countryside.

Bombs and rocket strikes caused tremendous amounts of damage to the built environment, scattering debris throughout the city, impeding transportation, and posing a safety risk. In December 1944, Lieutenant Colonel Barnes assisted with the formation of a provincial coordinating committee to increase the amount of manpower and equipment available for bomb site clearance. Though led by Belgian officials, Major A.J. Dunn, a Civil Affairs technical specialist on loan from II Canadian Corps Headquarters, oversaw operations and successfully negotiated the loan of 100 trucks and 3 cranes from the British Ministry of Home Security to accelerate clean-up efforts.[63] Swift clean-up restored the normal running of services and a sense of normalcy.

Essential services kept running despite the bomb and rocket attacks. With Civil Affairs' support, the PLB enhanced utility crews and borrowed vehicles and repair equipment from military and civilian sources to keep these systems functioning.[64] Utility companies kept the water supply flowing and the trams running. Gas, though in short supply, did not break down. The city lights stayed on, and Antwerp experienced only one power outage.[65] With electricity, water, and gas running reliably, there was a semblance of normal daily life, and the port and other businesses continued to operate.

By the end of the war in May 1945, the performance of the PLB and associated services had improved remarkably. Despite the persistent hail of rockets, no significant population flight from the city had occurred. Civilians continued to work in the docks amidst the dangers. Though rocket strikes had reduced port discharge tonnage, it had remained operational even after receiving 302 rocket strikes. However, the port of Antwerp did not meet the planned discharge targets[66] and the Allies were obligated to open an additional port at Ghent.[67]

In the six months since October 1944, detachment 325 had helped the city establish a comprehensive civil defense and emergency response system. A Civil Affairs postwar report modestly summarized the unit's extensive work in Antwerp as having "assisted and guided" local authorities.[68] Belgian authorities recognized the assistance provided by civil affairs officers. In a May 1945 letter, the head of Antwerp's PLB, wrote to detachment 325 to express his gratitude:

> I fully realize that it is mainly due to your great efforts, to your help, and to your previous experience that it has been possible to develop the PLB into a solid organization and that thousands of civilians could be rescued alive.[69]

Analysis and Conclusion

The task facing Civil Affairs in Antwerp in the autumn of 1944 was a mammoth one: Standing up a civil defense network in a city under bombardment by novel weapons in a country emerging from Nazi occupation and historically divided. Belgium was a challenging social environment to operate within, but Civil Affairs had several advantages. The port installations were still intact, and the city was habitable. Antwerp was a strategic priority for the Allies and diverted resources for the city's protection. Civil Affairs could also draw upon additional expertise within II Canadian Corps and SHAEF. Although there were inevitable frictions, the population was overall friendly towards the Allies and not actively undermining Civil Affairs work.

The absence of effective government at national and local levels meant Civil Affairs took on considerable responsibilities and commanded authority. They could centralize services and governing bodies and issue safety advisories. Belgians respected Civil Affairs officers and heeded their advice. The material resources of the Allies and the amount of goods flowing through Antwerp meant that Civil Affairs officers could requisition necessary equipment and vehicles to fill critical needs. Civil Affairs officers could thus rectify supply shortages for Antwerp's civil defense with relative ease and speed. Civil Affairs gained experience working with populations and local governments in Italy and France as an organization and brought their best practices to Belgium. The structure of Civil Affairs enabled detachment 325 to remain in the city for a prolonged period, allowing for building working relationships and trust.

The nature of V-weapons impeded the interdiction of rocket strikes on the port and the city, and the strikes succeeded in disrupting the pace and quantity of Allied cargo shipping. However, a well-organized civil defense organization could minimize loss of life, provide swift medical treatment for the injured, and maintain public order in the aftermath of bombings. Orderly incident management boosted public confidence, and people remained in the city.

Civil Affairs officers did not—and could not—rectify Allied logistics challenges nor arrest the v-weapon strikes. They helped develop local capacity and create conditions enabling civilian dock workers to remain in the city despite near-constant bombardment. This kept critical national logistics infrastructure functioning, albeit at reduced volume, and supplies moving towards the front lines—critical for ending the war. Eighty years on, Civil Affairs' experience in Antwerp retains relevance as it demonstrates the challenges of protecting civilians and working with local organizations to build capacity and keep critical logistics and national infrastructure functioning during air strikes on a key urban center.

Endnotes

1. Michael J. Neufeld, *The Rocket and the Reich*, (New York: Free Press), 1995.
2. Ben King, "Antwerp and the German Attack on Allies' Supply Lines, 1944-1945," US Army School of Transportation. https://transportation.army.mil/history/pdf/studies/antwerp.pdf
3. Richard J. Backhus, "The Defense of Antwerp Against the V-1 missile," Army Command and General Staff College, Fort Leavenworth, Kansas, 1971.
4. Freeman, A. G. "Effect on Troops of the "V" Weapon Bombardment of Antwerp." *British Medical Journal* 1,no. *4436.58*. https://doi.org/10.1136.58
5. Examples include: https://www.the-low-countries.com/article/remembering-the-v2-attack-on-cinema-rex and http://www.v2rocket.com/start/others/antwerp.html; There are photographs and maps of the V-1 and V-2 rocket strikes in the Canadian War Museum and Imperial War Museum collections.
6. F.S.V. Donnison, Civil Affairs and Military Government: Central Organisation and Planning, (London: Her Majesty's Stationary Office), 1966.
7. Terry Copp and Michelle Fowler, "Heavy Bombers and Civil Affairs First Canadia Army in France, July-September 1944." Canadian Military History 22, 2 (2013), 4-18. https://scolars.wlu.ca/cgi/viewcontent=cgi?article=1693&context=cmh.
8. Matthew S. Wiseman, "Civil-Military Relations and Ethics," in *Small Armies, Big Cities: Re-thinking Urban Warfare*, ed Louise Tumchewics (Boulder: Lynne Rienner Publishers, 2022), 133-156.
9. Kirk W Goodlet (2014). In the Shadows of the Sea: The Destruction and Recovery of Zeeland, the Netherlands, 1940-1948. UWSpace. http://hdl.handle.net/10012/8758.
10. David A. Borys, Civilians at the Sharp End: First Canadian Army civil Affairs in Northwest Europe (Montreal: McGill-Queen's University Press), 2021.
11. Wiseman, "Civil-Military Relations and Ethics," 145-146.
12. Wiseman, "Civil-Military Relations and Ethics," 145.
13. Wiseman, "Civil-Military Relations and Ethics," 145.
14. Borys, Civilians at the Sharp End, 51.
15. Wiseman, "Civil-Military Relations and Ethics," 145.
16. Borys, Civilians at the Sharp End, 54-55.
17. Wiseman, "Civil-Military Relations and Ethics," 145.
18. Wiseman, "Civil-Military Relations and Ethics," 147.
19. Borys, Civilians at the Sharp End, 54-55.
20. Mark Zuehkle, *Terrible Victory.* Toronto: Douglas & McIntyre, 2007, 44-45.
21. King, "Antwerp and the German Attack on Allies' Supply Lines, 1944-1945,"4.
22. King, "Antwerp and the German Attack on Allies' Supply Lines, 1944-1945,"3.
23. Borys, *Civilians at the Sharp End*,123.
24. King, "Antwerp and the German Attack on Allies' Supply Lines, 1944-1945," 2.

25. The failure to clear the Scheldt was acknowledged by Churchill in his recollections of World War II. World War II historian Antony Beevor also places responsibility for the delayed clearance of the Scheldt on Montgomery; Antony Beevor, *Ardennes 1944: Hitler's Last Gamble,* New York: Viking, 2015.
26. R. Daniel Pellerin "You Have Shut Up the Jerries" Canadian Counter-Battery Work in the Clearing of the Breskens Pocket, October–November 1944." Canadian Military History 21, 3 (2015), 17-35. https://scholars.wlu.ca/cgi/viewcontent.cgi?referer=&httpsredir=1&article=1660&context=cmh.
27. Mark Zuehkle, *Terrible Victory,* 120-121.
28. Zuehkle, *Terrible Victory* 75, 76, 124.
29. Zuehkle, *Terrible Victory* 443, 453.
30. A. Vigarié, "From break-bulk to containers: the transformation of general cargo handling and trade," *GeoJournal* 48, 3–7 (1999). https://doi.org/10.1023/A:1007024300877.
31. King, "Antwerp and the German Attack on Allies' Supply Lines, 1944-1945,"3. The port was expected receive 22,400 tons of American Cargo and 17,500 tons of British cargo daily.
32. Neufeld, *The Rocket and the Reich*, 274.
33. King, "Antwerp and the German Attack on Allies' Supply Lines, 1944-1945,", 4.
34. Bory, *Civilians at the Sharp End,* 124.
35. On an average day, the number of dock workers at the port ranged between 9,000-13,000. Archival sources consulted for this paper do not indicate the particular political persuasion of dock workers, however, as mentioned, former Nazi collaborators were actively being sought by various resistance groups.
36. Borys, *Civilians at the Sharp End*, 110.
37. Wiseman, "Civil-Military Relations and Ethics," 147.
38. Borys. *Civilians at the Sharp End*, 107.
39. Borys. *Civilians at the Sharp End,* 113-114 and "Report on Civil Affairs in Belgium," November 1944, WO 219/3738, 15, The National Archives, Kew, London, U.K.
40. Borys, *Civilians at the Sharp End,*111.
42. Borys, *Civilians at the Sharp End* 112.
42. King, "Antwerp and the German Attack on Allies' Supply Lines, 1944-1945,"12; Borys, *Civilians at the Sharp End,* 103.
43. King, "Antwerp and the German Attack on Allies' Supply Lines, 1944-1945,"12.
44. King, "Antwerp and the German Attack on Allies' Supply Lines, 1944-1945,"12-13.
45. King, "Antwerp and the German Attack on Allies' Supply Lines, 1944-1945,"13-14.
46. King, "Antwerp and the German Attack on Allies' Supply Lines, 1944-1945,"14.
47. A. G. Freeman "Effect on Troops of the "V" Weapon Bombardment of Antwerp," 58, 59.
48. King, "Antwerp and the German Attack on Allies' Supply Lines, 1944-1945," 6.

49. Borys *Civilians at the Sharp End*,125.
50. Borys, *Civilians at the Sharp End* ,124.
51. Borys, *Civilians at the Sharp End*,124,125-126; "Civil Defense in Antwerp," May 1945, WO 171/7982, 2, The National Archives, Kew, London, U.K.
52. Borys, *Civilians at the Sharp End*, 126.
53. King, "Antwerp and the German Attack on Allies' Supply Lines, 1944-1945," 9.
54. Borys, *Civilians at the Sharp End*, 132.
55. "Civil Defense in Antwerp," May 1945, WO 171/7982, 18, The National Archives, Kew, London, U.K.
56. "Civil Defense in Antwerp," May 1945, WO 171/7982, 9, The National Archives, Kew, London, U.K.
57. Borys, *Civilians at the Sharp End*, 128.
58. "Civil Defense in Antwerp," May 1945, WO 171/7982, 9, The National Archives, Kew, London, U.K.
59. Borys, *Civilians at the Sharp End*,131.
60. King, "Antwerp and the German Attack on Allies' Supply Lines, 1944-1945," 14.
61. Borys, *Civilians at the Sharp End*.
62. Borys, *Civilians at the Sharp End* 134-135.
63. Borys, *Civilians at the Sharp End* 136.
64. Borys, *Civilians at the Sharp End* 131.
65. "Civil Defense in Antwerp," May 1945, WO 171/7982, 22, The National Archives, Kew, London, U.K.
66. King, "Antwerp and the German Attack on Allies' Supply Lines, 1944-1945,"16.
67. King, "Antwerp and the German Attack on Allies' Supply Lines, 1944-1945,"16.
68. "Civil Defense in Antwerp," May 1945, WO 171/7982, 35, The National Archives, Kew, London, U.K.
69. "Letter to Major Foreshew from Major E. Van Cappelen," June 1945, WO 171/7982, The National Archives, Kew, London, U.K.

CHAPTER 3
Urban Disaster Wrought by Man: The Battle for Manila, 1945

Russell W. Glenn

Introduction

Manila today stands as Earth's sixth most populous urban area.[1] The city and its surrounds offer much found in any 21st-century megalopolis, e.g., vibrancy born of hosting its country's brightest, most motivated, and entrepreneurial citizens drawn by the magnetism of professional, economic, and social opportunities. This is despite the Philippine capital's often cheek-by-jowl living and traffic congestion second only to India's Bangalore.[2] Such magnetism proved attractive even during the dark days of Japanese occupation during World War II, if for different reasons. People were so impoverished in the countryside that the city beckoned despite the looming threat of fighting for its recapture, limited food availability, and proximity to occupier cruelty. It was, in retrospect, an ill-fated attraction given the suffering to come.

Manila in 1945 demonstrates the brutality of urban combat, violence the innocent often experience in far greater numbers of killed and wounded than the opposing combatants. Unfortunately, little has changed, as Iraq, Syria, and Ukraine have demonstrated in recent years. If there is an unseen benefit in this dark cloud, it is the fungibility of lessons available when combat visits cities. Warfare is but one among urban disaster's many forms. It differs from other types in that targeting decisions made during its waging can dramatically impact the experience and the cost, duration, and difficulty of recovery in its aftermath. Yet urban disaster brought about by combat offers much in the way of lessons pertinent to calamities borne of other causes. Given that no megacity (commonly understood to mean urban areas with a population of ten million or more) has ever suffered major wartime devastation, it is the destruction resultant of combat in one of the world's most populous cities in 1945 that we look for insights into future contingencies.

Urban Combat: The Nature of the Beast

Combat is often feral. That in cities, however, is exceptional, possessing a primordiality our prehistoric ancestors would have found familiar. Urban struggles tend to be intimate. If the soldier does not see the faces of those he (and, increasingly, she) kills—and he frequently will—the individual will hear the screams following the grenade thrown through an open door or muffled groans of those suffering limbs and organs crushed in the aftermath of the bomb, artillery round, or thermobaric blast he called for to avoid the high-risk, often deadly activity of clearing building after building floor-by-floor, room-by-room.

Though hell for the soldier, the victims of urban combat's ferocity are rarely the province of combatants alone. It might be because of physical immobility, incomprehension of the challenges awaiting those who do not evacuate, or sheer misfortune. Noncombatants—the innocent—are all but inevitably caught up in the fighting that invades their neighborhoods. The consequences are often as much or more a disaster than the devastation due to earthquake, tsunami, flood, fire, terrorism, or volcano. The number of attacking Americans killed during the battle of Manila totaled 1,010. Some 14,000 Japanese defenders lost their lives.[3] Terrible numbers, but nothing like the 100,000 Filipinos perishing during those days of fighting in early 1945, one in ten from a population of about one million as the battle began. Many others were injured, widowed, or orphaned.[4] Urban combat remains hyper-lethal for civilians today. International Committee of the Red Cross research found that urban casualties numbered eight times the number of civilians killed in rural environments during fighting to defeat the Islamic State of Iraq and Syria (ISIS) in March 2017—July 2018 Iraq and Syria.[5]

Japanese forces occupied Manila after General Douglas MacArthur declared the Philippine capital an open city in December 1941. Many of the pre-war population remained during the interim years. Others joined them as months went by, some involuntarily as prisoners of the occupiers, with others seeking shelter, food, or the work that made the formers' purchase possible. Some idea of how hard it was to survive in the countryside is evident in Manila having achieved the urban area's largest wartime population in early 1944 despite the oppressive policies of the Japanese. Only with the beginning of Allied bombing in the autumn of that year did numbers start to lessen, though not so much as to reduce the population level to that seen before the occupiers' arrival.[6] The worst was yet to come as US Army forces approached from north and south. Manila's 1945 defenders had no intention of declaring the Philippine capital an open city a second time. Manileños would see no repeat of 1942's reprieve from combat's devastation.

MacArthur had made good on his promise to return. Three divisions accompanying him would engage those 14,000 Japanese army and navy defenders in the capital. MacArthur and his staff underestimated the difficulties ahead, planning for a grand victory parade soon after entering the city. At first, they placed severe restrictions on artillery and air bombardment, hoping to save civilian lives and minimize damage.[7] Yet years of advancing from island to island meant the Americans were unpracticed in urban combat. Commanders at echelons below MacArthur's learned vital lessons at the cost of soldiers' lives. For example, the staff drew boundaries along either side rather than down the middle of a street to avoid confusion in times of limited visibility. Exhausted soldiers peering into darkness, dust, or smoke would otherwise not know whether the vague forms approaching were the enemy or those from the American unit across the way. Assigning the street to one team meant the Americans owning the thoroughfare knew those vague forms were either enemies or innocents unless their leaders had informed them to expect some of their own. Barring this, anyone carrying a weapon was a target.

The US Sixth Army's XIV Corps moved into Manila from the north with two divisions on February 3, 1945 (the 1st Cavalry and 37th Infantry). General Robert L. Eichelberger and his Eighth Army's 11th Airborne Division advanced from the opposite direction several days later. American soldiers found an enemy sometimes poorly—if at all—trained in ground combat tactics but rich in automatic and large-caliber weapons stripped from naval vessels.

Japanese commanders positioned relatively few defenders in the northern parts of Manila, expecting the Americans to attack from the south or via an amphibious landing from the bay to the west. A post-battle summary noted that fifty US soldiers, from the 1,010 who would eventually fall, were killed in the earlier fighting.[8] American leaders continued to insist on restricted use of artillery, considering the initial low casualty numbers. Losses quickly mounted as the attackers approached Manila's core, however. MacArthur felt he had no option but to let loose those bigger dogs of war. The army's official history recalls:

> Casualties were mounting at a much too alarming rate among the infantry units….If the city were to be secured without the destruction of the 37th and the 1st Cavalry Divisions, no further effort could be made to save the buildings; everything holding up progress would be pounded, although artillery fire would not be directed against structures such as churches and hospitals that were known to contain civilians. Even this last restriction would not always be effective, for often it could not be learned until too late that a specific building held civilians. The lifting of the restrictions on support fires would

result in turning much of southern Manila into a shambles [On the other hand, restrictions on aerial bombardment would remain in effect though Army Air Corps aircraft did strike targets on the city's periphery to deny the enemy resupply and reinforcement].[9]

Ultimately, the exchanges of artillery fire caused the most significant loss of civilian life.[10]

The Spanish-era Intramuros fortress, with forty-foot-thick and twenty five-foot-high walls, proved particularly tough to reclaim. Were those walls not challenging enough, Japanese defenders took advantage of the fort's tunnel system to move from one part of the massive structure to another without exposure to American fire. Innovation became critical to the attackers' success. Artillery firing unfused rounds from short-range knocked holes in walls. (Unfused rounds did not dissipate their energy by exploding on impact, instead transferring all momentum onto the target.) Progress was slow; creating passage for infantrymen's final assaults required 150 or more rounds. Elsewhere, the use of flamethrowers or the expedient of pouring gasoline into subterranean passageways and igniting it proved effective in dealing with trapped enemy forces. US soldiers dusted off doctrinal manuals, advising them to clear a building from the top down. The guidance proved wise. Units unable or choosing to do otherwise found their foes on upper stories and had cut holes in floors so defenders could toss grenades down onto their attackers. Nor was enemy fire the only threat faced by MacArthur's soldiers. The Japanese had strewn streets and alleys with mines and booby traps, including buried anti-ship mines. Elsewhere, they blocked passages with earth-filled barrels and steel rails driven into the ground, hindering supporting tanks and artillery's ability to keep pace with infantry forces.

American soldiers soon learned to minimize time in open areas, avoiding the city's broad boulevards and even narrower streets when possible. Moving between buildings only after hacking holes through walls using hand tools was a slower but more survivable way of advancing. A grenade or blast from a flamethrower preceded room entry through these mouse holes, barring knowledge of civilian presence. Attackers also found that firing their weapons when moving into rooms assisted both in seizing the initiative and causing defenders to open fire prematurely, helping the Americans to detect where the enemy awaited in ambush. The tactics unquestionably reduced US casualties, but the approach was far less helpful in preserving the lives of unfortunate Filipinos caught between the opposing forces. The Japanese used noncombatants as human shields when they realized the Americans refrained from firing when Manileños were in a building.

Those defenders' weeks of preparation meant Americans would repeatedly advance to find themselves under fire from within nearby buildings where the enemy had cut openings in walls to ambush the attackers. US tanks accompanied the advancing foot soldiers when possible, providing overwatch and eliminating defenders. The American two-pronged north-south advance meant that by February 8th commanders designated a boundary between Sixth and Eighth Army units across which neither could fire to avoid friendly fire casualties. Trying to prevent such fratricide proved more complicated than first realized, especially when artillery was involved. Limited distances to access targets and the toughness of materials used in construction meant artillery engaged from as close as 150 yards. American soldiers were happy for the support…unless they were on the receiving end of fragmented debris, ricocheting rounds, or those passing over a target to land among their own.

Filipino civilians fortunate enough to escape the fighting quickly became a concern of a different sort. Japanese defenders set fire to neighborhoods, flooding the streets with noncombatants fleeing flames and smoke. These civilians unwittingly helped enemy soldiers infiltrate American lines by concealing themselves in the crowds. At times, noncombatants' behavior surprised US soldiers. Civilians would casually stroll Manila's streets once they thought themselves sufficiently distant from combat, unaware of how far modern weapons could reach out to kill or maim. (Americans in early 21st-century Iraq found the same behavior during fighting in Baghdad and other cities.) Elsewhere, Manileños sheltering in the hoped-for safety of their homes became unintended casualties when bullets passed through the walls of thatched or other thin-skinned dwellings with hardly a notice.

Most people dwelling in those or more substantial structures hungered for the Americans' return after years of Japanese abuse. Some risked passing vital information to US soldiers despite the potential consequences if caught.

Enemy soldiers and Manileño noncombatants were not the only concerns for the attackers. The city's internment camps held American and other prisoners in the thousands suffering severe malnutrition and lack of medical care. Santo Tomas University alone, long since turned into a prison, held some four thousand. Soldiers from the 1st Cavalry Division raced forward to seize the camp given fears the enemy might slaughter its occupants. The Japanese camp commander took two hundred prisoners as the Americans arrived, demanding free passage to his men and himself without surrendering their weapons. Refusal would mean the hostages' execution and a defense to the death. The American commander agreed, taking on the difficult task of feeding the newly freed once the Japanese departed. The task proved harder than expected as prisoner digestive systems initially rejected the rich military rations after prolonged dietary deprivation.

Caring for these and other civilians was a responsibility and a hindrance to attackers trying to maintain their momentum. Pauses became necessary as civilian masses overwhelmed the soldiers' capacity to care for their new trusts and continue the assault. Some amidst the population were fortunately able to relieve the burden somewhat. Marcial Lichauco and his wife converted their home and a nearby property into a makeshift aid facility. The Lichaucos and fellow volunteers would provide care to over twelve hundred Filipinos. The local Red Cross director likewise converted his organization's headquarters into a refugee center. Military units set up to feed US soldiers and hospitals found themselves providing journalists, aid workers, and other unexpected guests. Some locals turned to looting. To MacArthur's disgust, some former prisoners profited by selling army handouts to others in more dire need.

Post-combat fighting destroyed 11,000 of Manila's buildings, leaving 200,000 Filipinos homeless in addition to the 100,000 killed. Death and the spread of disease were both possibilities if—among other prophylactic initiatives—the attacking Americans could not maintain the flow of potable water.[11] Controlling sources, treatment facilities, and significant pipelines pulled additional soldiers away from street fighting. Water sources were sometimes many kilometers distant from the capital and exposed to possible interdiction by enemy forces. Survivors initially had no running water despite the efforts to secure its flow. Nor were electricity and sewage treatment available. The combination left one army doctor amazed that the city had no cholera epidemic. Rats thrived where humans suffered, posing yet another potential source of disease.

Capitalizing on Urban Disasters' Commonality

It took four weeks to clear Manila of occupiers. Recovery took much longer. Civilians continued to die after the fighting ended, many as victims of not-yet-removed enemy mines and booby traps. Thousands of unexploded artillery rounds required disarming, detonation in place, or movement to locations for safe neutralization. Aircraft flew overhead, spraying insecticide to subdue mosquitos feasting on the weakened population and a fly population gorging on carcasses, corpses, and untreated waste. The line between civilized behavior and anarchy was sometimes a knife's edge thin under such conditions. Other efforts to relieve suffering included military civil affairs units hiring over 27,000 Manileños to provide some income; the War Damage Corporation stepped in to cover losses insurance would not.

The above often have parallels in disasters spawned by other causes. Structural collapse threatens anyone returning to earthquake-damaged homes in hopes of recovering belongings no less than Manila's lingering explosives, and some are sure to ignore warnings just as others discount alerts advising them of dangers when disturbing unexploded ordnance. Combat produces types of wounds that demand specialized expertise during treatment. So, too, other catastrophes inflict injury types disproportionate to normality. Crush wounding over-presents in the aftermath of tremors. Respiratory ailments characterized those suffering from Tokyo's 1995 sarin nerve agent terrorist attacks. Similar disorders will be threatened when future accidents or terrorist episodes involve chemical or biological hazards. Such was true during 9/11 when escapees and responders inhaled pulverized concrete and other materials after the Twin Towers collapsed in New York City (NYC). The lesson is clear: plans should identify injury types coincident with various disasters and align these with procedures to link victims with locations and personnel best able to treat them.[12]

Just as military preparations seek to identify expected challenges and effective responses before combat, better civil disaster plans account for difficult choices best made before a calamity. An assembly of pre-COVID New York City experts recommended who should receive medical attention during crises when personnel, equipment, pharmaceutical, or other shortages overwhelm capabilities. Those with little—if any—chance of recovery consume limited resources while the more robust succumb. Individuals die when policies fail to provide guidance or decision-makers lack the courage to enforce well-advised triage procedures. Such was, at times, unfortunately the case in 2020 COVID-plagued NYC.[13]

Care provided by Marcial Lichauco and Manila's Red Cross chapter demonstrates a ubiquitous truth: Select residents will voluntarily assist fellow urban dwellers in times of crisis. It is a reality oft-noted in highlighting individual actions; local newspapers, radio, television, and—indeed today—social media find and draw attention to these cases. The result can be a mistaking of the commonplace as exceptional. The presumption of exceptionality helps to explain why authorities too seldom formally prepare those who might become first-responders (volunteers who come to the aid of neighbors and other disaster victims) before calamities occur. Some thirty-eight percent of victims making their way to hospitals during the 1995 Tokyo sarin attack did so not in ambulances or other official vehicles but via taxis or rides offered by private citizens.[14] Another thirty-five percent walked alone or assisted.[15] An estimated 270,000 of Lower Manhattan's workers and residents evacuated not by a formal plan on 9/11; those departing did so via largely spontaneous maritime transport piloted by private or public providers.[16] Contrast this with Tokyo where formal arrangements between a civilian boat service and the city exist to evacuate personnel should a large earthquake preclude ground escape. Dictates also require local Tokyo authorities to prepare and distribute disaster preparedness maps. These identify areas notably exposed to earthquake damage, fire, liquification, flooding, or other hazards. The maps and related citizen training also facilitate providing citizen aid to others during disasters. Preparing residents and visitors to protect themselves is wise. Preparing them to assist fellow residents in times of need borders on the brilliant. These examples are only a few demonstrating the fungibility of wartime lessons applicable to other disaster types and vice versa. Manila offers others further when it comes to recovering from an urban disaster.

Wartime Manila's Lessons for Recovery from 21st-Century Urban Combat

Manila foretold events regarding ongoing Ukrainian urban combat: Too little has changed when war visits today's cities, towns, and villages, regardless of whether the conflict predominantly features conventional or irregular forces. Coalition soldiers in early 21st-century Iraq found it necessary to secure water sources remote from urban areas as did those in the Philippines. Controlling access to Tigris River dams upstream of Mosul and Baghdad became a priority, albeit as much to prevent the enemy's destroying the dams and flooding civilian communities as to maintain water supplies (a concern that brings the June 2023 Kakhovka Dam breach in Ukraine to mind).[17] Fighting to secure Mosul in 2016-2017 provided parallels in safeguarding noncombatant life. Civilians in the Iraqi city became virtual prisoners. ISIS denied noncombatant occupants medical care and other essentials, targeting them during attempts to flee the city, in some cases spreading corrugated metal sheets on streets, the noise of which would reveal civilians trying to escape after dark. In a revolting variation on using civilians as shields, ISIS positioned injured infants as bait during daylight hours to lure noncombatants into snipers' engagement areas.[18]

Writing years after the liberation of Manila, one author looked back on the physical damage to the Philippine capital, observing the battle for the city dramatically:

> Showed a need for planning post-combat [recovery] operations in detail. Foremost among many competing requirements is the disposal of health-threatening human remains…. While front-line units fought and moved on, logistics forces moved into areas contaminated by disease resulting from large numbers of unburied dead. Traumatized civilians tried to care for their own dead…. Planning for mortuary affairs for US casualties only is insufficient…. Medical support for noncombatants heavily taxes standard military medical organizations…. Other aspects of the urban combat environment require early planning, especially the restoration of public services. Efforts to restore food, water, electrical, fire, police, and sanitation services need the work of specialists…. It is not a task to be handed off lightly to an infantry division that has just fought through the city.[19]

As the world has increasingly urbanized, so too have its wars. More so than with disasters due to other causes, mankind has much to say regarding the extent of a population's suffering and the type and extent of damage wrought. The nature of targeting will impact both immediate and longer-term recovery. Are they military targets, infrastructure of dual use in character, or undeniably civilian or proscribed facilities such as schools and hospitals? Urban complexity can stupefy military leaders. US forces bombing targets in 1991 Baghdad consciously avoided the destruction of medical facilities while disabling power plants, transportation nodes, and fuel supplies that might benefit the adversary. Urban infrastructures' inherent interdependency nevertheless significantly restricted the provision of civilian medical care as hospitals lacked power once backup generators ran out of fuel and doctors, nurses, and critical support personnel could not travel to work. How a force inflicts destruction will similarly have a dramatic effect on recovery. Using chaff (shredded metal strips dropped from the air) to cause temporary shorting in Baghdad power stations rather than destroying generators that could take years to replace sought to quicken post-combat restoration of electricity in 1991.

Conclusion

Lessons from 1945 Manila have much to offer today's leaders whose cities suffer warfare's devastation or on whom responsibility for planning recovery falls. Preventing disease outbreaks, mobilizing resident cooperation, constraining the darker side of human behavior, bridging the gap between immediate provision of necessities and permanent restoration, identifying critical components of and prioritizing infrastructure repairs: These are merely a handful of the challenges that lie ahead whose solutions have seeds in the urban disaster that was Manila. That the Philippine capital was one of the world's most populated cities in 1945 hints at the magnitude of such challenges should primary combat operations occur in a megacity for the first time. Lessons from that World War II battle certainly have insights of value for Ukrainian leaders confronting the challenges inherent in restoring damaged physical and social urban infrastructure. How national and local leaders—and those rendering international assistance—bring their resources to bear during and after the devastation will significantly influence the extent of resident suffering and recovery duration. These decisions should not await the end of combat or, for urban catastrophes yet to come in Ukraine or elsewhere, disaster's arrival.

Endnotes

1. Wendell Cox Consultancy, *Demographia World Urban Areas*, 18th annual edition, July 2022, 21, http://www.demographia.com/db-worldua.pdf.
2. TomTom International BV; "Traffic Index 2019"; https://www.tomtom.com/trafficindex/ranking/.
3. Robert Ross Smith, *Triumph in the Philippines* (Washington, D.C.: Center of Military History, 1963), https://history.army.mil/html/books/005/5-10-1/CMH_Pub_5-101.pdf; Assistant Chief of Staff, G-3, Headquarters, Sixth Army, *Combat Notes Number 8*, June 1945; Assistant Chief of Staff G-3, Headquarters, Sixth Army, *Combat Notes Number 7*, May 1945; Edwin B. Jeffress, *Operations of the 2nd Battalion, 511th Parachute Infantry (11th Airborne Division) in the Battle for Southern Manila, 3-10 February (Luzon Campaign), (Personal Experience of a Battalion Intelligence Officer)*, Advanced Infantry Officers Course, 1948-1949 (Fort Benning, GA: The

Infantry School, undated), https://mcoecbamcoepwprd01.blob.core.usgovcloudapi.net/library/DonovanPapers/w wii/STUP2/G-L/JeffressEdwinB%20%20CPT.pdf; Richard Connaughton, John Pimlott, and Duncan Anderson, *The Battle for Manila: The Most Devastating Untold Story of World War II* (Novato, CA: Presidio, 1995); Douglas MacArthur, *Reminiscences* (NY: Crest, 1964); Herald H. Smith, *The Operations of the 148th Infantry Regiment (37th Infantry Division) at Manila, Luzon, Philippine Islands, 9 January-3 March 1945 (Luzon Campaign)* Advanced Infantry Officers Class Number 1, 1947-1948 (Fort Benning, GA: The Infantry School, undated), https://fhl.omeka.net/items/show/542; Kevin T. McEnery, "The XIV Corps Battle for Manila, February 1945" (master's thesis, US Army Command and General Staff College, 1993), https://apps.dtic.mil/sti/pdfs/ADA273960.pdf; James M. Scott, *Rampage: MacArthur, Yamashita, and the Battle of Manila* (NY: Norton, 2018); Milton T. Hunt, *Use of Armor in Luzon*. General Instruction Department (Fort Knox, KY: The Armored School, 1948), https://mcoecbamcoepwprd01.blob.core.usgovcloudapi.net/library/Armorpapers/AST UP/G-L/HuntMilton%20T.%20MAJ.pdf; Thomas A. Barrow, *Breakthrough to Manila*. Advanced Officers Class #1 military monograph, April 22, 1948, https://mcoecbamcoepwprd01.blob.core.usgovcloudapi.net/library/Armorpapers/AST UP/A-F/BarrowThomas%20A.pdf; William S. McElhenny, William D. Beard, Alfred W. Bruneau, David D. Fleming, Leo J. Nawn, Jr., William A. Burke, Robert S. Ferrari, Francis J. Kelly, and John H. Cleveland, *Armor on Luzon: Comparison of Employment of Armored Units in the 1941-1942 and 1944-1945 Luzon Campaigns*, Research report by committee 9, Officers Advanced Course 1949-1950 (Fort Knox, KY: The Armored School, May 1950), https://mcoecbamcoepwprd01.blob.core.usgovcloudapi.net/library/Armorpapers/AST UP/A-F/Committee%209%20Armoron-Luzon.pdf; Samuel T. Fuller, *The United States Army and Large Cities Prior to the Global War on Terror* (Fort Leavenworth, KS: School of Advanced Military Studies, US Army Command and General Staff College, 2013), https://www.armyupress.army.mil/Portals/7/Primer-on-UrbanOperation/Documents/The-United-States-Army-and-Large.pdf; Assistant Chief of Staff, G-2, Headquarters, Sixth Army, *Japanese Defense of Cities as Exemplified by the Battle for Manila*, July 1, 1945, https://cgsc.contentdm.oclc.org/digital/collection/p4013coll8/id/2947; Nelson H. Randall, "The Battle of Manila," *The Field Artillery Journal* 35, no. 8 (August 1945): 451-456, https://tradocfcoeccafcoepfwprod.blob.core.usgovcloudapi.net/fires-bulletinarchive/1945/AUG_1945/AUG_1945_FULL_EDITION.pdf.

4. Russell W. Glenn, Randall Steeb, John Matsumura, Sean Edwards, Robert Everson, Scott Gerwehr, and John Gordon, *Denying the Widow-Maker: Summary of Proceedings, RAND-DBBL Conference on Military Operations on Urbanized Terrain* (Santa Monica, CA: RAND, 1998), 6, https://www.rand.org/content/dam/rand/pubs/conf_proceedings/2007/CF143.pdf.

5. Andrew Bell, "Civilians, Urban Warfare, and US Doctrine," *Parameters* 50, no. 4 (Winter 2020): 36, https://doi.org/10.55540/0031-1723.2686; International Committee of the Red Cross, "New Research Shows Urban Warfare 8 Times More Deadly for Civilians in Syria and Iraq," news release, October 1, 2018, https://www.icrc.org/en/document/new-research-shows-urban-warfare-eight-timesmore-deadly-civilians-syria-iraq.

6. Smith, *Triumph in the Philippines*, 237 and 239.

7. Smith, *Triumph in the Philippines*, 249.

8. Randall, *The Battle of Manila*. 451-456.

9. Smith, *Triumph in the Philippines*, 264.

10. McEnery, 'The XIV Corps Battle for Manila', 115.

11. There were wells throughout Manila, but US estimates concluded that these resources would run dry after two weeks. Buddy Buck, Anselmo Avenido, John Benedict, Norm Benninghoff, Dick Demers, Jim Groce, Jim Harpole, Mike Kussman, Gary Richardson, Pete Rodda, Pete Verga, Bill Whiteley, Bob Wiese, Skip Wigner, and Yoshihiro Yamaguchi, *Combat Studies Institute Battlebook 13-B* (Fort Leavenworth, KS: Combat Studies Institute, May 1984), III-4, https://apps.dtic.mil/sti/pdfs/ADA165904.pdf. Scott also mentions water resources, to include pipelines: Scott, *Rampage*, 192.

12. Local or national policies and preparations may dictate the character of medical treatment in response to casualties in the field. Doctors in 1995 Tokyo hospitals waited for victims of the nerve agent attack to come to them as was specified procedure. Preparations and policy in 2015 Paris saw both evacuation of patients to medical facilities and the dispatch of medical provider teams to victims' locations, this in keeping with plans.

13. Russell W. Glenn, *Come Hell or High Fever: Readying the World's Megacities for Disaster* (Canberra, Australia: Australian National University Press, 2023), 189. The book is available for free download at https://press.anu.edu.au/publications/comehell-or-high-fever.

14. Tetsu Okumura, Kouichiro Suzuki, Atsuhiro Fukuda, Akitsugu Kohama, Nobukatsu Takasu, Shinichi Ishimatsu and Shigeaki Hinohar, "The Tokyo Subway Sarin Attack: Disaster Management, Part 1—Community Emergency Response," *Academic Emergency Medicine* 5, no. 6 (1998): 614, doi.org/10.1111/j.1553-2712.1998.tb02470.x.

15. Okumura, et al., "The Tokyo Subway Sarin Attack," 614.

16. L. Douglas Keeney, *The Lives They Saved: The Untold Story of Medics, Mariners, and the Incredible Boat Lift that Evacuated Nearly 300,000 People from New York City on 9/11* (Guilford, CT: Lyons Press, 2021), xii. Other sources cite higher numbers of evacuees.

17. William Wallace and Kevin C. M. Benson, "Beyond the First Encounter: Planning and Conducting Field Army and Corps Operations," in *Bringing Order to Chaos: Historical Case Studies of Combined Arms Maneuver in Large-Scale Combat Operations*, ed. Peter J. Schifferle (Fort Leavenworth, KS: Army University Press, 2018), 4, https://www.armyupress.army.mil/Portals/7/combat-studies-institute/csibooks/bringing-order-to-chaos-lsco-volume-2.pdf.

18. Center for Civilians in Conflict, *Policies and Practices to Protect Civilians: Lessons from ISF Operations Against ISIS in Urban Areas*. October 1, 2019, 21, https://civiliansinconflict.org/publications/research/policies-practices-to-protectcivilians/; Trevor Keck, "Episode #31 When War Comes to Cities with Jenny McAvoy and Sahr Muhammedally," produced by the International Committee of the Red Cross, podcast, https://blogs.icrc.org/intercross/2017/09/12/episode-31-when-war-comesto-cities-with-jenny-mcavoy-and-sahr-muhammedally/#sthash.0niYFSTc.dpbs=.

19. McEnery, 'The XIV Corps Battle for Manila', 122-23.

CHAPTER 4
Virtual Urban Siege: Modern Urban Siege and Swarming in Culiacán 2019 & 2023

Daniel Weisz Argomedo, Nathan P. Jones, and John P. Sullivan

Introduction

The two Battles of Culiacán between Mexican state forces and elements of the Cártel de Sinaloa in 2019 and 2023 provide examples of the challenges states face when criminal armed groups (CAGs) employ sophisticated urban battle techniques such as urban siege and swarming attacks. These challenges are a component of the operational complexity found in high-intensity criminal violence, such as that found in crime wars, criminal insurgencies, and the Novo Cangaçao tactics employed by territorial gangs in Brazil.[1] Specifically, urban siege can be viewed as a metaphor for urban swarming as an evolved urban campaign.[2] John Arquilla and David Ronfeldt trace the history of swarming techniques from the animal kingdom all the way through decades of warfare.³ The authors trace the evolution of swarming techniques and predict that these tactics will increase in popularity because of the evolution of communication systems and their effectiveness in modern conflict.⁴ The concept of modern urban siege was first articulated in relation to the 26th of November Mumbai Attack.⁵ This style of attack was later employed in the Westgate Mall Attack (Kenya 2013), the Paris *Charlie Hebdo* and Hyper Cacher attacks (January 2015), and the (November 2015) Stade de France and Bataclan attacks.⁶ In addition to these classic events, the swarming tactics, techniques, and procedures (TTPs) applied in these innovative events continue to influence urban combat by criminals and terrorists alike. In addition to swarming, these influences include armed assaults, combined arms attacks, hostage-taking and, more recently, the use of weaponized aerial drones.⁷ This operational mix has been seen in criminal actions ranging from high-intensity robberies in Brazil's Novo Cangacão to terrorist acts such as the Siege of Marawi by ISIS affiliates in the Philippines (2017).⁸ This framework sets the stage for exploring the incidents in Culiacán.

This chapter compares the two arrests of Ovidio Guzmán and their implications for urban warfare by criminal networks in response to state high-value targeting (HVT). In October 2019, the Mexican military captured Ovidio Guzmán, one of the leaders of the Chapitos faction of the Sinaloa Cartel. The Sinaloa Cartel response was a comprehensive siege of the city of Culiacán, which involved heavy weaponry, street blockades, threats delivered electronically, a prison break, and sufficient violence that the Mexican government at the Presidential level chose to release Ovidio Guzmán to prevent further bloodshed. This incident became known as the *Culiacanazo*. While these tactics were not new, the scale was unprecedented, and the intervening years saw other Mexican cartels mimic this response. Later, in early 2023, the Mexican government recaptured Ovidio Guzmán and was better prepared to withstand the coming onslaught. The authors call this incident *Culiacanazo* 2.0 in their comparison in this article. This article uses the two events as case studies to compare criminal network urban warfare in response to state high value targeting. It supplies tactical and operational comparisons of the events and their strategic implications. It also concludes with policy recommendations for how states can address criminal network urban warfare in response to high-value targeting by states. Ultimately, the Mexican government successfully applied many lessons from the 2019 Siege of Culiacán to the January 2023 capture of Ovidio Guzmán. Still, future Mexican administrations must answer what strategic framework successful HVT operations will serve.

Our assessment will proceed by (1) contextualizing the two attempts to capture Ovidio Guzmán and the urban environment of the city of Culiacán, (2) briefly discussing the recent scholarship on urban security of relevance, (3) elucidating the case study and data gathering methods; (4) presenting the cases in chronological order; (5) analyzing and comparing the cases in their geopolitical context; and (6) providing conclusions and policy recommendations.

Contextualizing the Urban Siege of Culiacán

Ovidio Guzmán López (*El Ratón*) is the son of Joaquin (*El Chapo*) Guzmán and is accused of having a significant role in the Sinaloa Cartel, according to the Treasury Department of the United States.[9] In April 2018, the United States Department of Justice accused Ovidio and his brother Joaquín Guzmán López of trafficking large shipments of cocaine, methamphetamines, and marijuana to the United States.[10] In 2021, the US State Department offered a 5-million-dollar reward for information leading to the arrest of four of El Chapo's sons, including Ovidio.[11] The other three sons that comprise the Chapitos are Iván Archivaldo Guzmán Salazar, Jesús Alfredo Guzmán Salazar and Joaquín Guzmán López.

Two operations by the Mexican government have attempted to capture Ovidio Guzmán. The first attempt in 2019 failed, resulting in his capture and subsequent release. The second attempt in 2023 would result in his capture and transfer to the Altiplano maximum security federal prison (the same prison his father escaped from in 2015). Security expert Alejandro

Hope explains that Mexico opened no judicial investigation against Ovidio and that most of the judicial case to arrest Ovidio emerges from the United States.[12] He believes that the Mexican judicial system will only be able to legally detain him for a few months, which means the government will likely seek to extradite him to the United States.[13] The Mexican judicial system gave the United States until March 5, 2023, to formally request his extradition and present evidence against Ovidio.[14] On February 27, 2023, the United States government officially requested the extradition of Ovidio. Both operations to capture Ovidio serve as valuable case studies to explore modern urban sieges that employ swarming tactics, techniques, and procedures (TTPs).

Culiacán is the Capital City of Sinaloa. Historically and presently, Sinaloa is known as the heart of Mexican drug trafficking, with many of the original cartel-leading families hailing from the state where poppy and marijuana grew the first significant traffickers. The Sinaloa Cartel also dominates it. The sons of Chapo Guzman now essentially lead the cartel. Culiacán is a city of one million people. It has dense urban zones in addition to bridges and high toll booths that can serve as chokepoints, allowing a powerful non-state actor with command control over its forces to shut down the possibility of Mexican government reinforcements.

Recent Scholarship

There has been significant recent scholarship on urban security, and the role cities will play in the future of conflict, of which this current special issue on urban security, the authors hope, will become a core component.[15] In his seminal 2015 book *Out of the Mountains*, David Kilcullen argues that militaries' fixation on rural warfare is ill-considered given the megatrends he identifies, such as coastal city growth, climate change, and increased urbanization, all of which lead us to forecast increased urban conflict. Given that likelihood, understanding the role of violent non-state actors (VNSAs)—specifically CAGs—in using urban siege tactics to prevent high-value targeting (HVT) of their leadership is critical to global, regional, and local security and an understanding of illicit network resilience.[16]

Urban Operations Planning

Military and police urban operations are challenging due to the intricate interplay between the competing forces—state services against arms bearers: Criminals, terrorists, insurgents, or military forces—population density, and the complexity of the terrain and the built environment. When these factors converge, operations become difficult, the distinction between combatants (or arms bearers) blurred, and the population is at risk.[17] Planning is the key to effective procedures that protect the populace and minimize risk to security forces and their adversaries. This planning must be based on effective intelligence to understand the potential threats and risks faced during a specific operation, the nature of the threat group, and the terrain where the operation(s) will occur.[18]

The relative success of urban operations depends upon detailed intelligence, planning, and execution. This preparation must be sufficient to overcome the natural defensive advantage of local criminal groups on their turf, where they have an advantage on terrain knowledge, can prepare defenses and strongholds, and rely on local support.

Police-Military Interaction in the Urban Environment

Crime, including violent gang crime, is a feature of many cities. Urban crime is often a significant policy concern. When territorial and third generation gangs dominate the local space criminal enclaves, characterized by criminal governance, may exist.[19] When CAGs confront the state, well-honed interaction between civil police agencies and state military forces is necessary. This interaction, however, is often problematic due to bureaucratic competition, perceptions of corruption, and lack of capacity. Mexico has profoundly experienced these challenges over the years.[20] These challenges are exacerbated by the organizational complexity of both the military and the police, with the military divided among the army under the *Secretaría de la Defensa Nacional* (SEDENA or Secretariat of National

Defense) and naval forces under the *Secretaría de la Marina* (SEMAR or Naval Secretariat). On the police side, the First Battle of Culiacán occurred just weeks after the *Policia Federal* (Federal Police) dissolved and merged into the new *Guardia Nacional* (National Guard).[21]

The Guardia Nacional (National Guard) and the Military

The establishment of the Guardia Nacional was controversial and remains so. Some view The National Guard as a step toward militarizing Mexican law enforcement, and its critics prefer establishing civil policing institutions.[22] Essentially, the issue is one of military versus civilian control. To contain corruption and enhance citizen perceptions of legitimacy, Mexican president Andres Manuel Lopes Obrador (AMLO) sought to place the National Guard under military leadership (SEDENA); the Mexican Supreme Court has rejected military control as being unconstitutional.[23] Nevertheless, there is a role for both police and army operations (supported by intelligence) to contain the threat of CAGs and the extreme violence they present. Both civil police and military-type capabilities are necessary at various parts of the violent contest between the state and CAGs. That is one reason the government constructed the Guardia Nacional as a paramilitary or gendarmerie-type force. Further police reform and discussion about the framework for policing in Mexico are needed. Notwithstanding that necessary policy debate, the operational effectiveness of security forces needs to be calibrated by the government to address the threat of CAGs in a range of missions, including urban operations.

Presentation of the Case Studies

This comparative case study analysis relies on open-source materials describing the two events. These include opensource media reports, court documents, videos of the incident where available, and documents made public by the *Guacamaya* hackers, including a trove of Mexican Military (*Secretaria de Defensa Nacional* (SEDENA)) documents related to the incident. Additionally, this operational and tactical analysis utilized timelines presented by the Mexican government and the New York Times, which painstakingly pieced together relevant social media videos, posts, and other data to create a timeline replete with maps. The cases are compared utilizing chronological analysis and the method of structured, focused comparison wherein the same questions were asked of all cases to ensure their comparability.[24]

Culiacanazo (The Siege of Culiacán 2019)

The first and failed attempt to capture Ovidio happened on October 17, 2019, in Culiacán, the capital of the state of Sinaloa. Mexicans refer to this attempt popularly as the *Culiacanazo* or *Jueves negro* (the Black Thursday). The Mexican government gave several official versions of what happened. Alfonso Durazo, head of the secretary of security and citizen protection, would report that 30 elements of the National Guard and the army were conducting a routine patrol when they were attacked from a home.[25] The security forces proceeded to repel the attack and surround the house, where four people, including Ovidio Guzmán, were detained.[26]

The video recorded by authorities in 2019 showed Ovidio coming out of a residence with his hands in the air. Once arrested, Ovidio Guzmán received a cell phone from security forces so that he could order the Sinaloa Cartel to stop the violence. He did so but to no avail as his Sinaloa Cartel compatriots fought.[27] The cartel would proceed to begin an operation to release Ovidio, and only an hour after his reported detention, the authorities released him back to the cartel.[28] President Andrés Manuel López Obrador contradicted Durazo and declared this had been a purposeful operation to capture Ovidio due to an extradition order for his apprehension.[29] After significant pressure due to contradicting reports on the arrest, the government would provide a minute-by-minute operation breakdown that justified Ovidio's release as a decision to "protect the lives of citizens" in Sinaloa.[30]

Chronology of Events

The operation began at 1 pm Pacific time in Mexico City, where members of the National Guard presented a report to the prosecutor's office to justify a search warrant and alerted the armed forces to prepare for the operation.[31] Around an hour later, at 2 p.m., Ovidio arrived at a house in Culiacán, and 30 minutes later, the operation began by surrounding the place where Ovidio and his family were located.[32]

The house is in the neighborhood of *Tres Rios* within Culiacán.[33] This neighborhood has a high urban density and is close to the city's most famous park, Las Riberas, shopping center, *Plaza Fórum,* and several education and government buildings.[34] Mexican security forces reported getting fired upon at 2:50 p.m. As a result, the search warrant under process in Mexico City was deemed no longer needed, and the operation to capture Ovidio began.[35]

In 2022, reporter Carlos Loret de Mola reported on documents his news agency (*Latinus*) had received from a hacker group called *Guacamaya* that uncovered previously unknown information about this military operation.[36] The army reported that Ovidio's capture occurred at 3:15 p.m. Still, the hacked documents report that the army arrived at 3 p.m. At 3:17 pm, state security forces captured Ovidio to persuade his older brother Iván Archivaldo Guzmán Salazar to stop hostilities.[37] As soldiers attempted to surround Ovidio's home, news around Sinaloa spread, and by 3:30 p.m., the first reports of injured soldiers began to come in. Culiacán was under siege, with all highways in and out blocked.[38] Figure 1 represents all blockades conducted during this operation by criminals with blue points and any violent confrontations with red points.

Figure 1. Map of blockades and violent confrontations in Culiacán during Ovidio's first arrest.[39]

The cartel members surrounded the house where the operation occurred by 3:47 p.m.[40] The group of criminals surrounding the house consisted of 40 armed men in eight vehicles, two of which had bulletproof windows and armor.[41] On a larger scale, the criminals also blocked strategic points around the city with burning vehicles. They successfully secured a perimeter in which soldiers, federal agents, and the population of Culiacán could not escape.[42] Overall, the cartel placed barricades and burning vehicles at 19 different points across Culiacán, and the violence took the lives of nine people.[43]

There are reports that as the cartel set up blockades, a military helicopter trying to support the armed forces on the ground received several bullet impacts.[44] At 3:50 pm, armed cartel members aboard vehicles surrounded the military bases in Culiacán and kidnapped several military personnel.[45] Cartel members blocked the highways North and South of Culiacán to prevent land reinforcements from reaching Mexican armed forces.[46] The federal forces could only recapture and hold one of the access points by *Avenida Universitarios* of the nine available in the area of the operation.[47]

To create more chaos and replenish their numbers, cartel members targeted the Aguaruto prison at 5:04 p.m. and successfully orchestrated a massive prison break.[48] The cartel members liberated around fifty convicts, of which several belonged to the cartel, and joined in the fight against the armed forces.[49] The cartel members successfully kidnapped soldiers protecting a highway towards Mazatlán and targeted the barracks where soldiers' families live.[50] The criminals threatened to execute the families of the soldiers, and twenty cartel members with automatic weapons in four vehicles were able to repel the troops sent to support the barracks.[51]

The criminals penetrated four apartments to kidnap their inhabitants as part of a broader strategy to exchange soldiers for Ovidio.[52] The cartel targeted the military and kidnapped nine soldiers and two officers, two of whom were taken by 15 armed men in the Crucero de Jesús María about 30 km from Ovidio's house.[53] The cartel members also created blockades from vehicles taken from the armed forces. They surrounded the military bases in Cosalá, El Fuerte, and Cosa Rica, where 150 cartel members kidnapped 24 soldiers and two officers.[54]

At 6:49 pm, the cabinet of security of México, supported by AMLO, ordered the armed forces to fall back and liberate Ovidio.[55] The violence would begin to diminish after security forces released Ovidio. By 7:17 pm, an officer and four soldiers kidnapped at a highway toll booth in Costa Rica, located South of Culiacán, were released.[56]

Overall, around 700-800 armed cartel members successfully defeated 350 members of security forces around the city.[57] The army also reported the criminal use of eight vehicles, of which at least two were armored, and the use of Barrett sniper rifles and machine guns, some of which were vehicle mounted.[58] Secretary of Defense Crescencio Sandoval explained how the criminals had overtaken the four strategic points close to the home of Ovidio that the army had tried to secure.[59] Juan Carlos Montero, a security expert, believes that either someone prewarned the criminals or the army didn't have enough manpower.[60]

Culiacanazo 2.0

This operation occurred in the early hours of January 5, 2023.[61] This time, the army was able to target Ovidio in the rural community of Jesús María, a small town of 5,062 people located North of Culiacán.[62] This location is better suited for the capture as it has fewer civilians and is far enough away from Culiacán to avoid the armed forces being under siege inside the capital of Sinaloa (Culiacán).

The operation began with members of the National Guard supported by the army identifying several armed people in pickup trucks with homemade armor commonly used by organized crime.[63] The Mexican security forces formed a perimeter around the vehicles. They tried to persuade the people inside the vehicle to descend, at which point the armed individuals opened fire against the security agents.[64] The armed individuals then proceeded to take refuge in three different homes, from which they continued attacking the agents of the National Guard with 50caliber machine guns.[65] The high caliber power of the criminal's weapons forced the security forces to call for air support, which resulted in the emergency landing of a plane used by the army from the damage caused by the .50-caliber weapons.[66] A UH-60M helicopter, better known as a 'black hawk' with a Gatling Dillon Aero M134D machinegun capable of shooting 3,000 rounds a minute was able to successfully defeat the armed individuals and provide aerial cover for the ground units capturing Ovidio Guzmán.[67]

During Ovidio's detention, security forces found him possessing weapons legally restricted to the Mexican army and air force in Mexico at 5:20 a.m. Pacific Standard Time, according to the national registry of detentions in

Mexico.⁶⁸ Around 7 a.m., two military planes took off from the airbase in Santa Lucía, located in the State of Mexico, towards Sinaloa to help provide air support for the operation.⁶⁹ Immediately after his detention, members of the Sinaloa Cartel set up 19 blockades and aggressions in different parts of Culiacán. Figure 2 shows blockades in red and aggressions in yellow and grey.⁷⁰

Figure 2. Government map of the blockades and violent confrontations in Culiacán during Ovidio's second detention.⁷¹

As soon as federal agents captured Ovidio, the Air Force transported him by a plane to extract him quickly from Sinaloa to Mexico City for detention.[72] This successful operation resulted from six months of surveillance and was better organized and supported than the first attempt to detain Ovidio.[73] The Sinaloa Cartel members reacted similarly to the 2019 '*culiacanazo*' and blocked all roads heading toward Culiacán.[74]

Criminal members stole 250 vehicles in Sinaloa and burned 51 to blockade Culiacán.[75] Juan José Moreno Orzúa, colonel of infantry and two soldiers, were ambushed and killed by cartel members in the municipality of Escuinapa, Sinaloa.[76] To stop Ovidio from leaving Sinaloa, cartel members attacked the international airport in Culiacán and forced its closure.[77] Some videos show cartel members firing at planes from the Mexican air force and commercial planes parked at the international airport.[78] Cartel members also attacked a military air base in Sinaloa in a failed attempt to recapture Ovidio.[79] The operation resulted in the detention of 21 cartel members and the capture of several weapons and 40 pickup trucks, of which 26 were armored.[80] Twenty-nine people died in this operation, including ten soldiers and nineteen cartel members. Thirty-five soldiers also sustained injuries in the operation.[81]

Case Comparison and Discussion

Table 1. *Culicanazo* 1.0 in October 2019 to the *Culiacanazo* 2.0 in 2023

	Culiacanazo (Oct. 2019)	***Culiacanazo* 2.0** (Jan. 2023)
Urban versus Rural	Urban	Primarily Rural
Time of Day	Mid-Afternoon	Early Morning
Location	Culiacan (pop. 1 million)	Santa Maria (pop. 5,000)
Military or LEA Deaths	2	10
Cartel Member Deaths	8	19
Civilian Deaths	2	0
Wounded	21	35
Total deaths	14[82]	29
Arrests	~49[83]	21
Air support	No	Yes
Aerial exfiltration of HVT	No	Yes
Total Troops or LEAs Used	350	3500
Narco Blockades or Burning Vehicles	Yes (19)	Yes (9)
Sniper Rifles	Yes	Yes
.50 Cal Machine Guns	Yes	Yes
Successfully detain and hold Ovidio Guzmán?	No	Yes

Numerous areas of comparison emerge when comparing *Culicanazo* 1.0 in October 2019 to the *Culiacanazo* 2.0 in 2023. A point-by-point summary comparison of the two *Culiacanazo* incidents is provided in Table 1.

Most importantly, Mexican security forces had learned lessons from the earlier failure. It is also highly likely that the earlier failure was a humiliation for the military or law enforcement and a political defeat for the government of AMLO. His political enemies had hotly criticized the failure to capture

Ovidio Guzmán and the decision to release him, though it is highly likely this decision saved civilian lives.[84] Further, other cartels became emboldened by the success of the Sinaloa Cartel in securing the release of one of their high-value members after an apprehension by the government.

This later played out in August 2022, when in the states of Jalisco and Guanajuato, the Cártel de Jalisco Nueva Generación (CJNG) engaged in widespread simultaneous violent responses to what appeared to be the apprehension of high-value members of the CJNG.[85] A similar wave of violence occurred in Tijuana a few days later.[86] Thus, these violent responses to high-value target apprehensions became commonplace and automated. Therefore, a significant cost to the public release of Ovidio Guzmán as the high-profile event may have emboldened copycats. The Mexican military understood the failures of the previous attempt to apprehend and hold Ovidio Guzmán and adapted in numerous ways.

It is important to note that these events happened before the 2019 *Culiacanazo*. In 2012, the CJNG set extensive roadblocks and large-scale violence in Guadalajara to thwart the capture of its leader, El Mencho.[87] In 2017, the Tlahuác-Chalco Cartel had a similar response to the 2017 arrest of its leader.[88] Thus, the *Culiacanazo* event is part of an ongoing trend. Still, given its size and media coverage, it likely inspired all organized crime in Mexico to double down on the strategy.

The Government Response and AMLO Critics

Some AMLO critics like Jorge Castañeda have argued that the *Culiacanazo* of 2019 resulted from the history of the US-Mexico relationship and the Wikileaks release of US diplomatic cables in 2010.[89] The release revealed a situation wherein the US government provided SEDENA with the location of Arturo Beltran Leyva, leader of the Beltran-Leyva Organization (BLO). The Mexican Military, likely due to risk aversion or corruption, did not act on the intelligence. US officials then funneled the information to the Mexican Marines (SEMAR), which acted on the intelligence. The WikiLeaks revelations of the United States playing different Mexican security agencies off each other gave the appearance of a sovereignty issue and resulted in the resignation of Pascual, the US ambassador to México.[90]

Castañeda argues that experience may have been why the Mexican government half-heartedly went into the *Culiacanazo* event. It wanted to show the US government it would act on the intelligence in the run-up to the negotiations of the USMCA, which became the successor trade deal to NAFTA. It feared that US agencies would use it to sabotage the trade deal if it did not. Nonetheless, AMLO had long overtly rejected the kingpin strategy of targeting cartel leaders because Mexico's experience over the previous decade was that it only increased violence.[91] Thus, the Mexican government pursued Ovidio with a small number of troops and was caught off guard by the Sinaloa Cartel response, according to Castañeda.[92]

Implications and Lessons Learned Culiacanazo 1.0

The authors assess that Sinaloa Cartel had a preplanned response to a high-value apprehension in the city of Culiacán. In hindsight, the preplanned response is not surprising given the 2017 extradition of Chapo Guzmán to the United States and the desire of his sons to avoid that fate.

The Sinaloa Cartel plan went into effect within minutes of the apprehension of Ovidio Guzmán, leading some reporters to speculate that the cartel may have been alerted by some corrupt official.[93] Videos of the event show elements of the Sinaloa Cartel that had bulletproof vests, helmets, and heavy weaponry such as sniper rifles, .50-caliber machine guns (some mounted on the back of trucks), and, more importantly, a radio system to coordinate their efforts. The Sinaloa Cartel took control of critical chokepoints throughout the city to cut off military reinforcements. It used *narcobloqueos* or narco-blockades using vehicles at key choke points. They then lit the vehicles on fire with gasoline. The plumes of smoke added to the sense of chaos for all involved and may have limited air visibility and air support.

Despite the preplanned nature of the response, there may have been improvisation. There were reports of young men being recruited on the spot with offers of 20,000 pesos or about US $1,000 to join the fight. The prison break may also have been improvised, with the intent of sowing added chaos to pressure the government to release Ovidio Guzmán.[94]

Operational Lessons Learned and Implemented

The Mexican government learned many lessons from the failed operation in 2019. These lessons led to the second and final operation to capture Ovidio. The first lesson applied was not to conduct an operation in the middle of the day. In an urban environment, operations conducted in the middle of the day can pose an additional risk for civilians in public places, as seen during the first operation to capture Ovidio.

Mexican security force's second lesson targeted Ovidio Guzmán in a rural area. This highlights the urban security issue, namely that in an urban environment, there are more choke points, more opportunities for a violent response, more potential hostages, and more potential for collateral damage. On the other hand, in the rural environment, there is far less opportunity for collateral damage and less urban environmental density to mount a defense in. Again, in the urban environment, one of the reasons why the Mexican government chose to release a video of Guzmán was to avoid significant civilian casualties.[95]

The third lesson applied led the Mexican security forces to adapt by recognizing that Ovidio Guzmán would immediately need to be extracted by security forces from the areas under the protection and control of the Sinaloa Cartel. The failure to capture Ovidio during the first operation was partly because the security forces could not extract him from the city before criminals surrounded them. Rapid aerial exfiltration made easier by the rural environment was thus an essential adaptation.

The fourth lesson applied resulted in the government understanding it must be ready for and accept the inevitable violent backlash and prepare accordingly. This required the military and the AMLO Administration's political will to take casualties and violence. By preparing for this immediate backlash, in part by rapidly moving Ovidio Guzmán of Sinaloa Cartel-controlled territories, the Mexican government limited the ability of the cartel to engage in a highly violent response. This would force the Sinaloa Cartel to engage in a perilous game, to inflict suffering on the local population whose support it on some level needs, as earlier research has shown, or continue pressing the government with violence.[96]

Simply by engaging in this second attempt to capture Ovidio Guzmán, the Mexican government was effectively signaling that it was willing to accept any violent response by the Sinaloa Cartel. Otherwise, it would simply not have tried to arrest him. Thus, by successfully capturing, rapidly moving, and holding Ovidio Guzmán, the Mexican government was dealing a psychological blow to the Sinaloa Cartel that would deflate cartel members and, thereby, the length and level of violent response. It is also highly likely the Mexican security apparatus had its analysts assessing the level of response by the Sinaloa Cartel, which would likely determine that the Sinaloa Cartel would be constrained in the amount of violence it could use in any attempt to recapture Ovidio Guzmán based on its need for the support of the population. This would force the cartel into a calculus, a violent response versus other potential mechanisms, such as legal machinations to retrieve Ovidio Guzmán via the legal system.

As a tactical operation, *Culiacanazo* 2.0 was a success for the Mexican government and military. The military was able to capture, detain, and hold Ovidio Guzmán. The stain of the embarrassment of his release in the *Culiacanazo* 1.0 of 2019 had, on some level, been avenged by the government, reestablishing some level of deterrence by demonstrating Mexican government and security forces capabilities vis-à-vis violent cartels. Whether or not México can consider it a long-term operational success will also depend on the Mexican legal institutions' success in determining whether he can be extradited to the United States or by trying him successfully and legally in México and then incarcerating him for an extended period. The arrest and detention of Ovidio Guzmán is not likely to be considered a strategic success for the Mexican government insofar as the Mexican drug war will continue, and the leadership of the Chapito's faction of the Sinaloa Cartel is sufficiently decentralized that his arrest in a vacuum will have limited disruptive impact.

The authors assess that targeting the families in the military barracks as hostages in the *Culicanazo* 1.0 may have been successful in that event but triggered a strong state reaction from the military.[97] It is important to note that the military has played an essential role in Mexico's battle with organized crime. In the Cienfuegos affair, it has demonstrated that the Mexican army has political leverage and support.[98] The targeting of military families in the *Culiacanazo* 2019 was no doubt viewed as an affront and necessitated a response from the military, making the events of January 2023 inevitable.

Conclusion

Finally, a comparison of the two attempts to apprehend Ovidio Guzmán, a significant leader of the Sinaloa Cartel, supplies illuminating lessons learned. In the first attempt, a failure, the Mexican government faced the realities of poorly planned urban operations against highly organized, well-financed, violent non-state adversaries. The coordinated response by the non-state adversary suggested preplanning, strong communications, command and control, including pre-existing radio systems, a factor earlier research has shown assisted major Mexican cartels in controlling territory.[99] The urban dimension supplied many challenges. For example,

1. The well-coordinated adversary could use the city's geography, including bridges and other chokepoints such as highway toll booths, to control and cut off the flow of reinforcements to the government.

2. The urban dimension allowed the cartel to respond rapidly with many belligerent forces. In an improvised fashion, the cartel's

ability to offer 20,000 pesos for every volunteer willing to fight allowed it to surge its numbers rapidly in a matter of hours. This suggests that the cartel violence has left México with a glut of willing young killers seeking employment opportunities.[100]

3. The urban environment supplied more hostage opportunities, including the family military barracks.

4. While a lack of planning was also likely to blame, the lack of air support and air exfiltration of Ovidio Guzmán was likely a key component of the failed operation.

5. The Mexican government was more accepting of casualties and the lethality of a high-value apprehension in January 2023 than in the 2019 *Culiacanazo*. Twice as many people died, but civilian casualties and the threat to civilian lives were far lower than in the first attempt.

6. The time of day may have also aided the second response. Targeting the apprehension in the early morning may have helped to catch the cartel off guard. The time of day, combined with the rural environment, meant that much of the cartel response was not in the location of the apprehension; in other words, the Sinaloa Cartel targeted and fired upon planes to prevent Guzman's exfiltration via air but he was nowhere close to their attacks.

Taking a step back from the success of the second HVT operation, what is the strategic orientation an HVT operation fits into? These are the questions the AMLO Administration, and any future Mexican Administration must ask broadly before it engages in these strikes, lest Kingpin apprehensions appear *ad hoc* and in foreign interests (US government pressure or trade related). Strategically, the Mexican government must answer this fundamental policy question before any operational lessons learned from these events will matter as part of a coherent policy to reduce violence and criminality in Mexico

Endnotes

1. John P. Sullivan, "Crime Wars: Operational Perspectives on Criminal Armed Groups in Mexico and Brazil." *International Review of the Red Cross* 105, no. 923 (2023): 849–75, https://www.cambridge.org/core/journals/international-review-of-the-red-cross/article/crime-wars-operational-perspectives-on-criminal-armed-groups-in-mexico-and- brazil/2A788ED54A033AA-299C5A473721F8716.

2. John P. Sullivan, "Policing Urban Conflict: Urban Siege, Terrorism and Insecurity," *Stratfor*, April 19, 2018, https://www.academia.edu/36721271/Policing_Urban_Conflict_Urban_Siege_Terrorism_and_Insecurity.

3. John Arquilla and David Ronfeldt, "Swarming & The Future of Conflict," *RAND,* 2000, https://www.rand.org/content/dam/rand/pubs/documented_briefings/2005/RAND_ DB311.pdf.

4. John Arquilla and David Ronfeldt, "Swarming & The Future of Conflict."

5. John P. Sullivan and Adam Elkus, "Postcard from Mumbai: Modern Urban Siege," *Small Wars Journal*, February. 16, 2009, https://smallwarsjournal.com/blog/journal/docs-temp/181-sullivan.pdf; John P. Sullivan and Adam Elkus, "Preventing Another Mumbai: Building a Police Operational Art," *CTC Sentinel* 2, no. 6, June 2009, https://ctc.westpoint.edu/wpcontent/uploads/2010/06/Vol2Iss6-Art2.pdf.

6. David Killcullen, "Westgate mall attacks: urban areas are the battlegrounds of the 21st century," *The Guardian*, September 2013, https://www.theguardian.com/world/2013/sep/27/westgate-mall-attacks-al-qaida; John P. Sullivan and Adam Elkus, "Urban Siege in Paris: a Spectrum of Armed Assault," *Small Wars Journal*, February 2, 2015, https://www.academia.edu/10660299/Urban_Siege_in_Paris_A_Spectrum_of_Arme d_Assault; Jean-Charles Briard, "The Paris Attacks and the Evolving Islamic State Threat to France," CTC Sentinel 8, no. 11, November/December 2015, https://ctc.westpoint.edu/the-paris-attacks-and-the-evolving-islamic-state-threat-tofrance/.

7. Sullivan, "Policing Urban Conflict"; Robert J. Bunker and John P. Sullivan, eds. Criminal Drone Evolution: Cartel Weaponization of Aeria IEDs (Bloomington, IN: Xlibris, (2019), https://www.amazon.com/Blood-Concrete-Conflict-MegacitiesAnthology/dp/1984573756.

8. John P. Sullivan, José de Arimatéia da Cruz, and Robert J. Bunker, "Third Generation Gangs Strategic Note No. 48: "Novo Cangaço" Style Urban Raid in Guarapuava, Paraná (PR), Brazil," *Small Wars Journal*, May 9, 2022, https://smallwarsjournal.com/jrnl/art/third-generation-gangs-strategic-note-no-48novo-cangaco-style-urban-raid-guarapuava; Ervin C. Divinagracia, "Urban Terrorism: The Siege of Marawi City," Master of Military Art and Science Thesis (Ft. Levenworth: US Army Command and General Staff College, 2018), https://cgsc.contentdm.oclc.org/digital/collection/p4013coll2/id/3785/.

9. "¿Quién es Ovidio Guzmán López, hijo del Chapo Guzmán?," [Who is Ovidio Guzmán López, son of Chapo Guzmán?]. *CNN*, January 5, 2023, https://cnnespanol.cnn.com/2023/01/05/quien-es-ovidio-guzman-lopez-hijo-delchapo-guzman/.

10. Isaías Alvarado, "Quién es Ovidio Guzmán: el hijo de 'El Chapo' recapturado a tres años después de una fracasada operación policial," [Who is Ovidio Guzmán: the son of 'El Chapo' recaptured three years after a failed police operation]. *Univision*, January 5, 2023, https://www.univision.com/noticias/narcotrafico/quien-es-ovidioguzman-el-hijo-de-el-chapo-captura-

do-otra-vez-en-culiacan.

11. Alvarado, "Quién es Ovidio." [Who is Ovidio].

12. "Nadie ha construido una investigación judicial: el dardo de Alejandro Hope a la detención de Ovidio." [Nobody has built a judicial investigation: Alejandro Hope's dart at Ovidio's arrest]. *Infobae*, January 9, 2023, https://www.infobae.com/america/mexico/2023/01/09/nadie-ha-construido-unainvestigacion-judicial-el-dardo-de-alejandro-hope-a-la-detencion-de-ovidio/.

13. "Detención de Ovidio." [Ovidio's arrest].

14. "Otorgaron suspension definitiva contra extradición de Ovidio Guzmán a EEUU," [Definitive suspension granted against extradition of Ovidio Guzmán to the United States]. *Infobae*, January 25, 2023, https://www.infobae.com/mexico/2023/01/25/otorgaron-suspension-definitivacontra-extradicion-de-ovidio-guzman-a-eeuu/.

15. John P. Sullivan and Nathan P. Jones, "Bandits, Urban Guerrillas, and Criminal Insurgents: Crime and Resistance in Latin America," in *The Routledge Handbook of Latin America and the Caribbean (Twentieth and Twenty-First Century)*, ed. Pablo Baisotti (New York: Routledge, 2021); Dave Dillege et al., eds., *Blood and Concrete: 21st Century Conflict in Urban Centers and Megacities*, A Small Wars Journal Anthology (Bloomington, IN: Xlibris, 2019), https://www.amazon.com/BloodConcrete-Conflict-Megacities-Anthology/dp/1984573756.

16. Rene M Bakker, Jörg Raab, and H Brinton Milward, "A Preliminary Theory of Dark Network Resilience," *Journal of Policy Analysis and Management* 31, no. 1 (2012): 33– 62; Nathan P. Jones, *Mexico's Illicit Drug Networks and the State Reaction* (Washington, D.C.: Georgetown University Press, 2016).

17. Anthony King, *Urban Warfare in the Twenty-First Century* (Cambridge: Polity Press, 2021); John P. Sullivan, "Protecting the Populace: Humanitarian Considerations in Urban Operations," *Stratfor*, June 2, 2018, https://www.academia.edu/36953769/Protecting_the_Populace_Humanitarian_Cons iderations_in_Urban_Operations.

18. John P. Sullivan and Nathan P. Jones, "Intelligence and Analytical Approaches for the Crime-Gang-Terrorism Nexus," *International Journal on Criminology* 10, no. 1, Fall 2022/Winter 2023, https://www.criminologyjournal.org/intelligence-and-analyticalapproaches-for-the-crime-gang-terrorism-nexus.html; Nathan P. Jones, Irina A, Chindea, Daniel Weisz Agromedo, and John P. Sullivan, "A Social Network Analysis of Mexico's Dark Network Alliance Structure," *Journal of Strategic Security* 15, no, 4 (2022), https://digitalcommons.usf.edu/jss/vol15/iss4/5/.

19. John P. Sullivan and Nathan P. Jones, "Bandits, Urban Guerillas and Criminal Insurgents) in Pablo A. Baisotti, ed. *Problems and Alternatives in the Modern Americas* (New York, Routledge, 2022), https://www.taylorfrancis.com/chapters/edit/10.4324/9781003045342-7/banditsurban-guerrillas-criminal-insurgents-john-sullivan-nathan-jones; John P. Sullivan, "The Challenges of Territorial Gangs: Civil Strife, Criminal Insurgencies and Crime Wars," *Revista do Ministério Público Militar* (Brazil), Edição n. 31, November 2019, https://www.academia.edu/40917684/The_Challenges_of_Territorial_Gangs_Civil_S trife_Criminal_Insurgencies_and_Crime_Wars.

20. John P. Sullivan, "Police-Military Interaction in Mexico's Drug War," *Air & Space Power Journal – Spanish Edition*, Third Trimester 2009, https://www.academia.edu/1113223/Police_Military_Interaction_in_Mexico_s_Drug _War.

21. The Federal Police were dissolved on October 1, 2019, and the first Battle of Culiacán occurred on October 17, 2019. Additional complexity in Mexican policing results from the federal nature of the republic with states having their won state police agencies. Municipalities often maintain their own police as well. Furthermore, the Mexican police service is divided among preventive (patrol) and investigative Detectives) police with different agencies handling different aspects of policing. On the transition from the Federal Police to Guardia Nacional (National Guard; Patricia H. Escamilla-Hamm, "The *Guardia Nacional* (National Guard): Why a New Militarized Police in Mexico," Small Wars Journal, December 8, 2020, https://smallwarsjournal.com/jrnl/art/guardia-nacional-national-guard-why-newmilitarized-police-mexico.

22. Marco Leofrigo, "The Mexican National Guard: a solution to ensure security or a strong escalation in the process of militarization?" Small Wars Journal, October 9, 2022, https://smallwarsjournal.com/jrnl/art/mexican-national-guard-solution-ensuresecurity-or-strong-escalation-process; John P. Sullivan and Nathan P. Jones, "The Establishment of the Mexican Guardia Nacional (2012-2019): A Gendarmerie Force for Crime Wars and the Fourth Transformation of Mexico," in *Forza Alla Legge Studi Storici Su Carabinieri, Gendarmerie e Polizie Armate*, vol. 14, FVCINA DI MARTE (Rome: Società Italiana di Storia Militare: Nadir Media, 2023), 413–39, https://www.namsism.org/Fucina%20di%20marte/Carbone%20(cur)%20Forza%20alla%20legge%20St udi%20storici%20su%20Carabinieri%20Gendarmerie%20e%20polizie%20armate%20 n%20 14.pdf

23. "Mexico Supreme Court strikes down law to put National Guard under Army control, Reuters, April 18, 2023, https://www.reuters.com/world/americas/mexico-supremecourt-strikes-down-law-put-national-guard-under-army-control-2023-04-18/.

24. Alexander L. George and Andrew Bennett, *Case Studies and Theory Development in the Social Sciences* (Cambridge: MIT Press, 2005); Stephen Van Evera, *Guide to Methods for Students of Political Science* (Ithaca: Cornell University Press, 1997); Sarah Miller Beebe and Randolph H. Pherson, *Cases in Intelligence Analysis: Structured Analytic Techniques in Action* (Thousand Oaks: C.Q. Press, 2014).

25 "¿Qué pasó en el Culiacanazo? Se cumplen tres años," [What happened in Culiacanazo? Three years have passed]. *La silla rota*, October 17, 2022, https://lasillarota.com/nacion/2022/10/17/que-paso-en-el-culiacanazo-se-cumplentres-anos-397523.html.

26. "Cumplen tres años." [Three years have passed].

27. "Ovidio Guzmán: cómo fue el 'Culiacanazo', la fallida operación tras la que las autoridades mexicanas dejaron escapar al hijo del Chapo en 2019," [Ovidio Guzmán: what the "Culiacanazo" was like, the failed operation after which the Mexican authorities let Chapo's son escape in 2019]. BBC, January 6, 2023, https://www.bbc.com/mundo/noticias-america-latina-64186716.

28. "'Culiacanazo', el intento fallido en 2019 para capturar a Ovidio Guzmán," ['Culiacanazo', the failed attempt in 2019 to capture Ovidio Guzmán]. *El Universo*, January 5, 2023, https://www.eluniverso.com/noticias/internacional/culiacanazo-elintento-fallido-en-2019-para-capturar-a-ovidio-guzman-nota/.

29. "Chapo en 2019." [Chapo in 2019].

30. Arturo Ordaz Díaz, "'Culiacanazo', la batalla que ganó el crimen organizado a las fuerzas federales de AMLO," ['Culiacanazo', the battle that organized crime won against AMLO's federal forces]. *Forbes*, October 17, 2020, https://www.forbes.com.mx/noticias-culiacanazo-batalla-ga-

no-crimen-organizadofuerzas-federales/.

31. For more on the establishment of Mexico's National Guard and its close relationship with the military, John P. Sullivan and Nathan P. Jones, "The Establishment of the Mexican Guardia Nacional (2012-2019);" Patricia Escamilla-Hamm, "The Guardia Nacional (National Guard)."; "Así fue el 'Culiacanazo', la fallida operación de 2019 para capturar a Ovidio Guzmán," [This was the 'Culiacanazo', the failed 2019 operation to capture Ovidio Guzmán]. *CNN*, January 5, 2023, https://cnnespanol.cnn.com/2023/01/05/asi-fue-el-culiacanazo-la-fallida-operacionde-2019-para-capturar-a-ovidio-guzman-orix/.

32. "Así fue el 'Culiacanazo'." [This is what happened during the 'Culiacanazo'].

33. "Cumplen tres años." [Three years have passed].

34. "Así se vivió el Culiacanazo en 2019: el día más negro en la historia de Sinaloa," [This is how Culiacanazo was experienced in 2019: the darkest day in the history of Sinaloa]. *Infobae*, January 5, 2023, https://www.infobae.com/america/mexico/2023/01/05/asise-vivio-el-culiacanazo-en-2019-el-dia-mas-negro-en-la-historia-de-sinaloa/.

35. "Así fue el 'Culiacanazo'." [This is what happened during the 'Culiacanazo'].

36. Carlos Martínez, "Así se 'dobló' AMLO en 'Culiacanazo'… documentos filtrados revelan cómo Ovidio Guzmán fue puesto en Libertad," [This is how AMLO 'gave up' in 'Culiacanazo'… leaked documents reveal how Ovidio Guzmán was released]. *Vanguardia*, September 30, 2022.

37. Carlos Martínez, "Así se 'dobló' AMLO." [This is how AMLO 'gave up'].

38. "Así se vivió el Culiacanazo." [This is how the Culiacanazo was experienced].

39. Javier Cabrera Martínez, "Despiertan entre miedo y vestigios de una Guerra en Culiacán," [They wake up between fear and vestiges of a War in Culiacán]. *El Universal*, October 19, 2019, https://www.eluniversal.com.mx/nacion/despiertan-entre-miedo-yvestigios-de-una-guerra-en-culiacan.

40. "Así fue el 'Culiacanazo'." [This is what happened during the 'Culiacanazo'].

41. "Así se vivió el Culiacanazo." [This is how the Culiacanazo was experienced].

42. "Así se vivió el Culiacanazo." [This is how the Culiacanazo was experienced].

44. "Cumplen tres años." [Three years have passed].

44. "Ovidio Guzmán."

45. "Así fue el 'Culiacanazo'." [This is what happened during the 'Culiacanazo'].

46. "Así se vivió el Culiacanazo." [This is how the Culiacanazo was experienced].

47. "Así se vivió el Culiacanazo." [This is how the Culiacanazo was experienced].

48. "Así fue el 'Culiacanazo'." [This is what happened during the 'Culiacanazo'].

49. "Ovidio Guzmán."

50. "Ovidio Guzmán."

51. "Así se vivió el Culiacanazo." [This is how the Culiacanazo was experienced].

52. "Ovidio Guzmán."

53. "Así se vivió el Culiacanazo." [This is how the Culiacanazo was experienced].

54. "Así se vivió el Culiacanazo." [This is how the Culiacanazo was experienced].
55. "Así fue el 'Culiacanazo'." [This is what happened during the 'Culiacanazo'].
56. "Así fue el 'Culiacanazo'." [This is what happened during the 'Culiacanazo'].
57. "Así se vivió el Culiacanazo." [This is how the Culiacanazo was experienced].
58. "Así se vivió el Culiacanazo." [This is how the Culiacanazo was experienced].
59. "El minuto a minuto del operativo para arrestar al hijo del Chapo en Culiacán," [The minute by minute of the operation to arrest Chapo's son in Culiacán]. *Noticias de Navarra*, October 30, 2019, https://www.noticiasdenavarra.com/actualidad/2019/10/30/video-minuto-minutooperativo-arrestar-2344131.html.
60. "El minuto a minuto." [The minute by minute].
61. "Así se logró la captura de Ovidió Guzmán, hijo de El Chapo: Todos los detalles de la operación en Culiacán," [This is how the capture of Ovidió Guzmán, son of El Chapo, was achieved: All the details of the operation in Culiacán]. *El Comercio*, January 1, 2023, https://elcomercio.pe/mundo/mexico/ovidio-guzman-asi-se-logro-capturar-alhijo-de-el-chapo-todos-detalles-de-la-operacion-en-culiacan-sinaloa-mexico-loschapitos-noticia/.
62. Fanny Padilla, "¿En dónde capturaron a Ovidio Guzmán en Culiacán, Sinaloa?," [Where was Ovidio Guzmán captured in Culiacán, Sinaloa?]. *La Razón*, January 5, 2023, https://www.razon.com.mx/estados/capturaron-ovidio-guzman-culiacansinaloa-fotos-512532.
63. "Ovidio Guzmán López: qué se sabe del operativo para capturar al hijo del Chapo que dejó 29 muertos en Culiacán," [Ovidio Guzmán López: what is known about the operation to capture Chapo's son that left 29 dead in Culiacán]. *BBC*, January 6, 2023, https://www.bbc.com/mundo/noticias-america-latina-64182714.
64. "29 muertos en Culiacán." [29 dead in Culiacán].
65. "Los detalles de la captura de Ovidio Guzmán: 29 muertos, un black hawk y armas de alto poder," [The details of the capture of Ovidio Guzmán: 29 dead, a black hawk and high-powered weapons]. *Infobae*, January 6, 2023, https://www.infobae.com/america/mexico/2023/01/06/los-detalles-de-la-captura-deovidio-guzman-9-militares-muertos-un-black-hawk-y-armas-de-alto-poder/.
66. "Los detalles de la captura." [The details of the capture].
67. "Así es el helicóptero artillado usado en la captura de Ovidio Guzmán," [This is the gunship used in the capture of Ovidio Guzmán]. *Milenio*, January 5, 2023, https://www.milenio.com/politica/helicoptero-artillado-usado-captura-ovidioguzman.
68. "29 muertos en Culiacán." [29 dead in Culiacán].
69. "Los detalles de la captura." [The details of the capture].
70. "29 muertos en Culiacán." [29 dead in Culiacán].
71. "Culiacanazo 2.0 dejó 29 muertos, 35 heridos y 21 detenidos, confirma Sedena," [Culiacanazo 2.0 left 29 dead, 35 injured and 21 detained, confirms Sedena]. *Debate*, January 6, 2023, https://www.debate.com.mx/policiacas/Culiacanazo-2.0-dejo-29muertos-35-heridos-y-21-detenidos-confirma-Sedena-20230106-0029.html.
72. "Los detalles de la captura." [The details of the capture].

73. "29 muertos en Culiacán." [29 dead in Culiacán].
74. "29 muertos en Culiacán." [29 dead in Culiacán].
75. Cristanta Espinosa Aguilar, "Así le hemos contado la recaptura de Ovidio Guzmán, el hijo de El Chapo," [This is how we have told you about the recapture of Ovidio Guzmán, the son of El Chapo]. *El Pais*, January 7, 2023, https://elpais.com/mexico/2023-0105/la-recaptura-de-ovidio-guzman-en-vivo.html.
76. "Los detalles de la captura." [The details of the capture].
77. "Confirmado Aeropuerto de Culiacán no dará servicio el 6 de Enero," [Confirmed Culiacán Airport will not provide service on January 6]. *Debate*, January 5, 2023, https://www.debate.com.mx/sinaloa/culiacan/Confirmado-Aeropuerto-de-Culiacanno-dara-servicio-el-6-de-enero-20230105-0152.html.
78. "Ovidio Guzmán, hijo de "El Chapo", fue detenido en Culiacán; se desata el caos en la ciudad," [Ovidio Guzmán, son of "El Chapo", was arrested in Culiacán; chaos breaks out in the city]. *Marca*, January 5, 2023, https://us.marca.com/actualidad/2023/01/05/63b6ff42e2704ecc618b4579.html.
79. "Así se logró." [This is how it was achieved].
80. "Culiacanazo 2.0."
81. "Culiacanazo 2.0."
82. "Battle of Culiacán," *Wikipedia*, https://en.wikipedia.org/wiki/Battle_of_Culiacán#cite_note-2.
83. Around 49 cartel prisoners, including Ovidio Guzmán López reportedly escaped from detention during this incident. Sieff, "The failed arrest of El Chapo's son turned a Mexican city into an urban war zone."
84. Paulina Villegas, "After Soldiers Surrender El Chapo's Son, a Shocked Mexican City Sighs With Relief," *New York Times*, October 20, 2019, https://www.nytimes.com/2019/10/20/world/americas/culiacan-mexico-chaposon.html.
85. Luis Chaparro, "Mexico Allegedly Arrested CJNG Leader 'El Doble R' and All Hell Broke Loose," *Vice News*, 86. August 10, 2022, https://www.vice.com/en/article/bvmjnq/cjng-el-doble-r-gunajuato-firefight.
86. "Wave of Violence in Tijuana, Baja California Creating Nightmare Scenario for Residents," *CBS Los Angeles*, 2022, https://www.cbsnews.com/losangeles/video/wave-of-violence-in-tijuana-bajacalifornia-creating-nightmare-scenario-for-residents/.
87. "Nemesio Oseguera Cervantes, Alias' El Mencho,'" *InSight Crime*, April 17, 2015, https://insightcrime.org/mexico-organized-crime-news/nemesio-oseguera-ramosalias-el-mencho/.
88. Phillip Luke Johnson, "Revisiting the Battle of Culiacán," *NACLA*, November 22, 2019, https://nacla.org/news/2019/11/22/culiacan-chapo-mexico-drug-violence.
89. Jorge G. Castañeda, "The Bigger Story Behind the Humiliating Release of El Chapo's Son," *New York Times*, October 23, 2019, sec. Opinion, https://www.nytimes.com/2019/10/23/opinion/el-chapo-son-mexico.html.
90. Castañeda, "The Bigger Story Behind the Humiliating Release of El Chapo's Son."
91. Johnson, "Revisiting the Battle of Culiacán."

92. Castañeda, "The Bigger Story Behind the Humiliating Release of El Chapo's Son."

93. *The Siege of Culiacán*, Episode 20, *The Weekly* (*New York Times*, 2019), https://www.nytimes.com/2019/11/15/the-weekly/el-chapo-guzman-son.html.

94. The Siege of Culiacán.

95. Paulina Villegas, "After Soldiers Surrender El Chapo's Son, a Shocked Mexican City Sighs With Relief," *New York Times*, October 20, 2019, https://www.nytimes.com/2019/10/20/world/americas/culiacan-mexico-chaposon.html.

96. John P. Sullivan, "Criminal Insurgency: Narcocultura, Social Banditry, and Information Operations," *Small Wars Journal*, December 12, 2012, http://smallwarsjournal.com/jrnl/art/criminal-insurgency-narcocultura-socialbanditry-and-information-operations; Robert J. Bunker and John P. Sullivan, "Mexican Cartel Strategic Note No. 29: An Overview of Cartel Activities Related to COVID-19 Humanitarian Response," *Small Wars Journal*, May 8, 2020, https://smallwarsjournal.com/jrnl/art/mexican-cartel-strategic-note-no-29-overviewcartel-activities-related-covid-19.

97. Jones, *Mexico's Illicit Drug Networks and the State Reaction.*

98. General Cienfuegos was the former Mexican Secretary of Defense and a high-ranking general in SEDENA. His arrest at the Los Angeles International Airport on charges of assisting the H-2 Cartel (Beltran Leyva Organization splinter group) was highly embarrassing and triggered a major Mexican diplomatic effort. The US DOJ dropped the charges, and the Mexican government exonerated Cienfuegos. It then publicly argued the evidence against the General was weak. Tim Golden, "The Cienfuegos Affair: Inside the Case That Upended the Drug War in Mexico," *New York Times*, December 8, 2022, https://www.nytimes.com/2022/12/08/magazine/mexico-general-cienfuegos.html.

99. Nathan P Jones, "The Unintended Consequences of Kingpin Strategies: Kidnap Rates and the Arellano-Félix Organization," Trends in Organized Crime 16, no. 2 (2013): 156–76, https://doi.org/10.1007/s12117-012-9185-x. *Witness to History: Operation Shadow Game* (Washington, D.C., 2016), https://www.youtube.com/watch?time_continue=7&v=gwH6eeOwC4k.

100. Javier Valdez Cárdenas, *The Taken: True Stories of the Sinaloa Drug War*, trans. Everard Meade, Latin American and Caribbean Arts and Culture Initiative (Norman: University of Oklahoma Press, 2017).

CHAPTER 5
Implementing NIMS: Lessons Learned from the Boston Marathon Bombing

James M. Duggan, John Petrozzelli, and Jay Slattery

Introduction

The 2013 Boston Marathon bombing was the first successful terrorist attack on American soil since September 11, 2001. The targeting of a televised event in a densely populated urban area captured the public's attention and spread fear throughout the greater Boston region. The response and investigation of the bombing present critical learning opportunities that have yet to be realized. Lessons have been offered in official reviews of the response and investigation, and another focused on information sharing before the bombing.[1] Physicians and medical researchers have provided voluminous articles on the types of injuries suffered by victims of the bombing and techniques used to save their lives.[2] Public safety professionals and security pundits have provided opinions and insights on lessons to be learned from the response and investigation.[3] The latter are often derived from interviews with current and former law enforcement executives and politicians encumbered by policies and pressure to defer to the official narratives of the time.

This article employs the qualitative research method of collaborative autoethnography to examine lessons learned within the context of the National Incident Management System (NIMS) and Incident Command System (ICS). The authors were intimately involved in the response and investigation of the bombing. They have since separated from service to their respective agencies, allowing them to express personal views on their experiences. The focus on learning opportunities within the context of NIMS and ICS supports the objective analysis of processes and mitigates subjective perceptions of the performance of individuals involved in the response and investigation.

The prior research and official reviews have not revealed essential lessons to be learned from the Marathon bombings. The infrequency of incidents such as the Marathon bombings contributes to the importance of capitalizing on the available learning opportunities. Official reviews of the attacks and the subsequent manhunt have been informative but do not offer the granular lessons learned by those immersed in the daily operations of the response and investigation. The information contained in this article provides details on critical lessons learned throughout the incident. The lessons learned from this article will assist policymakers in preparing for and responding to terrorist attacks and other mass casualty incidents (MCIs) in urban areas.

A review of the prior literature follows an overview of NIMS and ICS. The authors present the literature review in two sections:

1. A presentation of the scholarship on NIMS and ICS

2. Research and official reviews of the response and investigation of the Marathon bombing

The literature review specific to the Marathon bombings focuses on previously identified issues and best practices. The authors gleaned most of the information from the official after-action review conducted by the Massachusetts Emergency Management Agency (MEMA) and present findings within the context of the three major components of NIMS:

1. Resource management
2. Command and coordination
3. Communications and information management[4]

The authors explain the methodology used for the study, followed by a presentation of lessons learned. The Lessons Learned section presents novel lessons learned and expands upon concepts presented in the Literature Review by providing detail and context not provided by the prior research. The lessons learned are presented within the context of the three major components of NIMS, as was done in the Literature Review section. The authors further disaggregated information presented in the Lessons Learned section into three parts:

1. Things done well
2. Issues needing improvement
3. Recommendations

The authors discuss their findings and the implications for practitioners and policymakers in the conclusions section of this article.

Overview of NIMS and ICS

Since 2004, NIMS has provided various government and private sector levels with a framework to "prevent, protect against, mitigate, respond to, and recover from incidents."[5] NIMS evolved from a system developed in the 1970s to combat forest fires in California. In the wake of the 2001 terrorist attacks, the Department of Homeland Security (DHS) recognized and promoted the system nationally.

The characteristics of NIMS make it applicable to all levels of government and the private sector for all sorts of planned and unplanned events. NIMS's standardized framework and vocabulary equip disparate federal, state, local, and tribal partners to work together effectively.6 The system is scalable and flexible, allowing users to adjust their level of response as incidents expand and contract.7

The ICS component of NIMS offers a framework to command and manage incidents of any type.8 Unified Command is a command structure within ICS that effectively manages incidents involving functional or jurisdictional overlap.9 Terrorist attacks in urban areas are often multijurisdictional, and MCIs are inherently interdisciplinary. In a Unified Command, individuals chosen by their respective agencies jointly determine objectives and manage resources.10 Among Unified Command's benefits are promoting a common operating picture among the involved agencies and unity of effort, a guiding principle of NIMS. Unity of effort is defined as "coordinating activities among various organizations to achieve common objectives."11

The Command and General Staff in a Unified Command are critical to effective incident management. A typical Command Staff includes a Public Information Officer (PIO), a Liaison Officer, and a Safety Officer.[12] General Staff positions are held by Section Chiefs appointed by the Incident Commander or Unified Command. Those sections are Operations, Planning, Logistics, and Finance and Administration.[13] The Operations Section Chief is responsible for designating a staging area proximate to but away from the Incident Command Post (ICP).[14] A staging area manager assigns and tracks resources, including personnel, ready for deployment.[15]

Literature Review

NIMS and ICS

The empirical research on NIMS and ICS is relatively new and growing.[16] Prior research findings on the topic indicate disagreement on the framework's utility. Practitioners tend to recognize the system's benefits.[17] Practitioners' support is contrasted with scholars, who often contend that such command-and-control models are archaic and ineffective.[18] Scrutiny of arguments presented by both sides indicates a common theme: That commitment to the system coupled with training and experience implementing the framework is critical to its success.

Practitioners supporting NIMS and ICS cite the framework's flexibility and scalability, making the system applicable to routine calls for service and significant events.[19] Routine use of the system, training, and interdisciplinary joint exercises with partners at all government levels equip practitioners to implement the framework during a crisis effectively. The ICS framework provides structure to multi-jurisdictional, multidisciplinary responses to crises that may otherwise devolve into chaos.[20]

Arguments against the efficacy of NIMS and ICS often deride the use of command-and-control structures. Those opposed to ICS often favor incident management models using collaborative networks rather than the top-down, bureaucratic characteristics of the current system.[21] Academics dislike ICS partly due to their misperception of it as a rigid, command-and-control military model that curbs decision-making by those in the field.[22]

Networks are essential to incident management but lack the structure to maintain control over MCIs, such as terrorist attacks in urban areas. At least one empirical study found that existing collaborative networks were important to effective emergency management.[23] MEMA's after-action report of the Marathon bombing cited the existing interagency relationships as a strength of the response efforts.[24]

Those opposed to the frameworks also cite refusal to accept the system or poor implementation as weaknesses of the model. For example, a metaanalysis of the prior research on ICS presented evidence of the system's ineffectiveness: "The ICS may not work as designed all of the time. More than one study identified variation in the degree to which the ICS was used, if it was used at all, in incident response, as well as a lack of use daily."[25] This argument against the efficacy of ICS suffers from faulty logic. A reasonable inference from the evidence presented indicates support for the inverse of the original idea: That acceptance of the system coupled with proper training and experience are critical to the successful implementation of the system. Nonetheless, the refusal to fully adopt NIMS and ICS persists.[26] Others have found that ineffective training and lengthy times between training and use of the system curb its utility.[27] The core principles of NIMS and ICS "cannot be compromised without losing the effectiveness and performance for which ICS and NIMS have become so highly regarded."[28]

At least one prior study found that ICS worked best for events limited in duration, objectives, and scope.[29] However, any incident management system would work best under the stated conditions. Rather than accepting the assertion as an indictment of ICS, it is crucial to recognize that the vulnerability is not within the system but the user's knowledge and experience. Implementing ICS properly is critical to effectively managing a protracted, complex incident such as the Marathon bombing.

The Boston Marathon Bombing Response and Investigation

Various agencies and individuals have conducted official reviews and studies of the Marathon bombing response and investigation. Concepts and themes outside the boundaries of NIMS and ICS are beyond the scope of this article. For instance, the Inspectors General of the Intelligence Community reviewed the handling and sharing of information before the attacks.[30] The House Homeland Security Committee Report focused on internal FBI investigative processes and addressed restrictive language in memoranda of understanding with Joint Terrorism Task Force partner agencies.[31] Only the review conducted by the Massachusetts Emergency Management Agency (MEMA) addressed operational management issues.[32] Although MEMA's study offers many lessons to be learned, the information provided is of a higher level. It lacks the granularity offered by those on the ground for 24x7 operations.[33] The MEMA review also emphasizes the positive aspects of the response phases and ignores command and control issues that plagued day-to-day operations.[34]

Resource Management

Boston's public safety and medical professionals did an admirable job preparing for events such as the Marathon bombing, especially regarding qualifying and certifying personnel. Numerous greater Boston and Massachusetts exercises prepared the region for MCIs.[35] In 2011, Operation Falcon II prepared Boston hospitals to respond to MCIs and identify their response deficiencies.[36] Urban Shield Boston is an annual exercise held just five months before the Marathon bombings and included more than 600 individuals from 50 agencies of assorted disciplines spanning the various levels of government.[37] The 2012 Urban Shield event revealed weaknesses in the interagency communications between the Boston Police and Fire Departments that were rectified before the 2013 Marathon.[38] The Boston hospitals' extensive emergency preparedness efforts and response capabilities saved many lives. The hospitals' participation in multi-disciplinary drills contributed to the speedy and effective treatment of the many injured.[39] Finally, the annual Pre-Boston Marathon Tabletop Exercise hosted by the Massachusetts State Emergency Operations Center promoted partnerships and the opportunity to practice with the Web EOC emergency management software used during the Marathon.[40]

Formal mutual aid agreements between law enforcement and EMS agencies were critical to effectively responding to the bombings.[41] Explosive Ordinance Disposal assets throughout New England were acquired via the New England State Police Compact.[42] The Boston Police Department (BPD) activated mutual aid from surrounding communities and the Transit Police.[43] Robust mutual aid agreements among EMS agencies facilitated a speedy response from many assets.[44]

Despite the utility of existing mutual aid agreements, self-deployment by law enforcement officers created chaotic and dangerous situations. Self-deployment contributed to the disarray and poor muzzle discipline in the shootout with the bombing suspects and the following day, when officers opened fire on the boat the second suspect was hiding in.[45] Incidents of self-deployment violated NIMS' tenets regarding mutual aid and created officer safety issues.[46] In 1956, sociologists coined the term "convergence" to explain humans' desire to provide help by converging on disaster areas.[47] Officers must resist the innate desire to converge on disaster areas and remain aware of the threat posed by multi-pronged, Mumbai-style attacks. In addition to creating a chaotic response to the immediate threat, self-deploying officers expose their assigned area of responsibility to risk.

The MEMA report recognized the failure to provide adequate relief for state and local law enforcement officers.[48] It is commendable that the developers of the report acknowledged the stress and fatigue experienced by officers. Still, the importance of this deficiency is minimized by the short thrift it was afforded in the report. In their review of the Marathon bombing, Leonard et al. recommended "depth of leadership" to allow proper rest for senior management.[49] The authors present further details in the Lessons Learned section of this article.

Command and Coordination

MEMA's review relative to the implementation of ICS focused overwhelmingly on the positive while acknowledging some deficiencies. Executive leadership was commended for establishing a Unified Command Center (UCC) at the Westin Hotel within approximately forty minutes of the explosions.[50] The UCC provided a location for executive leadership of the various agencies to meet with elected officials and disseminate information to the public.[51] The site of an appropriate UCC should have been identified during the planning phase.[52] The generosity of the Westin Hotel was appreciated, but the venue lacked the telephones, electrical outlets, and computers required by responding personnel.[53] By approximately 6:30 p.m., there was agreement that the responsibility for the investigation would transition from BPD to the FBI's Joint Terrorism Task Force.[54] An incident command post (ICP) was established at FBI Boston headquarters, and the UCC at the Westin Hotel was closed the next day.[55] The review ignores that another UCC wasn't established until the manhunt in Watertown, four days after the attacks. Leonard et al. opined that senior management effectively implemented the core principles of NIMS and that implementation suffered at the operational level.[56]

Nonetheless, MEMA did acknowledge that leadership at the Watertown UCC failed to brief or provide direction to the thousands of officers who responded to assist.[57] The review also observed that a Logistics Section Chief and Staging Area Manager should have been established to manage resources.[58] Further details are provided in the Lessons Learned section of this article.

Communications and Information Management

The loss of cellular service after the explosions and ineffective radio communications were two deficiencies identified by the MEMA review.[59] After the explosions, the many calls to and from individuals around the finish line overwhelmed the available cellular service. The after-action report acknowledged that cellular voice communications were unavailable but that text messaging remained available.[60] However, the availability of text messaging was intermittent at best. A Cell-On-Wheels was transported to the scene within an hour of the blast and facilitated cellular communications.[61] "Wireless Priority Service (WPS) is a White House-directed cellular communications service provided and managed by CISA in compliance with Federal Communications Commission (FCC) Report and Order, FCC-22-36."[62] The service would have been available to many first responders but was not active on many of their devices.[63] Radio communications were saturated because of poor radio discipline and the failure to utilize channels designated for Marathon Operations.[64]

Public messaging was best during the two phases when a UCC was established. The MEMA review acknowledged that the partners should have found a Joint Information Center (JIC) on Tuesday after they shut down the Westin Hotel UCC.[65] The failure to implement a JIC resulted in uncoordinated, often conflicting public messaging.

Methodology

This article employs collaborative autoethnography to examine and draw conclusions from the authors' experiences. This qualitative approach is "grounded in the simple yet potent proposition that a deep understanding of social phenomenon resides in the individuals who can make sense of their own experiences."[66] Autoethnography has been an accepted research method since the 1980s and is grounded in three critical characteristics.[67] First, the research is based on "insider self-knowledge."[68] Second, it emphasizes participation and crucial assessment of personal and joint experiences.[69] Finally, the experiences of the researchers are understood within one of many interdisciplinary contexts.[70]

Using established theoretical frameworks in empirical studies provides structure to complex topics. In addition to guiding and organizing the examination of the topic, using established frameworks equips future researchers to build upon the prior research more readily. Rather than using a theoretical framework, this article considers the authors' experiences within the operational frameworks of NIMS and ICS. Using an operational rather than theoretical framework contributes to the utility of this article by deviating from the abstract in favor of the concrete.

As with any research, this study has limitations. The qualitative methods employed in the study provide thick descriptions not found in quantitative studies but lack the objective measurement of quantifiable data. The information contained herein is limited to the experiences of the three authors and their perceptions of those experiences. The authors' experiences are not necessarily generalizable or predictive.

Lessons Learned

The lessons presented in this section include new themes and the elaboration of concepts presented in the literature review. Further detail, context, and emphasis are applied to issues identified by the prior research. The authors organized this section by each of the three major components of NIMS:

1. Resource management,
2. Command and coordination, and
3. Communications and information management

The authors explain things done well, issues needing improvement, and recommendations for each component.

Resource Management

Things Done Well

The FBI Boston Division fostered an environment that embraced partnerships with their state and local partners. The two partners contributing the most significant number of personnel to the FBI Boston Division Joint Terrorism Task Force (JTTF) were the Massachusetts State Police (MSP) and the BPD. The MSP and BPD also administer the two fusion centers within the Commonwealth of Massachusetts, with local, state, and federal partners embedded within each. The particularly robust daily activities at each fusion center forged partnerships among stakeholders at the various levels of government.

The inclusive environment promoted by the FBI and the fusion centers, coupled with extensive planning and preparation, resulted in proper certifying and credentialing of personnel. The overclassification of intelligence products often obfuscates information sharing, especially between federal agencies and their state, local, and tribal partners.[71] The FBI and DHS mitigated issues of overclassification by proactively credentialing state and local partners with the appropriate security clearances.

Issues Needing Improvement

Several issues presented in the Literature Review section are worthy of elaboration. The intense, protracted response and investigation revealed a critical weakness: the failure to rest personnel sufficiently. Worth noting is that 24-hour operations continued for 11 days, or one week after the second suspect was taken into custody. Also, the bombs exploded towards the end of a long day for many of the personnel assigned to FBI Boston's JTTF. Twelve-hour shifts were implemented by the FBI, BPD, and MSP but were not effectively enforced. Dedicated investigators and analysts were exhausted within days because superiors did not require them to leave when their shifts ended.

Comprehensive mutual aid agreements are exceedingly necessary for urban areas, where incidents such as terrorist attacks are inherently multijurisdictional and multidisciplinary. The critical concepts of NIMS and ICS must be incorporated into mutual aid agreements. Executive leadership must ensure that funding mechanisms are established and vendors identified to provide supplies, food, and office equipment (the authors provide details of these deficiencies in this article's Command and Coordination section). Plans should also incorporate funding for hotels or identification of other facilities to rest personnel not residing in the immediate area.

Executive leadership must prepare to establish command and control quickly to manage the influx of responding mutual aid resources.[72] It is estimated that as many as 2,500 officers converged on Watertown to assist with the search for the second suspect.[73] Although some responded from as far away as New York, terrorist attacks in densely populated urban areas will likely spawn a rapid, overwhelming response from neighboring communities that managers must be prepared for. The authors provide more detailed information on resource management issues in this article's Command and Coordination section.

Recommendations

All personnel should leverage fusion centers and task forces to build meaningful relationships. Individuals should not be handing out business cards during a crisis. To mitigate fatigue in the case of an incident occurring during a pre-planned event, stagger shifts when possible or assign personnel as alternates so they may relieve others as necessary. Supervisors and managers must enforce strict adherence to restrictions on work hours.

Executive leadership should collaborate with state and local partners to devise funding mechanisms and assign expense responsibility. Executives should establish relationships with federal partners at DHS and the Department of Justice to identify and remain abreast of possible disaster funding mechanisms. Consistent with the recommendations made by MEMA, the management of mutual aid resources requires training and policies that emphasize the orderly response of assets as directed by an identified incident commander.[74]

Command and Coordination

Things Done Well

Detective supervisors from the BPD and MSP responding to the scene of the bombing quickly established an ad hoc command post at the California Pizza Kitchen one block from the finish line. The investigation began immediately, with the field supervisors coordinating efforts and maintaining a common operating picture. Detectives coordinated with special agents from the FBI and ATF to respond to investigative leads, including following at least one suspect to the hospital. The California Pizza Kitchen command post was closed in deference to the UCC established by executive leadership several blocks away at the Westin Hotel. Personnel assigned to the command post established at FBI Boston for Marathon operations expanded the space within several hours to serve as the Incident Command Post (ICP). The ICP would accommodate the influx of partners from all levels of government.

Issues Needing Improvement

Critical concepts of NIMS were implemented well during the initial response but much less so during the protracted response and investigation. The contention that senior management effectively implemented the core principles of NIMS was inaccurate.[75] Beyond the initial establishment of the UCC at the Westin Hotel, NIMS was implemented poorly by senior management of the involved agencies and never improved throughout the event. The situation deteriorated as consequences of the poor implementation of NIMS became increasingly evident throughout the eleven days of 24x7 operations.

Unified Command

The benefits of the structure provided by Unified Command and the flexibility of NIMS were needed but rarely utilized in Boston. Although the FBI assumed primary jurisdiction the evening of the attack, the investigation remained a joint effort between the FBI, BPD, and MSP. In addition to being the major partners for FBI Boston's JTTF, the crime scene was within the jurisdiction of BPD, and evidence processing took place at Black Falcon Pier, within the MSP's jurisdiction. The need for a Unified Command structure was amplified when it became apparent that one of the bombers was suspected of an unsolved triple homicide being investigated by MSP detectives assigned to the Middlesex District Attorney's Office.[76] A prosecutor and detectives from the Middlesex District Attorney's Office became a regular presence at the ICP.

Executive leadership only implemented Unified Command in purely tactical applications rather than using the command structure to manage the rapidly evolving environment throughout the first four days. The speedy implementation of a UCC within 40 minutes of the attack was commendable. However, after the UCC at the Westin Hotel was closed the day after the attack (Tuesday), another wasn't established until Friday morning. The partners established the second UCC in Watertown to manage the search for the remaining suspect after the killing of Officer Sean Collier and the subsequent shootout.[77]

An active UCC at FBI Boston would have mitigated some of the issues of mutual aid and jurisdiction arising from the Watertown incident. FBI and MSP superiors both declared command over the extensive crime scene. The FBI assumed the Watertown suspects were also the Marathon bombers, and the MSP made no such assumptions. The MSP recognized the incident as a likely homicide and multiple officer-involved shootings to be investigated by MSP detectives assigned to the Middlesex District Attorney's Office. Troopers from the MSP Anti-Terrorism Unit maintained custody of the suspect until he was declared deceased and transferred to the control of the Chief Medical Examiner. Having senior representatives from the FBI and MSP seated in a UCC would have promoted the need to work together towards a common goal. The authors provide further details of the Watertown incident in this article's Communications and Information section.

Intelligence and Investigations

The failure to implement NIMS and ICS in Boston precluded the proper placement of investigations and intelligence within the command structure. It curbed the appropriate sharing of information and intelligence among stakeholders. ICS recognizes that terrorist attacks in urban areas may require the intelligence and investigations function to be moved from the Operations or Planning Section to a more prominent position in the Command Staff or as a separate function within the General Staff.[78]

Regular briefings at the ICP to update partners were not enough to overcome weaknesses created by the lack of formal structures provided by NIMS and ICS. Informal back-channel networks filled the vacuum created by ineffective information sharing, which impacted the promoting of a common operating picture for the involved stakeholders. The authors provide further details regarding the sharing of information in the Communications and Information Management section of this article.

The partners' failure to formally establish a command structure to manage the investigation impacted NIMS's unity of effort principle. The duration and multi-pronged investigation contributed to varying viewpoints among the many individuals involved. The leadership of partner agencies sometimes allowed contrarian subordinates to pursue alternative investigative angles intended to disprove the FBI plan.

Staging Area

The failure to establish a staging area away from the command post at FBI Boston impacted several aspects of the response and investigation. The many federal agencies arriving at FBI Boston offering help were welcomed and given a seat in the ICP. Boston Police Department and MSP detectives not assigned to FBI task forces also responded to FBI Boston, awaiting the assignment of tips and leads.

The FBI's benevolence, coupled with the failure of the partners to establish a staging area away from the ICP, resulted in too many people in the ICP. The number of people granted access to the ICP overwhelmed resources and FBI Boston's facilities. Elevators and bathrooms closest to the ICP were intermittently but frequently out of service from overuse. As the investigation continued, personnel assigned to the ICP were forced to walk increasingly further distances to find operable bathrooms. Copy machines also became inoperable in order of their proximity to the ICP. Scanners were then used to make copies, rendering the scanners out of service. FBI management's failure to plan for the increased activity also resulted in overflowing trash receptacles throughout the facility.

The number of superfluous individuals allowed access to the ICP likely impacted operational security (OPSEC) and may have contributed to the frequency of leaks to the media. Investigators were concerned about sharing sensitive information during operational briefings due to the frequency of that information appearing on the news in the minutes and hours after the briefing. The leak of the suspects' images to the media likely influenced their crime spree that began with the murder of a police officer and culminated in a shootout with police in Watertown. The authors discuss the leaks in greater detail in this article's Communications and Information Management section.

Safety

The primary duty of ICS leadership is to promote the safety of all personnel involved in an incident.[79] The Safety Officer holds a position within the

Command Staff of the ICS framework and is tasked with ensuring the safety of the operation.[80] The failure to implement a staging area away from the ICP weakened routine security protocols at FBI Boston. The FBI had unarmed security staff in place to regulate access to the ICP but did not deploy armed security to the exterior of the building until the manhunt for the second suspect, four days after the bombings.

Logistics Section

The proper implementation of ICS would have included appointing a Logistics Section Chief.[81] The Logistics Section's functions include providing food and repairing facilities and office equipment.[82] Establishing a Logistics Section in Boston would have mitigated some of the issues presented by the absence of a staging area. In addition to addressing problems with the facilities and office equipment, a Logistics Section would have facilitated the provision of food for investigators and intelligence analysts assigned to the ICP.

Food was provided intermittently through donations from local businesses near the ICP and was most often quickly consumed by onlookers from federal and state agencies not assigned to the ICP. None of the partner agencies had established accounts to fund food purchases. Rather than establishing funding mechanisms and vendors in the planning stage, managers of the Marathon bombing investigation relied on the intermittent charity of neighboring restaurants to feed their personnel.

Recommendations

The ICS is a system of interdependent components that works well when properly implemented. A deficiency in any component will affect the others. All stakeholders must embrace ICS as their incident management model and commit to training and practicing the system in frequent, interagency, interdisciplinary exercises. The flexibility and modularity of the system make it amenable to regular use in all types of situations, which facilitates opportunities to practice implementing the system.

Practitioners should take advantage of opportunities to employ ICS during pre-planned events to improve their proficiency with the system during an emergency.[83] The partners should have established and maintained a UCC at FBI Boston throughout 24x7 operations. The failure to implement a staging area away from the ICP in Boston is a compelling learning opportunity. Establishing a staging area away from the ICP will help to manage resources and dissuade onlookers. When presented with a largescale incident such as the Marathon bombing, do not overlook the obvious, such as providing security for the involved facilities and personnel. The assigned personnel must be fed and hydrated, no matter how tough and dedicated. Managers and supervisors must establish protocols in the planning phase to identify vendors, establish funding mechanisms, and determine financial responsibilities amongst partner agencies.

Communications and Information Management

Things Done Well

Public messaging was at its best during the two periods that a UCC was established: Immediately after the attacks and during the search for the second suspect. However, communications and information management were most often handled quite poorly. Issues needing improvement are presented in the following section.

Issues Needing Improvement

The failure to implement NIMS and ICS impacted public messaging and communications internally among stakeholders. The lack of a JIC affected the ability of officials to manage voluminous requests for information from media outlets.[84] Also, the partners never established the Command Staff positions of Public Information Officer (PIO) and Liaison Officer, despite their necessity in Boston.

Internal Communications

A Liaison Officer would have facilitated the sharing of information with partner agencies. Although a Unified Command structure would have been ideal in Boston, a Liaison Officer appointed by a single Incident Commander would have mitigated issues created by the unstructured information sharing that occurred. Failing to establish a Liaison Officer and provide structured information to stakeholders fomented distrust among the partner agencies.

The official review by MEMA acknowledged weaknesses in radio communications in the immediate aftermath of the bombing. It explained that personnel were not aware of channels made available for Marathon Day.[85] Although genuine, supervisors' inability to message and direct subordinates to a specific channel required establishing those backup channels before the event. The intermittent and infrequent availability of text messaging exacerbated the situation, contrary to the MEMA report that claimed text messaging was available.[86]

External Communications

The lack of a PIO in Boston was problematic throughout the response and investigation. The appointment of a PIO would have mitigated two critical issues that impacted operations in Boston:

1. The PIO would have established a JIC
2. Establishing a PIO would have reinforced the need for one voice to provide information to the public

The partners' failure to provide structured information to the public through a JIC created a vacuum that likely contributed to the frequency of leaks to the media. The leaks often occurred in near real-time. A prime example of this happened when the US Attorney for the District of Massachusetts, Carmen Ortiz, addressed the issue of leaks during a scheduled briefing at the ICP. She admonished those present (including authors of this article) and reinforced the need for OPSEC, threatening to prosecute anyone determined responsible for leaking information. Attendees stood dumbfounded as the breaking news of them being threatened with prosecution appeared on televisions positioned throughout the ICP soon after the US Attorney left and the briefing proceeded.

At least one official review identified uncoordinated messaging via social media by the various partners.[87] The messy, often conflicting messaging took a dangerous turn when a partner agency publicly announced the arrests of several associates of the surviving suspect moments before the execution of the operation. The offending agency's reckless dissemination of information increased the danger for the arrest teams deployed at different locations.

The leak of the suspects' images to the media violated the tenets of NIMS and may have contributed to the killing of Officer Sean Collier of the Massachusetts Institute of Technology (MIT) Police Department. The FBI identified video and still images of the suspects within approximately 32 hours of the attack, but their identity remained unknown to investigators. The BPD pressured the FBI to release the photos of the suspects to the media, but their partners refused. The partners were confident the suspects would soon be identified, and releasing the images would forfeit the element of surprise necessary to take them into custody without incident. The FBI was notified by a Boston media outlet on Thursday (three days after the bombing) that it had the images and planned to release them. The FBI could not convince the media outlet to reconsider and agreed to release the photos during the evening news. Unfortunately, none of the brothers' associates contacted law enforcement to advise of their identity.[88]

As many feared, the brothers went on the offensive shortly after the images were released. Text messages later retrieved from the bombers' phones indicated that the release of the images forced them into action. They first assassinated Officer Collier as he sat stationary in his patrol car on the MIT campus. The bombers then carjacked a Mercedes SUV and kidnapped the operator. Law enforcement tracked the vehicle to a residential area of Watertown, where officers from the Watertown Police Department engaged in a firefight with the older suspect as the younger of the two hurled improvised explosive devices at responding officers.

There has never been an investigation into who leaked the images to the press. The source of the leaks remains unknown, and it would be unfair to assess blame on any individual or agency. Far too many people had access to the investigation's intimate details, and the leaks may not have originated from law enforcement sources.

Recommendations

To mitigate the risk of being unable to communicate up and down the chain of command, supervisors and managers should establish specific backup radio channels before pre-planned events. A rallying point should also be established in case all communications become inoperable. Frequent, coordinated public messaging is a must. Ineffective information provision creates a vacuum that exacerbates the risk of information being leaked. The officer safety situations associated with the leaking of information, including the murder of Officer Collier, are a forceful reminder of the importance of OPSEC.

Conclusion

The intensity and duration of the Marathon bombing response and investigation revealed gaps in the preparation and response that present learning opportunities for practitioners and policymakers. Celebrating a job well done must be tempered by the realization that it can be done better. The authors' experiences during the eleven days of 24x7 operations provide critical context and detail not found elsewhere. This study's information and analysis of critical details augment the prior scholarship and official reviews of the 2013 Boston Marathon bombing and investigation. Opportunities to learn from such incidents are thankfully rare. A better understanding of the response and investigation in Boston better prepares the community of first responders and emergency managers to administer future incidents more effectively.

The presentation of lessons learned within the framework of NIMS and ICS reinforces the utility and importance of the model. The difficulties experienced in Boston resulting from the failure to properly establish the critical concepts of ICS reinforce the importance of the framework. Practitioners and policymakers should embrace NIMS and ICS and endeavor to implement the frameworks whenever possible. Executive leadership must develop detailed mutual aid agreements that include protocols facilitating a speedy but managed response under the direction of a clearly identified incident commander. Mutual aid agreements should also articulate financial responsibilities among partner agencies and identify funding mechanisms for essentials such as food, water, rest, and the facilities required for a UCC or ICP. Staging areas must be established away from the ICP to avoid overwhelming the facilities and affecting OPSEC. Finally, all personnel must ensure that the time and pressure of protracted incidents do not impact the unity of effort principle.

Endnotes

1. Massachusetts Emergency Management Agency. *After Action Report for the Response to the 2013 Boston Marathon Bombings.* (2014), https://www.mass.gov/doc/afteraction-report-for-the-response-to-the-2013-boston-marathon-bombings/download; Inspectors General of the Intelligence Community, Central Intelligence Agency, Department of Justice, and Department of Homeland Security. *Unclassified Summary of Information Handling and Sharing Prior to the April 15, 2013 Boston Marathon Bombings.* (2014), https://www.dni.gov/files/documents/ICIG_Forum_Boston_Marathon_Bombings_R eview_-_Unclassifed_Summary.pdf; Majority Staff of Committee on Homeland Security. *Preventing Another Boston Marathon Bombing: Reviewing the Lessons Learned from the 2013 Terror Attack* (Washington, DC.: U.S House of Representatives, 2015), https://www.hsdl.org/c/view?docid=764936

2. Jonathan D. Gates, Sandra Arabian, Paul Biddinger, Joe Blansfield, Peter Burke, Sarita Chung, Jonathan Fischer, Franklin Friedman, Alice Gervasini, Eric Goralnick, Alok Gupta, Andreas Larentzakis, Maria McMahon, Juan Mella, Yvonne Michaud, David Mooney, Reuven Rabinovici, Darlene Sweet, Andrew Ulrich, George Velmahos, Cheryl Weber, and Michael B. Yaffe. "The Initial Response to the Boston Marathon Bombing." *Annals of Surgery* 260, no. 6 (December 2014): 960–66, https://doi.org/10.1097/SLA.0000000000000914; Ann M. Hoppel, "Lessons from Boston: How a City Survived by Working Together," *Clinician Reviews* 23, no. 6 (June 2013): 24–29, https://web-p-ebscohostcom.proxy18.noblenet.org/ehost/pdfviewer/pdfviewer?vid=6&sid=8e53584d-07c44180-8436-2f57b72f4860%40redis; Jonathan D. Gates, Sandra Arabian, Paul Biddinger, Joe Blansfield, Peter Burke, Sarita Chung, Jonathan Fischer, Franklin Friedman, Alice Gervasini, Eric Goralnick, Alok Gupta, Andreas Larentzakis, Maria McMahon, Juan Mella, Yvonne Michaud, David Mooney, Reuven Rabinovici, Darlene Sweet, Andrew Ulrich, George Velmahos, Cheryl Weber, and Michael B. Yaffe, "The Initial Response to the Boston Marathon Bombing," *Annals of Surgery* 260, no. 6 (December 2014): 960–66, https://doi.org/10.1097/SLA.0000000000000914.

3. Juliette Kayyem, "The Day 'Stop the Bleed' Entered Civilian Life," *The Atlantic*, April 16, 2023, https://www.theatlantic.com/ideas/archive/2023/04/boston-marathonbombing-disaster-management-stop-the-bleed-tourniquet/673689/; Herman B. Leonard, Christine M. Cole, Arnold M. Howitt, and Philip B. Heymann, "Why Was Boston Strong? Lessons From the Boston Marathon Bombing," (Cambridge, MA: Harvard College, 2014), https://www.hks.harvard.edu/sites/default/files/centers/rappaport/files/BostonStron g_final.pdf.

4. Massachusetts Emergency Management Agency. After Action Report for the Response to the 2013 Boston Marathon Bombings.

5. United States Department of Homeland Security. *National Incident Management System*, 1.

6. Bogucki, Sandy, and Kevin J. Schulz. "Incident Command System and National Incident Management System." In *Emergency Medical Services*, eds David C. Cone, Jane H. Brice, Theodore R. Delbridge, and J. Brent Myers, 255–63. (Chichester, UK: John Wiley & Sons, Ltd, 2015), 260, https://doi.org/10.1002/9781118990810.ch100; Jessica Jensen and Steven Thompson, "The Incident Command System: A Literature Review," *Disasters* 40, no. 1 (January 2016): 158–82, https://doi.org/10.1111/disa.12135; Nicholas B. Hambridge, Arnold M. Howitt, and David W. Giles, "Coordination in Crises: Implementation of the National Incident Management System by Surface Transportation Agencies" Homeland Security Affairs 13, no.3 (March 2017), https://www.hsaj.org/ articles/13773; United States Department of Homeland Security. *National Incident Management System*, 3.

7. Bogucki and Schulz, "Incident Command System and National Incident Management System," 258; Hambridge et al, "Coordination in Crises: Implementation of the National Incident Management System by Surface Transportation Agencies," 4; United States Department of Homeland Security. *National Incident Management System*, 3.

8. Bogucki and Schulz, "Incident Command System and National Incident Management System," 263; Hambridge et al, "Coordination in Crises: Implementation of the National Incident Management System by Surface Transportation Agencies," 2; Jensen and Thompson, "The Incident Command System: A Literature Review," 159; United States Department of Homeland Security. *National Incident Management System*, 1.

9. Bogucki and Schulz, "Incident Command System and National Incident Management System," 258-259; Hambridge et al, "Coordination in Crises: Implementation of the National Incident Management System by Surface Transportation Agencies," 6; United States Department of Homeland Security. *National Incident Management System*, 4-5.

10. Bogucki and Schulz, "Incident Command System and National Incident Management System," 258-259; Jensen and Thompson, "The Incident Command System: A Literature Review"; United States Department of Homeland Security. *National Incident Management System*, 4-5.

11. United States Department of Homeland Security. *National Incident Management System*, 3.

12. United States Department of Homeland Security. *National Incident Management System*, 27.

13. United States Department of Homeland Security. *National Incident Management System*, 27.

14. Federal Emergency Management Agency. IS-0200.c Basic Incident Command System for Initial Response, ICS 200 - Instructor Guide, (2020), 307-09, https://training.fema.gov/emiweb/is/is200c/english/instructor%20guide/is0200c%2 0ig.pdf

15. United States Department of Homeland Security. *National Incident Management System*, 31.

16. Jensen and Thompson, "The Incident Command System: A Literature Review," 159.

17. Dick A. Buck, Joseph E. Trainor, and Benigno E. Aguirre, "A critical evaluation of the Incident Command System and NIMS," *Journal of Homeland Security and Emergency Management* 3, no.3 (September 2006): 1–27, https://doi.org/10.2202/15477355.1252; Jensen and Thompson, "The Incident Command System: A Literature Review," 162; William L. Waugh and Gregory Streib, "Collaboration and Leadership for Effective Emergency Management," *Public Administration Review* 66, no. s1 (December 2006): 131–40, https://doi.org/10.1111/j.1540-6210.2006.00673.x.

18. Thomas E. Drabek, *Emergency Management and Homeland Security Curricula: Contexts, Cultures, and Constraints*, (Alberta, Canada: Department of Homeland Security, 2007), https://doi.org/10.1177/028072701803600204; Waugh and Streib, "Collaboration and Leadership for Effective Emergency Management."

19. Ryan P. Burke, "Command and Control: Challenging Fallacies of the 'Military Model' in Research and Practice," *International Journal of Mass Emergencies & Disasters* 36, no. 2 (August 2018): 149-78, https://doi.org/10.1177/028072701803600204; Hambridge et al, "Coordination in Crises: Implementation of the National Incident Management System by Surface Transportation Agencies."

20. Anice I. Anderson, Dennis Compton, and Tom Mason, "Managing in a dangerous world: the National Incident Management System," *Engineering Management Journal* 16, no. 4 (2004): 3–9, DOI: 10.1080/10429247.2004.11415260; Jensen and Thompson, "The Incident Command System: A Literature Review"; Ronald W. Perry, "Incident management systems in disaster management," *Disaster Prevention and Management* 12, no. 5 (December 2003): 405–12, https://doi.org/10.1108/09653560310507226

21. Burke, "Command and Control: Challenging Fallacies of the 'Military Model' in Research and Practice"; Drabek, *Emergency Management and Homeland Security Curricula: Contexts, Cultures, and Constraints*; Brenda Phillips, Dave Neal, and Gary Webb, *Introduction to Emergency Management,* (Boca Raton, FL: CRC Press, 2012); Branda Nowell and Toddi Steelman, "Beyond ICS: How Should We Govern Complex Disasters in the United States?" *Journal of Homeland Security and Emergency Management* 16, no. 2 (May 27, 2019), https://doi.org/10.1515/jhsem-2018-0067; Waugh and Streib, "Collaboration and Leadership for Effective Emergency Management."

22. Burke, "Command and Control: Challenging Fallacies of the 'Military Model' in Research and Practice."

23. Naim Kapucu and Qian Hu, "Understanding Multiplexity of Collaborative Emergency Management Networks," *The American Review of Public Administration* 46, no. 4 (July 2016): 399–417, https://doi.org/10.1177/0275074014555645; John P. Sullivan & Robert J. Bunker, "Multilateral Counter-Insurgency Networks," *Low Intensity Conflict and Law Enforcement* 11, no. 2-3 (January 2007): 353-368.

24. Massachusetts Emergency Management Agency. After Action Report for the Response to the 2013 Boston Marathon Bombings, 9.

25. Jensen and Thompson, "The Incident Command System: A Literature Review," 173.

26. Buck et al, "A critical evaluation of the Incident Command System and NIMS," 21; Hambridge et al, "Coordination in Crises: Implementation of the National Incident Management System by

Surface Transportation Agencies"; Jensen and Thompson, "The Incident Command System: A Literature Review," 173; Donald P. Moynihan, "From Intercrisis to Intracrisis Learning," *Journal of Contingencies and Crisis Management* 17, no. 3 (August 2009): 189–198, https://doi.org/10.1111/j.1468-5973.2009.00579.x; Donald P. Moynihan, "The Network Governance of Crisis Response: Case Studies of Incident Command Systems," *Journal of Public Administration Research and Theory* 19, no. 4. (December 2008): 895–915, https://dx.doi.org/10.2139/ssrn.1311597; Mohammad Hossein Yarmohammadian, Golrokh Atighechian, Lida Shams, Abbas Haghshenas, "Are Hospitals Ready to Response to Disasters? Challenges, Opportunities and Strategies of Hospital Emergency Incident Command System (HEICS)," *Journal of Research in Medical Services* 16, no. 8 (August 2011): 1070–1077, https://www.ncbi.nlm.nih.gov/pmc/articles/PMC3263085/

27. Buck et al, "A critical evaluation of the Incident Command System and NIMS," 21; Jensen and Thompson, "The Incident Command System: A Literature Review," 174; Leslie D. Lutz, and Michael K. Lindell, "Incident Command System as a Response Model Within Emergency Operation Centers during Hurricane Rita," *Journal of Contingencies and Crisis Management* 16, no. 3 (August 2008): 122–134, https://doi.org/10.1111/j.1468-5973.2008.00541.x; Moynihan, "From Intercrisis to Intracrisis Learning"; Moynihan, "The Network Governance of Crisis Response: Case Studies of Incident Command Systems."

28. Bogucki and Schulz, "Incident Command System and National Incident Management System," 257.

29. Buck et al, "A critical evaluation of the Incident Command System and NIMS," 14; Jensen and Thompson, "The Incident Command System: A Literature Review," 174.

30. Inspectors General of the Intelligence Community. *Unclassified Summary of Information Handling and Sharing Prior to the April 15, 2013 Boston Marathon Bombings.*

31. Majority Staff of Committee on Homeland Security. *Preventing Another Boston Marathon Bombing: Reviewing the Lessons Learned from the 2013 Terror Attack.*

32. Massachusetts Emergency Management Agency. *After Action Report for the Response to the 2013 Boston Marathon Bombings.*

33. Massachusetts Emergency Management Agency. *After Action Report for the Response to the 2013 Boston Marathon Bombings.*

34. Massachusetts Emergency Management Agency. After Action Report for the Response to the 2013 Boston Marathon Bombings.

35. Federal Emergency Management Agency. *Boston Marathon Bombings: The Positive Effect of Planning and Preparation on Response,* (2020), https://www.hsdl.org/c/abstract/?docid=741742

36. Federal Emergency Management Agency. *Boston Marathon Bombings: The Positive Effect of Planning and Preparation on Response.*

37. Federal Emergency Management Agency. *Boston Marathon Bombings: The Positive Effect of Planning and Preparation on Response.*

38. Federal Emergency Management Agency. *Boston Marathon Bombings: The Positive Effect of Planning and Preparation on Response.*

39. Massachusetts Emergency Management Agency. *After Action Report for the Response to the*

2013 Boston Marathon Bombings, 75.

40. Federal Emergency Management Agency. *Boston Marathon Bombings: The Positive Effect of Planning and Preparation on Response.*
41. Massachusetts Emergency Management Agency. *After Action Report for the Response to the 2013 Boston Marathon Bombings*, 75-76.
42. Massachusetts Emergency Management Agency. *After Action Report for the Response to the 2013 Boston Marathon Bombings*, 68.
43. Massachusetts Emergency Management Agency. *After Action Report for the Response to the 2013 Boston Marathon Bombings*, 44.
44. Massachusetts Emergency Management Agency *After Action Report for the Response to the 2013 Boston Marathon Bombings*, 76.
45. Leonard et al, "Why Was Boston Strong? Lessons From the Boston Marathon Bombing," ii-iii; Massachusetts Emergency Management Agency. *After Action Report for the Response to the 2013 Boston Marathon Bombings.*
46. Massachusetts Emergency Management Agency. *After Action Report for the Response to the 2013 Boston Marathon Bombings*, 117-18.
47. Waugh and Streib, "Collaboration and Leadership for Effective Emergency Management," 133; Buck et al, "A critical evaluation of the Incident Command System and NIMS," 20.
48. Massachusetts Emergency Management Agency. *After Action Report for the Response to the 2013 Boston Marathon Bombings*, 91.
49. Leonard et al, "Why Was Boston Strong? Lessons From the Boston Marathon Bombing," ii.
50. Massachusetts Emergency Management Agency. *After Action Report for the Response to the 2013 Boston Marathon Bombings*, 4.
51. Massachusetts Emergency Management Agency. *After Action Report for the Response to the 2013 Boston Marathon Bombings*, 4-5.
52. Massachusetts Emergency Management Agency. *After Action Report for the Response to the 2013 Boston Marathon Bombings*, 88.
53. Massachusetts Emergency Management Agency. *After Action Report for the Response to the 2013 Boston Marathon Bombings*, 88.
54. Massachusetts Emergency Management Agency. *After Action Report for the Response to the 2013 Boston Marathon Bombings*, 23.
55. Massachusetts Emergency Management Agency. *After Action Report for the Response to the 2013 Boston Marathon Bombings*, 24.
56. Leonard et al, "Why Was Boston Strong? Lessons From the Boston Marathon Bombing," i-ii.
57. Massachusetts Emergency Management Agency. *After Action Report for the Response to the 2013 Boston Marathon Bombings*," 10.
58. Massachusetts Emergency Management Agency *After Action Report for the Response to the 2013 Boston Marathon Bombings* 117-18.
59. Massachusetts Emergency Management Agency. *After Action Report for the Response to the*

2013 Boston Marathon Bombings, 96.

60. Massachusetts Emergency Management Agency After Action Report for the Response to the 2013 Boston Marathon Bombings, 96.
61. Massachusetts Emergency Management Agency. After Action Report for the Response to the 2013 Boston Marathon Bombings, 96.
62. Cybersecurity and Infrastructure Security Agency, "Wireless Priority Service (WPS)," accessed August 11, 2023, https://www.cisa.gov/resources-tools/services/wirelesspriority-service-wps.
63. Massachusetts Emergency Management Agency. After Action Report for the Response to the 2013 Boston Marathon Bombings, 96.
64. Massachusetts Emergency Management Agency After Action Report for the Response to the 2013 Boston Marathon Bombings, 97.
65. Massachusetts Emergency Management Agency. After Action Report for the Response to the 2013 Boston Marathon Bombings, 107.
66. Kathy-Ann C. Hernandez, "Collaborative Autoethnography as Method and Praxis: Understanding Self and Other in Practice," in *Autoethnography for Librarians and Information Scientists,* ed Ina Fourie. (London and New York: Routledge, 2021), 62.
67. Kathy-Ann C. Hernandez, "Collaborative Autoethnography as Method and Praxis: Understanding Self and Other in Practice," 62.
68. Kathy-Ann C. Hernandez, "Collaborative Autoethnography as Method and Praxis: Understanding Self and Other in Practice," 62.
69. Kathy-Ann C. Hernandez, "Collaborative Autoethnography as Method and Praxis: Understanding Self and Other in Practice," 62.
70. Kathy-Ann C. Hernandez, "Collaborative Autoethnography as Method and Praxis: Understanding Self and Other in Practice," 62.
71. 111th Congress. *Public Law 111-258 Reducing Overclassification Act.* (2010), https://www.congress.gov/111/plaws/publ258/PLAW-111publ258.pdf.
72. Massachusetts Emergency Management Agency. *After Action Report for the Response to the 2013 Boston Marathon Bombings,* 117-18.
73. Massachusetts Emergency Management Agency. *After Action Report for the Response to the 2013 Boston Marathon Bombings,* 10.
74. Massachusetts Emergency Management Agency. *After Action Report for the Response to the 2013 Boston Marathon Bombings,* 117-18.
75. Leonard et al, "Why Was Boston Strong? Lessons From the Boston Marathon Bombing," i-ii.
76. Michael S. Schmidt, William K. Rashbaum, and Richard A. Oppel Jr., "Deadly End to F.B.I. Queries on Tsarnaev and a Triple Killing," *The New York Times,* May 22, 2013, https://www.nytimes.com/2013/05/23/us/officer-involved-in-shooting-of-man-tiedto-tsarnaev.html.
77. Massachusetts Emergency Management Agency. *After Action Report for the Response to the 2013 Boston Marathon Bombings,"* 6-7.
78. United States Department of Homeland Security. "National Incident Management System," 30.

URBAN OPERATIONS

79. Federal Emergency Management Agency. IS-0200.c *Basic Incident Command System for Initial Response, ICS 200 - Instructor Guide*, 70.
80. Federal Emergency Management Agency. *IS-0200.c Basic Incident Command System for Initial Response, ICS 200 - Instructor Guide*, 87.
81. Federal Emergency Management Agency. IS-0200.c *Basic Incident Command System for Initial Response, ICS 200 - Instructor Guide*, 87.
82. Federal Emergency Management Agency. IS-0200.c *Basic Incident Command System for Initial Response, ICS 200 - Instructor Guide*, 88.
83. Leonard et al, "Why Was Boston Strong? Lessons From the Boston Marathon Bombing," 41-42.
84. Massachusetts Emergency Management Agency. *After Action Report for the Response to the 2013 Boston Marathon Bombings*, 11.
85. Massachusetts Emergency Management Agency. *After Action Report for the Response to the 2013 Boston Marathon Bombings*, 97.
86. Massachusetts Emergency Management Agency. *After Action Report for the Response to the 2013 Boston Marathon Bombings*, 96.
87. Massachusetts Emergency Management Agency. *After Action Report for the Response to the 2013 Boston Marathon Bombings*, 107.
88. Majority Staff of Committee on Homeland *Security. Preventing* Another Boston Marathon Bombing: Reviewing the Lessons Learned from the 2013 Terror Attack, 13.

CHAPTER 6
Urban Warfare: The Recent Israeli Experience

Nadav Morag

Introduction

Israel has been engaging in urban warfare for several decades to support counterterrorism and counterguerrilla objectives on various fronts, including the West Bank, the Gaza Strip, and Lebanon. Israel's experience conducting urban warfare has been characterized by a significant evolution in tactics and strategies. Over time, urban warfare took the place of warfare in open terrain as Israel's primary type of warfare, a process that mirrored developments in other parts of the world, including US counterinsurgency efforts in Iraq and Afghanistan and the Syrian Civil War.

This chapter briefly addresses modern urban warfare's nature and constraints. It examines Israel's early experience with urban warfare during the 1982 Lebanon War, where urban warfare was still a corollary to warfare in open terrain. It then describes and assesses a range of Israel's wars and operations—starting with Defensive Shield in the West Bank and moving to the Second Lebanon War and concludes by addressing several conflicts between Israel and Hamas in the Gaza Strip between 2007 and 2021. Between 1982 and 2021, the Israel Defense Forces (IDF) became increasingly focused on urban warfare as the main air and ground operations arena. The IDF developed specific tactics and technologies designed to provide advantages to enable it to leverage its capabilities more efficiently within the constraints of the urban environment. Additionally, the author will identify a few overarching trends in the evolution of Israeli urban warfare.

Urban Warfare

Urban warfare, whether in cities or—to broaden the definition to all confined man-made spaces—in forts and castles, has been a feature of warfare since antiquity. Many of the principles recognized as characterizing urban warfare today were largely applicable in the premodern period, except for aerial assets or, farther back in time, explosives. While not exhaustive, John Spencer offers a useful list of eight rules and the major principles of modern urban warfare:

1. Defenders almost always have a tactical advantage, particularly in cities, though this does not imply that they will necessarily succeed at the operational or strategic level of a conflict

2. The urban terrain inhibits the attacking force's ability to use intelligence, surveillance, reconnaissance, deploy aerial assets, and engage the defenders from a distance

3. Attacking forces have trouble achieving the element of surprise as they are monitored by the defending troops, which can remain hidden from the attackers

4. Buildings, particularly those made of steel-reinforced concrete or stone, serve as fortified bunkers from which defending forces can fire upon attacking forces

5. Attackers often use munitions, sometimes powerful ones, to access buildings and deny them to defending forces

6. Defenders have the advantage of comparatively free movement within the city and intimate knowledge of its streets, alleys, and warrens—when not under surveillance or attack by unmanned aerial vehicles or via other means

7. Defenders can build tunnels, arms depots, and a range of other facilities underground and use these to access multiple locations in and around the city. Attackers often have no or little knowledge of these

8. Neither attacking nor defending forces can mass their assets in a concentrated location. The concentration of forces is one of the deciding factors in conventional battlefield warfare in that, historically, the objective of field operations was to concentrate one's force to decimate the enemy's army. The inability to use mass forces has disadvantages for both sides, but if it is the defending force that is an irregular force and the attacking force that is a modern military—which has in the case in many instances of postWorld War II modern urban warfare—the technological, numerical, training, and equipment advantages of a modern military cannot, in many cases, be brought to bear as effectively as it can in open warfare. Thus, the modern military force is often forced to skirmish with irregular fighters, with both sides being largely matched because they carry similar types of equipment, and the training advantage that a modern soldier has can be somewhat negated by the knowledge of the terrain afforded to an irregular defending fighter. Also, the irregular defenders usually have a significant amount of time to prepare their city for conflict, including taking measures such as: Digging tunnels, building ammunition dumps, establishing sniper positions, deploying booby-traps, and planning ambushes.[1]

Since much of modern warfare is asymmetric, irregular forces such as guerrillas and insurgents cannot hope to best their adversaries in warfare on open terrain. and thus, must rely on the advantages afforded by extensive cover, whether in natural environments such as jungles, mountains, deserts, or other locations that are hard to access and control or in cities.[2]

Of course, as noted above, urban warfare is not new. However, even in the modern period, as during World War II, urban warfare was largely noholds-barred and did not take into consideration in any meaningful way the issue of collateral damage, both in terms of egregious damage to property and especially in terms of loss of life among non-combatants. Hence, for example, in the great urban battles of World War II, such as those of Stalingrad, Warsaw, and Berlin, the city in its totality served as a military target and, therefore, anyone or anything in it was in danger of becoming collateral damage. The same was true of the strategic bombing of cities such as Hamburg, Dresden, and Tokyo during the War. The goal was either to capture the city in ground operations or to massively bomb from the air to degrade its ability to contribute to the war effort and weaken the morale of its inhabitants. Moreover, with the noted exception of the Battle of Stalingrad—which involved the trapping and destroying of German troops in and around the city, the most impactful battles of World War II (Midway, Kursk, Overlord, Guadalcanal, El Alamein, and others) did not occur in urban environments.

Of course, the approach that views a city as a legitimate target for all military activity has not entirely disappeared—witness the current Russian tactics in cities in the Ukraine—but it is largely unacceptable, particularly for democracies, to treat a city full of civilians as essentially one big military target. Modern legal conventions and ethical considerations make it necessary to try and distinguish between the peaceful inhabitants of a city and regular or irregular enemy forces. Of course, the irregular forces are aware of this and thus often masquerade as peaceful citizens to maximize their tactical advantages and minimize their vulnerabilities vis a vis the invading force.

These new legal and ethical considerations attached to urban warfare have been buttressed by the even newer phenomenon of the Information Revolution and the possession of cell phone cameras in the hands of most inhabitants of a city and access to social media to upload video and photographs of combat and atrocities. In addition, the phenomenon of lawfare in which parties to a conflict, sometimes using cell phone footage, try to initiate legal actions against individuals or organizations plays an increasing role in modern warfare. The problem with close-quarter urban combat in and around the homes and businesses of noncombatants, of course, is that it is impossible to guarantee the safety of noncombatants. This limits the freedom of movement of conventional invading forces and makes them more vulnerable to attack, while civilian deaths and property damage can benefit the irregular defending forces by drawing global attention and ire towards the invading forces. The death of innocents in a city can sway public opinion on the part of the inhabitants in the direction of providing increasing support to the irregular forces and stoke greater hatred towards the invading forces. Hence, urban defenders enjoy a large range of advantages, not just tactically but also in terms of local, national, and global opinion, something that can influence the politics of the invading country as well as its relationships with its allies and trading partners.

The key, then, for a modern military of a democratic state that wants to attack and gain control of an urban environment is to significantly degrade the enemy's ability to conduct operations in the city while minimizing its own casualties while reducing to an absolute minimum the loss of life of noncombatants, and minimizing, to the degree possible, the destruction of property. The invading force must accomplish all of this without turning the masses of the urban population against it in a way that might produce a secondary insurgency. Clearly, accomplishing all the objectives is a tall order and difficult, if not effectively impossible, to achieve all at once. Israel's approach to urban warfare provides a good case study of some of the pitfalls of urban warfare and ways to cope with its challenges.

The Israeli Experience with Urban Warfare: The Early Years to Defensive Shield

In the early decades of Israel's existence, Arab-Israeli warfare was characterized largely by conventional clashes in open terrain, particularly in the Sinai and on the Golan Heights. At the same time, virtually all of Israel's wars featured some manifestations of urban combat. Examples include the battle of Jerusalem during Israel's War of Independence, Israel's conquest of east Jerusalem, the cities of the West Bank, and the cities of the Gaza Strip during the Six Day War, or the Battle of Suez during the Yom Kippur War. However, most of the fighting in these cases occurred in the streets of the cities and not in or from the buildings themselves.[3]

Despite the fact that urban combat of some kind featured in these wars, most of the military activity and the most important clashes occurred outside urban environments. This began to change with Israel's 1982 war against the Palestine Liberation Organization (PLO) and Syria in Lebanon. In that war, the most serious military clashes occurred during tank battles between Israel and Syria on open terrain in the Bekka Valley. The 1982 Lebanon War nevertheless featured widespread clashes with irregular PLO fighters who primarily fought in cities or the urban environments of large villages.

At that time, Israel's urban warfare doctrine, largely like other militaries, called for encircling, cutting off, and bypassing cities. Furthermore, the Israeli military's traditional emphasis on the use of armor resulted in a shortage of infantry and a resulting reliance on tanks in combat, and these were not thought to be as useful in constrained urban environments.[4] Fortunately for Israel, when it came to dislodging the Palestinians from their strongholds in Beirut, most of the PLO fighters were deployed in the Palestinian refugee camps in more open terrain on the margins of the city where tanks and armored vehicles could operate more easily, and were furthermore easily viewed from the mountains south and east of Beirut, where the IDF had placed its artillery batteries.[5]

The shift in focus to urban combat occurred gradually. After the 1979 peace treaty between Israel and Egypt, the conventional Arab military threat to Israel, which afforded possibilities to concentrate forces on the battlefield, using combined infantry, air, artillery, and armor assets and deliver decisive victories, albeit sometimes at a high cost to Israeli forces, essentially began to dissipate. Ultimately, the Egyptian decision to pursue peace with Israel effectively negated the Arab option of waging another combined conventional war against Israel. Over time, the weakening of Iraq, owing to its war with Iran and then its defeat at the hands of the

United States, removed yet another conventional adversary from the Israeli threat picture. With the signing of a peace treaty between Israel and Jordan in 1993 (though Jordan had not been a real military threat to Israel in decades and secretly cooperated with it), only Syria presented any real conventional threat to Israel—however, Damascus could not realistically take on Jerusalem on its own. With the collapse of Syria in 2011 and the onset of the brutal civil war in that country, the last realistic conventional threat facing Israel evaporated. The Egyptian military is still formidable and will be a major conventional threat in the highly unlikely event that Egypt decides to tear up the long-standing peace treaty and go to war, but, even when under a Muslim Brotherhood-affiliated government (June 2012 to July 2013), Egypt did not demonstrate any real desire to abandon the peace treaty with Israel.

As the traditional battlefield military threat to Israel decreased dramatically from 1979 to 2011 and subsequently effectively disappeared, there was a gradual concomitant rise in the threat from irregular forces— terrorist groups and guerrilla or insurgent forces. These forces were unable to field manned aircraft or even battlefield-grade artillery or tanks in anything approximating the numbers required or capability needed to represent any sort of battlefield threat to the Israel Defense Forces (IDF). Consequently, the only locations in which irregular forces could try and level the playing field with the IDF was in crowded urban environments, where the IDF was unwilling to concentrate its fire and otherwise take full advantage of its conventional capabilities. Indeed, urban warfare partially deprived the IDF of one of its greatest tactical advantages, air support.[6] Consequently, because Israel's current primary adversaries are ensconced, either almost totally in the case of Hamas and other Palestinian groups, or largely, as in the case of Hezbollah, in urban environments, the Palestinian and Lebanese cities and large villages have become Israel's main battlefield —leaving aside the scenario of long-range Israeli air and sea strikes against Iran's nuclear program.

Unlike Arab armies in the early decades of Israel's existence, these irregular forces pose no existential threat to Israel, as a state, but they do, in many ways, pose a greater existential threat to the individual citizens of the State of Israel. Irregular forces can manufacture or smuggle missile and rocket technology, as well as drones, and deploy these against Israeli military and civilian targets. This poses an increasing threat due to continual advances in the technology behind these weapons systems. Israeli citizens in their homes and businesses, are now the targets of explosive projectiles launched by Hezbollah and various Palestinian factions in Lebanon and Hamas, Palestinian Islamic Jihad, and other factions in the Gaza Strip. This was initially a novel experience for Israeli civilians as, under the traditional warfare model that Israel had followed during its conventional wars with the Arab states, the Israeli Air Force dominated the skies above the battlefield and hence, with a few exceptions, prevented Arab aircraft from bombing Israeli cities. Lebanese Hezbollah being far better equipped (with an arsenal of some 150,000 rockets and missiles), trained, and enjoying more mobility in comparison to Hamas or other Palestinian organizations, has come to pose a major threat to Israel's cities, infrastructure, and civilian population.

The response to the outbreak of the Second Intifada in October 2000 and Operation Defensive Shield (March-May of 2002), launched to temporarily retake most of the cities of the West Bank from the direct control of the Palestinian Authority, featured extensive urban warfare. Operation Defensive Shield represented the largest Israeli military mobilization since the 1982 Lebanon War with some 30,000 reservists called up. Most of the fighting was against small groups of Palestinian fighters ensconced in buildings among the civilian population. During the operation, the IDF faced significant resistance, preventing it from utilizing the full range of its air assets or employing concentrated fire from armor and artillery. The ground forces were thus compelled to engage in house-to-house combat to flush out Palestinian fighters. The IDF used Caterpillar D9 armored bulldozers to clear routes and destroy IEDs on the roads and inside buildings, though these frequently caused significant material damage in the areas in which they operated, particularly where the roadways were narrow, such as in the Casbah districts of Palestinian cities such as Nablus.[7] The IDF also employed what were, for it, novel tactics such as blasting through walls to move horizontally or floors and ceilings to move vertically, thus allowing infantry soldiers to avoid stairwells and avoid exposing themselves to sniper fire or IEDs in the streets and warrens of the cities.[8] This tactic had the advantage of forcing Palestinian fighters out into the streets where they were more vulnerable to Israel's overwhelming advantage in firepower, but it also caused significant physical damage to homes and businesses.[9] The Israeli military also employed large numbers of undercover personnel that masqueraded as Palestinian civilians in order to foil plots, gather intelligence, and make arrests.[10]

In the wake of Defensive Shield, the IDF increasingly came to view a capability to wage effective urban warfare as important and, three years later, it built a 60-acre urban warfare training center at an IDF base in southern Israel, that can accommodate an entire brigade at a time.[11] This training capability came none too soon as, during the 2006-2009 period, the IDF definitively shifted to focusing on urban warfare as a result of The Second Lebanon War (July-August 2006), and those new techniques were then employed for the first time during Operation Cast Lead (December 2008-January 2009).

The Second Lebanon War and its Aftermath

During the summer of 2006, the Second Lebanon War featured numerous engagements in urban environments within large villages, along with Israeli bombing of Hezbollah positions in southern Beirut and other cities. Unlike classical guerrilla tactics, which involve ambushes in which the guerrillas quickly retreat after the attack to avoid being crushed by conventional forces, some Hezbollah fighters in urban environments, as well as in rural outposts, attempted to hold ground for extended periods of time.[12] Hezbollah guerrillas made effective use of urban environments in towns and large villages but, unlike subsequent operations in Gaza, most of the towns and villages that were attacked by IDF forces during the Second Lebanon War had already been evacuated by their civilian inhabitants and thus coping with civilians during ground engagements was less of a problem.[13]

Many viewed Israel's performance during the Second Lebanon War critically, both at the military and the governmental levels, particularly within Israel. Public outrage, stemming from the perceived paltry results of the war at the time, compelled the Prime Minister to appoint a commission to investigate the war's multiple failures. The Winograd Commission concluded that Israel's poor performance was a combination of the failure of civilian and military leadership, poor preparedness and training, poor intelligence, poor operational doctrine, and an overreliance on air power.[14] Perhaps unsurprisingly, Israel, in coping with the Second Intifada, was focused on Low-Intensity Conflict (LIC) and not prepared for what might be termed guerrilla warfare plus. One of the features of Israel's LIC approach was that time constraints in accomplishing an operation were less of a factor that avoiding casualties among IDF forces or Palestinian civilian casualties.[15] This was essentially the opposite of Israel's past approach to conventional warfare, which involved hitting the enemy decisively to end the war as quickly as possible, given Israel's limited resources.

In 2006, in response to Israeli failures in effectively execute urban warfare during the Second Lebanon War, the IDF revised its approach. Active duty and reserve forces were provided with new equipment (including equipment for breaching buildings), the aforementioned urban warfare training center was built, and there was a greater emphasis on combined arms in the urban environment. Israel increased its procurement of Merkava IV tanks, viewing the Merkava as a more effective troop carrier for coping with anti-tank missiles than normal armored troop carriers.[16] Greater coordination between the Israeli Air Force and ground forces was also emphasized and tactical air control, which had been denied the ground forces prior to the

Second Lebanon War on the grounds that it was not needed in LIC urban environments, was re-instated at the brigade level.[17] IDF training emphasis shifted from a three to one ratio in favor of LIC versus high intensity conflict (HIC) to 80 percent of training being devoted to combined-arms HIC training because the military had concluded that it would have to prepare for a 'hybrid' threat in which it would have to deal not only with low-level tactical teams of Palestinian fighters, but also with higher-end 'professional' guerrilla forces such as those of Hezbollah.[18] In this hybrid context, at the lower-end, the IDF had to learn to better exploit unconventional tactics by focusing on disrupting the enemy rather than holding territory, and, on the other side of the hybrid equation, it had to abandon concepts such as 'front lines' or 'rear staging areas' as the battlefield was potentially everywhere in the urban environment.[19]

In changing its doctrine to emphasize urban warfare, the Israeli Air Force had to focus on surgical strikes using accurate and low yield munitions, as opposed to its previous focus on destroying enemy formations on the battlefield. This also necessitated the use of more attack helicopters and unmanned aerial vehicles (UAVs), alongside manned fixed-wing aircraft. The IDF ground forces also had to prepare for urban warfare in a combined arms approach in which infantry advanced in, and along with, heavy and light armored personnel carriers (APCs), tanks, armored bulldozers, and combat engineers. In the case of the latter, the military utilized combat engineers to blast through buildings and neutralize tunnels.[20]

One of the lessons from the Second Lebanon War was that the IDF could not rely on infantry alone in urban environments as this could dramatically increase the number of casualties, and hence armor, including tanks, was still essential. In addition, tactical intelligence-gathering and dissemination would need to change. The IDF shifted to technological platforms and an intelligence doctrine that emphasized the provisions of real-time tactical intelligence from multiple sources (agents in the area, electronic interceptions, drones, fixed and rotary wing aircraft, and troops) to provide commanders on the ground with information about enemy positions.[21] Given the presence of civilians, techniques also had to be developed to ensure a minimization of loss of life among civilians. These included low yield munitions which were fired from a drone or helicopter into a room of a building via a window to kill a target without others in the building realizing that the building was under attack. Additionally, the IDF adopted tactics to warn civilians of pending attacks and to encourage them to leave the target area. These include roof knocking, which involves the firing of a low yield or non-explosive munition at the roof of a building to frighten the civilians in it and thus encourage them to flee the building before it comes under actual attack. Israel also started experimenting with dense inert metal explosives that create a highly concentrated blast without expelling shrapnel to contain damage to the actual blast zone.[22] Israel would have a chance to test these new approaches, technologies, and tactics less than a year and a half later in the Gaza Strip.

Operation Cast Lead

Israel transferred power to Fatah forces representing the Palestinian Authority upon its unilateral withdrawal of troops and settlers from the Gaza Strip in September 2005. The Palestinian Authority was unable to maintain control and its forces were overthrown violently by Hamas forces in June 2007. Although rocket fire from Gaza was not unheard of in the 1990s and early 2000s, an increase of rocket fire into Israel after the Hamas takeover eventually drove the Israeli government to authorize a military operation in Gaza. Thus, in December 2008, during Operation Cast Lead, the IDF had a chance to test the changes it made to its training regimen, equipment, and doctrine against another hybrid opponent, albeit one that enjoyed far fewer advantages than those enjoyed by Hezbollah. Unlike Lebanon, Israeli and Egyptian territory surrounds the Gaza Strip. In addition, the Israeli Navy controls its coastline. Hence Hamas, Palestinian Islamic Jihad, and other Palestinian organizations in the Gaza Strip do not benefit, as Hezbollah does, from the use of porous borders with Syria or control of seaports and airports from which it can smuggle in arms from Iran. Moreover, Hamas also does not control a sovereign state government, as does Hezbollah in

Lebanon, with all that this entails for the ability to operate in a country's territory. From an intelligence perspective as well, Israel has much better penetration of the Gaza Strip (and West Bank) than it does of Lebanon. To make matters even worse from the Palestinian perspective, unlike southern Lebanon's difficult to traverse terrain, the Gaza Strip is flat and easily accessible from Israel. However, Hamas does enjoy one advantage, it rules one of the most densely populated areas of the world and this means nearly all fighting in Gaza takes place in dense urban areas where Hamas and its allies have built networks of tunnels, arms depots, and sniper positions, and otherwise prepared IEDs, smuggled in anti-tank missiles, and taken other measures to ready the urban battlefield.

Unlike the Second Lebanon War, Cast Lead had been planned as a ground operation and Israel mobilized needed reserves early on, as, by this time, ground operations were seen as a necessary part of the effort to defeat a hybrid opponent.[23] Once the IDF crossed into Gaza, Hamas fighters attempted to pull them into densely populated areas in order to conduct filmed ambushes and kidnapping of troops.[24] Israeli operations were characterized by an attempt to avoid collateral damage by selecting the appropriate munitions for specific targets, employing intelligence assets— including informants and airborne sensors—and active warning of impending operations to civilians via the aforementioned 'roof knocking' as well as warnings phoned in to people.[25] As a result, Hamas and other operatives had to be constantly on the move to avoid detection and this severely disrupted their ability to effectively respond to IDF assaults while also increasing the likelihood that these fighters would expose themselves to IDF fire or capture.[26] The Israeli Air Force also destroyed pre-planned fixed targets while also interdicting targets of opportunity—such as Hamas personnel—and then shifted to on-call close air support when called in by IDF forces on the ground.[27]

Operation Cast Lead ended in January 2009 after 22 days of fighting with ten deaths among IDF soldiers—four in friendly fire incidents. Israel killed only a small number of Hamas personnel and leadership and thus left the organization largely functioning. Israel's objectives in the operation were unclear beyond a vague desire to restore deterrence and degrade Hamas's military infrastructure, with the latter objective being in keeping more with a counterterrorism policy that seeks to, *mow the grass*, in Israeli parlance, with ongoing operations to degrade enemy capabilities, rather than a hybrid war policy with a near-state actor. As noted, the conflict had vague objectives, which have both the advantage and the disadvantage of being hard to measure. This is an advantage because, unlike the situation during the Second Lebanon War when clear Israeli objectives, as described by the Prime Minister at the time, were completely unmet and helped thus create a sense that Israel had lost its war with Hezbollah, fuzzy objectives cannot be proven to *not* have been achieved. On the other hand, major military operations without clear objectives can lead to questions as to the necessity and justifiability of such operations—as were indeed raised by quite a few people inside and outside Israel at the close of fighting.[28] Nevertheless, if the objective was to significantly curtail rocket and missile fire into Israel from Gaza, this objective was achieved, for a time, during the period of 2009-2012—though there were flareups in the summer of 2011 and in early 2012. Developments that made the Israeli home front more resilient, thus creating more operations options for Israel's leadership, had a major impact on the next engagement with Hamas, Operation Pillar of Defense.

Pillar of Defense

By 2012, Israel had deployed its new Iron Dome anti rocket system, and this weapons system would gradually give Israel the ability to withstand the bulk of Hamas's rocket fire on population centers and thus give Israel more time and options in deciding how to respond to Palestinian attacks. Increasing Palestinian fire at Israel during 2012 and Israeli military responses eventually escalated and led to the eight-day operation Pillar of Defense in November 2012. As with Cast Lead, Israel's objectives were to restore deterrence and degrade Hamas's military capabilities—objectives that were vague enough, as noted earlier with respect to the previous conflict, to allow Israel to declare a victory at a point in time of its choosing. Israel had to accomplish these vague objectives while minimizing damage to the Israeli home front and avoiding negative international political fallout, particularly with respect to the Muslim Brotherhood-affiliated Egyptian government of Muhammad Morsi.[29] Had fighting with the Palestinians led to a breakdown of the peace agreement between Israel and Egypt, this would have been a grave outcome for Israel and thus this outcome needed to be avoided at all costs.

Unlike Operation Cast Lead, Pillar of Defense was largely an air campaign—though with some special forces' activity on the ground. It also involved the deployment of new intelligence capabilities vis a vis urban areas in Gaza to allow for more pinpoint attacks, including a reported increase of 25 percent in the number of military intelligence officers in the IDF and greater use of manned and unmanned aircraft to create situational awareness.[30] Attempts were made to reduce civilian casualties from air strikes through the dispersal of leaflets, roof-knocking, and automated calls to residents, and many urban targets had to be vetted and approved by IDF lawyers.[31] Despite the focus on air operations, Israel called up a total of 57,000 reservists—most of whom were ground forces, and this was comparable to the call up of reserves for the Second Lebanon War and much larger than the number mobilized for Cast Lead. This large number of reservists was mobilized both to prepare for the possibility of the need for a large ground operation and to demonstrate to Hamas, Egypt, and other actors, that Israel was serious about curbing Hamas rocket fire and prepared to undertake a major ground operation.[32]

Ultimately, Israel chose not to order its reservists to enter the Gaza Strip, a decision that has been attributed both to Israel's lack of desire for a major ground engagement in the cities of the Gaza Strip and also due to the success of Iron Dome in intercepting rocket fire and thus maintaining normality in most of Israel, outside sparsely populated areas near the Gaza Strip.[33] As with Cast Lead, Pillar of Defense restored quiet for a time. It demonstrated the desirability and effectiveness of anti-rocket systems, the utility of using air assets in urban operations (to the degree that these systems may obviate the need for a major ground operation), the importance of precision weapons, and the criticality of command-and-control capabilities and cyber assets.[34] However, Hamas's advances in creating a subterranean network of tunnels, both to protect its assets and to launch attacks in Israeli territory, ultimately pushed the pendulum back in the direction of ground operations in urban environments in the Gaza Strip.

Protective Edge

Pillar of Defense brought a measure of quiet to Israel's border with Gaza that lasted for about a year and a half, but in July 2014, the next round of fighting broke out between Israel and Hamas due to increased rocket fire and an increasing tempo in Israeli operations. Operation Protective Edge, which began on July 8, lasted 51 days and was by far the most lengthy and destructive conflict between Israel and Hamas to date. Protective Edge began with an extensive air campaign targeting Hamas assets and individual Hamas commanders. However, Hamas had learned from Pillar of Defense that it needed to deploy more of its assets underground and as a result, Hamas was comparatively less vulnerable to Israeli air operations, and this similarly allowed the organization to hide command and control capabilities, and rockets and other assets from Israel.[35] Hamas and other groups in the Gaza Strip based their operational concept on the use of tunnels to safeguard personnel and materiel.[36] As a result, Israel's air operations were comparatively less effective than in previous engagements.[37] Moreover, once all the pre-approved targets had been hit, it took some time for Israel to acquire new targets and have them vetted and approved by the IDF's legal team.[38] By this time, Israel's approach to targeting in the urban environment had been solidified. For preplanned targets, the process involved:

1. Collecting intelligence on the target to validate that it is a legitimate military target under the Law of Armed Conflict

2. Determining the objective in attacking the target—for example, destroying an infrastructure or eliminating an individual

3. Developing options for the strike, including minimization of collateral damage

4. Requesting professional advice on the target, including legal opinions

5. Obtaining command approval for hitting the target.[39]

Unlike the process for preplanned targets, the process for hitting a target that suddenly presented itself in real time was much more expeditious and often did not involve lawyers. However, after the operation, Israel's State Comptroller and Ombudsman determined that for future operations, the IDF should stipulate in a Supreme Command Order the obligation to receive legal accompaniment in the process of formulation of orders, and at least in respect of orders dealing with employing firepower, which may have implications for human life.[40]

While Israeli tactics, including legal review of operations, were developing, Hamas was also honing its tactics. Hamas established three lines of defense to try and cope with Israeli operations. The first line of defense was located up to 2 km inside the border fence and involved a network of mines, improvised explosives, ambush sites, and mortar targets.[41] The second line of defense was at the outskirts of the major cities in the Gaza Strip, where heavy mortars, machine guns, and anti-tank weapons were deployed—along with snipers and suicide bombers.[42] The final line of defense was the tunnel network inside the cities designed to allow movement of fighters and material and to surprise IDF forces, as well as the use of boobytraps and mines. Hamas also developed the capacity to attack Israeli territory via amphibious assault, paragliders, and, most worryingly, via tunnels. The tunnel threat into Israel, in particular, led to an Israeli push to uncover these tunnels—many of which started 3 km inside the Strip- and thus authorize a major ground incursion.[43] Israel ultimately uncovered and destroyed some 100km of tunnels during the operation—one third of which extended into Israeli territory, and the pursuit of these led IDF forces to enter urban areas, resulting in some significant urban battles.[44] All of this resulted in a larger IDF death toll (66 soldiers) as well as a significant number of Palestinian fatalities (approximately 2,133, of whom 1,489 were civilians).[45]

During many of the pitched battles in urban areas, tanks and other armored vehicles with active protection systems proved their worth in protecting troops while providing mobility and demonstrated that air power cannot compensate for armored vehicles on the ground.[46] The campaign resulted in significant losses to Hamas in terms of tunnel infrastructure and other assets, but left Hamas fully intact. Protective Edge led to a longer period of Israeli deterrence of Hamas. In December 2021, Israel attempted to finally put an end to the tunnel threat through its completion of an anti-tunnel barrier, equipped with sensors, along the border with the Gaza Strip, and this has thus far been successful. The destruction left in the wake of Protective Edge also arguably led Hamas to opt for less direct means of confrontation with Israel including encouraging (sometimes violent) mass demonstrations at the border with Israel as well as shifting the location of the 'battlefield' via authorizing more Hamas operations against Israeli civilians and soldiers in the West Bank.

Protective Edge also saw significant improvements in the provision of tactical intelligence at the brigade level, with commanders having access to signals intelligence, human sources, and UAV cameras.[47] At the same time, these shed little light on Hamas's tunnel networks and, at the strategic level, there was little insight into what Hamas might do in various scenarios.[48] In the wake of Protective Edge, the IDF began reinvesting in armored vehicles and the fighting reinforced the arguments in favor of the benefits of active protection systems such as the Trophy Active Protection System deployed on Merkava tanks and Namer armored personnel carriers. The system not only addresses the threat posed by rocket propelled grenades and anti-tank missiles, but also provides immediate intelligence on the location from which a rocket-propelled grenade or missile was fired.[49] The next round of fighting did not feature any major new developments in urban warfare and returned to a reliance on air power in the urban environment. The new round of fighting did, however, evidence greater Hamas capabilities to target more Israeli cities, but the success of Iron Dome batteries largely neutralized these greater attack capabilities.

Operation Guardian of the Walls

The next—and at the time of this writing last—major round of Israel-Gaza fighting erupted on May 10, 2021. In 11 days of fighting Palestinian groups fired more than 4,000 rockets from Gaza and Israel killed over 200 Hamas and Palestinian Islamic Jihad members. However, the IDF did not destroy much of the enemy infrastructure, only destroying approximately 850 rockets of the estimated 15,000 rockets in the hands of Hamas and other Palestinian factions.[50] At the same time, Iron Dome missiles neutralized approximately 90 percent of the rockets fired at Israel, and over 100 km of tunnels that made up about one third of Hamas's underground infrastructure—known in the IDF as "the Metro" were destroyed by the Israeli Air Force, something that will perhaps prompt Hamas to reconsider the value of its reliance and focus on underground logistics and operations.[51] According to some reports, the IDF had actually planned to draw hundreds of Hamas members into the tunnels via faking a ground invasion and then kill them via air strikes, yet Israel apparently showed its hand with some early air strikes on tunnels coupled with weak efforts to convince Hamas that a ground invasion was imminent.[52]

Operation Guardian of the Walls once again illustrated the IDF's desire to avoid entering urban areas with ground forces and to try and address threats via precision bombing. As noted above in the discussion of the four major military operations in Gaza, reliance on air power to neutralize urban threats has come in and out of favor. The fact that the IDF, and Israel's civilian leadership, allowed themselves the relative luxury of relying on the Air Force in Guardian of the Walls is likely a combination of advances in intelligence, targeting, and the use of precision munitions coupled with the reduced threat to Israeli citizens from rocket fire due to Iron Dome, and Hamas's inability to use tunnels to initiate cross-border kidnapping or terrorism operations.

Yet Hamas, demonstrated both resilience and an ability to improve its capabilities, as manifested by its increasing operational capacity to engage in sustained rocket fire that targeted deeper into Israel than ever before, threatening Tel Aviv, Jerusalem, and other major population centers in Israel. While not a direct result of Hamas efforts, Guardian of the Walls also saw the most widespread civil strife in Israel, with major riots flaring up in Israeli-Arab towns and mixed Jewish-Arab cities, and, while civil strife in Israel is outside the scope of this study, Hamas may come to view the potential for civil strife inside Israel as another tool to use in its ongoing conflict with Israel. For now, the significant damage to infrastructure in the Gaza Strip due to air strikes, coming in the wake of previous operations, has given Hamas leaders an interest in focusing on rebuilding and maintaining calm with Israel. This, of course, does not solve the underlying conflict (assuming it can be solved) and it is likely that as long as the asymmetric power relationship exists between Israel and Hamas, the Palestinian organization and its affiliates in the Gaza Strip will continue to look for ways to force the IDF into the streets, alleyways, and warrens of the cities of the Gaza Strip, where the Palestinians can take advantage of the urban environment to level the playing field with the IDF and extract a more significant human, economic, and political 'price' from Israel.

Conclusion: Israel and the Challenges of Urban Warfare

As evidenced from the above discussion, Israel's approach to urban warfare has evolved dramatically over time and has gone through periods focusing on ground operations to periods in which the bulk of its efforts were in air operations. While urban warfare had been a feature of all of virtually all of Israel's wars, it had previously involved regular (and sometimes irregular) forces fighting in the streets of towns and cities and did not start to qualify as urban warfare, in the sense used here, until the 1982 Lebanon War—though even at this time, the most important military engagements still occurred on the battlefield, in clashes between Israel and Syria. Gradually, the focus of the main battle space shifted from the battlefield to urban environments in the 1990s as urban warfare became a major feature of Israel's military operations. Operation Defensive Shield in the West Bank, the Second

Lebanon War, and the four Israel-Hamas clashes in the Gaza Strip, from Cast Lead to Guardian of the Walls, all involved new tactics, technologies, and efforts to leverage the urban environment to one side's advantage at the expense of its enemy. The overarching trend in the evolution of Israel's approach to urban warfare has been one of:

1. A greater focus on accurate battlefield intelligence to pinpoint adversaries and minimize collateral damage,
2. Increased use of accurate, low yield weapons systems for surgical strikes and defensive weapons systems to protect IDF forces in urban environments,
3. Greater use of air defense systems (once developed) to protect the civilian population from rocket and missile attacks thus enabling a more flexible response with comparatively less time pressure,
4. Greater willingness to mobilize large numbers of reservists for ground operations to demonstrate intent and to deploy them if needed,
5. The increased use of combined arms including infantry, combat engineers, fixed and rotary aircraft, tanks, armored personnel carriers, artillery, armored tractors, and special forces,
6. A greater understanding of the need to ensure that operations do not run afoul of the Laws of War or other international legal conventions.

Post-Guardian of the Walls, Israeli Police are likely to deploy in greater numbers to prevent civil strife within Israel during future major IDF operations against Hamas in Gaza. Notwithstanding the above, there is also a significant possibility that the type of hybrid warfare that Israel has engaged in since 1982 will move increasingly towards a more conventional military approach, in the early stages of a future war. As noted above, thus far, advances in Israel's anti-rocket and anti-missile systems have allowed Israel to use force more sparingly and wait for some targets to present themselves, thus minimizing civilian casualties and reducing physical destruction. At the time of this writing, there is an increased likelihood that Israel will face a coordinated multi-front war against Iranian proxies in Syria, Hezbollah, and Hamas and other Palestinian factions—all orchestrated to some degree by Teheran.[53] In this scenario, the sheer number of rockets and missiles in the hands of Hezbollah, Iranian proxies in Syria, and Palestinian groups in the Gaza Strip, will quickly overwhelm Israel's rocket and missile defense systems and cause significant damage and loss of life in Israel. It is therefore highly likely that Israel will revert to a more traditional approach of hitting the enemy quickly with maximum force to end the conflict as soon as possible. In such a situation, concern about collateral damage will play a much less significant role and Israel is likely to view the conflict, while not existential, as one that it needs to end quickly to limit the damage that it will suffer. Thus, while Israel has drawn conclusions from the accumulated engagements noted above, and thus developed an operational doctrine for dealing with hybrid warfare in urban environments, its enemies are continuing to evolve and present it with new challenges that may necessitate significant changes in this operational doctrine.

Endnotes

1. John Spencer, The Eight Rules of Urban Warfare and Why We Must Work to Change Them, Modern War Institute at West Point, (West Point, NY: United States Military Academy, January 12, 2021), https://mwi.usma.edu/the-eight-rules-of-urban-warfareand-why-we-must-work-to-change-them/
2. Eyal Weizman, "Interview with Eyal Weizman," Interview by Vincent Bernard and Ellen Policinski, International Review of the Red Cross (2016), 98 (1), 21-35.
3. John Spencer, "The Israeli Way of Urban Warfare," May 13, 2022, Urban Warfare Project. Modern War Institute, podcast audio, May 13, 2022, https://mwi.usma.edu/the-israeli-way-of-urban-warfare/.
4. Kendall D. Gott, Breaking the Mold: Tanks in the Cities (Ft. Leavenworth, KS: Combat Studies Institute Press, 2006), p. 49, https://www.armyupress.army.mil/Portals/7/Primer-onUrban-OOperation/Documents/Breaking-the-Mold.pdf.
5. Gott, Breaking the Mold, pp. 61-62.
6. Shai Levy, "International Experts in Urban Environments: This is How the IDF Fights in the Alleys," Mako, Translated by Nadav Morag, June 17, 2014, https://www.mako.co.il/pzm-soldiers/Article-a6fc203ba19a641006.htm.
7. Thomas H. Henriksen, The Israeli Approach to Irregular Warfare and Implications for the United States, JSOU Report 07-3 (Hurlburt Field, FL: Joint Special Operations University, 2007), pp. 37-38, https://apps.dtic.mil/sti/citations/ADA495467

8. Henriksen, "The Israeli Approach," p. 39.
9. Henriksen, "The Israeli Approach," p. 39.
10. Henriksen, "The Israeli Approach," p. 40.
11. AP and TOI Staff, "'Mini Gaza': The IDF's Urban Warfare Training Center, a Town that's Known Only War," The Times of Israel, June 22, 2022, https://www.timesofisrael.com/mini-gaza-the-idfs-urban-warfare-training-center-atown-thats-known-onlywar/#:~:text=Officially%2C%20it's%20known%20as%20the,of%20the%20second%20Palestinian%20intifada.
12. Stephen D. Biddle and Jeffrey A. Friedman, The 2006 Lebanon Campaign and the Future of Warfare: Implications for Army and Defense Policy (Carlisle, PA: US Army War College Press, 2008), pp. 34-35, https://press.armywarcollege.edu/monographs/641/
13. Biddle and Friedman, The 2006 Lebanon Campaign, pp. 43-44,
14. Winograd Commission, The Second Lebanon War, Final Accounting, Vol 1, Translated by Nadav Morag, (Jerusalem: Government of Israel, January 2008), https://cdn.exiteme.com/exiteto-go/www.pro-aware.com/userfiles/files/PDF/%D7%93%D7%95%D7%97%2520%D7%A1%D7%95%D7%A4%D7%99.pdf
15. David E. Johnson, Hard Fighting: Israel in Lebanon and Gaza (Santa Monica, CA: RAND, 2011), p. 38, https://www.rand.org/pubs/monographs/MG1085.html [16] Johnson, Hard Fighting. p. 98.
16. Johnson, Hard Fighting. p. 101.
17. Johnson, Hard Fighting. p. 101.
18. Johnson, Hard Fighting. p. 101.
19. Ariel Siegelman, "From Lebanon to Gaza: A New Kind of War," Colloquium, Vol 2., No. 1 (2009): 1-9, https://apps.dtic.mil/sti/citations/ADA497594.
20. Spencer, The Israeli Way.
21. Spencer, The Israeli Way.
22. Benjamin S. Lambeth, Air Operations in Israel's War Against Hezbollah: Learning from Lebanon and Getting it Right in Gaza (Santa Monica, CA: RAND, 2011), p. 244, https://www.rand.org/pubs/monographs/MG835.html.
23. Johnson, Hard Fighting. p. 124.
24. Johnson, Hard Fighting. pp. 118-119.
25. Johnson, Hard Fighting. p. 128.
26. Johnson, Hard Fighting. p. 134.
27. Lambeth, Air Operations, pp. 240-241.
28. Stuart Cohen, The Futility of Operation Cast Lead, BESA Center Perspectives, Paper No. 68, https://besacenter.org/the-futility-of-operation-cast-lead/.
29. Ephraim Kam, Following the Operation: The Balance Between the Two Sides," in In the Aftermath of Operation Pillar of Defense: The Gaza Strip, November 2012, Memorandum 124, Shlomo Brom (ed) (Tel Aviv: Institute for National Security Studies, 2012), p. 17, https://www.inss.org.il/wpcontent/uploads/systemfiles/memo124f027134590.pdf.

30. Raphael S. Cohen, David E. Johnson, David E. Thaler, Brenna Allen, Elizabeth M. Bartels, James Cahill, and Shira Efron, From Cast Lead to Protective Edge: Lessons from Israel's Wars in Gaza (Santa Monica, CA: RAND Corporation, 2017), p. 41, https://www.rand.org/pubs/research_reports/RR1888.html.
31. Cohen et al., From Cast Lead to Protective Edge, pp. 44-45.
32. Cohen et al., From Cast Lead to Protective Edge, p. 49.
33. Cohen et al., From Cast Lead to Protective Edge, p. 59.
34. Cohen et al., From Cast Lead to Protective Edge, pp. 63-64.
35. Udi Dekel, "Operation Protective Edge: Strategic and Tactical Asymmetry," in The Lessons of Protective Edge, Anat Kurz and Shlomo Brom (eds.) (Tel Aviv: Institute for National Security Affairs, 2014), p. 17, https://www.inss.org.il/publication/the-lessonsof-operation-protective-edge/
36. Gabi Siboni, "Operations Cast Lead, Pillar of Defense, and Protective Edge: A Comparative Review," in The Lessons of Protective Edge, Anat Kurz and Shlomo Brom (eds.) (Tel Aviv: Institute for National Security Affairs, 2014), p. 31, https://www.inss.org.il/publication/the-lessons-of-operation-protective-edge/.
37. RAND Arroyo Center, Lessons from Israel's Wars in Gaza (Santa Monica, CA: RAND, 2017), p. 9, https://www.rand.org/content/dam/rand/pubs/research_briefs/RB9900/RB9975/RA ND_RB9975.pdf.
38. Cohen et al., From Cast Lead to Protective Edge, p. 95.
39. Cohen et al., From Cast Lead to Protective Edge, p. 146.
40. The State Comptroller and Ombudsman of Israel, Operation "Protective Edge" – IDF Activity From the Perspective of International Law (Jerusalem: The State Comptroller's Office, 2014), p. 64, https://www.mevaker.gov.il/he/reports/pages/622.aspx#.
41. Yoram Cohen and Jeffrey White, Hamas in Combat: The Military Performance of the Palestinian Islamic Resistance Movement, Policy Focus #97 (Washington, D.C.: The Washington Institute for Near East Policy, 2009), p. 9. https://www.washingtoninstitute.org/media/3416.
42. Cohen and White, Hamas in Combat, pp. 9-10.
43. Cohen et al., From Cast Lead to Protective Edge, pp. 96-97.
44. Daniel Rubenstein, Hamas' Tunnel Network: A Massacre in the Making (Jerusalem: Jerusalem Center for Public Affairs, n.d.), https://jcpa.org/the-gaza-war-2014/hamastunnel-network/
45. RAND Arroyo Center, Lessons from Israel's Wars in Gaza (Santa Monica, CA: RAND, 2017), p. 6, https://www.rand.org/content/dam/rand/pubs/research_briefs/RB9900/RB9975/RA ND_RB9975.pdf.
46. Cohen et al., From Cast Lead to Protective Edge, p. 168.
47. Cohen et al., From Cast Lead to Protective Edge, p. 139.
48. Cohen et al., From Cast Lead to Protective Edge, p. 140.
49. Cohen et al., From Cast Lead to Protective Edge, pp. 169-170.

50. Judah Ari Gross, "'Guardian of the Walls' Wasn't the Resounding Victory the IDF Had Hoped For," The Times of Israel, May 21, 2021, https://www.timesofisrael.com/guardian-of-the-walls-wasnt-the-resounding-victorythe-idf-had-hoped-for/.

51. Gross, "Guardian of the Walls."

52. Assaf Orion, Sword of Jerusalem vs. Guardian of the Walls: Gaza and the Next Lebanon War, PolicyWatch 3501 (Washington, DC: The Washington Institute for Near East Policy, 2021), https://www.washingtoninstitute.org/policy-analysis/sword-jerusalemvs-guardian-walls-gaza-and-next-lebanon-war.

53. Ben Caspit, "Multi-front war with Iran proxies irks Israel despite deterrence," ALMonitor, April 25, 2023, https://www.al-monitor.com/originals/2023/04/multi-frontwar-iran-proxies-irks-israel-despite-deterrence.

CHAPTER 7
Artificial Intelligence and Urban Operations

Anthony King

Introduction

Artificial intelligence (AI) is about to revolutionize the conduct of warfare, as gunpowder, tanks, aircraft, and the atom bomb have in previous eras. Today, states are actively seeking to harness the power of AI for military advantage. China, for instance, has announced its intention to become the world leader in AI by 2030. Its New General AI Plan proclaimed that "AI is a strategic technology that will lead the future."[1] Similarly, Vladimir Putin declared, "Whoever becomes the leader in this sphere will become ruler of the world."[2] In response to the challenge posed by China and Russia, the United States has committed to a Third Offset Strategy. It will invest heavily in AI, autonomy, and robotics to sustain its advantage in defense. Eric Schmidt, the former chief executive officer of Google, declared that the United States is in an AI arms race.[3] In September 2018, the Defense Advanced Research Projects Agency announced a $2 billion campaign to develop the next wave of AI.[4] The Department of Defense (DOD) issued its AI strategy in 2019 with a major increase in AI funding; In 2020, the DOD budget included a request for $927 billion for AI.[5] Smaller states are equally committed to the military development of AI; the United Kingdom and Israel, for instance, are developing their capabilities in this area.

Artificial intelligence is not always easy to define because there are many types of AI. Rather, it is a field rather than one specific object. However, the term Artificial Intelligence refers to computer software that can develop (to some level) the ability to process data independently of immediate human direction. The distinctive feature of most AIs today is that they can develop or refine their own programs to more effectively complete the data-processing tasks they have been set.

To understand the military significance of AI, it is useful to be aware of the history of AI. In the past fifty years, there have been two main types of AI: Good Old-Fashioned AI (GOFAI) and Second Wave AI. Good Old-Fashioned AI developed in the 1950s and 1960s. Following the celebrated Dartmouth seminar on AI in 1956, attended by luminaries like Alan Turing, computer scientists explored the possibility of programming computers to process data autonomously using symbolic logic. Scientists assigned symbolic values to the variables which they wanted analyzed. They then programmed computers to calculate those symbols based on mathematical logic. Good Old-Fashioned AI was successful on limited tasks. However, because it relied on heavily curated input, GOFAI was narrow. It tended to collapse when confronted with the real world. The real world inevitably exceeded the symbolic coding of programmers. Consequently, after some initial success, the AI program faltered. From the 1970s to the 1990s, an AI winter fell on the field.

In the 1990s and especially after 2000, there has been a revolution in AI. Second Wave AI has generated some remarkable success. Second Wave AI operates quite differently to GOFAI. Second-generation AI relies on three key components: Data, computing power, and algorithms. Data refers to digital information held in cyberspace; it consists ultimately of an almost infinite store of binaries. The explosion of data is the key element in the advance of AI in the last few decades. Since the creation of the internet and digital communications and the proliferation of digital sensors across the globe, there has been a data explosion. Almost every activity now leaves a digital trace somewhere. It would be impossible for humans to sift through and analyze all these data. Here AI becomes crucial. Harnessing massive computing power, AI programs process these data to identify patterns or signatures. Contemporary AI does this on a purely inductive and statistical basis. Based on its data, an AI program calculates the most probable correlations. The more data, the more accurate its calculations become. AI understands nothing. It does not know what reality is; it cannot comprehend meaning. It only recognizes the frequent co-appearance of binaries within its data. However, because it can process vast quantities of data, it is able to provide unique insights into the activities that are recorded digitally in cyberspace. It sees numerical correlations and connections within the data, which are impossible for humans to see.

Second-generation AI algorithms have typically operated on various forms of machine learning: Supervised, unsupervised, or reinforcement learning. Each of these is slightly different; supervised learning asks the program what to predict narrowly, and unsupervised learning allows the program to classify data itself, while reinforced learning specifies the reward. The three techniques are a little different. Yet, in each case, machine learning algorithms have all operated by pure induction. The second generation has developed deep learning neural networks that allow programs to weigh different bits of data with greater or lesser numerical significance in order to generate a more accurate answer. The more data, the more accurate AI becomes. Second-generation AI knows nothing. However, because there is now so much data, it has become increasingly powerful. Its inductions are increasingly accurate, and AI can now make sound predictions based on past cases.

The potential of second-generation AI for security and defense purposes is clear. It potentially allows the armed forces to process an unimaginable quantity of data. Because second-generation AI is based on such prodigious quantities of computing power, there is almost no limit to the data; it can collate and analyze. It can process data from sources such as diverse satellites, ground sensors, and mobile phones to provide an accurate situational picture. AI may allow commanders to see further, more accurately, and more quickly across the battlespace. AI may be able to accelerate decision-making.

Given the potential of AI, the prospect of states harnessing AI for military purposes has been the focus of profound professional and scholarly concern. A large and growing literature has already developed which has addressed many aspects of the debate. Many commentators fear that AI will have major global security implications, especially as great power competition between China and the United States intensifies.[6] These discussions are a starting point. However, the primary research question of this article addresses the implications of AI for urban security, especially for urban operations. Sub questions are: how might the application of second-generation AI change the character of urban warfare, and how might urban warfare evolve in the next decade as AI becomes ever more potent and ubiquitous?

Supercomputers and Killer Robots

In light of these dramatic developments, scholars working on global security have become deeply interested in the military application of AI. For instance, in their recent monograph on AI, Ben Buchanan and Andrew Imrie have claimed that AI represents a potentially revolutionary military development.[7] For Buchanan and Imbrie, AI is the new fire. It is the equivalent of ancient Greek fire or the gunpowder weapons of late medieval Europe. AI will transform the destructive power of weapons. Under AI, lethal autonomous weapons will dominate. AI will enable the rise of killer robots and swarms of autonomous drones.

It may seem an extreme, even unwarranted, view. The armed forces may soon be able to exploit lethal autonomous systems to monitor, strike, and kill their opponents and even civilians at will. In fact, there have already been experiments with autonomous drone swarms. In October 2016, US DOD demonstrated a swarm of 103 Perdix micro-drones capable of "advanced swarm behaviors such as collective decision-making, adaptive formation flying and self-healing."[8] Clearly, the United States' opponents are attempting to develop this technology. The Chinese have also made significant advances in swarm intelligence. In 2017, a formation of 1000 UAVs flew at Guanghzhou Airshow. In 2017, China Electronic Technology Group flew a 119 fixed-wing UAV swarm.[9]

Many scholars have been worried that the armed forces will apply AI-enabled lethal autonomous weapons to urban areas.[10] For instance, the British urban geographer Stephen Graham describes the proliferation of new security technologies in cities. He believes that the security forces are actively seeking to submit cities to total control. They are apparently obsessed with technophilic desire and fetishistic urges for mastery and control, adjusted to the new imperatives of urban counter-insurgency [sic] warfare.[11] AI-enabled autonomous surveillance and weapons systems will enable them to fulfill their ambitions of dominating cities.[12]

Stuart Russell has been a leading figure opposing the proliferation of AI-enabled weapons. He played an important role in the development of AI from the 1980s. As a result, he has campaigned vociferously for the regulation of AI-enabled lethal autonomous weapons. Russell was particularly concerned about the possibility of autonomous swarms of lethal drones and the urban threat they posed. On 12 November 2017, he released a short film called *Slaughterbots*.[13] The film dramatizes the potential of killer drones that assassinate a senator and invade a university campus. The implication is that once they have been authorized, humans will lose control of these swarms, which will kill without constraint.[14]

In 2020, Stuart Russell gave the BBC Reith Lectures in the United Kingdom. He dedicated one of his talks to the question of the military potential of AI. Once again, he returned to the theme of *Slaughterbots* and killer robots in the urban environment, "All the ingredients to Lethal Autonomous Systems existed in 2015: Autonomous drones, the ability to swarm and to be armed."[15] He described a scenario in which a lethal quadcopter the size of a jar could be armed with an explosive projectile device, "A million could be shipped. It is inevitable. The endpoint is that autonomous systems become cheap selective weapons of mass destruction."[16] He continued, "Anti-personnel mines could wipe out all the males in a city between 16 and 60 or all the Jewish citizens in Israel, and unlike nuclear weapons, it would leave the city infrastructure."[17] As evidence, he cited the Turkish recent use of the Khargu-2 autonomous drone in Libya in March 2021. Russell concluded, "There will be 8 million people wondering why you can't give them protection against being hunted down and killed by robots."[18] According to Russell, autonomous armed drone swarms will be clever enough to target cities. Armed drones will be able to identify and kill individual humans–or small groups of them–in streets and buildings.

Other scholars share Russell's vision of the urban threat that AI-enabled autonomous weapons may pose. David Hambling, the drone expert, has described the potential of swarms in urban areas[19]: "A swarm of ten thousand small drones could level a town…A small perching drone could deliver multiple incendiaries the size of bats…Acting together drones might bring down a bridge or skyscraper, but they could do more than that."[20] Similarly, Paul Scharre has claimed:

> Militaries around the globe are racing to deploy robots at sea, on the ground, and in the air – more than ninety countries have drones patrolling their skies. These robots are increasingly autonomous and many are armed. They operate under human control for now, but what happens when a Predator drone has as much autonomy as a Google car?[21]

His anxiety is that "in future wars, machines may make life and death engagement decisions."[22] Ken Payne, the British security studies scholar, predicts the rise of warbots:

> AI systems will allow autonomous decision-making by networked computer agents, enabling extremely rapid sequential action, even in uncertain environments…Soon autonomous and intelligent platforms will be able to maneuver faster, with more precision than those operated by humans.[23]

Soon, the armed forces will be able to dominate cities targeting at will. As a result, many scholars call for a regulation on these weapons, restricting drones to "kill box operations" away from civilians in urban areas.[24]

A consensus is emerging. Soon, AI-enabled autonomous swarms of lethal drones will transform the urban battle. Swarms of drones will fly autonomously over and through urban areas, hunting and killing their enemies with complete efficiency. Sensors will find targets and strike their targets independently of human direction. However, although these authors approach the prospect of autonomous swarms from a different ethical position, their unanimity about the future of urban operations is striking. In the coming decades, the introduction of AI-enabled weaponry will transform urban warfare. Soon, swarms of drones will have substantially replaced human combatants. As a result, the tempo of urban operations will accelerate, the accuracy and simultaneity of strikes will increase, and it will become increasingly easy to attack urban areas. Every city will become the potential victim of the autonomous swarm attack, identifying and destroying their human targets by means of algorithms.

These observers are correct to highlight the importance of second-generation AI to warfare. The development of AI is likely to have profound effects on the conduct of urban war in the coming decades. They have laid out a compelling vision of what that future conflict in cities might look like; swarms of autonomous drones capable of ubiquitous surveillance and guaranteed strike in urban environments will transform military operations in urban areas and urban warfare itself. We are indebted to them. But are they right?

AI and Urban Operations

There is no doubt that remote systems have already become an important part of military operations. Azerbaijan forces used them very successfully during the Second Nagorno-Karabakh War. They have played a vital role in the Russo-Ukraine War. Both sides have employed them ubiquitously in attack and in defense to conduct surveillance and strike missions. Indeed, the Ukrainians are reported to be expanding some 10,000 drones a month. Some of these are loitering munitions intended for destruction, but the Russians shot down many. Lethal autonomous weapons have existed since the Second World War. Many capable autonomous weapons are currently in use, such as Aegis, Patriot, Israel's Iron Dome, and South Korea's SGR-AI. In the coming decade, lethal autonomous weapons—including drone swarms—will likely appear in greater numbers on the battlefield. It is possible that they might have some impact on urban warfare.

Nevertheless, despite the possibility that in the future AI-enabled autonomous weapons might be deployed routinely on urban operations, the armed forces are a long way from that point now. Robots and drone swarms are unlikely to play a decisive role in urban warfare soon. The environment is too complex:

> In high-intensity and dynamic combat environments such as densely populated urban warfare–even where well-specified goals and standard operating procedures exist–the latitude and adaptability of "mission command" remains critical, and the functional utility of ML-AI tools for even routine "task orders" (i.e. [sic] the opposite of "mission command") problematic.[25]

Even the most successful second-generation AI programs rely on large sets of well-curated data. develop excellent inductive models for stable closed situations. However, because the urban environment is so complex and dynamic, it is difficult to see how a contemporary AI program could learn effectively so that it could execute operations effectively. Moreover, commentators vastly exaggerate the capabilities of drone swarms. In reality, its range and payloads would be limited; a rocket salvo might do far more damage more easily. Advocates ignore the inevitable counter-vailing measures. For instance, in their strategic bombardment of Ukrainian cities with drones and loitering munitions, most airframes were jammed or shot down. The vision of autonomous drone swarms swooping through ruined, burning streets to eliminate targets at will is science fiction, not computer science.

However, just because lethal autonomy is likely to be elusive in urban environments, this does not mean that AI will not be important to future urban operations. On the contrary, AI has already played an important role in urban operations over the last two decades. As the power of AI increases, it seems inevitable that it will become even more important in the next decade. Yet, in the near future of the next decade or so, the primary application of AI is unlikely to be lethal autonomy. Lethal autonomous drone swarms are improbable. As several scholars have already noted, the primary application of AI is likely to be more mundane, but no less important; it is most probable in intelligence.[26] Second-generation AI processes data on a massive scale. Consequently, it has a paramount ability to analyze a phenomenon and provide insights into it. It is noticeable that recent defense strategy documents have emphasized not lethal autonomy as the primary use of AI but the way AI may facilitate a transformation, even a revolution in military intelligence.[27] AI can be used to process a mass of data so that commanders have a better understanding of the battlespace and are able to plan and target more effectively. Indeed, by harnessing vast data sources with the help of AI, military commanders will be able to perceive the urban environment more deeply, more accurately, and faster than ever before. They will be able to identify enemy forces more quickly and precisely. Moreover, even if lethal autonomous swarms do indeed emerge thereafter, they will rely on data to provide them with an intelligence picture of the battlespace. It is useful to provide some examples of this application of AI to urban operations.

Joint Special Operations Command

The armed forces have exploited data and AI with increasing effect for nearly two decades. An increasing number of examples are now available. However, it is useful to go back to one of the earliest employments of data and AI by a Western military force in an urban operation. The Joint Special Operations Command's operations in Baghdad between 2004 and 2008 is an obvious example here. In 2004, a Joint Special Operations Command (JSOC) stood up in Baghdad with General Stanley McChrystal as its commander.

The mission of JSOC between 2004 and 2008 was the destruction of al-Qaida in Iraq and the hunt for al-Zarqawi the leader of the organization in Iraq. JSOC instituted an industrial-level counterterrorist operation in which troops, mainly from the US Delta Force and the U.K.'s SAS, conducted missions every night against al-Qaida networks in Baghdad, Ramadi, and Fallujah. They raided houses and bases to kill or capture al-Qaida terrorists and to acquire intelligence on the networks. It was a remarkable operation, and JSOC became a uniquely networked, interagency, global organization. It played a key role in the elimination of al-Zarqawi in 2006. Data played an important role.

Early in the campaign, there were several mistakes that underscored the importance of improving their intelligence collection and fusion. For instance, on September 16, 2004, al-Qaida captured a British civil engineer in Baghdad. He was subsequently beheaded by al-Zarqawi on October 7, 2004. For three weeks, JSOC were searching for his location, which they failed to find. Yet, retrospectively, it emerged that the evidence was there to locate Bigley; his handler had been identified in JSOC's data, but human analysts missed it, claiming "It was unacceptable then, now even more so."[28] If JSOC had had a more efficient system for combining its data with machine learning, it would have found this evidence and saved Bigley.

To prosecute its campaign, JSOC employed every available intelligence feed. It received intelligence from the Central Intelligence Agency (CIA), the National Security Agency, the U.K.'s MI6, and other national intelligence agencies. It drew on satellite imagery, signal intelligence, phone intercepts, open-source intelligence, and human intelligence. It was a deluge of information. Many traditional techniques of collation and analysis are applied. JSOC was dealing with complicated information and evidence. Consequently, JSOC also applied machine-learning AI to the problem where they could. Many of the intelligence feeds consisted of information that was data or could be rendered as data: That is, quantifiable, computable information. Joint Special Operations Command, therefore, fused all the intelligence it could into data, to which it applied algorithms to identify patterns and to provide warnings for situations.

Eventually, JSOC brought in several data experts to help. A team from Rhombus Power led by Dr. Anshu Roy played an important role. Roy earned his PhD from the University of Michigan in computing. He invented a patented platform for solid-state subatomic particle detection. He has also applied his programming expertise to security problems, setting up the company Rhombus Power and building the Guardian program. Rhombus Power is one of the leading tech companies assisting the US DOD in security and defense issues. It has developed algorithms that are able to identify patterns in data that can assist in finding terrorists or enemies.

Roy provided an interesting account of how his team helped JSOC in this process, "There is an order in turbulence. It is possible to discern that order so that you can intervene in a complex problem."[29] Roy's team took all the data from tactical units and developed an automated system for fusing data from across intelligence sources and analyzing it at speed, "We aggregated and geolocated that data."[30] McChrystal determined the mission and, on that basis, identified his critical information requirements, but Rhombus accelerated the solution, "We mathematized it. We were able to quickly and reiteratively put into a maths [sic] construct that could be encoded and put into an AI system."[31]

Using machine learning and algorithms, Roy's team was able to identify anomalies and signatures in the data, from which they were able to infer what would happen. Roy summarized what they had done, "Capture everything you can, mathematize it, encode it so that the next set of people have a far easier time."[32]

The use of data, data analysis, algorithms, and machine learning by JSOC was not a panacea. JSOC succeeded because it had a clear mission and gained a deep understanding of the insurgency in Iraq and al-Qaeda. Human intelligence, signal intelligence, and physical evidence harvested from nightly SOF raids also proved crucial. However, McChrystal's data-centric, AI-enabled method augmented these traditional methods so that JSOC was able to identify Zarqawi in a complex urban environment. The use of big data and machine learning to process it accelerated the decision cycle and made it more accurate. As McChrystal said, "As a commander, you check data, then trust it. You develop leaders who know about AI. This information being connected, it makes sense to them."[33]

AI was employed to harness the deluge of information that was in danger of swamping, allowing JSOC to follow Zarqawi's digital footprints, correlating them with other evidence. JSOC eventually tracked Zarqawi to a safe house in a small village called Habib north of Baqubah on 6 June 2006. Two US Air Force F-16 dropped two laser-guided bombs on the building, killing Zarqawi and five associates, including his lieutenant.

The Israeli Defense Force

The Israeli Defense Force is equally advanced in its use of data. Since the first Intifada in 1987, the Israeli military's main mission has been to suppress Palestinian terrorist cells in Gaza and the West Bank. Many deplore the political situation in Israel; they describe it, with good evidence, as an apartheid state. However, whatever the political situation, the Israeli Defense Forces (IDF) provides a perspicuous example of how data has been employed for urbanized operations. Since the 1980s, the IDF has monitored Palestinian groups like Fatah and Hamas closely. In the last fifteen years, it has also explicitly sought to exploit data as a way of tracing and targeting Palestinian terrorists. Palestinians employ mobile phones for communications which, no matter how many counter-measures they employ, leave a digital signature in cyberspace. In addition to traditional methods of intelligence collection, Israeli sensors saturate the West Bank and Gaza Strip, including satellites, radar, and cameras:

> The data revolution has led to a massive amount of operational data being collected [sic] from cameras, microphones, networks, information systems, and devices. The human factor is no longer sufficient, as soldiers cannot physically keep up with the amount of incoming data.[34]

In addition, Open Source data has become a rich means of collecting intelligence but the amount of potential data it offers is vast. Israeli Defense Officers emphasize the problem: "The data is endless, reaching into petabytes (one million gigabytes) in some areas."[35]

Consequently, the IDF has created several specialist units to harness the potential of data, such as Units 8200 and 9900, J6 or C4I Directorate's Lotem Unit, and the Sigma Branch IDF. As the commander of the Sigma Branch has noted, "the goal is to improve the effectiveness of the IDF." The IDF has trained AI applications to sift through this mass of data to recognize the important information. The IDF's AI programs can analyze hundreds of videos at a time and automatically flag suspicious activity. For instance, after Operation Protective Edge in 2014, a punitive assault upon Hamas in Gaza following rocket strikes, the Lotem Unit developed an app that learned from field sensors and other data, "We collected what are the most likely areas launchers will be set up and at what hours. That enables us to know in advance what will happen and what areas should be attacked in order to fight them more effectively."[36]

By 2017, the IDF had already developed a sophisticated descriptive AI program; its algorithms could automatically identify objects of interest in the operating space. The aim was to create predictive AI. AI programs would not only recognize targets for the IDF, which were already operating but also make predictions about the movements of Palestinian operatives and recommend courses of action.

In 2021, the IDF mounted yet another major operation against Hamas in Gaza, Operation Guardian of the Walls. The Israeli armed forces described the action as the first AI war. Building on the work of its specialist units from 2014, the IDF incorporated AI fully into the targeting process. This was essential because the Israelis employed a network of electronic sensors on drones, F-35s, seismic monitors, and other systems over the course of several years. The IDF had collected billions of pieces of signal and other intelligence on Hamas and the Palestinian Islamic Jihad. The IDF fused these diverse data sets,

> By employing AI algorithms and machine learning, paired with intelligence analysts in 'man-machine teams' to flag and review potential targets, the IDF synthesized extensive amounts of data into pre-conflict target folders that were significantly more detailed, accurate, and timely than in 2014.[37]

Artificial intelligence allowed for increasingly dynamic targeting, which was also more accurate than in the past. Leveraging data and AI, the IDF developed a system of 'intelligence-drive combat' which disseminated intelligence to combat units in real-time using a digital battlespace management system that matched the targets with precision-guided munitions, "The IDF could conduct highly accurate airstrikes, substantially mitigating risks to civilians."[38]

For instance, during the operation, the Israelis targeted Muhammed Bawab, the leader of Hamas's east Rafah brigade, who was responsible for abducting two IDF soldiers in 2014. His house was acting as a command post. The IDF wanted to strike the building. However, a variety of feeds—some processed by AI—showed that there were civilians sheltering under a palm tree just outside the house. Shin Bet, the Israeli secret service, rang Bawab's neighbors, warning them in Arabic, "You are under the palm tree, near the house. Go away, there's a one-ton bomb coming, and you are going to get hurt."[39] Artificial intelligence helped the IDF prosecute a precise lethal campaign, yet civilian casualties were still high: 120 were killed. However, Israel's strikes were certainly more accurate than in the past; 99 confirmed enemy kills, while 40 more deaths may have been enemy. The IDF claimed a 1:1 civilian-to-belligerent casualty ratio.[40] Data and AI had allowed the IDF to target precisely in a complex, dense urban environment.

Conclusion

In the last two decades, the armed forces have increasingly sought to harness the potential of second-generation AI. Each year, the military potential of AI becomes more apparent and potent. Many scholars, therefore, fear that AI is about to unleash a wave of lethal autonomous weapons that will transform the urban battlespace. Swarms of killer drones will replace human combatants, striking targets in urban areas with remorseless precision and lethality. This article takes an alternative view. AI has become increasingly important for urban operations. However, as the example of JSOC in Baghdad and the IDF show, the real potential of AI lies not in lethal autonomy but in data processing and, therefore, in intelligence and targeting. The resources of digital information held in cyberspace, from open sources, satellites, mobile phones, and a panoply of other sensors, potentially provide commanders with unparalleled oversight across the depths of the battlefield. They can see further and more accurately than ever before. However, to exploit the potential of data, it is essential to employ AI programs for all this material; it is a task that quite defies humans. Data and AI have become key resources for urban operations and will become more so in the future.

Both examples involved military operations against terrorists; they were lower-intensity operations. According to many scholars, the appearance of lethal autonomous drones will accelerate high-intensity combat between states. Battles will become quick, easy, and decisive as swarms fight each other autonomously. Robotized combat will eliminate friction and chaos. This seems highly unlikely. The campaign against Al Qaeda in Iraq was long and hard. Despite its AI-enabled targeting, the IDF is locked into an interminable struggle with Palestinian opponents. Operation Guardian of the Walls may have been precise– but it was not decisive, as the current intervention into Jenin shows.

The Russo-Ukraine War is instructive here. This is a genuine interstate war between two well-equipped forces. With intimate United States support, the Ukrainians have employed a data-centric targeting system that echoes JSOC and the IDF closely. Ukrainian forces have been able to target Russian command posts and logistical hubs to an impressive depth and accuracy by exploiting the power of data and AI processing. Nevertheless, the fighting in this war has congealed into a series of grueling battles in and around the towns and cities of Ukraine. Sieges, not lightning maneuvers, have predominated. This pattern will likely continue as the Ukrainians continue their counter-offensive.

The armed forces are increasingly using data to gain a battlefield advantage, but combat, especially in urban areas, has slowed down. The relatively small size of Russian and Ukrainian forces is relevant here; they converge of decisive, often urban locations. Long-range precision artillery and drones have made it difficult for them to move. Data is also crucial. Both sides–and especially the Ukrainians can target accurately and rapidly in the deep. Attritional, positional fighting has therefore predominated. There is an irony today, then. With the use of data, forces may indeed now be able to target at the speed of light, but combat operations themselves, especially in urban areas, have slowed to a glacial pace. Twenty-first-century warfare has decelerated to the pace of medieval combat.

Endnotes

1. Kania, Elsa, Battlefield Singularity: Artificial Intelligence, Military Revolution and China's Future Military Power (New York: Center for a New American Security, 2017.
2. Horowitz, Michael, Elsa B. Kania, Gregory C. Allen, and Paul Scharre, *Strategic Competition in an Era of Artificial Intelligence* (Washington, DC: Center for a New American Security, 2018), 16.
3. Gonzalez, Robert, *War Virtually* (Oakland, CA: University of Oakland, 2022), 62.
4. Waltzman, Rand *Maintaining the Competitive Advantage in Artificial Intelligence and Machine Learning* (Santa Monica, CA: Rand, 2020), 3; James Baker *Centaur's Dilemma* (Washington, DC: Brookings Institute Press, 2021).
5. Wyatt, Austin, "Charting Great Power Progress Toward Lethal Autonomous Weapon System Demonstration Point," *Defense Studies* 20, no. 1 (2019): 10, https://doi.org/10.1080/14702436.2019.1698956.
6. Scharre, Paul, Four Battlegrounds: power in the age of artificial intelligence (New York: WW Norton and Co, 2023.
7. Buchanan, Ben and Andrew Imbrie *The New Fire: War, Peace and Democracy in the Age of AI* (Cambridge, MS: MIT Press, 2022), 1-2. Watch spacing after number. You have 2 here. It should be 1.
8. Jürgen Altmann and Frank Sauer 'Autonomous Systems and Strategic Stability' *Survival* 95(5), 120
9. Kania *Battlefield Singularity*, 22-23; Kania, Elsa 'Chinese Military Innovation in Artificial intelligence: hearing of the US-China Economic and Security Review Commission' Center for a New American Security 7 June 2019
10. Williams, John 'Locating LAWS: lethal autonomous weapons, epistemic space and "meaningful' human control' *Journal of Global Security Studies* 6(4) 2021, 1-17; James Johnson, James 'Inadvertent escalation' *European Journal of International Security* 7(3) 2022, 337-359; Garcia, Denise 'Lethal Artificial Intelligence and Change' *International Studies Review* 20(2) 2018, 334-341; Bode, Ingvild and Hendrik Huelss, 'Autonomous Weapons and changing norms in international relations' *Review of International Studies* 44(3) 2018, pp.393-413; Arkin, Ronald 'The case for Ethical Autonomy in Unmanned Systems' *Journal of Military Ethics* 9(4) 2010332-341; Haas, Michael-Carl and Sophie-Charlotte Fischer 'The evolution of targeted killing practices' *Contemporary Security Policy* 38(2) 2017, 281-306; See Michael Horowitz 'When Speed Kills: lethal autonomous weapon systems, deterrence and stability' *Journal of Strategic Studies* 42(6) 2019, pp.764-788; Henry Kissinger, Eric Schmidt and Daniel Huttenlocher, *The Age of AI*

and our Future (London: John Murray 2021); Altmann, Jürgen and Frank Sauer 'Autonomous Systems and Strategic Stability' *Survival* 95(5), p120;

11. Graham, Stephen, *Cities under Siege* (London: Verso, 2010), 162.
12. Amoore, Louise, 'Algorithmic Warfare: everyday geographies of the war on terror' *Antipode* 41(1) 2009, 49-62.
13. 'Sci-Fi Short Film: Slaughterbots' YouTube 17 October 2019, https://www.youtube.com/watch?v=O-2tpwW0kmU.
14. Russell, Stuart, Human Compatible: artificial intelligence and the problem of control (London: Allen Lane, 2019)
15. Russell, Stuart 'AI and Warfare', Reith Lecture 2021. https://www.bbc.co.uk/programmes/m00127t9
16. Russell 'AI and Warfare'
17. Russell 'AI and Warfare'
18. Russell 'AI and Warfare'
19. Hambling, David *Swarm Troopers* (Hambling, 2015), 203.
20. Hambling *Swarm Troopers*, 223, 226,238.
21. Sharre, Paul *Army of None: autonomous weapons and the future of war* (New York: W.W. Norton and Company, 2019), p.4.
22. Sharre *Army of None*, p.4.
23. Payne, Kenneth, 'Artificial Intelligence: a revolution in military affairs?' *Survival* 60(5) 2018, 7-32.
24. Krishnan, Armin 'Automating War: the need for regulation' *Contemporary Security Policy* 2009 30(1), p.179; Horowitz, Michael 'The ethics and morality of robotic warfare' *Daedalu*s Fall 2016, pp.145, 25-
25. Johnson, James 'Automating the OODA Loop in the age of intelligence machines: reaffirming the role of humans in command-and-control decision-making in the digital age' *Defence Studies* 23(1) 2023, 51.
26. Jensen, Benjamin, Christopher Whyte, Scott Cuomo 'Algorithms at War: the promise, the peril and limits of artificial intelligence' *International Studies Review* September 2020 22(3), 540.
27. National Security Commission on Artificial Intelligence Final Report 2021 https://nscai.wpenginepowered.com/wp-cointent/uploads/2021/03/Full-ReportDigital-1.pdf.
28. Anonymous source, ex-SOF officer, personal interview, 8 July 2022.
29. Lopez, Nick and Atwell, Kyle 'Artificial Intelligence in Counter-Terrorism and Counterinsurgency with retired General Stanley McChrystal and Dr Anshu Roy', Modern Warfare Institute, 1 January 2021. https://mwi.usma.edu/artificialintelligence-in-counterterrorism-and-counterinsurgency-with-retired-gen-stanmcchrystal-and-dr-anshu-roy/
30. Lopez and Atwell, 'Artificial Intelligence in Counter-Terrorism and Counterinsurgency with retired General Stanley McChrystal and Dr Anshu Roy'
31. Lopez and Atwell, 'Artificial Intelligence in Counter-Terrorism and Counterinsurgency with retired General Stanley McChrystal and Dr Anshu Roy'.

32. Lopez and Atwell, 'Artificial Intelligence in Counter-Terrorism and Counterinsurgency with retired General Stanley McChrystal and Dr Anshu Roy'
33. Lopez and Atwell, 'Artificial Intelligence in Counter-Terrorism and Counterinsurgency with retired General Stanley McChrystal and Dr Anshu Roy'
34. 'The Future of Artificial Intelligence in the IDF' *Israel Defence* 2 July 2017 https://www.israeldefense.co.il/en/node/30189
35. Eliran Rubin 'Tiny IDF Unit Is Brains Behind Israeli Army Artificial Intelligence' *Haertz* 15 August 2017 https://www.haaretz.com/israel-news/2017-08-15/ty-article/tiny-idf-unit-is-brains-behind-israeli-army-artificial-intelligence/0000017fe35b-d7b2-a77f-e35fc8f40000
36. Rubin 'Tiny IDF Unit Is Brains Behind Israeli Army Artificial Intelligence'.
37. Jewish Institute for National Security of American, 'Gaza Conflict 2021 Assessment: observation and lessons' https://jinsa.org/jinsa_report/gaza-conflict-2021assessment-observations-and-lessons/, 10.
38. Jewish Institute for National Security of American, 'Gaza Conflict 2021 Assessment', 16.
39. Jewish Institute for National Security of American, 'Gaza Conflict 2021 Assessment'
40. Jewish Institute for National Security of American, 'Gaza Conflict 2021 Assessment'

CHAPTER 8
Wide Area Motion Imagery and the Colonial Antecedents of Surveillance

Dinesh Napal

Introduction

Since the September 11, 2001 terrorist attacks on the World Trade Center and the ensuing invasion of Iraq and Afghanistan under the Bush administration's global war on terror, surveillance across territories, communities, and cyberspaces has enhanced.[1] In the context of visual mapping of cities and towns, new technologies have been deployed to embed post-2001 security techniques.[2] The Uniting and Strengthening America by Providing Appropriate Tools Required to Intercept and Obstruct Terrorism Act (PATRIOT Act), passed in response to the attacks, established unprecedented levels of surveillance as part of law enforcement strategies, much of which would be shielded from the public and free of judicial oversight.[3] Similar rationales behind the PATRIOT Act of protecting

American lives and liberties through legitimated mass surveillance persist today.[4] In 2023, New York City's Police Department partnered with Amazon Ring as part of their Domain Awareness System to establish access channels to Ring devices, which include the collection of biometric information, including face shape, skin color, and odor recognition to determine whether patterns of behavior constitute "suspicious activity."[5] These innovations categorize different individuals and communities into those deemed risky, punishable, or suspect, marking them as deserving of surveillance and targeting.

Wide area motion imagery (WAMI) surveillance technologies have emerged as a new, efficient form of data collection and processing. These employ persistent surveillance that utilizes up to hundreds of compact cameras, which capture image and video recordings across an exceptional range.[6] The scale of WAMI projects shifts surveillance techniques into overdrive, enabling continual monitoring and recording of civilian settings under the guise of law enforcement. Perpetual surveillance relegates specific communities deemed suspect or risky to the margins of social life, replicating the architecture of colonial surveillance systems. Such surveillance repeats the methods of dehumanization and disposability inherent to imperial and colonial endeavors.

WAMI technology: Origins, Examples, and Implications

Defense industry leaders developed sophisticated technologies, including WAMI, in the 2000s for intelligence, surveillance, and reconnaissance (ISR) operations in Iraq and Afghanistan. Nascent forms, such as the E-8C Joint Surveillance Target Attack Radar System, flew army personnel as part of Operation Desert Storm in 1991 and Operation Iraqi Freedom in 2003.[7] In the latter, ISR was enhanced to merge capabilities around transporting personnel with wide-area surveillance coverage, spanning 19,000 square miles.[8] Once ground troops and commanders recognized the benefits of persistent and wide-ranging surveillance, wide-area coverage technologies for ISR missions were in demand and innovating. WAMI developed as a branch of technology, providing remote, continuous video coverage of several square miles at several frames per second and providing live image capture using an onboard array of cameras.[9]

Project Angel Fire was developed in the late 2000s to bring WAMI surveillance to Iraq, empowering troops with forensic and post-event analysis for roadside bombings.[10] BAE Systems, with the sponsorship of the Defense Advanced Research Projects Agency and the US Air Force, developed the Autonomous Real-Time Ground Ubiquitous Surveillance-Imaging System (ARGUS-IS) pod system, with its first test flight on a Black Hawk piloted helicopter in 2010.[11] The ARGUS-IS, equipped with a 1.8 gigapixel sensor, could cover an 8-by-8 kilometer field of view with 20-centimeter resolution, but weighed 1,000 pounds. With innovation in the field increasing, alongside resources and government and private sector support, the urgency to develop efficient, advanced, and compact WAMI systems became apparent.

Dr. Michael Eismann, chief scientist for electro-optical and infrared sensors at the Air Force Research Laboratory, explained that reducing space, weight, and power consumption was imperative to the longevity of WAMI development. Proponents of similar views express fears about the insidiousness of terrorism and extremist threats. They cite that WAMI capacities enable significantly enhanced "pattern-of-life" analysis, ascertaining the risk of terrorist activity and their precise location in complex, urban settings.[12] Many WAMI capabilities have been incorporated into uncrewed aerial vehicles (UAVs). In 2016, the global aerospace company Exelis launched a compact WAMI system titled CorvusEye 1500, with the capacity to monitor city-size areas atop UAVs, focus on specific target sections for suspicious activity, and record perpetually in real-time, without the need for a human operator and weighing less than 95 pounds.[13]

While innovation fulfilled the desires of efficiency, compactness, and scale, the perception of terrorism and extremism developed—fears of individuals being radicalized across cities into enemies of America flourished.[14]

Consequently, WAMI technologies, specifically Project Angel Fire, were positioned to solve domestic homeland security problems. These innovations operated as part of a broader trend of law enforcement militarization, including increased SWAT deployment and provision of surplus military equipment to local police forces.[15] Using Ross McNutt, Project Angel Fire founder, reconfigured Project Angel Fire into Persistent Surveillance Systems, developers of the Gorgon Stare Project and other perpetual WAMI operations in towns such as Dayton, Ohio, and Baltimore, Maryland.[16]

Such projects have significant legal implications that, while operating under the logic of preventing terrorism and undertaking anticipatory surveillance to enhance public safety, undermine its integrity. Although it is legal for surveillance to take place in US airspace, which falls into the same category as sidewalks, roads, and parks, and it is legal to take photographs of private property and private citizens from public space, there are implications for how privacy is undermined by ever-present technologies that can achieve precision imagery without detection.[17] Indeed, WAMI's capacity to capture high-resolution images today that may lend themselves to facial recognition[18] alongside pattern-of-life analysis may place doubt over the effectiveness of the right to record in public spaces to account for such developments to protect private citizens and property.[19]

In conflict settings, however, WAMI technologies, such as the BlackKite and RedKite from Logos Technologies, are designed to be light enough to be equipped onto a range of tactical aircraft and support ground troops in real time.[20] The Center for Strategic and Budgetary Assessments' 2020 report on deterrence by detection presented sophisticated ISR operations utilizing WAMI to ensure that US forces are prepared for any eventuality.[21] Tension persists between the protection of privacy under both domestic and international law, particularly in light of counterterrorism efforts and anticipatory action on behalf of states undertaking ISR operations beyond their borders.[22] With regard to the United Kingdom, the Investigatory Powers Tribunal handed down a controversial decision in *Human Rights Watch v Secretary of State*, which determined that individuals living abroad were not subject to the provisions of the European Convention on Human

Rights in the context of ISR.[23] Under the law of armed conflict, whether privacy rights guaranteed under international conventions and treaties, to which the United States is a party, can be violated by the United States in its counterterror ISR operations remains a thorny area of concern in international law.

Commentary on the legal and ethical dimensions of WAMI has undertaken little investigation into the capacity of such technologies to ascribe identities of suspicion and risk to specific individuals and communities. Proponents' own words refer to WAMI technologies as having the capacity to "identify threat activities" or flag individuals as suspicious.[24] In this context, it is critical to investigate how the inscription of such identities presents effects that replicate the dehumanization efforts of colonial surveillance efforts.

Colonial Surveillance on Mauritian Plantations and Beyond

In the early 19th century, 452,000 indentured people arrived in Mauritius from India, China, and other Asian and African nations to work on sugar plantations.[25] Indentured labor in Mauritius was designed as a colonial project to repair the rupture in capital production caused by the liberation of enslaved people and continue to meet the demand for raw materials in Britain, France, and The Netherlands.[26] Plantation estates reassumed their designation as sites for the ordering and reconstituting of individuals into disciplined objects of service toward the machinery of colonial production, with many owners expressing resistance to the establishment of jails or prisons, as they considered them to be refugees from the levels punishment and surveillance they would deploy on plantations.[27]

Plantation architecture confined indentured laborers into poor accommodations, just as the enslaved people who were imprisoned before them.[28] Many occupied a nucleated village landscape—the Trianon plantation followed a "big house and slave quarters" pattern, informed by racial stratification and surveillance.[29] The structure of plantations was expressly designed to address what colonialists perceived to be a problem of space and surveillance, whereby surveillance must be as simple as possible to regulate enslaved and indentured behavior efficiently.[30] Architecture on plantations invoked a panoptic gaze, in which the indentured person's vision of the central house and witnessing of the plantation overseer is inhibited. Yet, the owner retains the disciplinary power of the gaze, instilling fear and coercion through the potential that the overseer may always be watching.[31]

Archaeologists have analyzed the implications of space and surveillance as emblematic of the panopticon, wherein sight and lines of sight, and the capacity to be perceived, serve as tools of discipline across the landscape of the plantation.[32] Through the obscuring of sight lines and the concurrent perpetual sight of the plantation overseer, and disciplinarians, the status of indentured or enslaved is inscribed upon the existence of the surveilled community. In 1899, the US Consulate issued a report of plague in Port Louis, Mauritius, which exemplifies the desire for constant surveillance and control—200 indentured people afflicted with plague had "stampeded" to escape police surveillance.[33] These individuals would be hunted as they scattered across towns with friends who would conceal and protect them.

Critically, the Consulate employed the language of the indentured escaping surveillance and finding concealment as safety. The notion that concealing oneself manifests as some semblance of shelter demonstrates how the architectures of existence in the plantation acted as a disciplinary mechanic to pacify and pathologize the surveilled community. In the context of the panoptic gaze, the plantation environment created new territories of being, stratifying life according to whether one's existence warranted disciplinary treatment and control. Such systems constructed those who experience surveillance as deviant if they were to try to escape the territory of the plantation or the reach of colonial officials. If they were to obey the ordering of life on the plantation, the system would consider them disciplined or captured, with little between these poles of being.

Surveillance in colonial Mauritius also extended beyond indentured life on the plantation. The passage of Ordinance 31 in 1867 enforced a "pass system," through which older indentured migrants would have conditions imposed upon their continued residence on the island following completion of their contractual stay.[34] If anyone possessing a pass failed to display it when requested by an inspector or law enforcement, they were highly likely to be arrested under vagrancy laws.[35] Surveillance and its disciplinary capacity for managing life across the colony were indispensable to the enforcers of imperial repression.[36] Norms and discursive practices were produced through multiple intersecting matrixes of surveillance, movement recording, and encoding of suspect or deviant behavior. This combination of practices and regulatory schemes would set boundaries around legitimate, non-suspect citizens or residents, as opposed to suspect, risky groups of individuals and communities.

These enveloping practices of norm production, discourse, and surveillance stratified relations across the colonial landscape into the legitimate and the suspect. At the same time, the construction of the suspect category dehumanized and dispossessed the surveilled community of the same degrees of agency. In a literal sense, the dichotomy between the capacity of the surveilled to witness or gaze upon the overseer and the overseer's capacity to surveil embodies this dispossession. They became disposable to the overseer—they acted in service of the production of resources to serve the colonial metropole. Still, they cannot act outside their disciplined category, fearing further punishment, ostracization, and dehumanization.

WAMI and the Postmodern Plantation

As Katherine McKittrick has described, "The plantation provides the future through which contemporary racial geographies and violences make themselves known."[37] In this sense, the postmodern surveillance scape of post-9/11 paranoia makes it possible for imperial statecraft and national security discourse to return to the same dehumanization techniques of the plantation. WAMI technologies re-enact the colonial surveillance matrix to produce re-disciplined individuals and communities.

Perpetual WAMI surveillance was first employed in the homeland security landscape in Dayton, Ohio. Deputy Police Chief Richard Biehl supported

PSS's efforts to install WAMI systems by stating that he wanted the public "to be worried" that they were being watched and would never know when.[38] This statement exemplifies the totality of the plantation structure of surveillance and panoptic gaze—the insidious desire to maintain perpetual surveillance, with the capacity to act on information gathered in secret, replicates the extreme disparity between the overseer and the surveilled. This is reinforced by the Ohio American Civil Liberties Union's concern that the project lacked a warrant requirement, clear retention and sharing policies, or provisions for independent oversight.[39] This approach developed new geographies that extended the plantation landscape into the ephemeral, through which the capacity to witness or perceive the overseer from the position of the surveilled becomes impossible.

In Baltimore, WAMI technologies were first identified to be in operation across the city in 2015, following the Baltimore Police Department's (BPD) agreed 90-day trial period for PSS, initially conducted without public scrutiny or awareness.[40] The project deployed two planes equipped with a WAMI system of twelve 192 megapixel cameras, from which digital images would be stitched together to form a complete topological analysis of crime and deviance across the city.[41] In the recorded dialogue of a Community Support Program focus group, a participant describes the capacity of the PSS technology to act as an independent, neutral observer: "That's the eye in the sky just watching the two parties."[42] The eye-in-the-sky trope implies an almost superhuman level of observance, akin to divine imagery, through which everyone may be judged on equal footing. However, in the context of colonial surveillance architecture, it invokes the gaze of the overseer.

The overseer's gaze over the plantation, as established, does not observe a logic of justice and fairness—the priority of its capacity to observe is to maintain discipline and control over the population for capitalist production. With the PSS or BPD project in Baltimore, this is evidenced by the New York University's Policing Project's finding that the program strayed outside of its civil liberties assurances, tracking residents over multiple days and failing to delete images after 45 days.[43] The priority of the WAMI technology was to maintain persistent surveillance and relay information around the movements of people linked to crime scenes, not necessarily to protect private citizens from direct harm. At the time, the Baltimore City Council President, Brandon M. Scott, stated that the BPD had testified that the PSS surveillance planes "yielded zero pieces of evidence that could be used to fight crime."[44]

Like the overseer's gaze and the plantation's concurrent structure, the WAMI across Baltimore produced narratives around suspect individuals and communities. Communities with Solutions, a recipient of PSS donations in Baltimore, defended the level of investment into a second PSS WAMI project in 2020, with representative Archie Williams stating that "it helps the person that's innocent and it helps the person that's guilty."[45] However, in the broader context of reporting on BPD's history of targeted policing of Black communities and racial bias across their enforcement actions, it would be predictable that the BPD's arsenal of surveillance technologies would be deployed primarily in Black neighborhoods.[46] The WAMI's gaze encompasses and aggregates particular communities into categories of crime, deviancy, and unlawful behavior, searching for data that warrants investigation and interrogation of those becoming more suspect or risky over time. In this sense, just as the overseer intends to maintain the divergent status of the surveilled, the WAMI wants to preserve the status of the surveilled as potentially, or inevitably, criminal.

Conclusion

The post-2001 security landscape and its constitutive techniques are replicating the disciplinary techniques of colonial surveillance. Not only is this done through the employment of literal surveillance technologies, but their prominence in everyday life and the scale at which they can operate signifies a return to the panoptic gaze of plantations. WAMI technology is the most acute indicator of said return, in the capacity to operate perpetual and all-seeing surveillance and condensed recorded information for easy processing by operators of the WAMI systems. Utilizing such technology has accelerated the casting of different individuals and communities as suspect, deviant, or dangerous within the security landscape.

WAMI technology reopens colonial wounds and expands the panoptic scope. The plantation security scape enables unprecedented levels of intimate surveillance from exceptional distances through the level of ISR data collection offered by WAMI. It allows the operators to escape the returned gaze of the public. In legal reform, WAMI technology raises concerns around privacy law, the right to record, and law enforcement powers of surveillance, particularly as such technologies become more advanced and enhance the capacity to shield those conducting the surveillance.

To avoid and resist the continued integration of plantation geographies, legal scholarship and discussion must focus on destabilizing military practices in law enforcement and surveillance. The law of armed conflict's regulation of military technology continues to struggle with accounting for rapid innovation, and federal regulation of law enforcement will only replicate said struggles if militarization and enhancement of such techniques continue at the same rate. The discourse around WAMI technologies in the light of persisting colonial surveillance should contribute a flashpoint in such efforts to improve transparency and awareness around these practices. One can illuminate pathways toward avoiding the panoptic gaze through improved awareness and interrogation of these technologies.

Endnotes

1. Patrick Toomey and Ashley Gorski, "The Privacy Lesson of 9/11: Mass Surveillance is Not the Way Forward," *American Civil Liberties Union*, September 7, 2021, https://www.aclu.org/news/national-security/the-privacy-lesson-of-9-11-masssurveillance-is-not-the-way-forward; Albert F. Cahn, "20 Years After 9/11, Surveillance Has Become a Way of Life," *Wired*, September 8, 2021, https://www.wired.com/story/20-years-after-911-surveillance-has-become-a-wayof-life/.

2. Tate Ryan-Mosley, "A New Map of NYC's Cameras Shows More Surveillance in Black and Brown Neighborhoods," *MIT Technology Review,* February 14, 2022, https://www.technologyreview.com/2022/02/14/1045333/map-nyc-camerassurveillance-bias-facial-recognition/; Nicol T. Lee and Caitlin Chin, "Police Surveillance and Facial Recognition: Why Data Privacy is Imperative for Communities of Color," *Brookings Institution*, April 12, 2022, https://www.brookings.edu/research/police-surveillance-and-facial-recognitionwhy-data-privacy-is-an-imperative-for-communities-of-color/

3. Paul T. Jaeger, John C. Bertot and Charles R. McClure, "The Impact of the USA Patriot Act on Collection and Analysis of Personal Information Under the Foreign Intelligence Surveillance Act," *Government Information Quarterly* 20 (2003): 310, https://doi.org/10.1016/S0740-624X(03)00057-1; Maria A. Simone, "Give Me Liberty and Give Me Surveillance: A Case Study of the US Government's Discourse of Surveillance," *Critical Discourse Studies* 6, no. 1 (2009): 3, https://doi.org/10.1080/17405900802559977.

4. Simone, "Give Me Liberty," 6; Robert de Beaugrande, "Critical Discourse Analysis from the Perspective of Ecologism: The Discourse of the 'New Patriotism' for the 'New Secrecy'," *Critical Discourse Studies* 1, no. 1 (2004): 135, https://doi.org/10.1080/17405900410001674542 ; Robert K. Beshara, "A Critical Discourse Analysis of George W. Bush's 'War on Terror' Speech: The Rhetoric of (Counter)Terrorism and the Logic of Islamophobia," *Journal of Language and Discrimination* 2, no. 1 (2018): 105-6, https://doi.org/10.1558/jld.34307.

5. Daniel Schwarz and Simon McCormack, "The NYPD is Teaming Up with Amazon Ring. New Yorkers Should be Worried," *New York Civil Liberties Union*, January 11, 2023, https://www.nyclu.org/en/news/nypd-teaming-amazon-ring-newyorkers-should-be-worried.

6. Jefferson Morley, "A New Book Reveals Just How Sophisticated Surveillance Has Become," *Salon*, September 7, 2019, https://www.salon.com/2019/09/07/newbook-reveals-just-how-sophisticated-surveillance-has-become_partner/; Baynard Woods and Ciara McCarthy, "Baltimore Police Confirms Aerial Surveillance of City Residents," *The Guardian*, August 24, 2016, https://www.theguardian.com/usnews/2016/aug/24/baltimore-police-aerial-surveillance-cameras#-maincontent; Adil Robertson, "Lawsuit Fights New Baltimore Aerial Surveillance Program," *The Verge*, April 9, 2020, https://www.theverge.com/2020/4/9/21215090/aclu-aerialsurveillance-baltimore-police-department-pss-lawsuit.

7. Rebecca Grant, "JSTARS Wars," *Air and Space Forces Magazine*, November 1, 2009, https://www.airandspaceforces.com/article/1109jstars/.

8. Grant, "Wars."

9. Ilker Ersoy, Kannappan Palaniappan, Guna S. Seetharaman and Raghuveer M. Rao, "Interactive Target Tracking for Persistent Wide-Area Surveillance," *Geospatial InfoFusion* 2, no. 8396 (2012): 46, https://doi.org/10.1117/12.920815.

10. Stacia Zachary, "Angel Fire Surveillance a Key Tactical Asset," *Eglin Air Force Base*, January 23, 2009, https://www.eglin.af.mil/News/ArticleDisplay/Article/392767/angel-fire-surveillance-a-key-tactical-asset/.

11. Frank Colucci, "Wide Area Aerial Surveillance Technologies Evolve for Homeland Security and Other Applications," *Defense Media Network*, December 6, 2012, https://www.defensemedianetwork.com/stories/wide-area-aerial-surveillancetechnologies-evolve-for-homeland-security-and-other-applications/2/.

12. *Defense Update*, "The New Generation of Persistent Wide Area Motion Video Surveillance Systems," *Defense Update*, July 4, 2010, https://defenseupdate.com/20100704_persistent_wide_area_surveillance.html; Hugh McFadden, "Common Sense: Improving the Efficacy of Wide Area Surveillance," *Air and Space Power Journal* 28, no. 2 (2016): 75, https://www.airuniversity.af.edu/Portals/10/ASPJ_Spanish/Journals/Volume28_Issue-2/2016_2_09_McFadden_s_eng.pdf.

13. Jason Reagan, "Harris Unveils All-Seeing Drone," *Drone Life*, May 7, 2016, https://dronelife.com/2016/05/07/harris-unveils-all-seeing-drones-sensors/.

14. Murat Haner, Melissa M. Sloan and Cheryl L. Jonson, "Public Concern About Terrorism: Fear, Worry, and Support for Anti-Muslim Policies," *Socius: Sociological Research for a Dynamic World* 5 (2019): 11-12, https://doi.org/10.1177/2378023119856825.

15. Jeff Adachi, "Police Militarization and the War on Citizens," *American Bar Association Human Rights Magazine* 42, no. 1 (2017), https://www.americanbar.org/groups/crsj/publications/human_rights_magazine _home/2016-17-vol-42/vol-42-no-1/police-militarization-and-the-war-oncitizens/; Tonya Mosley and Serena McMahon, "Militarization of Police 'Ramped Up' After 9/11, 'Rise of the Warrior Cop' Author Says," *WBUR*, September 9, 2021, https://www.wbur.org/hereandnow/2021/09/09/post-9-11-policing.

16. *KnowledgeNuts*, "The All-Seeing Eye of Persistent Surveillance," *KnowledgeNuts*, December 5, 2015, https://knowledgenuts.com/2015/12/05/the-all-seeing-eye-ofpersistent-surveillance/.

17. Arthur H. Michel, "The Military-Style Surveillance Technology Being Tested in American Cities," *The Atlantic*, August 3, 2019, https://www.theatlantic.com/technology/archive/2019/08/military-stylesurveillance-air-often-legal/595063/; Margot E. Kaminski, "Privacy and the Right to Record," *Boston University Law Review* 97 (2017) : 171-72, https://www.bu.edu/bulawreview/files/2017/03/KAMINSKI.pdf.

18. Lee and Chin, "Police Surveillance;" Morley, "Sophisticated Surveillance."

19. Kaminski, "Right to Record;" Daxton R. Stewart and Jeremy Littau, "Up, Periscope: Mobile Streaming Video Technologies, Privacy in Public, and the Right to Record," *Journalism and Mass Communication Quarterly* 93, no. 2 (2016), https://doi.org/10.1177/1077699016637106.

20. Erik Schechter, "No Surprise Attacks: How Wide-Area Surveillance Enables "Deterrence by Detection," *Logos Technologies*, May 25, 2021, https://www.logostech.net/how-wide-area-surveillance-enables-deterrence-bydetection/.

21. Thomas G. Mahnken, Travis Sharp and Grace B. Kim, "Deterrence by Detection: A Key Role for Unmanned Aircraft Systems in Great Power Competition," *Center for Strategic and Budgetary Assessments*, 2020, https://csbaonline.org/uploads/documents/CSBA8209_(Deterrence_by_Detectio n_Report)_FINAL.pdf.

22. Kristian P. Humble, "International Law, Surveillance and the Protection of Privacy," *International Journal of Human Rights* 25, no. 1 (2021): 9-10, https://doi.org/10.1080/13642987.2020.1763315.

23. Human Rights Watch Inc. & Ors. v. Secretary of State for the Foreign & Commonwealth Office & Ors., UKIP Trib. 15, 165 (2016).

24. *Defense Update,* "A New Generation of Persistnet Wide Area Motion Surveillance Systems," *Defense Update,* July 4, 2010, https://defenseupdate.com/20100704_persistent_wide_area_surveillance.html; Arthur H. Michel, "How Big Tech is Helping Build the Pentagon's All-Seeing Eye-in the Sky," *Fast Company,* June 18, 2019, https://www.fastcompany.com/90342971/how-thepentagon-is-bringing-algorithmic-spycraft-and-big-tech-to-war.

25. Julia J. Haines, "Mauritian Indentured Labour and Plantation Household Archaeology," *Azania: Archaeological Research in Africa* 55, no. 4 (2020): 510-11, https://doi.org/10.1080/0067270X.2020.1841966.

26. Amit K. Mishra, "Indian Indentured Labourers in Mauritius: Reassessing the 'New System of Slavery' vs. Free Labour Debate," *Studies in History* 25, no. 2 (2009): 231-32, https://doi.org/10.1177/025764301002500203.

27. Clare Anderson, "The Politics of Punishment in Colonial Mauritius, 1766-1887," *Cultural and Social History* 5, no. 4 (2008): 415, https://doi.org/10.2752/147800408X341622.

28. Srilata Ravi, "Treatment of Foreign Workers Lends a Lie to Myth of the Mauritian 'Miracle'," *The Conversation*, November 1st, 2016, https://theconversation.com/treatment-of-foreign-workers-lends-a-lie-to-myth-ofthe-mauritian-miracle-67180.

29. Haines, "Plantation Household Archaeology," 515.

30. Maureen Harkin, "Matthew Lewis's Journal of a West India Proprietor: Surveillance and Space on the Plantation," *Nineteenth-Century Contexts* 24, no. 2 (2002): 141, https://doi.org/10.1080/0890549022000017832.

31. Mukesh Kumar, "Coolie Lines: A Bentham Panopticon Schema and Beyond," *Proceedings of the Indian History Congress* 76 (2015): 352, https://www.jstor.org/stable/44156601; Sabrina Axster, Ida Danewid, Asher Goldstein, Matt Mahmoudi, Cemal B. Tansel and Lauren Wilcox, "Colonial Lives of the Carceral Archipelago: Rethinking the Neoliberal Security State," *International Political Sociology* 15 (2021): 430, https://doi.org/https://doi.org/10.1093/ips/olab013; Nicholas Mirzoeff, "Artificial Vision, White Space and Racial Surveillance Capitalism," *AI & Society* 36 (2021): 1296, https://doi.org/10.1007/s00146-020-01095-8.

32. Lydia W. Marshall, "Slavery, Space, and Social Control on Plantations," *Journal of African Diaspora Archaeology and Heritage* 11, no. 1 (2022): 1, https://doi.org/10.1080/21619441.2022.2079251; Joshna Biju and Liss M. Das, "Rearticulating Foucault's Panopticon: A Study on *The Handmaid's Tale* and *Twelve Years a Slave*," *Aureole* 7 (2020): 55-56, https://aureoleonline.in/wpcontent/uploads/2021/08/61_Aureole-2020.pdf; Jacques-Alain Miller and Richard Miller, "Jeremy Bentham's Panoptic Device," *October* 41 (1987): 4-5, https://www.jstor.org/stable/778327.

33. John C. Campbell, "Mauritius: Report of Plague in Port Louis," *Public Health Reports (1896-1970)* 14, no. 21 (1899): 788, https://www.jstor.org/stable/41454935.

34. Sunanda Sen, "Indentured Labour from India in the Age of Empire," *Social Scientist* 44, no. 1/2 (2016): 43, http://www.jstor.com/stable/24890231;

35. Pravina B. Sain, "A Study of the Problems Faced by Indian Indentured Labour in Mauritius Due to Violation of Contract 1834-1878," *Proceedings of the Indian History Congress* 41, (1980): 7, https://www.jstor.org/stable/44141909.

36. Reshaad Durgahee, *The Indentured Archipelago: Experiences of Indian Labour in Mauritius and Fiji, 1871-1916* (Cambridge University Press, 2022), 6.

37. Katherine McKittrick, "On Plantations, Prisons, and a Black Sense of Place," *Social & Cultural Geography* 12, no. 8 (2011): 950, https://dx.doi.org/10.1080/14649365.2011.624280.

38. Craig Timberg, "New Surveillance Technology can Track Everyone in an Area for Several Hours at a Time," *Washington Post*, February 5, 2014, https://www.washingtonpost.com/business/technology/new-surveillancetechnology-can-track-everyone-in-an-area-for-several-hours-at-atime/2014/02/05/82f1556e-876f-11e3-a5bd-844629433ba3_story.html [quoted].

39. Jay Stanley, "Ohio Aerial Surveillance System Moving Forward Without Having to Wait for FAA Drone Rules," *American Civil Liberties Union*, April 4, 2013, https://www.aclu.org/news/national-security/ohio-aerial-surveillance-systemmoving-forward.

40. Benjamin H. Snyder, "'Big Brother's Bigger Brother': The Visual Politics of (Counter) Surveillance in Baltimore," *Sociological Forum* 35, no. 4 (2020): 10, https://doi.org/10.1111/socf.12649.
41. Benjamin H. Snyder, "'All We See is Dots': Aerial Objectivity and Mass Surveillance in Baltimore," *History of Photography* 45, no. 3-4 (2021): 376, https://doi.org/10.1080/03087298.2022.2108263.
42. Snyder, "Big Brother," 13.
43. Barry Friedman, Farhang Heydari, Emmanuel Mauleón and Max Isaacs, "Civil Rights and Civil Liberties Audit of Baltimore's Aerial Investigation Research (AIR) Program," *Policing Project, NYU School of Law* (2020), https://static1.squarespace.com/static/58a33e881b631bc60d4f-8b31/t/5fc290577a cac6192a142d61/1606586458141/AIR+Program+Audit+Report+vFI-NAL+%28redu ced%29.pdf; Joanne C. Simpson, "Civil Liberties Questions Plague Baltimore's 'Spy Plane' Experiment," *Pulitzer Center*, December 21, 2020, https://pulitzercenter.org/stories/civil-liberties-questions-plague-baltimores-spyplane-experiment. `
44. Brandon M. Scott, "Council President Brandon M. Scott's Statement on Announcement of Aerial Surveillance Pilot Program," *Baltimore City Council*, December 20, 2019, https://www.baltimorecitycouncil.com/content/councilpresident-brandon-m-scotts-statement-announcement-aerial-surveillance-pilotprogram.
45. Ethan McLeod, "City Council Members Grill Spy Plane Company, BPD over Privacy Concerns, Lobbying," *Baltimore Fishbowl,* October 17, 2018, https://baltimorefishbowl.com/stories/city-council-members-grill-spy-planecompany-bpd-over-transparency-lobbying-privacy-concerns/.
46. *US Department of Justice Civil Rights Division*, Investigation of the Baltimore City Police Department, *US Department of Justice*, August 10, 2016: 7, https://www.justice.gov/crt/file/883296/download;.Joanne C. Simpson and Ron Cassie, "Under Watch," *Baltimore Magazine*, March 2021, https://www.baltimoremagazine.com/section/historypolitics/under-watch-policespy-plane-experiment-over-but-growing-surveillance-baltimore-continues/.

CHAPTER 9
The Battles of Hue: Understanding Urban Conflicts through Wargaming

David J.H. Burden

Introduction

In trying to better understand past urban conflicts and better plan for future urban conflicts, wargaming offers a valuable approach to the challenge. Wargames allow for a "vicarious understanding of some of the strategic and tactical dynamics associated with real military operations," are active learning, and present players with decisions similar to those in actual engagements.[1] The renewed interest in urban warfare since Iraq, exacerbated by operations in Ukraine, has led to an increased focus on urban wargaming in the professional military world, for example, the Urban Warfare Planners Course in the United States of America.[2]

This article takes a comparative case-study approach to examine how valuable wargames could be to understanding and planning urban warfare and security. It looks at one urban battle in Vietnam, the Battle of Hue in 1968, and the wargames produced about it. After summarizing wargaming and the issues involved in wargame research, the article presents the reasons for choosing Hue, followed by a summary of the actual Battle of Hue. The article then introduces the wargames on Hue and analyzes their structural elements. This is followed by an identification of the critical characteristics of the battle (which may apply to other urban battles) and a discussion of how they are (or are not) represented in the wargames. The article concludes with a summative assessment of the wargames and how well they represent the characteristics of Hue and a broader discussion of how such wargames might help us better understand past battles such as Hue and plan for future urban conflicts.

Wargaming

The US Department of Defense defines wargames as "representations of conflict or competition in a synthetic environment, in which people make decisions and respond to the consequences of those decisions."[3]

The professional community (those involved in delivering wargames principally to militaries and governments) differentiates between using wargames for training and analysis.[4] Such categorization can also extend to wargames for entertainment, edutainment, and education.[5] In the last 12 months, the UK Secretary of State for Defense and the US Chairman of the Joint Chiefs of Staff have stated the importance of wargaming.[6] Beginning principally with the Prussian military, wargames have been used to help military planners evaluate options and to train their staff.[7] Wargames were used in the inter-war period by the US Navy to train senior officers and examine strategies for any future war with Japan.[8] During WW2, the Germans utilized wargames widely, from planning the 1940 invasion of France to reacting—live—to a United States attack in the Ardennes in 1944.[9]

In the immediate post-war period, wargaming was challenged by computer-based operational research, resulting in computer-assisted wargames such as the multi-day *Global Wargames* series to help inform Cold War strategy.[10] However, these ran alongside manual, tactical training wargames, such as *Dunn-Kempf* and *Blockbuster*. Although first-person computer-based virtual training systems (such as Bohemia Interactive's *VBS4*) are increasingly taking on some of the training roles, the use of manual wargames persists for both training and analytic purposes.[11]

Recent years have also seen the introduction of Matrix games – structured discussions – particularly for more strategic and operational wargaming.[12] Regarding the current conflict in Ukraine, the USMC was using their Operational Wargame Series (OWS) manual wargaming system to examine the course of the war in the weeks leading up to its outbreak, and wargames have been used during the war to evaluate possible Russian and Ukrainian actions and Western responses to them.[13]

Running a wargame, or even multiple wargames, will not provide a prediction of the future—or an exact recreation of the past—but they may give an idea of the shape and likelihood of possibilities and help analyze past and future conflicts and decisions.[14] In many wargames, rigor and plausibility are more useful reference points than a prediction; the purpose is often to stimulate player decision-making for insight rather than making predictions on outcomes.[15]

Challenges with Wargaming Research

One of the main challenges in wargaming research, particularly for professional wargames, is that they tend to be relatively ephemeral.[16] Even if the wargame leads to a filed report, the wargame itself may not be kept.[17] There can also be issues around classification, cloistering of data, and intellectual property issues with the wargame design.[18] Initiatives such as the History of Wargaming project and the Hoover Institution's new Wargaming and Crisis Simulation Initiative collection are beginning to help address the issue but have limited reach. Philip Sabin identifies that hobby wargames offer "three overwhelming advantages" compared to professional wargames:

Their number and availability; that they deal with the past (which most professional games do not) as well as the future; and that there is a better balance between manual and computer wargaming (the former being far more transparent in their workings).[19]

In addition, there has long been a porous boundary between hobby and professional wargames. Professionals have used hobby games as-is; for example, *Gulf Strike* by Mark Herman, used by the Pentagon during the Gulf War, or have commissioned hobby designers to create professional games, for instance, Jim Dunnigan and *Firefight* for the US Army. Professionals have created hobby games based on their experience and expertise, for example, *Urban Operations* by Sébastien de Peyret, a French Army Officer at their urban training school. Professionals have also evaluated hobby games for ideas and potential military applications, for example, the United Kingdom's Defence Science and Technology Laboratory's Blockbuster study into urban wargames.[20] The military has also used hobby wargames for professional military education.[21] This diffusion of ideas between the professional and hobby communities reinforces the argument that hobby games are a viable field of research. However, hobby games' different aims than professional games must be born in mind.

Why Hue?

Ongoing work to build a database of over 230 hobby and professional urban wargames has identified only five urban battles that are covered by five or more wargames: Stalingrad (27), Hue (10), Berlin 1945 (6), Budapest 1956 (5), Fallujah II (5), all of which are common urban conflict case-studies.[22] It is intended to produce comparative studies on the wargames of each battle in due course. This first study chose Hue since it presented elements of symmetric and asymmetric conflict, enabling aspects of different forms of urban combat to be studied in one battle. It would have enough games for analysis even if some were not suitable or obtainable for the study. This study also acts as a pilot before examining the significantly larger number of games on Stalingrad.

Methodology

While there are a few reviews of individual wargames within the academic literature, one on Budapest 1956 being a rare example[23], no examples of academic comparative studies for wargames of historic battles have yet been identified.[24] Apart from the more considered reviews in the hobby literature, for example, a review of 29 Eastern Front games in Moves magazine,[25] the closest is perhaps on the representation of air warfare in games in the book Zones of Control—although covering the picture from WW2 to the present.[26]

The method, therefore, developed for this initial study was to compare the structural elements of the games, examine any Designer's Notes to understand the intent of the games, and then, through a play of the games and a reading of the rules, examine how the games represented the previously identified key features of the battle. The study did not emphasize how closely the games' plays matched the historic battle and outcome since no meaningful view on this could be taken from one or two plays. As described above, wargames should not be seen as predictive tools—even retrospectively—although they should demonstrate the issues and choices that forces and commanders of the time faced.

The Battle of Hue

The Battle of Hue was part of the North Vietnamese Tet Offensive in early 1968. With a population of about 140,000, Hue was a culturally significant city split by the Perfume River, which was crossed by only two bridges. The large Citadel with a moat and high walls, north of the river, contains the Imperial Palace and the Tay Loc airfield. South of the river was the more modern part of the city, known as the Triangle, about half the area of the Citadel.

Before 31st January 1968, significant numbers of Vietcong (VC) had infiltrated the city. At 0233 on 31st January, the VC seized the gates to the city, and by the end of the day, some 10,000 VC and North Vietnamese

Army (NVA) troops had taken control of most of the city. The defending forces initially consisted only of HQ 1st ARVN Division, based within the northeast corner of Citadel, and 200 US troops south of the river in the Military Assistance Command, Vietnam (MACV) compound.

As the scale of the Communist (NVA and VC) operation gradually became apparent, the Allies (ARVN and USMC) began to drip-feed reinforcements into the city, the battle splitting into fights north and south of the river. In the Citadel, the ARVN managed to keep the airstrip secure, using it for reinforcement and resupply. The USMC started to clear the Triangle, taking four days to clear the first two blocks but securing it by February 10, 1968. The USMC used boats to cross the Perfume River and reach the walls of the Citadel, but it was not until 21st February that the USMC managed to secure a gate to help the ARVN. Concurrently, the Allies tasked the US 1st Air Cavalry Division to block the Communist supply lines north and west of the city, and they stumbled onto the Communist HQ at La Chu. However, the night before an assault on the HQ, the Communist's command slipped away. By 23rd February, the Communists started to leave the city as it became surrounded by Allied forces. The Allies completed the retaking of Hue on February 25, 1968. Military analysts and historians often use the battle as a case study of urban warfare.[27]

Wargames of the Battle of Hue

Ten wargames (all hobby games) have been identified on the Battle of Hue.[28] Table 1 provides essential information on these games, along with their scores for Complexity and Rating (roughly player satisfaction) on the comprehensive BoardGameGeek hobby website— although these scores have their biases.[29] Three of the games—*'65 Hue City Map Expansion*, *ATS: The Fight For Hue*, and *Fields of Fire 2*— are scenarios for more generic tactical level games (*ATS* works in 90second turns), and their scenario details being unavailable will not be considered further here. *A Bloody Business: The Battle of Hue, 1968* is an earlier version of *City of Confusion* and is not considered separately. Of the games that make up this case study:

- *Hue* came out only five years after the battle and used a traditional hex-and-counter mechanism.
- *Vietnam Battles: Hue!* is also a hex-and-counter game, published in *Strategy & Tactics* magazine. It is notable as the only game to include a significant area outside the city.
- *A Week in Hell: The Battle of Hue* is a hex-and-counter solitaire game published in *Battles* magazine.
- *City of Confusion: The Battle for Hue* uses areas rather than hexes to manage movement and a card-based activation mechanic.
- *The Battle of Hue!* is a solitaire hex-and-counter game based on the designer's previous *The Battle for Ramadi* game.
- *Block by Block* is an area-based game published in *Modern Warfare* magazine.

Table 1: Battle of Hue Wargames

Game	Date	Designer	Publisher	Complexity (/5)	Rating (/10)	Solitaire?
Hue	1973	John Hill	Mayfair	2.43	6.7	N
Vietnam Battles: Hue!	1999	Joseph Miranda	Strategy & Tactics	2.5	5.8	N
A Bloody Business: The Battle of Hue, 1968	2006	Perry Moore, Paul Rohrbaugh	Firefight Games	2.00	8.0	N
A Week in Hell: The Battle of Hue	2010	Laurent Guenette	Battles Magazine	2.41	7.1	Y
City of Confusion: The Battle for Hue	2012	Paul Rohrbaugh	High Flying Dice Games	2.5	6.9	N
'65 Hue City Map Expansion	2016	Mark H. Walker	Flying Pig Games	3.00	7.8	N
ATS: The Fight for Hue	2016	Critical Hit, Inc.	Critical Hit, Inc.	-	9.0	N
The Battle of Hue!	2019	Jay Ward	Tiny Battle Publishing	2.67	6.9	Y
Fields of Fire2	2019	Ben Hull	GMT Games	4.60	8.2	Y
Block by Block	2020	Nicholas Edwards	Modern Warfare Magazine	3.25	6.0	N

Source: Extracted from the individual game entries on the BoardGameGeek website and the game documentation.

Figure 1 shows images of each game used in this case study.

9: THE BATTLES OF HUE: UNDERSTANDING URBAN CONFLICTS THROUGH WARGAMING

Figure 1: Images of the Battle of Hue Wargames

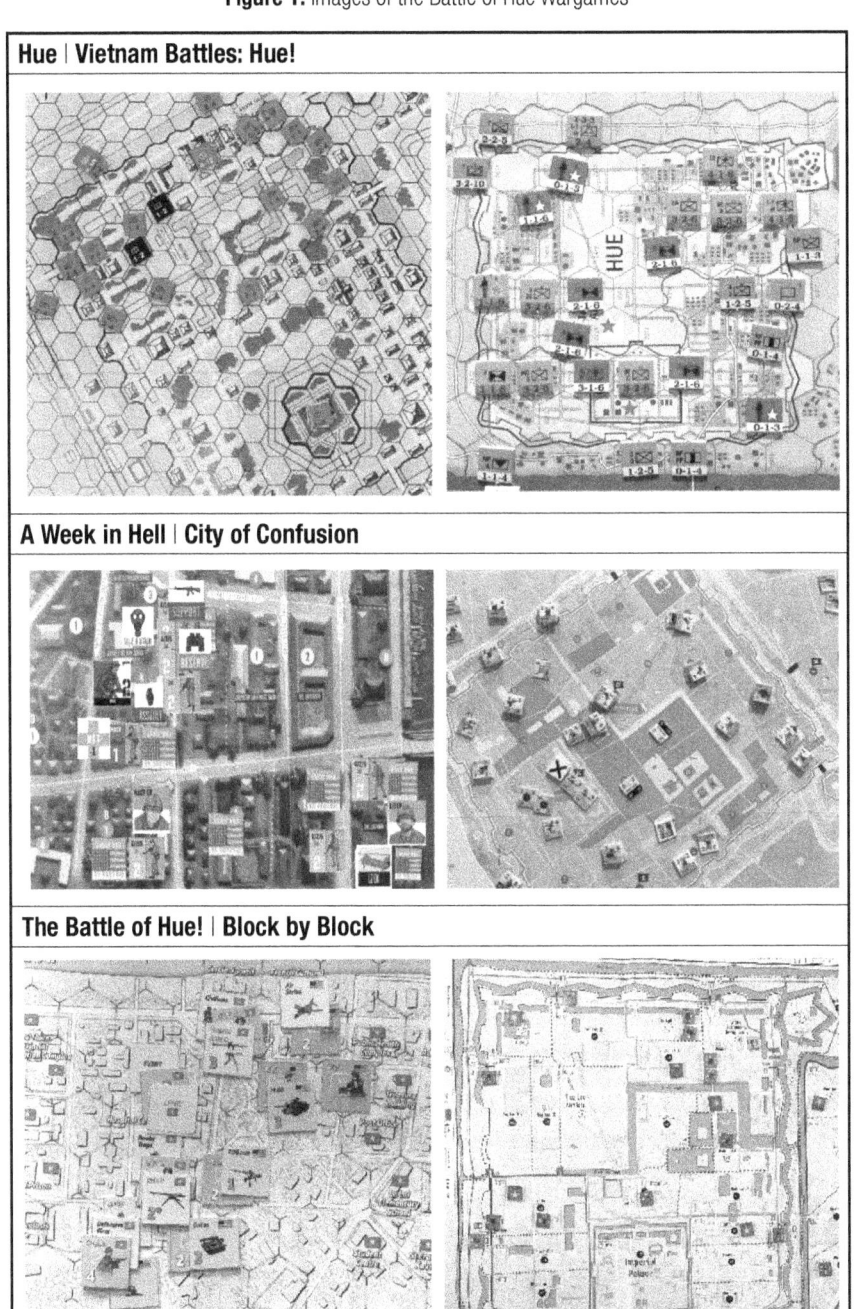

Source: Photographs by the author of games in the author's private collection.

Structural Comparison

Wargames use a variety of mechanisms to control actions in time and space and represent the forces and effects involved.[30]

Table 2: Key Characteristics of the Hue Wargames

Feature Game	Space Regulation	Space Scale	Turn Length	Number of Turns	Resolution
Hue	Hexes	~180m	One day	12+	Company
Vietnam Battles: Hue!	Hexes	~360m	One day	24	Company & Battalion
A Week in Hell	Areas	~100m	One day	7	Platoon
City of Confusion	Areas	~150m	2-3 days	10	Platoon
The Battle of Hue!	Hexes	~100m	½ day	15	Platoon
Block by Block	Area	~400m	Five days	5	Platoon to Battalion

Source: Analysis by the author of physical copies of the games and their documentation. Notes: Space scale is per hex, or more approximately, per area, depending on the space regulation used.

Figure 2 compares the areas covered by each of the games. *Vietnam Battles: Hue!* is notable for including a significant amount of terrain beyond Hue (and well beyond La Chu)—although most of that area has little impact on play. *The Battle of Hue!* and *A Week in Hell* only cover the USMC operations south of the Perfume River. Three games expect the play to represent all 25 days of the battle, and three cover only the first 12 days when the US was mainly engaged south of the river. The counters in the games cover the relevant orders of battle for each game's scope, but what each counter represents varies, as shown in the Resolution column in

Table 2. Each of these wargames is rigid—played to strict rules.[31] Both solitaire games are semi-open, with counters inverted or randomly drawn, so the player is unsure of exactly what enemy forces are where. In contrast, the competitive games are open with no mechanic to hide units from the other player—although *Hue* does suggest inverting the counters for Communist units.[32]

Figure 2: Comparative Areas covered by the Hue Wargames

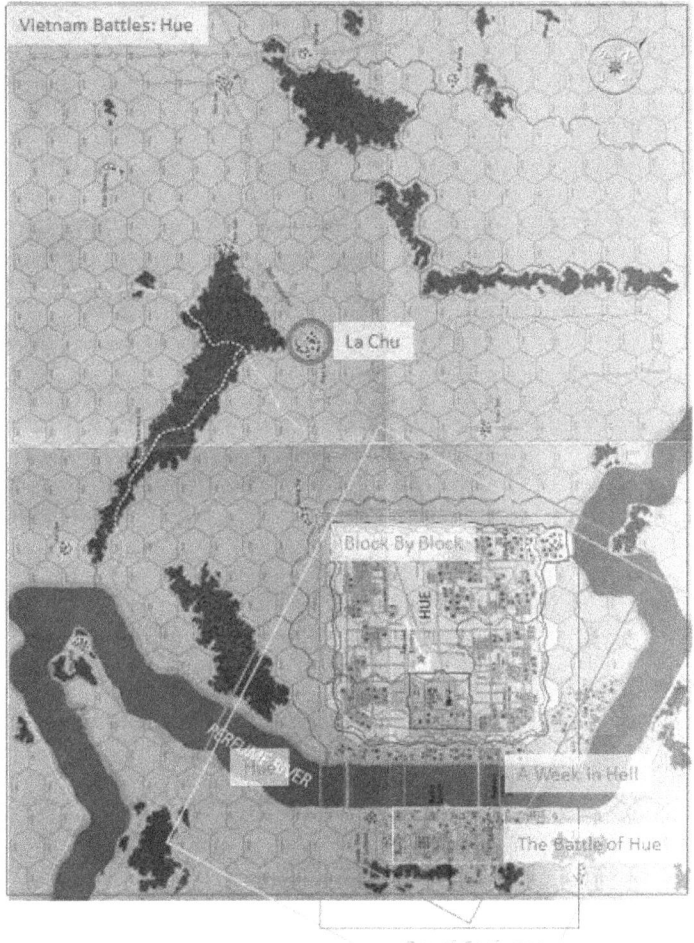

Source: Image created by the author based on photos and measurements by the author of game maps in the author's private collection.

Designer's Intent

The Battle of Hue! is the only game with formal Designer's Notes. In his notes, Jay Ward writes that the game is a follow-up to, and uses the same basic system as, his Iraqi Insurgency era *Battle of Ramadi* game. He sees command and control implemented through a command point system as critical. The player also has trade-offs– particularly in using heavy weapons in civilian areas. Ward notes that the victory conditions are "based on comparing progress in the game with the historical rate of progress" and encouraging the player to match the real-life operational priorities.[33]

In *A Week in Hell,* designer Laurent Guenette places short designer notes within relevant rules sections. Guenette comments on the block-by-block tactical approach making the area division of the city straightforward; the lack of training of the Marines; that counters represent combined arms units (including the Ontos); that narrow frontages limited combined attacks; the infiltration issues, and the order mechanism reflects the problems with communications in the city.[34]

Rather than a set of Designer's Notes, *Block by Block* has introductory comments by Joseph Miranda, the *Vietnam Battles: Hue!* designer, and an influential contemporary wargame designer. Miranda notes that: Movement is limited by enemy contact, not distance; there is a trade-off between using heavy weapons to destroy the enemy weapons and increasing collateral damage; each of the allied forces needs to fight separately due to command and control issues, and that the "Political Track" is an acknowledgment that Hue was a battle fought as much "in the press room and on television sets" as on the ground in Vietnam.[35]

The Key Features of the Battle of Hue

This section identifies the key features of the Battle of Hue and if and how the wargames represent them.

Combined Arms

The firepower of the M48 tanks was essential, particularly for blowing holes in walls. A typical pattern was to "first pump out the target building or complex with mortars... Then came a [CS] gas cloud, tanks, Ontos [self-propelled recoilless rifles], 106s [recoilless rifles], bazookas, and finally Marines." [36] In the Citadel, the narrow streets caused problems for the US armor, but more significantly, the ARVN did not have direct-fire heavy weapons available and suffered. [37]

A Week in Hell and *Block by Block* both only have infantry counters, although according to the accompanying notes, they are meant to represent combined arms groups. In *Hue* and *Vietnam Battles: Hue!* combat simply combines counter strengths but does not include a modifier for the infantry and armor operating in combination. *City of Confusion* gives assaults a positive modifier if tanks or Ontos are present. *The Battle of Hue!* treats all tank types as assets so they cannot make attacks on their own, forcing the players into a combined arms approach. In several games (notably *Hue* and *Vietnam Battles: Hue!*), the combination of hex-based mapping, rules, and a traditional combat results table means that the player is focusing more on counter positioning and unit values than on any combined-arms tactics.

The M50 Ontos, a small, lightly armored tank equipped with six 106mm recoilless rifles, was a crucial weapon in Hue.[38] "The tremendous firepower of the Ontos proved significantly more effective than other supporting arms, especially against heavy buildings or enemy positions in the Citadel wall." [39] The only *City of Confusion* and *The Battle of Hue!* have counters for the Ontos, but their role in combined arms has no distinctive effects beyond its essential combat factor.

CS Gas

CS gas proved invaluable in clearing buildings without causing any structural damage.[40] "The greatest difference in firepower for US forces in Hue relative to earlier battles was the extensive use of non-lethal gas." [41] There were problems, though, with it drifting into unprepared friendly troops.⁴² *Hue* includes using CS Gas, removing the Communist ability to fire back, but increasing the Communist Victory Points (VPs). In *A Week in Hell,* CS Gas reduces the enemy combat factor but can drift into neighboring spaces, adversely affecting other Allied units. *The Battle of Hue!* applies CS Gas as a benefit to the attacker—a random dice roll, which is significant but also uncertain, with no secondary effects.

Asymmetric Combat

Hue had elements of both symmetric and asymmetric combat, with the Viet Cong leading the infiltration and conducting covert guerilla-style operations alongside the more formal operations of the ARVN.⁴³ The games typically represent the VC troops as just being weaker counters. In *Hue,* the Communist player may play counters face down to hide their strength, so the Allied player knows where the enemy is but not how strong they are. In *City of Confusion,* only VC units have a "concealed" status, which gives them a bonus in combats and allows multiple activations. As solo games, both *A Week in Hell* and *The Battle of Hue!* use a common mechanism of drawing Communist counters from a pot as the USMC moves into each new area, and both also have an infiltration mechanism to allow the Communists to reappear behind the USMC lines. *The Battle of Hue!* also includes booby traps.

Staggered Reinforcements

Reinforcements and replacements on both sides were drip-fed into the city by land, river, and helicopter.⁴⁴ Many US reinforcements were unseasoned, and Lt Col Cheatham, CO 2/5ᵗʰ Marines, famously spent the night before his deployment rapidly reading US military urban doctrine.⁴⁵ All of the games have relatively detailed turn-by-turn reinforcement charts. *Hue, Vietnam Battles: Hue! A Week in Hell* and *City of Confusion* include the ability to do heliborne or air-landed reinforcements. *A Week in Hell* has an explicit reinforcement mechanism. New USMC units arrive in an off-map Phu Bai box and then move up to the MACV compound as trucks are available but being ambushed or flown directly in by helicopters. This gives the player some awareness of what is happening beyond the city.

Riverine Activity

The Perfume River and the landing stages around the city enabled the Allies to use Landing Craft to resupply and deploy units relatively unmolested.[46] Boats are operated in *Hue* and *City of Confusion* as an alternative way to bridge the Perfume River. *Vietnam Battles: Hue!* has one "Patrol Boat, Riverine" counter, but this is only a gun platform. *Block by Block* allows Allied units to move directly between dock symbols on the map—regardless of distance.

Co-ordination and Command Friction

The United States and ARVN command relationships "remained disjointed and confused throughout the battle."[47] *Vietnam Battles: Hue!* uses a system of Initiative Points to drive combat bonuses, but USMC troops can only gain them from nearby USMC HQ, and likewise for the ARVN. In City of Confusion, US and ARVN troops can occupy the same space but cannot deliver coordinated attacks. *A Week in Hell* and *The Battle of Hue!* both have a command-point style system to restrict how many units can activate each turn. *City of Confusion* uses cards to randomize which unit activates when, and not every unit will activate every turn. Each of the oppositional games use face-up counters, so there is no "fog of war." This contrasts to a game like *We Are Coming Nineveh* where both blocks and dummies are used to hide opposition locations and strengths.

Operations Beyond the City

The failure of the United States to isolate Hue is seen as "the most notable shortfall at Hue for American forces."[48] The fortunate discovery of the Communist Thung Front HQ at La Chu and the eventual fleeing of the Communist command staff had a significant negative effect on the resilience of the PAVN defense of Hue.[49] The only game with any specific consideration of isolation is *Block by Block* where Communist reinforcements are proportional to the number of Citadel gates that they still control. Whilst the *Vietnam Battles: Hue* map extends out beyond the Communist HQ at La

Chu, the size of the area and lack of forces make isolation and interdiction operations a formidable task. La Chu has no special significance in the game.

Fire Support and Rules of Engagement (ROE)

Despite the forces fighting in close proximity, indirect fire support (including naval gunfire support – NGS) played a significant role.[50] Observers brought fire down within 100 yards of their own troops, and only about half a dozen cases of casualties from friendly fire were reported.[51] Whilst air support was available, bad weather and rules of engagement made its contribution less significant.[52]

The United States was wary of the political ramifications of damaging important cultural sites: "The initial ROE played a key role in the difficulties incurred in the early days of the battle."[53] The Close Air Support (CAS) and NGS restrictions were gradually lifted but were not evenly applied, with the ARVN using CAS in the Citadel from the beginning.[54] In *Hue*, the Imperial Palace is off-limits to both artillery and armor, and weather strongly affects availability. In *City of Confusion,* a specific die roll after turn 5 is required to gain "US Free Fire release." Before this happens, no United States units may operate in the Citadel, or CAS or NGS be used within the Citadel. *The Battle of Hue!* has a 33 percent chance of supporting fires available from turn 3 onwards and automatically from turn 7. *Block by Block* has no ROE rules but makes all use of supporting fires subject to a 50 percent chance of also inflicting damage on one's own forces. It also combines a wide range of weaponry (Ontos, Artillery, CS Gas, CAS, NGS) into a single Heavy Weapons roll. None of the games use the card mechanics for additional but abstracted capabilities (such as fire support, close air support, and electronic warfare) found in more recent games such as *We are Coming Nineveh* and *Littoral Commander.*

Population & Infrastructure

It is estimated the fighting destroyed that 80 percent of the city, and around 116,000 (82 percent) of the population was made homeless.[55] As the fighting started, most residents sheltered in basements and caused little disruption to the combat itself, but emerged as areas were cleared, causing significant management issues.[56] Dead bodies (there were at least 5,800 civilian deaths) became a public health hazard.[57] The Communist forces used the population as human shields.[58] They also purged several thousand residents for political reasons.[59]

Vietnam Battles: Hue! has a random refugee event that can delay troop transport. *A Week in Hell* has a civilian random event that delays an attack. *The Battle of Hue!* has Civilian counters in its random pot, which a dice roll then converts into either rescues or casualties—the concurrent use of supporting fires increases the chance of the casualty result. *City of Confusion* creates rubble from some supporting fires which limits movement. In *Block by Block* the player chooses between two levels of supporting fires, the greater causing more enemy damage, but also increasing a Destruction count collateral damage, which counts against the player in victory terms. *Block by Block* is also unique in giving the Communist player a "Clearing" action to gain victory points and represent the political purges (although this can encourage some possibly unrealistic player behavior).

Political and Media

The Battle of Hue and the greater fate of the Tet Offensive led to a rapid erosion in public support in the United States of America for the Vietnam War.[60] While Hue may have been a tactical defeat for the Communists, it became part of their strategic victory. The populated and accessible location led to a significant media presence which put the USMC actions in the spotlight.[61] Most of the games use the Victory Point (VP) track as a way of reflecting the political and media dimensions alongside locations taken or forces lost or destroyed. In Hue, the Communists gain VPs if the United States uses CS gas. In *Vietnam Battles: Hue!*, the random events include an "Atrocity" event, which can affect Allied or Communist VPs. In *City of Confusion,* rubble can become an "atrocity" that has a variable (but always negative) and unlimited impact on VPs. *The Battle of Hue!* has Media counters in its pot, which can have a positive, neutral, or negative impact on VPs. *Block by Block* has separate tracks for "Publicity" and "Destruction," both of which contribute adversely to Allied VPs. Some more modern games, for example, *We Are Coming Nineveh,* have dedicated political tracks rather than binding them in with the combat results.

Summative Analysis

The conclusion from the above is that none of the games capture all the different aspects of the Battle of Hue. All the games represent staggered reinforcements, but only two games a-piece cover features such as Combined Arms, the Ontos, CS Gas, Command Friction, and Rules of Engagement. None of the games has any extensive representation of the Operations Beyond the City, Civilian Impact, or Media and Political considerations. *City of Confusion, The Battle of Hue!* and *Block by Block* possibly provide the best coverage overall, but *The Battle of Hue!* only focuses on the fight in the Triangle, and neither of the others includes the impact of CS Gas. *City of Confusion* includes minimal reference to the civilian population, and *Block by Block* is more abstract and does not include Rules of Engagement.

On the positive side, there are many elements of the wargames that could usefully inform the design of new urban wargames, for instance:

- The drift of CS Gas (or other toxic chemicals) and the negative political impact of its use
- The modeling of the reinforcement chain and the dock symbols and routes for riverine activity
- The inability of units from different Allies to coordinate attacks
- The ability for a commander to choose between different levels of support fires, and hence the potential for collateral damage
- Some representation of the Media—and particularly the real-life quotes in *The Battle of Hue!*
- The rubble creation in *City of Confusion,* although the same publisher's *Christmas in Hell* about the 1943 Battle of Ortona has a better approach to this

- Areas that perhaps any new game on Hue could model better include:
- The role of the direct-fire HE weapons such as the Ontos as part of the combined arms operations, particularly in the Citadel
- The different and changing Rules of Engagement
- A more sophisticated treatment of the civilian population, with civilians possibly appearing as each area is cleared, and even their use as human shields
- The operations outside of Hue on both sides to interdict supply lines, isolate the city, and disrupt enemy command and control

Implications for Wargaming Urban Conflict and Security

In considering how wargames might help us better understand past battles and plan for future urban conflict, reviewing these Hue wargames suggests four issues for consideration.

The first is that wargaming is an evolving art, and approaches to wargaming have changed significantly since the publishing of *Hue* in 1973. There has been increasing use of the area-type approach of *A Week in Hell, City of Confusion,* and *Block by Block.* The use of cards is also becoming more prevalent, both to manage random events and to abstract operations and capabilities outside of the main area of operations, for example, in *We Are Coming Nineveh.* The explicit tracking of the political domain is also more common, for example, in *Littoral Commander.*

While no one of the games provides a perfect example of what a wargame of Hue could achieve, there are a lot of good ideas in them which, when combined with more modern mechanics and a good reading of the critical features of the battle itself, could deliver a valuable game to help understand Hue, the decisions, and options that commanders' faced, and how they compare to those of more modern urban conflicts.

Second, Hue highlights the challenge of wargaming any urban engagement in that urban environments are complex, constrained, and changing, with multiple actors, conflicting demands, limited resources, and a population that has to live with the consequences.[62] Shoehorning all of this into a single wargame for any urban battle is a challenge, and the designer has to choose what they are going to focus on, what they are going to abstract, and what they are going to ignore - and ideally document this in the Designer's Notes. The game's intent should drive these choices—what it wants to achieve and who the audience is.

Third, these are all hobby games, and so are edutainment. It should be no surprise if they do not model the full complexity of urban combat. All the games start when the fighting starts and stop when the fighting stops. Put into a professional context, this is just one phase of the NATO doctrine of Understand-Shape-Engage-Consolidate-Transition (USECT).[63] If a game was aimed at a professional audience, then one could expect mechanisms (but not necessarily rigid wargame mechanics) to also explore the before and after of the battle, and in particular, the associated activities in the information and cognitive domains and the impact on the civilian population and the city infrastructure.

Finally, Hue was a battle won but a war lost. The consideration of the USECT model and the extension to the information and cognitive domains begins to put the battle (and wargame) in a wider operational, strategic, and even cultural context. While rigid wargames of battles can help to understand the detail at a tactical and possibly grand tactical level, examination of a broader scope may require different wargaming techniques. The concept of the nested game could be a useful approach.[64] *The Battle of Hue!* could give players some understanding of the issues and the sheer grind of the USMC operations in clearing the Triangle, whereas *City of Confusion* could help to situate that within the broader context of the whole city. Above this, a less rigid wargaming approach, such as a Matrix Game, could better explore operational and political issues.[65]

Conclusion

By developing a more analytic approach to the study of wargaming, such as through the comparative study of wargames on specific battles, there is the potential to develop better urban wargames. These can help professionals to better understand the complexity of urban operations and to better plan for future urban conflict. While each of these wargames of the Battle of Hue can contribute something to an understanding of the battle, such as the choices facing commanders and some of the general implications for urban conflict, none provides the complete picture. However, there are game mechanics in these and more modern games that could perhaps create a better game. For a professional audience, and particularly one concerned with urban security, all the games leave out what happens before and after the active combat phase of the battle. The complexity of urban conflict is such that no one game is ever going to capture it all, and a nested approach to wargaming urban issues, using different wargaming techniques at each level, seems an appropriate approach.

Endnotes

I want to acknowledge the support of my Supervisor, Dr. John Curry, and my fellow wargaming PhD students in preparing the original article published in the Journal of Strategic Security.

1. Philip Sabin, Simulating War: Studying Conflict Through Simulation Games (Continuum, 2012).
2. John Spencer, "Inside the World's Only Urban Warfare Planners Course," Modern War Institute, accessed July 27, 2023, https://mwi.westpoint.edu/inside-theworlds-only-urban-warfare-planners-course/.
3. US Department of Defense, *Joint Planning*, Joint Publication 5-0 (Washington D.C: Department of Defense, 2020), https://irp.fas.org/doddir/dod/jp5_0.pdf.
4. Graham Longley-Brown, *Successful Professional Wargames: A Practitioner's Handbook* (The History of Wargaming Project, 2019).
5. Paulo David da Silva Simões and Cláudio Gabriel Inácio Ferreira, "Military War Games Edutainment," (presentation, IEEE 1st International Conference on Serious Games and Applications for Health, SeGAH, Braga, Portugal, November, 16-18, 2011).
6. Mark A. Milley, "Strategic Inflection Point: The Most Historically Significant and Fundamental Change in the Character of War Is Happening Now—While the Future Is Clouded in Mist and Uncertainty," *Joint Force Quarterly* 110, 3rd Quarter, July 2023.

7. Matthew B. Caffrey Jr, *On Wargaming* (Newport, RI: Naval War College Press).
8. Jeff Appleget, Robert Burks, and Fred Cameron, *The Craft of Wargaming* (Annapolis, MD: Naval Institute Press, 2020).
9. Peter Perla, *The Art of Wargaming* (UK: History of Wargaming Project, 2011).
10. Peter Perla, The Art of Wargaming.
11. Tom Mouat, "The Use and Misuse of Wargames," *Scandinavian Journal of Military Studies*, Vol. 5 Issue. 1 (2022): 209–220, https://doi:10.31374/sjms.121
12. John Curry, Chris Engle and Peter Perla, *The Matrix Games Handbook* (UK: History of Wargaming Project, 2011).
13. James Lacey, Tim Barrick, And Nathan Barrick, "The Wargame Before the War: Russia Attacks Ukraine", War On The Rocks, accessed July 27, 2023, https://warontherocks.com/2022/03/the-wargame-before-the-war-russia-attacksukraine/; Phil Stewart, "US hosts war games for Ukraine ahead of next phase of Russia conflict", Reuters, accessed July 27, 2023, https://www.reuters.com/article/ukraine-crisis-usa-wargames-idAFKBN2V4225
14. Tom Mouat, "The Use and Misuse of Wargames".
15. Paul Webber, "Modern Operational Level Naval Wargames: Design Challenges and Techniques", YouTube, accessed May 25, 2023, 0https://www.youtube.com/watch?v=5JbSn5bevnI.
16. Philip Sabin, *Simulating War.*
17. Yuna Wong, Applying Design Thinking to Wargame Design, YouTube, accessed July 27, 2023, https://www.youtube.com/watch?v=xjwMrgsNfiE.
18. Andrew Reddie, From Art to Science: Analytical Wargaming and Behavioral Research, YouTube, accessed July 27, 2023, https://www.youtube.com/watch?v=e6W9tbHbEkE.
19. Philip Sabin, *Simulating War.*
20. Paul Beaves. "Blockbuster: Dstl Urban Manual Wargame COTS Assessment." Professional Wargaming, accessed July 27, 2023, https://www.professionalwargaming.co.uk/Blockbuster.pdf.
21. James Sterrett, Leveraging Commercial Games for Military Education by James Sterrett, YouTube, accessed July 28, 2023, https://www.youtube.com/watch?v=vaOY0cUDcqo.
22. "Urban Wargames Database," Airtable, accessed May 25, 2023, https://airtable.com/shreVPHaoJBpxGzFj.
23. Michael Peck, "Game Review: Operation Whirlwind – The Soviet Assault on Budapest, 1956, Blood and Concrete (Small Wars Journal).
24. Brian Train, "In magazines like Moves or Fire and Movement, there have been several pieces I can recall that were dedicated to games on specific conflicts or even battles…Nothing super-academic, though", WDDG, Groups.io, July 28, 2023, https://groups.io/g/WDDG/message/790.
25. Steve List, "On the EastFront," *Moves,* Nr. 50 (April/May 1980): 22-28.
26. Lee Brimmicombe-Wood, The Wild Blue Yonder: Representing Air Warfare in Games in *Zones of Control*, ed. Pat Harrigan & Matthew G. Kirschenbaum (Cambridge, MA: MIT Press); Steve List, "On The East Front - Twenty-Nine Games in Print: A Survey", *Moves #50, Apr-May 1980.*

27. John Spencer and Jayson Geroux, "Case Study #3, Hue", Modern Warfare Institute, accessed May 25, 2023, https://mwi.usma.edu/urban-warfare-project-case-study3-battle-of-hue/.
28. *Urban Wargames Database.*
29. Jeremy, "Guide to BoardGameGeek Weightings and Ratings, and How to Find Good Games," The Boardgame Detective, accessed May 25, 2023, https://tbgd.blog/2019/01/25/guide-to-boardgamegeek/.
30. Mike Markowitz, Wargame Graphic Design, YouTube, accessed May 25, 2023, https://www.youtube.com/watch?v=r0ir7yv7D7g.
31. Longley-Brown, Successful Professional Wargames.
32. Jennifer McArdle and Eric Hilmer. "Effectively Integrating Technology into Wargames," *2022 Interservice/Industry Training, Simulation, and Education Conference (I/ITSEC).*
33. Jay Ward, *The Battle of Hue!* (Flying Pig Games, 2020).
34. Laurent Guenette, *A Week in Hell: The Battle of Hue* (Battles Magazine, 2010).
35. Joseph Miranda, "Design Theory – Block by Block: The Battle of Hue," *Modern War #48, Jul-Aug 2020.*
36. Mark Bowden, *Hue 1968: A Turning Point of the American War in Vietnam* (New York, NY: Grove Press/Atlantic Monthly Press, 2018).
37. Alec Wahlman, Storming the City: US Military Performance in Urban Warfare from World War II to Vietnam (Denton, TX: University of North Texas Press, 2015).
38. Anthony King, *Urban Warfare in the Twenty-First Century.* (Cambridge, UK: PolityPress, 2021).
39. Wahlman, Storming the City.
40. Norm Cooling, Hue City, 1968 in *City Fights: Selected Histories of Urban Combat from World War II to Vietnam,* ed. John Antal, (New York, NY: Presidio Press, 2003).
41. Wahlman, *Storming the City.*
42. Cooling, Hue City, 1968.
43. Wahlman, *Storming the City.*
44. DiMarco, *Concrete Hell.*
45. DiMarco, *Concrete Hell.*
46. Willbanks, *The Battle of Hue 1968.*
47. Cooling, Hue City, 1968.
48. Wahlman, *Storming the City.*
49. DiMarco, *Concrete Hell.*
50. DiMarco *Concrete Hell.*
51. Wahlman, *Storming the City.*
52. Bowden, *Hue 1968.*
53. Willbanks, *The Battle of Hue* 1968.

54. Cooling, Hue City, 1968.
55. Cooling, Hue City, 1968.
56. Wahlman, *Storming the City*.
57. Willbanks, *The Battle of Hue* 1968.
58. Cooling, *Hue City*, 1968.
59. Bowden, *Hue 1968*.
60. Bowden, *Hue 1968*.
61. Cooling, Hue City, 1968.
62. Liam Collins and John Spencer, Understanding Urban Warfare, (Havant, UK: Howgate, 2022)
63. Department of Defense, *Joint Urban Operations,* Joint Publication 3-06 (Washington, D.C.: Department of Defense, 2013), https://www.jcs.mil/Portals/36/Documents/Doctrine/pubs/jp3_06.pdf
64. Philip Sabin, *Simulating War.*
65. John Curry, Peter Perla, and Chris Engle, *The Matrix Games Handbook the Matrix Games Handbook: Professional Applications from Education to Analysis and Wargaming* (Lulu.com, 2019).

CHAPTER 10
Why Cities Fail: The Urban Security Crisis in Ecuador

Jorge Mantilla, Carolina Andrade, and Maria Fe Vallejo

Introduction

Several factors explain the fall of Guayaquil, the largest city in Ecuador, in the most violent year (2022) in its history. The authors argue that state security, governance capacity dismantling, criminal wars resulting from kingpins' removal, and state-criminal arrangements were the underlying mechanisms behind the surge of violence. Parallel to state-sponsored protection rackets, state security, and justice capacity reduction in urban areas gave Organized Crime Groups (OCG) territorial control in the second most important city of the Andean country.

In short, dismantling the security governance capacities facilitated criminal encroachment and fragmentation. As a result, security and crime policies transformed from a clientelistic to a reactionary model, in which authorities implemented states of exceptions and militarized responses. However, criminal governance dynamics in peripheral neighborhoods and prisons prove state response ineffectiveness, creating more violence and political instability. This paper shows that after reaching a high-crime equilibrium situation characterized by powerful OCGs and weak state capacities—the *mano dura* (firm hand) course of action adopted by national and local authorities—fostered more violence in Guayaquil.

Previous Literature

This study builds upon literature on crime, security, and prison governance in Latin America. Bergman's crime equilibrium theory states that crime is a function of profit opportunities in illegal markets, and the strength of the criminal justice system and states to enforce the rule of law is a pillar of how the authors understand Ecuador's security landscape evolution. According to Bergman, the growth of criminal activity reflects a breakdown of the social equilibrium: A low crime equilibrium shifts to a violent high crime equilibrium at the point where the demand for illegal market goods is greater than the ability of local law enforcement to neutralize such demand, producing the growth of organized crime.[1]

Hence, crime waves between 2018 and 2022 occurred because of overwhelming profits generated by acquisitive crime or inadequate criminal justice institutional performance. Guayaquil presents both conditions: A spillover effect from the overlap of transnational and local drug markets prompts criminal factions to expand into new markets and systematically erodes criminal justice capacity at national and local levels.

The relationship between violence and criminal contagion is central to Guayaquil's security crisis. As the authors will further explain, despite the recent mano dura policy taken by the government in the city, such courses of action have proved ineffective. From a high crime equilibrium perspective, the contagion effect explains how a critical mass of delinquents forms and why changes in law enforcement rarely neutralize the powerful effects of imitation.[2]

The literature on drug violence and criminal wars in the region shapes this paper's approach to the dynamics of violence in Guayaquil and how different factions compete between them and with the state for governance, illicit economies, and territorial control. Central to organized crime dynamics in Latin America is the scale and scope of violence, which led to a debate about whether citizens are in front of a crime or a conflict challenge.

Recently, some authors have explored the operational implications of OCG tactics on the militarization of policing and the use of armed forces for citizen security purposes.[3] For Sullivan, crime wars refer to the broad range of criminal conflicts, while criminal insurgency refers to the influence of criminal conflicts and criminal governance on States and interstate institutions.[4] As criminal insurgencies are a form of crime wars, the scale of power, territorial control, and violence exhibited by OCGs becoming de facto guerilals has profound political implications.[5] In short, the appetite of OCGs in Guayaquil to gain economic and social control over marginalized urban sectors ended in hollowing state capacity and public services. Following Sullivan's typologies of criminal insurgencies, Ecuador's OCGs went from local criminal insurgencies controlling urban enclaves to engaging the state and even surpassing the military capacity of law enforcement, mining its legitimacy at a national and local level.

Ecuador is a country that transited from a low to a high crime equilibrium situation, violent competition, and where the tactics, techniques, and procedures used by OCGs will be central to the answer if Guayaquil turned into a criminal governance enclave defined as areas where lawbreakers (gangs, cartels, criminal warlords) exert political and social control.[6] Social control and operational sophistication are critical to this analysis.

The operational sophistication of OCGs speaks to the visibility and frequency of violence and how these groups communicate violence during criminal wars. Massacres, beheadings, dismemberments, and exposition of corpses with OCG messages have shocked Ecuadorian society in the past two years, signaling the dimension of the unstopped bloodbath.[7] Previous research on drug wars in Colombia and Mexico has shown that the frequency of violence increases as the illicit markets become more competitive and the visibility of violence as the state security apparatus fragments. A fragmented state sends the message it can no longer protect criminals nor dismantle criminal organizations. Durán Martinez argues that the visibility of violence depends primarily on how cohesive or fragmented the state's security apparatus is. Violence will be more visible in contexts where criminals do not expect protection or effective coercion from the state. In contexts where the market and criminal competition are fragmented, violence will be more frequent.[8]

Interactions between criminals and the state can also be open confrontation against the state or violence toward public officials and law enforcement. As per Lessing's research, OCGs deploy violence against the state when the benefits of doing so surpass the cost.[9] The prior is when states decide to launch unconditional crackdowns even more if such a course of action occurs in corrupt contexts. The conditionality of repression, how and when states use its coercive power, affects whether these groups opt for a violent rule of the underworld and, more importantly, to evade or confront the state.[10]

The city government's response to crime in Guayaquil is influenced by both the levels of violence, particularly homicide rates, and the patterns of armed territorial control. According to Monacada's findings, there are three types of political responses to territorial criminal control:

- Reactionary
- Participatory
- Clientelist

Reactionary responses involve mano dura approaches and low levels of social investment, while clientelist responses direct economic resources toward social projects to build and strengthen political support. These models are crucial to understanding and tracing the processes of security deterioration from the *Revolución Ciudadana* period to the current crime crisis in Ecuador.

Finally, the chapter states it is difficult to understand the relationship between urban features, governance, and violence amid criminal wars without looking at how the penitentiary crisis in Ecuador shapes interactions between criminal factions. To do so, the authors build on Skarberk's theory of prison governance to explore how what happens inside prisons in Guayaquil informs what happens in the streets. From the prison's governance perspective, all prisoners face the general problem of order and need for services, but how governance varies from prison to prison depends on local conditions.[11] For instance, Latin American prisons are way more crowded and violent than prisons in Western Europe, while they share the fundamentals of confinement. Political economy determines how prisons, prison life, and inmate populations are organized, which explains this variation.

Following Skarberk, prisons present a fundamental issue of the political economy related to how institutions emerge to control and distribute power. In the absence of formal institutions and scarce confidence, prisoners often create institutions as forms of self-help.[12] Challenges such as untrustworthiness and direct threats, corruption, and the lack of services or access to leisure are among the reasons prisoners might resort to mechanisms of extralegal governance.[13]

Hence, there are at least four formats of prison extralegal governance:

- Official governance regimes
- Co-governance regimes
- Self-governance regimes
- No governance regimes

According to the data, Guayaquil's prison extralegal governance stands between a co-governance and a self-governance regime.

Why Guayaquil? Security and Crime Context, 2018-2022

In 2005, Ecuador was under siege of violence; the homicide rate was 17.6 per 100,000 inhabitants. In the subsequent years, Ecuador became the second-safest country in the region, with a sustained reduction in homicide rates.[14] In 2015, international organizations wondered what happened to the best-paid police in Latin America.[15] The Interamerican Development Bank IDB highlighted the growth in public investment in security from 1 percent of the gross domestic product (GDP) to 2.3 percent. This translated into strengthening physical, human, technical, and technological capacities. The average salary of a recently graduated police officer went from $358 US dollars in 2006 to $933 in 2016.[16]

Legal and institutional reforms accompanied public investment growth. In 2004, the Ecuadorian government introduced the Modernization Plan of the National Police. In 2007, with the Police Modernization Commission and, in 2008, with the new Constitution, a fundamental reformation of the security institutions came into place, centered on a new constitutional approach to integral security.[17] During the following years, these changes translated into new regulatory frameworks and comprehensive security management models. It went from a military police model that privileged repression to one of community police transforming the security institutional landscape.

However, since 2018, the crime statistics trend has shifted. The number of intentional homicides suffered an increment of 347 percent between 2018 and 2022, reaching a rate of 25.6 homicides per 100,000 inhabitants, making 2022 the most violent year in Ecuador's history.[18] Violence has become more evident with a spiking homicide rate, primarily concentrated in the provinces of Guayas (35 percent), Manabí (10 percent), Los Ríos (9 percent), and Esmeraldas (9 percent).

Currently, Guayas amounts to 3642 homicides registered between 2018-2022. Within this province, Guayaquil concentrates 68 percent of the total homicides, making it the second most violent city in the country after Esmeraldas, which reached a 77.4 homicide rate in 2022.

Figure 1. Intentional Homicides in Guayaquil (2018-2022)

Elaborated by Authors with Data from National Police, 2022. Note: Data is available until August 2022.

Guayaquil, Ecuador's largest city, has 2.6 million residents and contributes 20 percent to the national GDP. It is the second-largest economic center, primarily due to its role as a major maritime port. Ranked 7th in Latin America, Guayaquil's port handles a significant amount of cargo, with an average throughput of 2.06 million between 2019-2021, accounting for 91.4 percent of the country's freight.[19] Ecuador's role in the global production of illicit economies tied to drug trafficking has put the State in a critical situation. The National Police has reported that in 4 out of 10 intentional homicides, the primary motivation is drug trafficking.[20]

Figure 2. Intentional Homicides per Motive (2018-2022)

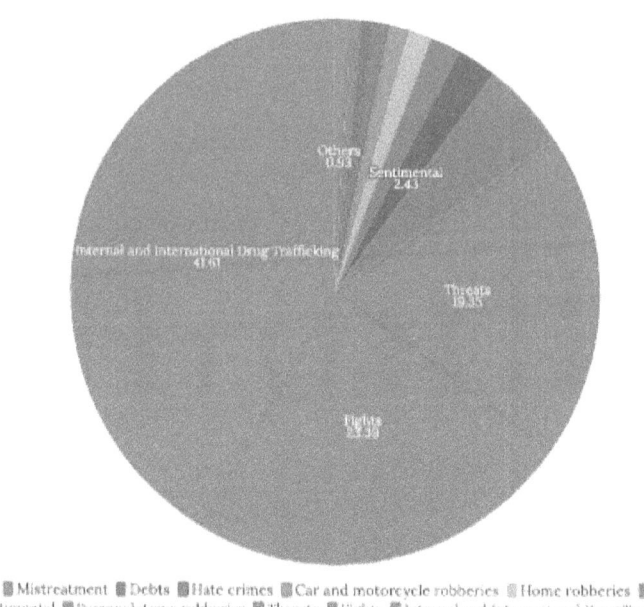

Elaborated by Authors with Data from National Police, 2022.
Note: Data is available until January 2022.

In all districts of Guayaquil, the National Police registers a growth of more than 200 percent in extortion, especially in Durán, Nueva Prosperina, and Pascuales. From the complaints made at the national level about extortion, less than 10 percent have received a favorable court ruling, while the rest continue to be investigated by the police.[21]

Figure 3. Number of Extortion Registered in Guayaquil per District (2018-2022)

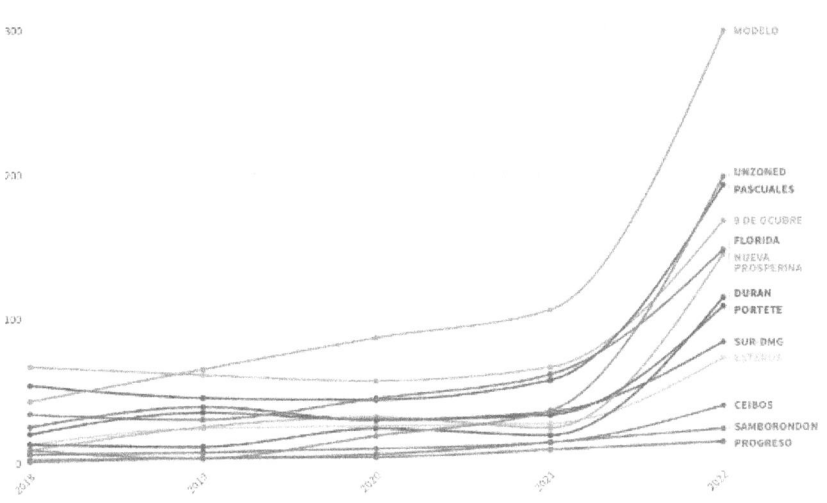

Elaborated by Authors with Data from National Police, 2022.

Until August 2022, there were 147 bomb attacks in the national territory. Over 49.7 percent of the attacks occurred in Guayaquil, Durán, and Samborondón, resulting in 72 explosions. In 2022, 50 attacks with explosives took place, mainly in the Pascuales district on the northern side of the city.[22] Such transformation marks the operational sophistication of OCGs and the way crime equilibrium shifted in the city.

Figure 4. Explosive Attacks by Metropolitan Districts, 2022

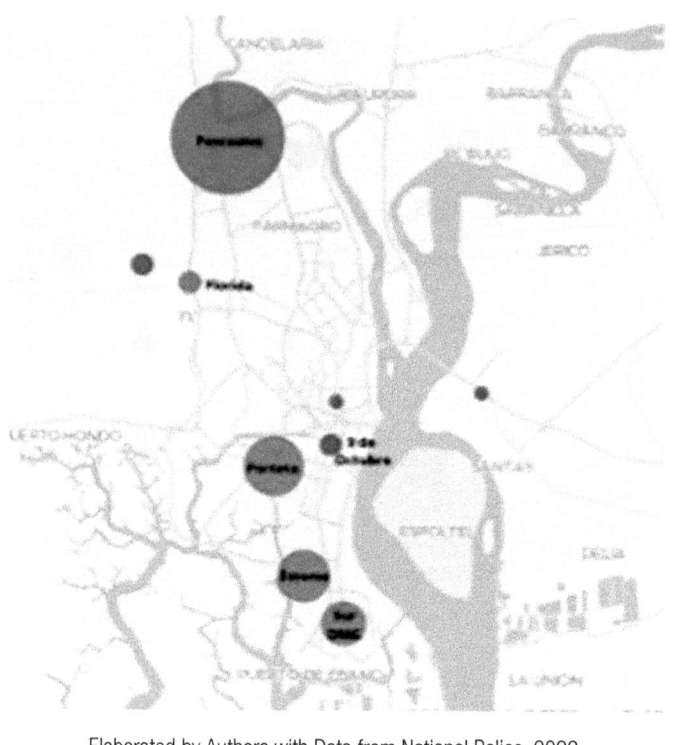

Elaborated by Authors with Data from National Police, 2022.

Confrontations between competing OCGs to control the growing cocaine trade are responsible for the violence spike. Additionally, Balkan traffickers have settled in Guayaquil, establishing supply lines to European markets.[23] In 2021, 33 percent of seized cocaine was destined for Europe, a significant increase from 9 percent in 2019. Despite not being a cocaine production site, Ecuador has witnessed record cocaine busts. From 2019 to 2021, cocaine seizures increased by 150 percent, totaling 210 seizures nationally, with Guayaquil contributing 96 tons.[24] In comparison, Colombia produced 972 tons of cocaine and seized 670 tons in the same period. Ecuador ranks third globally in cocaine interdiction, accounting for 6.5 percent of seizures, trailing behind Colombia (41 percent) and the United States (11 percent).[25]

Figure 5. Cocaine Seizures in Guayaquil (2018-2022)

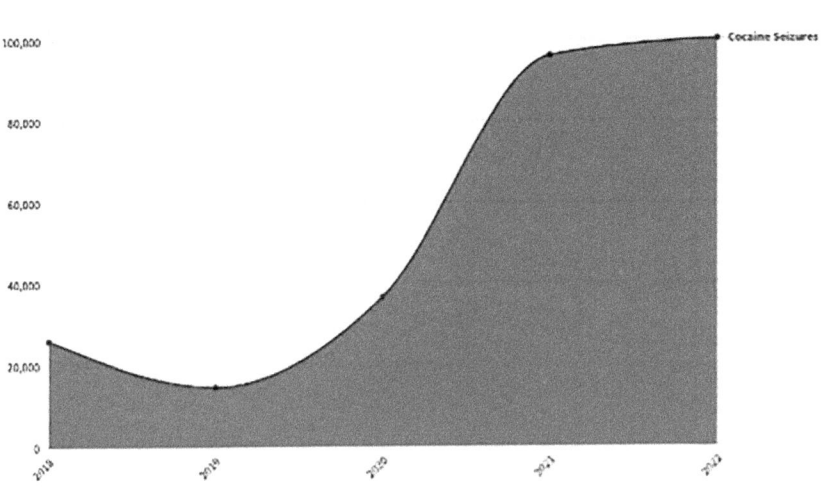

Elaborated by Authors with Data from National Police, 2022.

Due to its strategic location, Guayaquil has become a promised land for drug trafficking and criminal organizations. Through its ports, Guayaquil serves as a gateway of drugs to international markets and an ideal location for Albanian gangs to find partners.

Figure 6. Cocaine Seizures per District (2018-2022)

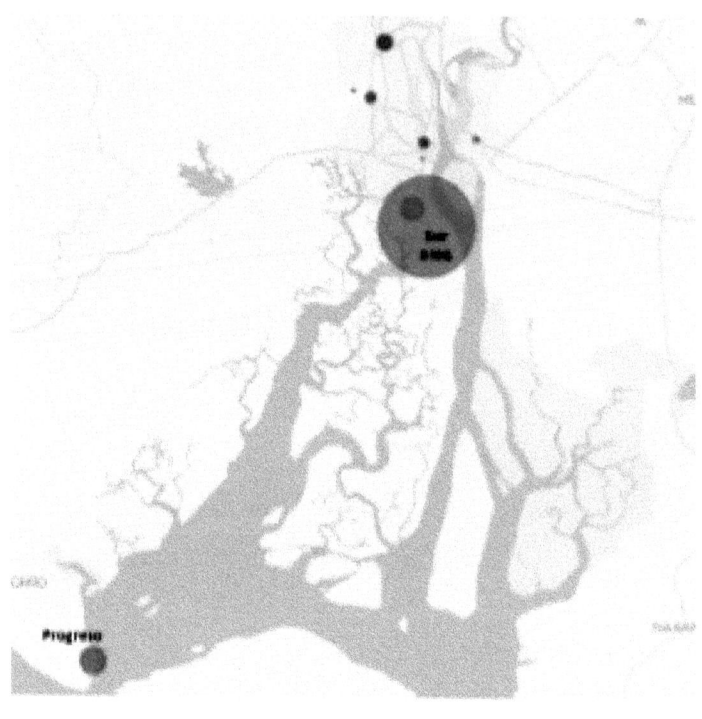

Elaborated by Authors with Data from National Police, 2022.

From its ports, cocaine is transported in ship containers, severely underinspected by authorities.[26] Lax border controls, corruption, dollarization, and the lack of an integrated security strategy have facilitated criminal enterprises. The growth of the international drug market embedded in the coastal urban setting and its port impacts the interactions among OCGs and the state.

Guayaquil's Criminal Map: Organizations and Crime-affected Areas

Organized crime and drug trafficking are not new threats in Ecuador. According to the Global Organized Crime Index, Ecuador ranks 11 below countries such as Colombia and Paraguay. Ecuador has the tenth highest level of crime, with an evaluation of 7.07, above the global average of 5.03, while countries like Mexico (7.57) and Honduras (7.05) have among the highest levels in Latin America.

Until 2020, the *Choneros* was the organization that monopolized criminal violence in Ecuador. In charge of the cocaine transfer routes to Ecuador's interior, shipments' security, and prisons' apparent peace, the *Choneros* were the privileged partners of Mexican and Colombian cartels. However, the release of its leader *Rasquiña* and his murder soon after would unleash a dispute over a new leadership and control in the monopoly of criminal violence.

Since 2020, two OCGs have operated at the national level: *Los Choneros* and *Los Lobos* control routes for the shipment of drugs to international markets. These OCGs are cartels' allies. On one hand, the *Choneros* work with the Sinaloa Cartel; on the other, *Los Lobos* are in alliance with the *Jalisco Nueva Generación Cartel*. These OCGs coordinate their criminal actions with local criminal gangs, mainly in the coastal zone. Los *Choneros*, for its part, maintains alliances with *Los Gangsters, Los Águilas, Los Fantasmas*, and *Los Fatales*; and *Los Lobos* work in criminal alliances with *Los Tiguerones, Los Lagartos, Los Chones Killers*, and *Los Ñetas*.

Figure 7. Location of Criminal Organizations in Guayaquil's Territory (2022)

Elaborated by Authors with Data from National Police, 2022. Note: Criminal Organizations distribute and compete the control of Prison wards in the Penitentiary Complex.

These organizations compete to control drug trafficking areas in multiple provinces. Although the criminal business revolves around international cocaine trafficking, each organization takes part in different criminal activities, whether controlling drug trafficking networks, crimes such as robberies, or providing criminal services such as assassination, kidnapping, and extortion linked to attacks with explosive devices. These criminal organizations have expanded into environmental crimes like illegal gold mining and logging related to money laundering networks.

Prisons and Massacres

Since 2021, Ecuador has witnessed over twelve massacres inside its prisons, in which over 400 inmates have died. Seven of these massacres occurred in the Guayaquil prison complex, killing approximately 260 inmates in a set of incidents provoked by what the director of Ecuador's penitentiary director called a struggle to keep the status quo inside prisons.[27] The previous toll represents a 587 percent increase in deaths under state custody compared to 2020. This section explains the status quo or prison order that has ruled prisons in Ecuador and Guayas. Then, it explores the governance of prisons in Guayaquil by OCGs and how fragmentation affected levels of violence within them.

Ecuador's incarceration rate has grown because of the excessive use of preemptive prison, obstacles to applying alternative sanctions, and the lack of a criminal and penitentiary policy centered on re-socializing and rehabilitating inmates. Until 2021, 44.24 percent of the population imprisoned in Ecuador were between 18 and 30 years old, while the majority were repeat offenders without the support of their families.[28] Approximately 56.8 percent (22,000) of the total inmates are already under a judiciary sentence, while 43.08 percent (17,000) are imprisoned preventively. Almost 50 percent (20,000) of the inmates have served between 40 and 80 percent of their time, which makes them eligible for reentry programs, including parole.[29]

Paradoxically, parallel to the steady increment of the incarcerated population and the rise of a penitentiary system crisis, the public budget and other resources allocated towards prisons were reduced by 64 percent only in 2021.[30] Such reductions are the continuation of the system's capacity dismantling and the culprit for prison extralegal governance. As stated by the Inter-American Commission on Human Rights, the absence of space can generate different problems inside prisons related to sanitation, violence, insecurity, prison subculture, and the reduction of essential services quality.[31]

The two prisons that are key to this analysis are *Litoral* and *La Roca*. While *Litoral* is the main prison complex, *La Roca* is a maximum security prison that closed in 2013 due to a massive escape but reopened in 2021 as a response to the prison crisis. The prominent leaders of the *Choneros*, *Lobos*, and R7 remain in *La Roca*, which has caused numerous incidents and a few massacres.[32] On the contrary, the *Litoral* penitentiary is where most inmates remain. The overcrowding in the prison system in Guayas is particularly critical. The five penitentiaries of the province, which can host 9553 inmates, host 39 percent (12,291) of the national inmate population (31,216), translating into an overpopulation rate of 29 percent and a 12 percent nationally, 12 percent.[33]

On February 23, 2021, a coordinated attack against *Choneros'* middle rank occurred in four prisons across the country, leaving a toll of 78 inmates assassinated. After the death of *Rasquiña* in December 2020, this was the first backlash in the process of *Choneros'* fragmentation from an OCG that transformed from a drug dealing organization to one of the most prominent prison gangs in the last decade. This was not the first episode of violence between prison gangs. However, it was the bloodiest prison massacre in Ecuadorian history. Journalist, Carolina Mella, explains:

> To survive in the jail, inmates must belong to one band. It is hard to pass a low profile, even more so in this penitentiary (Litoral), known as a hellhole. Families are afraid that anything they say can be misconstrued [sic] by the band's leaders. Because of that, what prevails is silence.[34]

Besides the institutionalization and expansion of the prison code, another repercussion of the intramural wars between OCGs was the degradation of violence and the communication of threats, killings, and terror. After the massacre of February, episodes of massive violence continued without authorities being able to stop them. Remarkably, on September 28 at *Litoral*, an incident in which *Lagartos* and *Tiguerones* entered Pavilion 5 under *Chonero*'s control claimed the lives of 125 inmates. Forensic authorities showed how the attack included beheadings, mayhem, and corpse incineration to the extent that some victims were not identifiable.

Guayaquil's underworld is prison-governed, necessitating power management and collective action within prisons to control street crime and drug trafficking. A violent reputation is critical to communicating power shifts in criminal fragmentation, corruption, and limited law enforcement contexts. To prevail, OCG must provide credible protection, which necessitates high levels of violence. Assessing the urban security crisis involves revealing spatial complexity and power circuits between the coast, prisons, and slums. As depicted in Figure 8, Pascuales, Prosperina, and the South DMG exhibit the highest homicide concentration. Notably, these districts house the critical urban assets for controlling illicit economies: Prisons, public housing ghettos, and the port. This geography shapes Ecuador's urban crisis.

Figure 8. Intentional Homicides by Metropolitan Districts 2018-2022

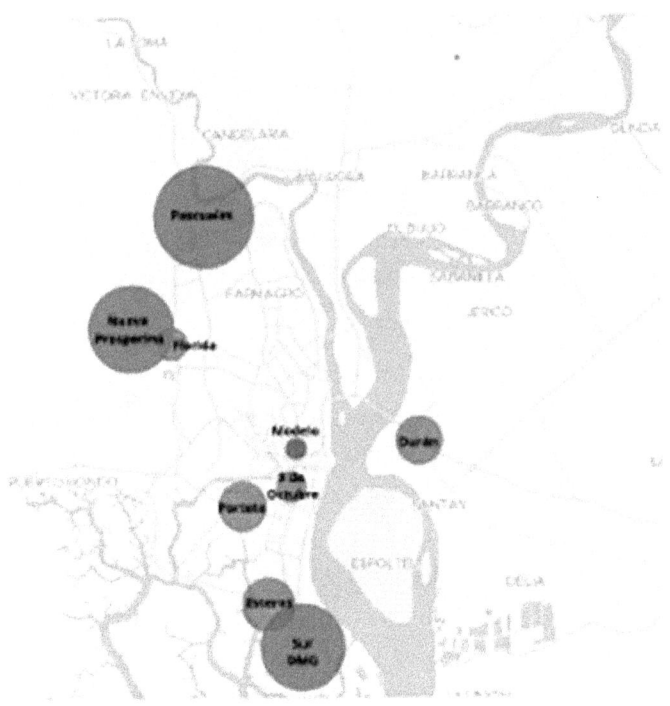

Elaborated by Authors with Data from National Police, 2022.

Regarding state criminal collusion, the Commission of Penitentiary Pacification stated that criminal fragmentation and systemic corruption within law enforcement and the penitentiary system made any intent of peace agreements with OCGs impossible. The report described the situation as an unequal system imposed by OCGs inside prisons: "The leaders of the groups force hunger strikes when they want to protest, while (them) receive excellent food in the max security pavilion at the *Regional*."[35] The privileges surrounding the bosses include barricades for protection and better armament than the army, all under the public force's protection.[36] In the next section, the authors analyze state-criminal interactions after President Lasso launched a mano dura campaign in Guayaquil, proving to be widely ineffective and increasing violence.

State Response: Mano Dura Narrative

The mano dura approach is common in Latin America. Despite lacking active armed conflicts, the region has become the world's most violent because of persistent violent democratic political systems with multiple parties in which elections are conducted periodically but have been unable to assure the monopoly of violence.[37] Consequently, insecurity and criminal violence are endemic across the region, and formerly peaceful countries now face significant security challenges.

In 2018, the destruction of the state's governance capacities and security governance began. This resulted in the elimination of the Coordinating Ministry of Security, responsible for strategic and intersectoral planning and public policies; the Ministry of the Interior, in charge of citizen security policy–which was integrated into political management under the figure of a Ministry of Government; the Ministry of Justice and Human Rights and Cults (MJDDH), in charge of the social rehabilitation system and management of prions; as well as the governing body of State Strategic Intelligence, in charge of coordinating the National Intelligence System. See Table 1.

Table 1. Modifications in the Security Institutional Framework, 2017-2022.

Date	Institutional Modification
May 2017	Through Executive Decree No. 7, the administration eliminated the Ministry of Security Coordination to reduce the state's spending.
January 2018	Ecuador registered the first terrorist attack in its history. A car bombing took place in San Lorenzo, Esmeraldas. After this event, OCG perpetrated multiple attacks against the National Police and journalists.
September 2018	The government announced the closure of the National Intelligence Secretariat. The Strategic Intelligence Center replaced it and took on the coordination of the National Intelligence System.
November 2018	The government announced the transformation of The MJDDH into the Human Rights Secretariat. Besides, its control over the prison turned over to the newly created SNAI.
December 2018	The Ministry of Interior, with all its functions, and the Public Management Secretariat merged under one entity, the Ministry of Government.
March 2022	Executive Decree No. 381 established the new configuration of the Ministry of Government. This entity remained but passed the public security management to the Ministry of Interior.
April 2022	Lasso presented the Strategic Plan for Security that assigns an investment of 1.2 million dollars to fight organized crime and drug trafficking.
August 2022	Executive Decree No. 514 created the National Secretariat of Public and State Security to create a new coordinating body of national security. This entity builds public policy, plans, and directs the Public Security System.

Note: Institutional modifications took place through executive decisions made by the administrations. Lenin Moreno was President between 2017-2021, and Guillermo Lasso came to power in May 2021. Elaborated by Authors.

These changes in public administration were not minor. There was a reduction, weakening, and elimination of qualified and professionalized human resources, appropriate financial resources, and technical and technological capabilities. The weakening of governance capacities generated comparative opportunities for the advancement of OCGs in a regional scenario with a historically increasing trend of crops for the illicit use of coca and a social and economic crisis post-COVID-19.

Institutional changes in 2018 should have resulted in a reorientation of the political-strategic vision of the Security Sector, not in eliminating governance capacities necessary to address existing threats. As a result, there was a shift from a model committed to prevention to one increasingly accustomed to repressive reactions that do not allow strategic thinking in medium and long-term scenarios at the state level.

Faced with a severe security crisis, the measures taken by the state were the declaration, via decrees, of forms of exception. This 'patch response' focused on trying to contain the accelerated growth of criminal violence–homicide rate–without addressing the structural causes of its increase. Proof of the failure of reactive-dispersed actions is that President Lasso decreed seven states of exception due to severe internal commotion, one revoked by the National Assembly.[38] Until April 2023, President Lasso enacted four states of emergency: three due to extreme internal unrest due to increasing crime and violence rates, and one due to public calamity.

In the case of Guayaquil, President Lasso announced a Special Security Plan from the *El Guasmo* slum in the Proserpina district in April 2022. The plan consisted of three pillars which were:

- Violence Contention
- OCGs dismantling
- Community empowerment.

In practice, the plan's focus, which cost $1.2 million, was dismantling OCGs, particularly incarcerating its members. President Lasso's orders were clear: "The important thing is to catch the heads of these bands that sow terror among the community. We need to catch them, send them to La Roca, and neutralize them."[39] Implementing the plan enhanced the prison crisis and empowered OCG in the penitentiary system.

The data reveals the failure of the actions classified as contingency, for example, states of exception, the militarization of streets, increased penalties, and the lack of a comprehensive security strategy. This is a set of mano dura actions that are not sustainable over time due to their limited focus limitations and mid- and long-term effectiveness. Likewise, it is an intervention that only contemplates a more excellent police and military presence to deter crime without planning a comprehensive intervention involving other sectors to recover the territories with their population under the control of organized crime.

Conclusion

Combining mano dura policies with fragmented criminal justice institutions exacerbates urban violence. When this happens in the context of systemic corruption and criminal fragmentation, crises emerge as violence toward state officials and organized crime groups gain power and sophistication. As the case of Guayaquil shows, these dynamics are spatially informed as while illicit economies take place in the streets, the decision-making of criminal wars takes place behind prison walls. For that reason, inmate transfer policies can ignite or contain violence, depending on the dynamics of alignment and fragmentation between OCGs. This chapter has made an essential contribution to urban security studies in Latin America by analyzing how cities fail in an unexplored setting such as Guayaquil.

Theoretically, the chapter connects the literature on criminal and prison governance, assessing how urban security policies must consider the spatial connections between prisons, violent slums, and illicit economic circuits—in this case, authors argued that the shifts in the role of Ecuador within the transnational drug market had drastic implications for prison violence and urban security. Contrary to politicians' assumptions in the region, despite how popular the tough-on-crime narrative might be, their implementation in high-crime equilibrium cities demands more than formal states of exception.

Policy-wise, Ecuador will need years to recover from the crime and violence spiral that it is currently undergoing. To do so, the country will need, in the first place, to solve the penitentiary crisis by moving toward a co-governance penitentiary regime that contains violence and manages criminal fragmentation. However, that would not be possible if the institutional infrastructure is not reinstalled in the midterm building capacities to prevent and control crime.

Endnotes

1. Marcelo Bergman, More Money, More Crime: Prosperity and Rising Crime in Latin America (New York: Oxford University Press, 2018).
2. Bergman, More Money, More Crime, 21.
3. John P. Sullivan, "Crime Wars: Operational Perspectives on Criminal Armed Groups in Mexico and Brazil," *International Review of the Red Cross* 105, no.923 (September 2022):1-27, https://doi.org/10.1017/S1816383122000558.
4. Sullivan, "Crime Wars," 3.
5. John P. Sullivan, "From Drug Wars to Criminal Insurgency: Mexican Cartels, Criminal Enclaves and Criminal Insurgency in Mexico and Central America. Implications for Global Security," *Working Paper No 9, Paris: Fondation Maison des sciences de l'homme*, April 2012, https://www.academia.edu/1539613/From_Drug_Wars_to_Criminal_Insurgency _Mexican_Cartels_Criminal.
6. John P. Sullivan, "Criminal Enclaves: When Gangs, Cartels, or Kingpins Try to Take Control," *Stratfor,* July 10, 2019, criminal-enclaves-when-gangs-cartels-orkingpins-try-take-control20190711-9925-166dxOo.pdf.
7. Sara España, "El Hallazgo de Dos Cadáveres Colgados en un Puente en Ecuador Dispara las Alarmas por la Violencia del Narcotráfico (The Finding of Two Bodies Hanging on a Bridge in Ecuador Triggers Alarms over Drug Trafficking Violence)," *El País* (Madrid), February 14, 2022, https://elpais.com/internacional/2022-0215/el-hallazgo-de-dos-cadaveres-colgados-en-un-puente-en-ecuador-dispara-lasalarmas-por-la-violencia-del-narcotrafico.html; "Hallan en Buena Fe Varios Cuerpos Desmembrados en Sacos de Yute (Several Dismembered Bodies Found in Jute Bags in Buena Fe)," *El Universo* (Guayaquil), April 27, 2023, https://www.eluniverso.com/noticias/seguridad/hallan-en-buena-fe-varioscuerpos-desmembrados-en-sacos-de-yute-nota/.
8. Durán-Martínez, The Politics of Drug Violence, 47.
9. Benjamin Lessing, Making Peace in Drug Wars: Crackdowns and Cartels in Latin America, (Cambridge: Cambridge University Press, 2018).

10. Lessing, Making Peace in Drug Wars, 277.
11. David Skarbek, The Puzzle of Prison Order: Why Life Behind Bars Varies Around the World (New York: Oxford University Press, 2020), 2.
12. Michelle Butler, Gavin Slade, and Camila Nunes Dias, "Self-governing Prisons: Prison Gangs in an International Perspective," *Trends in Organized Crime* 25, (March 2018), https://doi.org/10.1007/s12117-018-9338-7.
13. Skarbek, The puzzle of prison order, 6.
14. "Homicide Monitor," Igarapé Institute, accessed April 14, 2023, https://homicide.igarape.org.br/?l=es; Ministerio del Interior, *Análisis de Homicidios en Ecuador 1980-2017* (Homicide Analysis in Ecuador 1980-2017), October 2018, https://laverdadvencera.ec/wp content/uploads/2022/01/documento2seguridad.pdf.
15. Pablo Bachelet and Mauricio García, "¿Qué Ocurre con la Policía Mejor Pagada de América Latina? (What happens with Latin America's Highest-paid Police?)," *InterAmerican Development Bank* (blog), February 13, 2015, https://blogs.iadb.org/seguridad-ciudadana/es/que-ocurre-cuando-se-tiene-lapolicia-mejor-pagada-de-america-latina/.
16. Secretaría de Planificación y Desarrollo, *Informe a la Nación 2007-2017* (Report to the Nation 2007-2017), https://www.planificacion.gob.ec/wpcontent/uploads/downloads/2017/04/Informe-a-la-Nacion.pdf.
17. UNDP, *Human Development Report New Dimensions of Human Security*, (New York: Oxford University Press, 1994), https://hdr.undp.org/system/files/documents//hdr1994encompletenostatspdf.pdf.
18. Policía Nacional/ Estadísticas de Homicidios Intencionales; (2018-2022; accessed May 1, 2023), http://cifras.ministeriodegobierno.gob.ec/comisioncifras/inicio.php#.
19. CEPAL, "Informe Portuario 2021: Las Primeras Señales de Recuperación en el Transporte Marítimo Internacional Vía Contenedores de América Latina y el Caribe (Port Report 2021: The First Signs of Recovery in International Maritime Transport Via Containers in Latin America and the Caribbean)," *Facilitación Comercio y Logística en América Latina y el Caribe* 1, no.391 (2022).
20. Policía Nacional/ Estadísticas de Homicidios Intencionales; (2018-2022; accessed May 23, 2023), http://181.113.21.13:8080/registroinicialwar/metaMicrodatos.html.
21. Carolina Mella, "La Extorsión Crece un 300% en Ecuador y Sigue en Aumento (Extorsion Grows 300% in Ecuador and Continues to Increase)," *El País* (Madrid), February 20, 2023, https://elpais.com/internacional/2023-02-20/la-extorsioncrece-un-300-en-ecuador-y-sigue-en-aumento.html.
22. Policía Nacional, Análisis de Violencia y Delincuencia.
23. Global Initiative, "Western Balkans Criminal Groups Are Contributing to Drugrelated Violence in Ecuador," *Risk Buletin* 14 (February 2023), https://riskbulletins.globalinitiative.net/see-obs-014/02-western-balkanscriminal-groups-contributing-to-drug-related-violence.html.
24. Policía Nacional/ Estadísticas de Incautaciones de Cocaína; (2018-2022; accessed May 23, 2023); Ean Doherty and Douwe Den Held, "InSight Crime's Cocaine Seizure Round-Up 2022," *Insight Crime,* March 8, 2022, https://insightcrime.org/news/insight-crimes-cocaine-seizure-round-up-2022/.

25. Carolina Andrade, Mac Margolis and Robert Muggah, "Ecuador's Crime Wave and Its Albanian Connection," *Americas Quarterly,* April 12, 2023, https://www.americasquarterly.org/article/ecuadors-crime-wave-and-its-albanianconnection/.
26. Carolina Andrade, Mac Margolis and Robert Muggah, "Ecuador's Crime Wave and Its Albanian Connection."
27. Comisión Interamericana de Derechos Humanos (CIDH), *Personas Privadas de Libertad en Ecuador* (Persons Deprived of Liberty in Ecuador), (February 2022), https://www.oas.org/es/cidh/informes/pdfs/Informe-PPL-Ecuador_VF.pdf.
28. CIDH, Personas Privadas de Libertad en Ecuador.
29. Carla Morena, "Las Cárceles de la Muerte en Ecuador (Death Prisons in Ecuador)," *Nuso,* January, 2022, https://nuso.org/articulo/las-carceles-de-la-muerte-enecuado/.
30. Mario González, "El Gobierno Redujo en 64% el Costo del Plan de Mejoras Opara las Cárceles (The Government Cuts the Cost of the Prison Improvement Plan by 64%)," *Primicias* (Quito), August 19, 2021, https://www.primicias.ec/noticias/politica/carceles-reduccion-presupuesto-emergencia/.
31. Álvaro Castro Morales, "Estándares de la Corte Interamericana de Derechos Humanos en Materia de Imputados y Condenados Privados de Libertad (Standards of the Inter-American Court of Human Rights on Defendants and Condemned Persons Deprived of Liberty)," *Anuario de Derechos Humanos* no.14 (2018): 35-54, https://doi.org/10.5354/0718-2279.2018.49161.
32. "Estas son las Seguridades en la Cárcel La Roca, onde la Tarde de Este Martes, 4 de abril, se Generaron Incidentes entre Reos (These are the Security Measures at La Roca Prison, where on this Tuesday Afternoon, April 4, Incidents Occurred Between Inmates.)," *El Universo* (Guayaquil), April 4, 2023, https://www.eluniverso.com/noticias/seguridad/estas-son-las-seguridades-en-lacarcel-la-roca-donde-la-tarde-de-este-martes-4-de-abril-se-generaron-incidentesentre-reos-nota/.
33. "Estas son las seguridades en la cárcel La Roca," *El Universo.*
34. Fernanda Paúl and Ángel Bermúdez, "Ecuador: El Drama de los Familiares de los Presos Tras la Peor Masacre Carcelaria de la Historia del país, que Dejó al Menos 118 Muertos (Ecuador: The Drama of the Relatives of the Prisoners After the Worst Prison Massacre in the History of the Country, Which Left At Least 118 Dead)," *BBC,* September 30, 2021, https://www.bbc.com/mundo/noticias-america-latina58721703.
35. Comisión Para el Diálogo Penitenciario y la Pacificación, *Informe Primer Trimestre de Gestión* (First Quarter Management Report), March, 2022,
36. Comisión Para el Diálogo Penitenciario y la Pacificación, *Informe Primer Trimestre de Gestión* (First Quarter Management Report), March, 2022, https://www.planv.com.ec/sites/default/files/analisis_y_propuestas_de_la_comis ion_para_el_dialogo_penitenciario_y_pacificacion_version_final.pdf.
37. Desmond Arias and Daniel M. Goldstein, eds., *Violent. Democracies in Latin America* (Durham: Duke University Press, 2010).
38. Peter Appleby, et al., "Balance de InSight Crime de los Homicidios en 2022 (Insight Crime Balance of Homicides in 2022)," *InSight Crime,* February 8, 2023, https://es.insightcrime.org/noticias/balance-insight-crime-dhomicidios-en-2022/.

39. "Guillermo Lasso Presenta Plan de Seguridad para Guayaquil que Costará Cerca de $1.200 Millones (Guillermo Lasso Presents Security Plan for Guayaquil that Will Cost Nearly $1.2 Billion)," *Vistazo*, April 8, 2022, https://www.vistazo.com/politica/nacional/guillermo-lasso-presenta-plan-deseguridad-para-guayaquil-que-costara-cerca-de-1200-millones-Bl1569560.

CHAPTER 11
The Political Trajectory of Urban Violence: Organized Crime in Michoacán's Apatzingán

Fausto Carbajal

Introduction

Urban violence has swiftly become one of the most severe threats worldwide, mainly to democratic governance and citizen security on a local scale.[1] Specifically, homicidal violence perpetrated by violent nonstate actors—chief among them organized crime groups (OCGs)—is currently the dominant form of armed violence in the cities, from Medellin Rio de Janeiro to Cape Town, Lagos, and Karachi.[2] This trend is occurring in Mexican cities as well.[3]

Building on previous research,[4] the present article delves into the following questions: What are the underlying sources and drivers of large-scale violence in urban settings in Mexico? What role do Mexican OCGs play in today's urban violence? Answering these questions may contribute to research on urban security challenges in the 21ˢᵗ century, contemporary conflict-crime nexus, and future trends of organized political violence.[5]

To advance this research agenda, this article proposes the political trajectory of urban violence (PTUV) as an additional analytical category to nuance the developmental process of today's urban violence in Mexico. By adopting a historical perspective on urban violence, the PTUV posits that today's organized crime-related violence in multiple Mexican cities has unveiled—and exacerbated—intricate power tensions and reconfigurations among private legal actors (especially economic and political ones), which need to be explored.[6] As such, the historical evolution of these political processes at the local level is critical to explaining current cases of urban violence commonly associated with criminal activity. The PTUV regards organized crime-related violence as part of a continuum of a political complex in urban environments and not only because of criminal conduct or activity, per se.

A concrete case study is central to testing the PTUV; this article focuses on the city of Apatzingán, Michoacán. Indeed, this exploratory research suggests that recent outbreaks of organized crime-related violence in Apatzingán have resulted from a rooted local conflict over land access, economic hegemony, and political dominance. The case study research was based on the "intensive study of a single unit…to understand a larger class of similar units (a population of cases)."[7] This said, and building on Flyvbjerg's work on case study designs, the present case study of homicidal violence in Apatzingán seeks to produce more generalizable knowledge on the political, social, and economic factors associated with the micro-dynamics of violence in Mexico beneath the macro-cleavage known as criminal violence.[8]

The chapter has the following structure: After briefly describing the methodology, section two outlines Mexico's security landscape and highlights why Apatzingán is a helpful case study for this research agenda. Section three scrutinizes from a historical perspective different sources of urban violence in Apatzingán and the processes through which urbanization took place. Section four analyzes the multi-sourced nature of today's lethal violence in the city of Apatzingán. This section argues that four chronologically ordered processes (the democratization process, criminal pluralism, criminal fragmentation, and political fragmentation), have exacerbated conflicts over land access, political domination, and economic hegemony. The article concludes with final comments, policy implications, and the next steps in the research agenda.

Methodology

This chapter is based on field research conducted in Apatzingán, Michoacán from August to November 2021. It portrays the testimonies of six key participants—political and economic elites in Apatzingán—who were interviewed in a semi-structured fashion. Interviews were carried out on the following dates: Interviewee 1 (local politician) on 24 August 2021; Interviewee 2 (rancher) on 19 September 2021; Interviewee 3 (state-level politician/businessman) on 9 October 2021; Interviewee 4 (agricultural entrepreneur) on 17 October 2021, Interviewee 5 (local party leader) on 22 October 2021, Interviewee 6 (businessman) on 8 November 2021.

Although the information was not processed with qualitative data analysis software, these interviews were illustrative accounts of power dynamics and urban violence in Apatzingán. The participants came from different ideological, political, or economic backgrounds but shared similar viewpoints regarding the dynamics and cycles of urban violence in Apatzingán. To prevent potential data validity and reliability problems, the author employed open-source data from local and nationwide newspapers and literature on criminal violence, organized crime, and illicit networks in Michoacán.

The questionnaire included the following themes: the role of federal, state, and municipal governments; the War on Drugs and its impact on Apatzingán; the crime-government nexus; organized crime and political violence; democratization in Apatzingán; urbanization and inequality; disputes over natural resources; the role of economic and political elites at the local level; dynamics in homicidal violence; and criminal fragmentation.

I took notes during the interviews and recorded them with a voice recorder. The participants' safety was ensured at all times.

An Illustration of Mexico's Criminal Violence

In December 2006, the newly sworn-in president Felipe Calderon implemented a campaign against OCGs operating in Mexico.[9] The strategy—commonly known as kingpin strategy—comprised large-scale joint operations by federal forces aimed at dismantling the most powerful criminal cartels by then.[10] However, the use of military force caused an utter fragmentation and reconfiguration of the criminal underworld, as well as the creation of illicit economies and an unprecedented increase in homicidal violence.[11]

Michoacán has been one of the most affected states in Mexico by largescale violence ever since the fight against organized crime started.[12] In the words of a participant:

> During that time [2011] things got quite messy. Some places in Michoacán looked like a war zone. We don't need to go very far—you could see human corpses piled up in the middle of the streets and scenes like that here in Apatzingán. Yes, in the beginning I did support the government's actions against criminality, but eventually things turned out to be counterproductive, too much blood.[13]

Although considerable security improvements have been made since 2011, Apatzingán remains a violent municipality.[14] Between May 2022 and April 2023, it registered a rate of 27.7 homicides per 100,000 inhabitants.[15]

Recurrent turf disputes and waves of homicidal violence in Apatzingán also have a geographic explanation.[16] It is a strategic city as it is the region's closest urban hub to the Pacific coastline (see Figure 1), in particular to Lázaro Cárdenas, one of the most important city ports in México and a central point for criminal activities, chief among these drugdealing—particularly, synthetic drugs and precursor chemicals coming from China—as well as the creation of illicit economies such as the iron ore mining.[17]

Although this chapter focuses on its urban aspects, the city of Apatzingán is a clear example of the urban-rural dichotomy. On the one hand, Apatzingán is one the most important urban enclaves in the state of Michoacán as it is home to government offices, agricultural companies, wealthy businesses, and drug lords headquarters.[18] The rest of the municipality is predominantly rural.[19] The combination of these traits makes the municipality of Apatzingán a well-known agroindustry powerhouse in Mexico and, more importantly, the economic and political urban epicenter of Michoacán's *Tierra Caliente* (Hot Land region)—a region in the central and southern part of Michoacán which encompasses 14 municipalities of this state.[20] It also stretches to 9 municipalities of Guerrero and five municipalities of the state of Mexico. Overall, this region is known for its elevated levels of violence, the operation of multiple organized crime groups, and the production and distribution of illicit drugs.[21]

Figure 1: Central and southern Michoacán: Apatzingán and Lázaro Cárdenas.

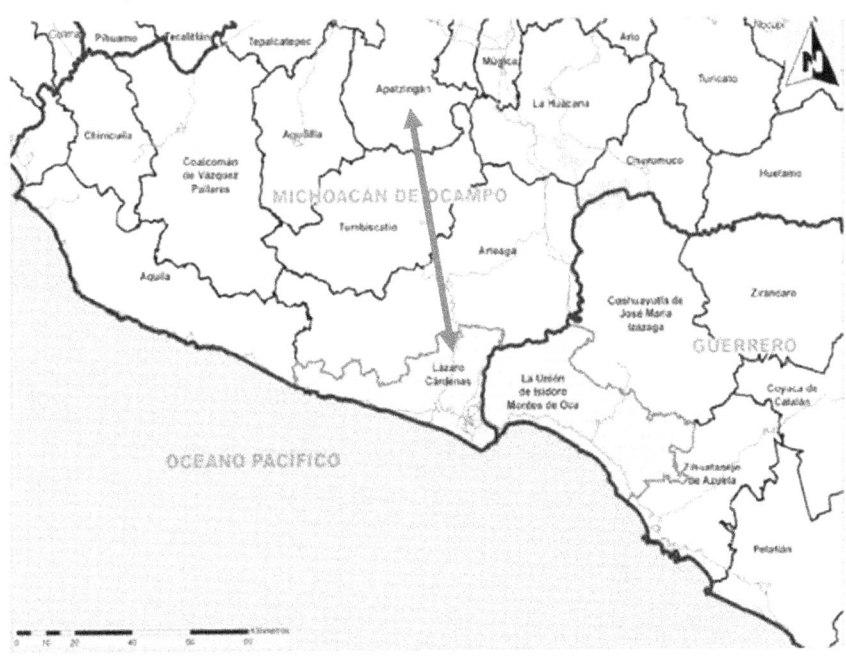

Source: Diario Oficial de la Federación, https://www.dof.gob.mx/nota_detalle.
php?codigo=5422684&fecha=14/01/2016#gsc.tab=0

As stated, the city has gone on and off intense waves of homicidal violence due to turf disputes among rival criminal groups. In 2007, for instance, violence surged after the Zetas cartel—a non-native and extremely prone to violence and brutality criminal organization—arrived in Michoacán and made the city of Apatzingán its stronghold.[22] According to a participant:

> Native criminal groups joined to expel the Zetas because that felt like a sort of an outside invasion by an alien criminal syndicate, something that made Michoacán one of the most violent states by then.[23]

In February 2013, the city would see another surge in large-scale violence when *grupos de autodefensas* (self-defense groups) popped up against the once-hegemonic *Caballeros templates* (Knights Templar) throughout *Tierra Caliente* region.[24] Through this period, Apatzingán reached a rate of 60 homicides per 100,000 residents.[25] Nowadays, a rather unstable mosaic of splintered local criminal groups under the banner of *Cárteles Unidos* have joined forces to fight Jalisco New Generation Cartel (CJNG) since 2019—a criminal group that once had allegedly financed many of those self-defense groups, as referred by two participants during fieldwork.[26] For example, Apatzingán witnessed another rise in criminal violence in late June—early July 2023 as a series of road blockades and shootings between the CJNG and *Cárteles Unidos* took place in and out of the city.[27] A symbolic event that attests to the worsening security situation in Tierra Caliente and that grabbed the Mexican headlines was the killing of the lemon farmer turned *autodefensa*, Hipólito Mora, in a municipality close to Apatzingán.[28]

The narco-centric explanation of violence would present armed violence in Apatzingán as a natural case of criminal groups warring against each other to control and expand a specific territory. This approach, however, assumes that Apatzingán is a politically neutral area whereas, actually, multiple actors with private interests interact with each other within a resource-rich geographic area.[29] In the words of a participant:

> We give criminal groups too much credit. Do you really think they are the only ones with interests here—political or economic ones?

They are not. Where are the politicians, the companies, the entrepreneurs, the central government?[30]

In this sense, violence—criminal violence being just one expression of it—has been a historical and useful means employed by private actors to harness political dominance, thwart economic competition, and solve land disputes. The central thesis of this article is best grasped by Interviewee 3:

> The security crisis in Apatzingán, adapting Gramsci, consists in the fact that old, historical dynamics of violence haven't died in their entirety while new have already born. This combination explains the morbid symptoms of today's violence.[31]

For this reason, the PTUV stresses the need to historicize large-scale violence in cases like Apatzingán to understand its multi-layered nature and linkages today.

A Violent History of Urban Life

Multiple cycles of violence coexisting in the city of Apatzingán today relate to its foundation as an urban enclave. Therefore, in order to provide a comprehensive interpretation of today's homicidal violence in the city of Apatzingán, it is paramount to adopt a historical perspective and briefly discuss a violent practice commonly referred to as *caciquismo*. *Caciquismo* has been a distinctive trait in the Mexican state-making process as well as a source of para-institutional power of social and political control.[32]

At the birth of the twentieth century, President Porfirio Díaz consolidated his power (1876-1911) through informal power brokers known as *caciques*. This network of local landowners-cum-patrons-cum-politicians exerted political, economic, and social influence in a geographic area starting at the municipality.[33] Although Porfirio Díaz was ousted after a 35-year hegemony by a revolutionary movement in 1911, *caciquismo* survived civil war. Moreover, once the revolution's political and social turmoil ended in the 1930s, and the Institutional Revolutionary Party (PRI) routinized the post-revolutionary regime in the 1940s, *caciques* were again fundamental to bring about peace and effective governance to the regime in a subnational scale.[34] The chieftains once again became the informal intermediary that, arguably, connected local politics to the national political project.[35] *Caciques* would operate—and still do—on a basis of coercion, co-optation, patronage, and consensual interaction between patrons and clients. As for coercion, the federal government would entrust *caciques* with control over public order to maintain socio-political discipline in remote areas with the help of the military.[36] In other cases, *caciques* would exert force primarily through the engagement of private militias or paramilitary forces that quickly suppress any uprising or political opposition.[37]

Now, as a predominantly rural region in the early twentieth century, Apatzingán was by no means exempt from *caciquismo*. Perhaps one of the most evident examples of this practice—and how the use of violent mechanisms permeated and conditioned the socio-political culture in the years to come—was the major land distribution that took place in the 1930s during Lázaro Cárdenas' presidency. Paradoxically, this distribution enabled local elites to further their economic control over land and, at the same time, to consolidate their political positions.[38]

As a result, land distribution in Apatzingán, as in other regions of Michoacán, generated in reality, land concentration by few *caciques* widening social inequalities.[39] Also, land concentration in Michoacán reinforced a system of norms, values and attitudes that contributed to the normalization of violence as means for controlling territory and solving disputes. Tied into this, according to the testimonies of Interviewees 4 and 6, violence has been functional to the interests of *caciques*, specifically to the concentration of power and social control.[40] During this time *caciques* in *Tierra Caliente* would form armed militias to terrorize small *ejido*-land owners—*ejidos* are areas of land held collectively by inhabitants of a Mexican village and farmed cooperatively or individually depending on the size—, and would employ tactics such as targeted assassinations, mass killings, and state-led violence.[41]

The land issue, as Guerra-Manzo labels this process, was a defining element in the formation of Apatzingán as an urban enclave as it inevitably paved the way for social grievances, civil unrest and, in time, organized crime and political violence in the municipality.[42] When asked about the sources of homicidal violence, Interviewee 1 stated the following: "You know, violence has always been present in Apatzingán. One thing that generated a lot of disagreements and discord was land distribution. Land access in the seventies set the tone for alliances among power groups— including organized crime—and for the use of violence. Even today the city has expanded in many ways."[43]

In this sense, Apatzingán is yet another case study where unequal urbanization has been a natural environment for conflict over resources. By 1960, common theft, homicides, and kidnappings were normal practices in *Tierra Caliente*. New breeds of violence popped up. For instance, the creation of self-defense groups became part of the culture among big landowners.[44] Interestingly, state authorities would allow only big landowners to harvest narcotics. According to a participant: "During the 1960s and the 1970s a culture of tolerance to organized crime groups and their activities permeated in municipal and state authorities."[45] Similarly, Interviewee 4 stated that through this time "the Army would grant permission to harvest the dope, during the PRI governments at the state and federal levels."[46] Soon, local drug-trafficking groups, political authorities, entrepreneurs, and landowners started what later on would become a network based on friendship and kinship to control illicit crops (particularly marijuana) and drug smuggling to the United States. This is how Apatzingán, as well as Aguililla, Coalcomán, Tepalcatepec, Arteaga, and Lázaro Cárdenas, became areas controlled by, what Maldonado-Aranda called, corporate groups focused on the drug business.[47]

In parallel, during this period the federal government started a process of urbanization with large infrastructure projects under the *Comisión de Tepalcatepec y Balsas* (Tepalcatepec and Balsas Commission). In Apatzingán, as in other parts of *Tierra Caliente*, the government opened several kilometers of highways and dirt roads, built large-scale crop irrigation systems, and carried out mining-metallurgy and hydroelectric projects in an effort to integrate the region into Mexico's national economy and politics.[48]

The development model, however, had two negative externalities. On the one hand, commodities production and export made not only entrepreneurs and political bosses wealthier but also benefited drug traffickers who took advantage of the new infrastructure and commercial networks to crop and transport narcotics.[49] On the other hand, the urbanization projects incentivized migration flows to *Tierra Caliente*.

According to one participant:

> Migration during this period was perhaps one of the most important negative transformations of Apatzingán and *Tierra Caliente* in general: it meant many people without access to economic benefits.[50]

This statement matches with Guerra-Manzo's research: During this period population growth became unsustainable causing insufficient job opportunities and a lack of land access.[51]

Eventually, there was a huge setback in the urbanization of Apatzingán when two major economic crises hit Mexico through the 1970s and 1980s, severely affecting the entire region's agroindustry—Mexico went through two serious economic crises characterized by an inflationary spiral, stagnant GDP growth, a large and growing foreign debt, a contraction of private investment, a financial sector in critical conditions, a devalued currency and an unstable exchange rate, and a loss of confidence in the State's ability to lead the country economically.[52] It is no surprise that during the mid-80s the first big criminal organization with regional and international capabilities emerged in Michoacán: The *Milenio* cartel.[53] Drug-trafficking boomed as local elites-landowners substituted watermelon and lemon exports with drugs (marihuana and, later on, poppy).[54] In turn, *Milenio Cartel* would diversify its portfolio of revenues in the real estate market and other commercial interests in municipalities like Apatzingán.[55]

The account of Interviewee 1 illustrates the situation:

> In addition to drug-trafficking, the *Milenio* cartel started creating companies and private business particularly in the construction, real state, and service sectors First they started with restaurants, bars, and

brothels. Then they made the numbers bigger and bigger for they started to build, hotels, apartments, and house residential zones.[56]

Similarly, according to one participant, this was something that eventually the *Familia Michoacana* (Michoacán Family cartel)[57] took to another level in the twenty-first century: "They even infiltrated the sports: One professional soccer team was financed by the Familia. Strikingly, the team was registered as part of a company based here in Apatzingán."[58]

Overall, dynamics of violence through the 1960s and 1980s were related to economic dominance through land concentration, an unequal as well as disorganized urbanization process, the establishment of a network of kinship among OCGs and political and economic actors, and the consolidation of organized crime in Apatzingán after two major economic crises. Up to this point, violence performed a means to guarantee a sense of stability and social control in Apatzingán. However, the democratization process provided another dynamic of violence that shook up the status quo. Something it will be necessary to delve into next.

Politics by Other Means

Carl von Clausewitz asserted that war is the continuation of politics by other means. Foucault, instead, inverted the statement saying that politics is the continuation of war by other means.[59] Although they feed each other at some point, the reasoning would suggest both belong to two opposite sides of a political spectrum. However, in Apatzingán such duality doesn't exist. Instead, violence and politics have coexisted at the same time and space. To a great extent, this has been a residual effect of the democratization process, particularly political and criminal pluralism as this article will now explain.

In 2000, the center-right National Action Party (PAN), the dominant opposition party at the time, ousted PRI from Mexico's presidency, thus ending its 70-year hegemony in the central government. The political changes associated with democratization at a national scale in Mexico "undermined the pyramidal composition of power structures (in other words, single-party government and centralized authority of the president) meaning the loss of social control."⁶⁰ However, at the local level the political system started to crack since the 1970s.⁶¹ By this time, state, and municipal authorities—often controlled by *caciques* themselves—gained more autonomy.⁶² Moreover, local political and economic elites adopted a more competitive approach in their relationship vis-à-vis the central government. In this sense, the democratization process made more evident that *caciquismo* was in reality a set of subnational regimes operating within the context of a national polity and economy.⁶³

As for the city of Apatzingán in the early stages of this political rupture, local elites consolidated yet again their predominance in the economic and political realms. Unexpectedly, it was in Mexico's democratic onset that coercive mechanisms of strongmen enjoyed a sort of parallel sovereignty the most.⁶⁴ Also, in municipalities like Apatzingán, PRI's decline at a national level strengthened local/regional arrangements between organized crime and state as well as municipal governments.⁶⁵

Things started to change dramatically when the regime's rupture brought about political pluralism in Michoacán. In the words of Interviewee 5:

> Violence has been present in our history. In recent times violence has been instrumental to politics. Now imagine when there is a multiplication of local *caciques* [local landowners-cum-patrons-cum-politicians]; everyone wants to be a boss. This anarchy demands the use of force, demands the elimination of the enemy to gain or maintain power.⁶⁶

In this sense, political alternation, and the rotation of parties in the state level undermined the informal networks of protection that had facilitated the cartels' operations under one-party rule.⁶⁷ As for Michoacán, this shift can be traced back to the late 1980s when Cuauhtémoc Cárdenas—son of Michoacán-born President Lázaro Cárdenas—founded the Democratic Revolution Party (PRD), a left-leaning splinter group from PRI. By the early 1990s, the PRD had already gained social traction in Michoacán by exacerbating historical social contradictions in the state—something relatively easy considering the dynamics of physical and structural violence mentioned in section 3. In cities like Apatzingán, the PRD soon became an appealing political alternative to the excluded people from the agrarian reform and urbanization.

The political tensions that entailed the existence of another political proposal added another layer of violence, where the use of coercive mechanisms was already common practice to harness political power. In Apatzingán, the appearance of another party inevitably meant the disruption of the local political environment, thus detonating political violence between the PRD's ideologically oriented mobilization, on the one hand, and PRI's resistance to hand in power, on the other. Some estimates suggest that violence in electoral strife in Michoacán caused as many as 50 murders between 1986 and 1993.[68] Eventually, the city of Apatzingán—and *Tierra Caliente* altogether—had become a bastion of political opposition led by the PRD. Malkin suggests that political opposition may well have served from the emergence of new generations of traffickers who opposed local elites still associated with the PRI.[69] Also, PRI in Michoacán started to implode due to diverging political aspirations from different inner factions. Interviewee 5 portrayed this idea in the following way:

> Party discipline in the state [Michoacán] relied to a great extent on the hegemonic power of the central government. In this sense, once one candidate as major was picked the other party members would join ranks. This changed when other parties became competitive enough to win an election. The angry political-economic actor that was not selected in the PRI's inner process would switch 'cap' [party], taking with him his political and social capital—sometimes criminal groups included. In some occasions local actors were not picked to run for office because they allegedly had ties to organized crime groups. They would go to other parties instead, and those parties were willing to compromise if that supposed winning an election.[70]

Accounts from other participants also reveal this trait in Mexico's democratization process. For instance, Interviewee 3 frequently talked about powerful political or economic actors who would knock on the opposition party's door after not having obtained a PRI candidacy for major or local congress:

> The PRD—and, eventually, other parties as they were having more presence in Michoacán—would welcome new party members with all its political scaffolding, including sometimes the support of a criminal group.[71]

Interviewee 2, for instance, stated that:

> Political alternation brought up a huge reconfiguration of *plazas* [turfs] in *Tierra Caliente*, benefiting criminal groups, more recently Jalisco New Generation Cartel.[72]

In consequence, a downside of political pluralism was the use of political connections to favor one organized crime group over another.[73] In this context, political pluralism made even more competitive—and violent— forthcoming electoral processes in urban areas insofar as they had the backing of a criminal group. None of Mexico's major parties remained ethically or genetically immune from this kind of corruption.[74] In a way, it was a natural response to political competitiveness: Political parties had to use additional sources of persuasion—and coercion—such as the ones provided by the already politically plural organized crime. By this time, the demise of rigid socio-political structures from the ancient regime, as Aguayo puts it, had emancipated the groups of power embedded in the Mexican political landscape, namely, unions, civil organizations, private sector and, certainly, criminal organizations.[75] In this new normal, criminal groups had more margin to choose any political group they thought best. This is how criminal pluralism became a decisive element in an already highly politically contested environment—especially in urban contexts like Apatzingán where most of the government offices, agricultural companies, wealthy businesses, and commercial opportunities were based.

Thus, democratization in Mexico took the crime-government nexus to a higher level—albeit eventually with highly unstable alliances because of criminal and political fragmentations, as the next paragraph will mention. As Interviewee 1 asserted, organized crime in Apatzingán "became a system of relations and acquaintances that reached the legal world via city contracts, the acquisition of public budget, or symbiotic connections with local law enforcement corporations. Politicians needed their support [criminal groups] to win an election, and so they made a deal with the devil that even changed the balance of power, of course, in organized crime's favor."[76] This nexus also affected social urban life, where organized crime became the enforcer of the political group in power. The criminal underworld implemented disciplinary mechanisms such as curfews, checkpoints, or bans on assembling in public squares in cities, to name some of them. Interviewee 6 describes these disciplinary mechanisms in the following terms: "Organized crime is functional to either local, state or national [political] power. To these powers, organized crime represents today an opportunity for control, stability, and security."[77]

However, the crime-government nexus eventually became more complex and an additional source of urban violence in Apatzingán. From 2006 onwards, in the context of the War on Drugs, the criminal underworld has gone through a severe process of fragmentation. Some recent estimates suggest that the number of criminal groups grew by 900 percent.[78] This reconfiguration of the criminal underworld—accompanied by internal fractures, defections, and shifts of alignment—was the outcome of increased competition between various organized crime syndicates and joint operations by the police and military.[79] Inevitably, the system of relations between organized crime and the government is also fragmented, with severe implications at the local level. In other words, the federal government's security strategy did not only contribute to a reconfiguration of the criminal landscape but also to a general political fragmentation in Apatzingán, hence generating a yet more unstable and competitive political and economic environment—and thus setting up the foundations for more homicidal violence. Interviewee 5 puts it in the following terms:

> The central government's notion of "order" at that time [in 2008] was not the same notion of "order" here [in Apatzingán]. They came here and faced a weak institutional framework that was not prepared to address Apatzingán's reality, say, for instance, the municipal police. The federal government crashed with the way things are done here, not now, since a long time ago....On the other hand, it was non-

sense, except from the armed forces, they came without institutions, and made the environment and the set of relationships here more divided, more complex.[80]

Le Cour Graindmason argues that instability and violence in places like *Tierra Caliente* have been due to a constant process of political reconfiguration generated by criminal groups.[81] In a subtle way, this viewpoint reproduces the narco-centric approach of violence: Any political reconfiguration relies on the existence of criminal groups. Although this thesis may have explained sources and dynamics of violence before the fragmentation of the criminal underworld, it falls short to bring granular knowledge on how, in turn, political fragmentation has caused a constant process of criminal reconfiguration as well. In this sense, the political trajectory of urban violence posits the need to analyze instability and criminal violence in a community as the result of a constant process of political reconfiguration, if not generated, at least fed by local elites. In other words, political or economic actors have employed organized crime groups to concentrate power, meaning that those local elites also contribute to the escalation—and perpetuation—of sub-national homicidal.[82] This is best portrayed by one participant: "Ok, for instance, there was a case of an alliance between big avocado producers and organized crime groups. This alliance favored the illicit appropriation of avocado orchards so that the big producers could expand their production area, hence benefiting economically from the 'green gold.'"[83]

Apatzingán as in other parts of *Tierra Caliente* cycles of violence and counter-violence include a range of different types of legal groups, chief among them rivalries between local elites. Interviewee 2 explains the idea in the following terms:

> In my perspective, the organized crime related violence is just the surface of homicides here—we have been killing each other for year, way before the war on drugs. And if you ask me, in many ways, different expressions of violence here are the result of rivalries among families whose interests—political or economic—have been affected.[84]

The most important flaw around the narco-centric approach of violence is in assuming that territories like Apatzingán in which criminal groups operate, or migrate to, are politically neutral. Instead, testimonies like the above suggest the intricate power relations—and tensions—among other groups with private interests in the same community (for example, local and national entrepreneurs, local political elites, syndicates, and multinational companies). Indeed, criminal groups undoubtedly play a political role in Apatzingán because they seize, concentrate, and exert power. It is not only that; criminal groups play a political role because they help other actors—illegal and legal—to seize, concentrate and exert power.

In other words, and contrary to common knowledge, criminal groups in Apatzingán may no longer be able to impose their will and conditions in strategic territories, even if these groups are more than willing to employ violence as their preferred means. Instead, to a great extent due to the fragmentation of the criminal underworld, criminal groups have been in the need to integrate themselves into the correlation of either political or economic forces, and to forge alliances with various actors operating at the local level.

Although possibly subtle, this epistemological turn in the political trajectory of urban violence demystifies a subordination of all actors to criminal groups. This is all the more relevant considering the criminal underworld's fragmentation as it has caused a considerable loss of leverage for criminal groups vis-à-vis other actors.[85] This dynamic of homicidal violence—and the role OCGs performs on it—represents a bigger challenge for urban security insofar as it is privatized by a legal actor. In this scenario, urban violence tends to perpetuate from the moment it is employed to achieve either political, economic, or environmental private interests.

Conclusion

This chapter put forward the idea that today's urban criminal violence in Mexico links to a long historical process of violence(s) and counter-violence(s). In other words, cases of contemporary urban violence in Mexico are a structural continuation of the political conflicts of the past. In particular, this case study research attested that homicidal violence in urban Apatzingán, Michoacán, has been historically related to disputes over access to land, political dominance, and economic hegemony. Also, Apatzingán attests why rapid urbanization processes have been frequently— and historically— connected with increasing rates of crime as well as urban and collective violence.

However, in more recent years Mexico's War on Drugs worsened these historical disputes in Apatzingán, as it has provided an unmatched platform for political and economic actors with local presence to redefine their positions of power in their own urban environments. In light of this, the article proposed the "political trajectory of urban violence" as an analytical category to juxtapose criminal violence nowadays to a historical continuum of the socio-political complex in urban settings.

The city of Apatzingán depicts how urban violence must be seen as a result of interactions where a multiplicity of actors—illicit and legal actors—have been permanently in search of the concentration of power. Indeed, criminal groups may play a political role in many Mexican cities as far as they seek, concentrate, and exert power. However, in addition to this, criminal groups play a political role at the local level as they help other private actors—legal and illegal ones—to seek, concentrate, and exert power through coercive means and high-intensity violence. Briefly put, the political trajectory of urban violence posits that organized crime-related violence is a fragment of a bigger power system.

Tied into this, this research emphasized that recent waves of large-scale violence in Apatzingán have not only been because of competition between organized crime groups, particularly those battling for the control of multiple illicit activities. Instead, violence in Mexico is also because of the constant reconfiguration of the political-economic-criminal factions in Apatzingán, fighting each other either for political or economic power. The pattern repetition in this exploratory research indicates this phenomenon. In this sense, the interviews that informed this article were illustrative accounts of power dynamics and urban violence in Apatzingán.

This said, the main findings of this case study have at least three important policy implications. First, any security crisis is, in essence, a political one. Deep-rooted and complex political issues, the most damaging of which are the weakness of local-level law enforcement institutions and social distrust in local government authorities, exacerbate any security crisis. In this sense, the use of military force by the central government has not delivered long-term political goals. It is worth reminding that the usefulness of force lies in its ability to generate conditions for state-building, economic development, generation of governmental capacity, and the establishment of rule of law, particularly at the local level.

Second, no institutional design will, on its own, be able to shape local politics and collective will. Aiming at imposing or re-imposing the State should bear in mind the limits of state building in complex urban settings. Moreover, any security policy from the central government should bear in mind the community's sociopolitical environment and its components, namely key groups, relationships, and tensions among groups, and narratives resonating within the community. In other words, the objectives, means, and ways of the national government must couple the realities and intricacies of local politics.

Third, any strategy attempting to pacify or stabilize violence in urban zones, such as the city of Apatzingán, will fail if it doesn't work as a mediator among local political and economic actors and balance their potentially conflicting interests. Any security strategy should aim to build local institutions but also to generate conditions for reconciliation at the local level. Ultimately, to consolidate institutions of local unity in urban enclaves—for example, a local police force—communities need a social covenant first. Otherwise, paradoxically, state-building could have undesired effects in divided communities where, most likely, a logic of existential politics will eventually beget political instability. After all, negotiation, reconciliation, peace-building processes, and post-conflict justice mechanisms are prerequisites to nation-building at the local level.

Avenues for further research should expand on how cycles of violence originate and persist across history in urban environments. In doing so, it will be necessary to delve into how historical processes of violence endure when new violence dynamics arise. Equally important will be to determine how this cocktail of violent dynamics can impact urban settings, especially those where organized crime groups operate.

Endnotes

1. Vincent Bernard, "War in the Cities: Towards a Holistic Response," ICRC, December 4, 2017, International Committee of the Red Cross, https://www.icrc.org/en/document/war-cities-towards-holistic-response; Achim Wennmann and Oliver Jutersonke, *Urban Safety and Peace Building: New Perspectives on Sustaining Peace in the City* (London: Routledge, 2019); Department of Social Development, Conflict, Crime and Violence, *Violence in the City: Understanding and Supporting Community Responses to Urban Violence*, (Washington DC: World Bank, 2011), https://openknowledge.worldbank.org/handle/10986/27454?show=full.

2. Fausto Carbajal-Glass, "The Micro-Geopolitics of Violent Non-State Actors," in *Higher Education Engages with SDF 16: Peace, Justice and Strong Institutions*, UNODC-IAU (Paris: International Association of Universities, 2021), 134-147, https://www.iauaiu.net/IMG/pdf/higher_ed_sdg16_iau_2021.pdf; Michael von der Schulenburg, "The Era of Armed Non-State Actors – Risks of Global Chaos," Changing Character of Conflict Platform, February 14, 2020, https://conflictplatform.web.ox.ac.uk/article/the-era-of-armed-non-state-actors.

3. John P. Sullivan, "Crime Wars: Operational Perspectives on Criminal Armed Groups in Mexico and Brazil," *International Review of the Red Cross*, no. 923 (2023): 1-27, https://doi.org/10.1017/S1816383122000558. Fausto Carbajal-Glass, "La Geografía de la Violencia Homicida en México 2015-2019 [The Geography of Homicidal Violence in Mexico 2015-2019]," Revista Nexos, November 18, 2019, https://seguridad.nexos.com.mx/la-geografia-de-la-violenciahomicida-en-mexico-2015-2019/; Fausto Carbajal-Glass, "Where the Metal Meets the Flesh: Organized Crime, Violence, and the Illicit Iron Ore Economy in Mexico´s Michoacán," in *Illegal Mining: Organized Crime, Corruption, and Ecocide in a Resource-Scarce World*, eds. Yuliya Zabyelina and Daan van Uhm, (London: Palgrave-Macmillan, 2020), 147-183, https://doi.org/10.1007/978-3-030-46327-4; Fausto Carbajal-Glass, "The Political Trajectory of Organized Crime in Mexico," in *Global Approaches on State Fragility & Organized Crime*, ed. Mauricio Vieira. (Costa Rica: University for Peace Press, 2023), 81-98, https://www.upeace.org/files/Publications/Vieira%202023-%20Global%20Approaches%20on%20State%20Fragility%20and%20Organized%20Cr ime.pdf.

4. Antonio Sampaio, "Criminal Governance During the Pandemic: A Comparative Study of Five Cities," Global Initiative Against Transnational Organized Crime, December, 2021, https://globalinitiative.net/wp-content/uploads/2021/11/GIZ-Criminal-governanceweb.pdf; David Kilcullen, *Out of the Mountains: The Coming Age of the Urban Guerrilla*, (Oxford: Oxford University Press, 2015); Simone Haysom, "Where Crime Compounds Conflict: Understanding Northern Mozambique´s Vulnerabilities," The Global Initiative Against Transnational Organized Crime, October, 2018, https://globalinitiative.net/wp-content/uploads/2018/10/TGIATOC-NorthMozambique-Report-WEB.pdf; Stathis Kalyvas, "How Civil Wars Help Explain Organized Crime

–And How Do They Not," *Journal of Conflict Resolution* 59, no. 8 (2015): 1517-40, https://doi.org/10.1177/0022002715587.

5. Carbajal-Glass, "The Political Trajectory".

6. John Gerring, "The Case Study: What Is and What It Does," in *The Oxford Handbook of Comparative Politics*, eds. Carles Boix and Susan Stokes (Oxford: Oxford University Press), 95.

7. Bent Flyvbjerg, "Five Misunderstandings about Case-Study Research," *Qualitative Inquiry* 12, no. 2 (2006): 219-245, https://doi.org/10.1177/1077800405284363.

8. Carbajal-Glass, "La Geografía de la Violencia".

9. Eduardo Guerrero, "Towards a Transformation of Mexico's Security Strategy" *The RUSI Journal* 158, no. 3 (2013): 6-12, https://doi.org/10.1080/03071847.2013.807579.

10. With regards to the particular case of illegal oil-tapping, Nathan P. Jones and John P. Sullivan, "Huachicoleros: Criminal Cartels, Fuel Theft, and Violence in Mexico," *Journal of Strategic Security* 12, no. 4 (2019): 1-24, https://www.jstor.org/stable/26851258; Gabriela Calderón; Gustavo Robles; Alberto Díaz-Cayeros and Beatriz Magaloni, "The Beheading of Criminal Organizations and the Dynamics of Violence in Mexico," *Journal of Conflict Resolution* 59, no. 8 (2015): 1455-1485, https://doi.org/10.1177/0022002715587053; Brian Phillips, "How Does Leadership Decapitation Affect Violence? The Case of Drug Trafficking Organizations in Mexico," *The Journal of Politics* 77, no. 2 (2015): 324-336, https://doi.org/10.1086/680209.

11. Carbajal-Glass, "La Geografía de la Violencia" [The Geography of Homicidal Violence].

12. Interviewee 6, 8 November 2021.

13. The lowest politico-administrative unit in Mexico before state and federal authorities.

14. Diego Valle-Jones, "Mapa de Homicidios de Mayo 2022 a Abril 2023 [Map of Homicides from May 2022 to April 2023]," May 12, 2023, https://elcri.men/mapa-dedelincuencia/.

15. For more about the "micro-geopolitical" dimension of organized crime in Mexico: Fausto Carbajal-Glass "Spaces of Influence, Power and Violence: The Micro-Geopolitics of Organised Crime," SHOC-RUSI, December 1, 2020, https://shoc.rusi.org/blog/spaces-of-influence-power-and-violence-the-microgeopolitics-of-organised-crime/.

16. Nathan P. Jones, "The Strategic Implications of the Cártel de Jalisco Nueva Generación," *Journal of Strategic Security* 11, no. 1 (2018): 19-42, https://doi.org/10.5038/1944-0472.11.1.1661; Fausto Carbajal-Glass, "The 'Global Power Competition – Transnational Organised Crime' Nexus: Lessons from Michoacán," SHOC-RUSI, March 7, 2023, https://www.rusi.org/explore-ourresearch/projects/strategic-hub-organised-crime-research-shoc/global-powercompetition-transnational-organised-crime-nexus-lessons-michoacan.; Carbajal-Glass, "Where the Metal," 166.

17. Salvador Maldonado-Aranda, "Stories of Drug-Trafficking in Rural Mexico: Territories, Drugs and Cartels in Michoacán," *European Review of Latin American and Caribbean Studies* 94 (2013): 43-66, https://www.jstor.org/stable/23408421.

18. As of 2018, roughly just 2.6% (42 km2) of the Apatzingán´s territory is considered an urban area out of the 1,632.8 km2 (Infonavit and UN-Habitat, "City Prosperity Index: Apatzingán, Michoacán, México", November 9, 2018, https://publicacionesonuhabitat.org/onuhabitatmexico/cpi/2018/16006_Apatzing%C3%A1n.pdf, p. 35).

19. Gerardo Vargas, "Apuntes para un Tipología de las Ciudades y la Urbanización en Michoacán

[Notes for a Typology of Cities and Urbanization in Michoacán]," Ciencia Nicolaita, Revista de la Coordinación de Investigación Científica (Universidad Michoacana de San Nicolás de Hidalgo, 1999), 43.

20. Congressional Research Service, "Mexico: Organized Crime and Drug Trafficking Organizations," June 6, 2022, https://sgp.fas.org/crs/row/R41576.pdf.
21. Maldonado-Aranda, "Stories of Drug Trafficking," 51.
22. As it was referred by Interviewee 2, 19 Sep. 2021.
23. Carbajal-Glass, "Where the Metal," 172.
24. Romain Le Cour Grandmaison, "'Vigilar y Limpiar': Identification and Self-Help Justice-Making in Michoacán, Mexico," *Politix* 115, no. 3(2016): 106, https://doi.org/10.3917/pox.115.0103.
25. As it was refereed by Interviewee 1 and Interviewee 5. Each participant was interviewed on 24 Aug. and 22 Oct. 2021, respectively. This statement was also present in nationwide newspapers such as David Vicenteño, "PGR: Cártel de Jalisco Arma a Grupos de Autodefensa [PGR: Cártel Jalisco Arms Self-Defense Groups]," *Excélsior*, March 8, 2013, https://www.excelsior.com.mx/2013/03/08/887952.
26. Redacción Infobae México, "¿Qué Está Pasando en Apatzingán y Por Qué el Ejército Mandó Cientos de efectivos a sus calles? [What Is Happening in Apatzingán and Why the Army Sent Hundreds of Troops to its Streets?]," *Infobae*, June 28, 2023, https://www.infobae.com/mexico/2023/06/28/que-esta-pasando-en-apatzingan-ypor-que-el-ejercito-mando-cientos-de-efectivos-a-sus-calles/.
27. Tom Phillips and Analy Nuño, "Mexico Vigilante Leader's Killing Highlights Failure to Curb Violence," *The Guardian*, July 16, 2023, https://www.theguardian.com/world/2023/jul/16/mexico-violence-vigilante-hipolitomora-amlo.
28. Carbajal-Glass, "The Political Trajectory".
29. Interviewee 2, 19 Sep. 2021.
30. Interviewee 3, 9 Oct. 2021. This was perhaps one of the most intellectually appealing statements during the research. Though, it was not surprising given the fact that the participant –albeit living and having its family in Mexico's periphery, namely, the city of Apatzingán– studied at one of the best universities in Mexico City. This statement illustrates the combination of a good education, a regionalist worldview and a robust ideological component.
31. Wil Pansters, Violence, Coercion, and State-Making in Twentieth-Century Mexico: The Other Half of the Centaur, (California: Stanford University Press, 2012), 25.
32. Vanda Felbab-Brown, "Peña Nieto's Piñata: The Promise and Pitfalls of Mexico's New Security Policy against Organized Crime", Brookings Institution, February 19, 2013, https://www.brookings.edu/research/pena-nietos-pinata-the-promise-and-pitfalls-ofmexicos-new-security-policy-against-organized-crime/; Antonio Ugalde, "Contemporary Mexico: From *Hacienda* to PRI, Political Leadership in a Zapotec Village," in *The Caciques: Oligarchical Politics and the System of Caciquismo in the Luso-Hispanic World*, ed. Roy Kern (New Mexico: University of New Mexico Press, 1973), 124.
33. Doug McAdam, Sidney Tarrow and Charles Tilly, *Dynamics of Contention*, (Cambridge: Cambridge University Press, 2001), 294. The post-revolutionary regime in Mexico was characterized by a single-party government; a centralized authority of the President; a corporatist pact among

the party-government, interest groups, and bureaucratic leaders; and a clientelist pyramid composed of political officials and local powerbrokers –*caciques*– to enhance State capacity in remote areas.

34. Lorenzo Meyer, "Los Caciques de Ayer, Hoy y Mañana [Caciques from Yesterday, Today and Tomorrow]," Letra Libres, December 31, 2000, https://www.letraslibres.com/mexico/los-caciques-ayer-hoy-y-manana.
35. Raúl Benítez-Manaut, "Seguridad Interior: Otro Dilema del 2017 [Homeland Security: Another 2017's Dilemma]," Revista Nexos, January 30, 2017, https://seguridad.nexos.com.mx/seguridad-interior-otro-dilema-del-2017/.
36. Maldonado-Aranda, "Stories of Drug Trafficking," 48.
37. Victoria Malkin, "Narcotráfico, Migración y Modernidad [Drug-Trafficking, Migration and Modernity]," in *La Tierra Caliente de Michoacán*, ed. José Eduardo Zárate (Ciudad de México: El Colegio de México. 2001), 549-584.
38. Enrique Guerra-Manzo, "La Violencia en Tierra Caliente, Michoacán, c. 1940-1980 [Violence in Tierra Caliente, Michoacán, c. 1940-1980]," *Estudios de Historia Moderna y Contemporánea* 53(2017): 59-75, https://www.redalyc.org/articulo.oa?id=94153158004.
39. Interviewee 4 and Interviewee 6, interviews were carried out on 17 Oct. and 8 Nov. 2021, respectively.
40. Jean Meyer, "Los 'Kulaki' del Ejido [The Ejido's Kulaki]," *Estudios de Historia y Sociedad* 29, no. 8 (1987), https://www.jstor.org/stable/j.ctt15vt914; Juan OrtizEscamilla, "El Desarrollo Económico-Social del Centro Ejidal Felipe Carrillo Puerto (La Ruana): 1952-1981[The Socio-Economic Development of Felipe Carrillo Puerto (La Ruana) Ejido: 1952-1981]," (PhD diss. UMSNH, 1983), 134.
41. Guerra-Manzo, "La Violencia en Tierra Caliente [Violence in Tierra Caliente]," 65.
42. Interviewee 1, 24 Aug. 2021.
43. Guerra-Manzo, "La Violencia en Tierra Caliente [Violence in Tierra Caliente]," 69.
44. Interviewee 3, 9 Oct. 2021.
45. Interviewee 4, 17 Oct. 2021.
46. Salvador Maldonado-Aranda, "Globalización, Territorios y Drogas Ilícitas en los Estados-Nación [Globalization, Territories and Illicit Drugs in Nation-States]," *Experiencias latinoamericanas sobre México. Estudios Sociológicos* XXVIII (2010): 421, https://www.redalyc.org/articulo.oa?id=59820673004.
47. Guerra-Manzo, "La Violencia en Tierra Caliente [Violence in Tierra Caliente]," 71.
48. Luis Astorga, "Transición Democrática, Organizaciones de Traficantes y Lucha por la Hegemonía [Democratic Transition, Trafficking Organizations and Struggle for Hegemony]," Razón Pública, May 18, 2009, https://razonpublica.com/mcotransiciemocrca-organizaciones-de-traficantes-e-inseguridad/.
48. Interviewee 6, 8 Nov. 2021.
49. Guerra-Manzo, "La Violencia en Tierra Caliente [Violence in Tierra Caliente]," 68.
50. Ricardo Peña-Alfaro, "La Política Económica Mexicana 1970-1976. Ensayo de

51. Interpretación Bibliográfica [The Mexican Economic Policy 1970-1976. Bibliographic Interpretation Essay]," *Nexos*, April 1, 1979, https://www.nexos.com.mx/?p=3321; Jeffrey L. Bortz and Salvador Mendiola, "El Impacto Social de la Crisis Económica de México [The Social Impact of Mexico's Economic Crisis]," *Revista Mexicana de Sociología* 53, no. 1 (1991): 43-69, https://doi.org/10.2307/3540828.

52. The *Milenio* Cartel, also known as the Valencia Cartel, was a family-run criminal organization that began with the exportation of avocado. However, later on they entered the drug business by planting marijuana and poppies for export to the United States.

53. Malkin, "Narcotráfico, Migración y Modernidad [Drug-Trafficking, Migration and Modernity]", 58.

54. Maldonado-Aranda, "Stories of Drug Trafficking," 59.

55. Interviewee 1, 24 Aug. 2021.

56. The criminal group that gave birth to the Knights Templar in 2011, after a series of internal disputes and divisions.

57. Interviewee 4, 17 Oct. 2021. The referred professional soccer team was called *Los Mapaches* (The Raccoons) and represented *Nueva Italia* (New Italy), a neighboring municipality of Apatzingán. In 2008, its owner was apprehended and the team disbanded.

58. Carl von Clausewitz, *On War*, (New Jersey: Princeton University Press, Ed. 1976); Michel Foucault, *Security, Territory, Population. Lectures at the College de France 1977–1978*, (London: Palgrave Macmillan, 2009.

59. Andrés Villarreal, "Political Competition and Violence in Mexico: Hierarchical Social Control in Local Patronage Structures," *American Sociological Review* 67, no. 4:(2007), 484, https://doi.org/10.2307/3088942.

60. Alan Knight and Wil Pansters, *Caciquismo in Twentieth-Century Mexico*, (London: University of London Press, 2005).

61. Maldonado-Aranda, "Stories of Drug Trafficking," 54.

62. Guillermo O'Donnell, "Cuatro Temas para Una Agenda de Debate: La Democracia en América Latina: El Debate Conceptual [Four Topics for a Debate Agenda: Democracy in Latin America: The Conceptual Debate]," PNUD, July 23, 2015, https://www2.ohchr.org/spanish/issues/democracy/costarica/docs/pnudseminario.pdf; James D. Cockroft, Andre Gunder Frank and Dale Johnson, *Dependence and Underdevelopment: Latin America's Political Economy*, (London: Doubleday, 1972), 12.

63. Maldonado-Aranda, "Stories of Drug Trafficking," 66.

64. Maldonado-Aranda, "Stories of Drug Trafficking," 65.

65. Interviewee 5, 22 Oct. 2021.

66. Guillermo Trejo and Sandra Ley, "Federalism, Drugs, and Violence: Why Intergovernmental Partisan Conflict Stimulated Inter-Cartel Violence in Mexico," *Política y Gobierno* 23, no. 1:(2016), 9-52, http://www.politicaygobierno.cide.edu/index.php/pyg/article/view/741/598; Guillermo Trejo and Sandra Ley, "Why Did Drug Cartels Go to War in Mexico? Subnational Party Alternation, the Breakdown of Criminal Protection and the Onset of Large-Scale Violence," *Comparative Political Studies* 51, no. 7:(2018), 900–937, https://doi.org/10.1017/9781108894807.003.

67. Pascal Beltrán del Río, Michoacán. Ni un paso atrás. La política de la intransigencia [Michoacán. Not one step back. The politics of intransigence], (Ciudad de México: Libros de Proceso, 1993), 19.
68. Malkin, "Narcotráfico, Migración y Modernidad [Drug-Trafficking, Migration and Modernity]", 57.
69. Interviewee 5, 22Oct. 2021.
70. Interviewee 3, 9 Oct. 2021.
71. Interviewee 2, 19 Sep. 2021.
72. Luis Astorga and David Shirk, "Drug Trafficking Organizations and Counter-Drug Strategies in the US-Mexican Context", *UC San Diego*, (2010): 40, https://escholarship.org/uc/item/8j647429.
73. Astorga and Shirk, "Drug Trafficking Organizations," 40.
74. Sergio Aguayo, *La Transición en México. Una Historia Documental 1910-2010* [The Transition in Mexico. A Documentary History 1910-2010], (Ciudad de México: Fondo de Cultura Económica, 2010), 262.
75. Interviewee 1, 24 Aug. 2021.
76. Interviewee 6, 8 Nov. 2021.
77. Carbajal-Glass, "Where the Metal," 165.
79. For a more comprehensive and recent analysis on the networked nature of organized crime in Mexico nowadays, Nathan P. Jones; Irina A. Chindea; Daniel Weisz Argomedo and John P. Sullivan, "A Social Network Analysis of Mexico's Dark Network Alliance Structure," *Journal of Strategic Security* 15, no. 4 (2022): 76-105, https://doi.org/10.5038/1944-0472.15.4.2046; Carbajal-Glass, Fausto, "Scope and Limits of COIN Doctrine in the Mexican Theatre," *Mexican Navy Institute for Strategic Research (ININVESTAM)* DA 46, no. 18: (2018), 12.
80. Interviewee 5, 22 Oct. 2021.
81. Aguayo, *La Transición en México* [The Transition in Mexico], 272.
82. Fausto Carbajal-Glass, "Criminal Violence in Mexico and South Africa: Mirrors of the Same Fate," *SHOC-RUSI*, August 12, 2019, https://shoc.rusi.org/blog/between-thedevil-and-the-deep-blue-sea-organised-crime-and-port-security/.
83. Interviewee 1, 24 Aug. 2021.
84. Interviewee 2, 19 Sep. 2021.
85. Carbajal-Glass, "The Political Trajectory".

CHAPTER 12
NATO's Path to Addressing Urban and Urban Littoral Operations

Alex Case and Gordon Pendleton

Introduction

In 2013, when the news, TV, and Western militaries were focused on counter-insurgency conflicts in Iraq and Afghanistan, NATO initiated a project to better understand urban conflict and operations. This was based on their own long term forecast study, Strategic Foresight Analysis (SFA), that predicted the urban environment as being key in future operations. More than 10 years in those same conflicts of Iraq and Afghanistan, along with Syria, Sudan, Ukraine, and, latterly, Gaza, have all proved the critical nature of the urban environment in determining the success or failure of military operations.

Between them, the two authors of this chapter contributed to the SFA of 2013, which indicated the emerging role of the urban environment, led the initial urbanization study team, supported both NATO's urban concept development efforts, and helped deliver four separate urban wargames to test and validate the study and concepts. The insight and experience gained from being continuously involved in the project from its infancy to delivery, both as NATO staff officers at Allied Command Transformation (ACT) in Norfolk, Virginia, and as consultants with Cordillera Applications Group,[1] who have provided services to NATO continuously since 2017, enables the authors to describe the process of 10 years' work and highlight the key lessons and outputs of the project. This will allow readers to appreciate the challenges of designing concepts and, ultimately, doctrine for an environment that is hard to exercise and experiment with due to its inherent characteristics of scale, infrastructure, and people.

Outline of the Urbanization Project

Key to understanding why urbanization was identified as a developing trend in NATO's SFA 2013 was a UN study on urbanization which stated:

Urban areas world-wide will absorb 3 billion new people in the next generation. Many of these people will go into under-governed, under-resourced and overstretched cities on coastlines. This is a recipe for conflict, security and crime issues, and governance, health and public order crises.[2]

Additionally, other military studies had identified global demographic trends suggesting that an increasing percentage of armed conflicts would most likely be fought in urban surroundings. Subsequently, the new NATO Framework for Future Alliance Operations (FFAO) 2015 highlighted the increased likelihood of NATO involvement in urban operations and included it as an Alliance threat. Based on this analysis the NATO Military Committee (MC) tasked HQ Supreme Allied Command Transformation (NATO HQ SACT) to deliver a conceptual study aimed at examining the impact of urbanization on NATO operations out to 2035. This conceptual study was delivered in 2016, and the development work included eighteen NATO Member Nations, nineteen NATO Centres of Excellence (COE),

International Organizations, Academic Institutions, and Industry.[3] The ideas and theories developed in the conceptual study were also tested in two major wargames conducted by the NATO Command Structure. The project included the development of a realistic 3D model of a future urban environment to allow the testing of new operating procedures and the conduct of military operations in a heavily congested civilian environment. The major findings from the 2016 Conceptual Study were:

- NATO needed to produce Joint Doctrine for future Allied Urban Operations

- NATO must commence strategic, operational, and tactical urban training/exercises and include higher levels of civil-military interaction to identify how resilience and the protection of civilians could be achieved

- A number of new capabilities and technologies were identified that were required to be included in the NATO order of battle to provide an advantage in urban operations

- Leadership education and training for future leaders at all levels should include aspects related to urban operations

- NATO should invest in joint urban training facilities to simulate the complexities of the urban and urban littoral environment

The Conceptual Study was well received by the Military Committee and the NATO Nations, and they again tasked NATO HQ SACT to produce a NATO Capstone Concept for Joint Military Operations in an Urban Environment (Capstone Concept).[4] The work was to further evaluate, analyze, initiate, and materialize the given recommendations in the conceptual study and was required to bridge future capability development, which could include operational and functional concepts as well as future Urban Doctrine.

The increasing awareness that the urban environment would likely be a potential future battleground for NATO led to huge interest and participation in the NATO Capstone Concept from across the Alliance. The program of work followed a similar approach to the Conceptual Study with a number of concept development workshops, research into historical urban operations, coordination with industry, and engagement/feedback from urban experimentation being carried out by individual nations. This development work culminated with a major operational-level wargame where the ideas, principles, and operational art identified in the Capstone Concept were rigorously tested and validated. The scope of the wargame was: *How should NATO forces be organized, trained, equipped, led and manned to comprehensively understand, execute and sustain joint operations, and create desired effects across the multiple dimensions of increasingly complex and dynamic urban environments?* In 2018, the new NATO Capstone Concept was accepted by NATO's Military Committee, and concept implementation commenced in early 2019 to facilitate the detailed Doctrine, Organisation, Training, Material, Leadership, Personnel, Facilities, and Interoperability (DOTMLPFI) requirements identified in the concept.

Urban Littorals

Academic research on behalf of the NATO urbanization project also identified that the majority of this urban growth would occur on the world's coastlines, so with an expansion of the current 80% of the global population living within 100km of the coast there would be an increased likelihood of urban littoral conflict.[5] Subsequently, NATO research considered the urban littoral to have nine-domain challenges—see Figure 1—and some distinct characteristics, including constricted sea approaches, shallow waters, chokepoints, narrow straits, jagged and rugged coastlines resulting in a vulnerability to global supply chains. These all made the urbanized, networked littoral an increasingly complex and difficult future operating environment for NATO and one that required specialized training.

Figure 1: The Nine-Domain Urban Littoral Challenge

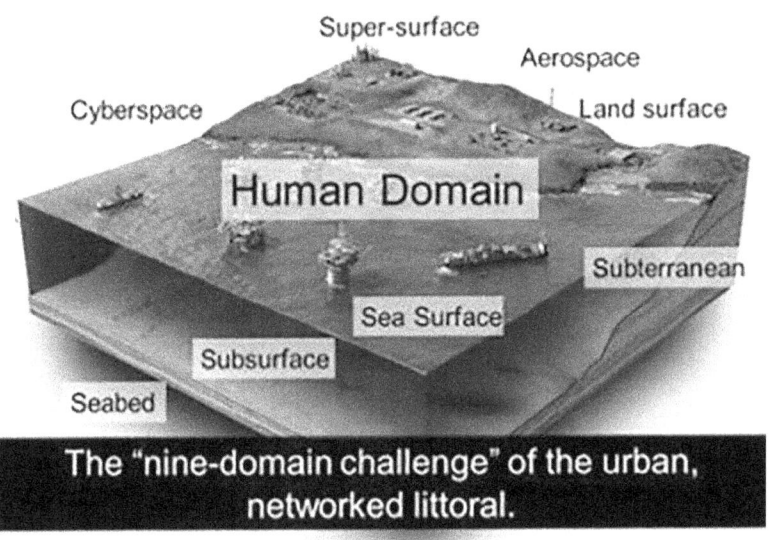

Courtesy of Dr David J. Kilcullen

The importance of the urban littorals led the NATO project team to commission five further studies in 2015, aimed at identifying the requirements for best replicating the future urban littoral environment for inclusion in a modeling and simulation system to support wargaming and training. These studies were:

- The Role and Relevance of the Maritime Domain in an Urban-Centric Operational Environment
- Concept for Harbour Protection During NATO Expeditionary Operations
- The Conduct of Future Operations in the Urban Littoral and its Implications for NATO
- Perspectives on Future Urban Environments
- Future Anti-Access and Area Denial (A2AD) Challenges Posed by Urban Centres to 2035

The research papers clearly identified that NATO faces unprecedented technological, environmental, commercial, and A2AD challenges when operating in the urban littoral approaches. The research also identified the significance of a fully functioning and protected port not only for military operations but for the free flow of commercial goods, food, and humanitarian aid for the urban population. In addition, the COE for Operations in Confined and Shallow Waters and the Combined Joint Operations from the Sea COE identified that dominating the maritime domain requires a comprehensive inter-agency approach that brings together the entire spectrum of relevant national institutions—navy, coast guard, customs, police, etc. This inter-agency approach would be cooperative or through bilateral, regional, or multinational initiatives. The project team was also granted permission to visit the heavily automated Ports of Los Angeles and Norfolk, where it quickly became apparent that any impact on port operations or access to the urban littorals around the port would be economically and socially disastrous and would lead to food shortages and a breakdown in law and order in as little as 5 days.

To create an urban and urban littoral environment, the project team worked with the Modelling & Simulation COE (M&S COE), Rome, and developed a 2D model based on the City of Naples, the surrounding Tyrrhenian Sea, and the Island of Sardinia. The City of Naples was chosen as the University of Rome, and the University of Naples was willing to share significant and existing urban and littoral data to assist with the creation of the PMESII6 data layers in ArcGIS. In addition, military and civilian subject matter experts worked directly with the M&S COE and created a realistic and futuristic environment called "Archaria" that contained the military, technological, and commercial littoral threats identified in the project research. An illustration of the 3D view of the Port of Naples is shown at Figure 2 and the blue/white circles in the picture are the data points for the PMESII information layers.

Figure 2: 3D Model of the Port of Archaria

Courtesy of the M&S COE, Rome

The completed model was used in 2016 and 2018 to deliver the NATO urban wargames and has since been used by the Australian, Canadian, German, Italian, the Netherlands, and United Kingdom militaries for urban training, concept development, and wargaming. For the NATO Multi-Domain Operations in an Urban Environment wargame in 2023, it was decided to add operational-level simulation to support the wargame. Additionally, the littoral environment had an increased level of critical national infrastructure modeled—Diagram 3—to enable both the protection and targeting of key assets and to understand the impact of the loss of this infrastructure on the ability to operate in the urban/urban littoral and its effect on the population.

Figure 3: Detailed M&S of Critical National Infrastructure

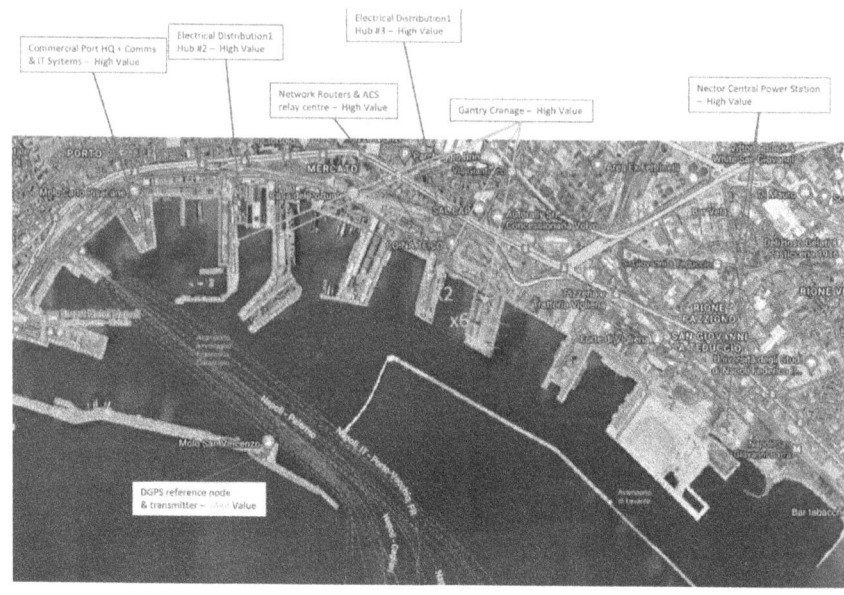

The Path Towards MDO and the Development of the MDO in UE Concept

As referred to earlier, in 2019, the Concept Development Branch in ACT, NATO's headquarters in the US, launched a concept development project to develop an operational level urban operations concept as tasked by NATO's MC based in the NATO Headquarters in Brussels. This was the next step within the Urban project and was designed to deliver a concept to be the basis for new operational-level urban doctrine. In 2019, Multi-Domain Operations (MDO) emerged as the new operational doctrine of the future, partly as a result of the development work involved in the development of NATO's Warfighting Capstone Concept (NWCC) published in 2021, which highlighted the role of MDO alongside others. While NATO and NATO nations were still scrambling to understand MDO, the MC directed that the next phase of the urban concept development was to include MDO as an overarching input to any future urban operational doctrine.

The problem statement the concept was required to answer was: *NATO does not possess sufficient capabilities for operations in the UE. Therefore, to increase NATO's readiness for operations in the UE, NATO requires an operating concept for the UE that is aligned with NATO's MDO concept.* This effectively resulted in one project team attempting to translate the existing NATO Urban Capstone Concept, delivered in 2018, into an operational-level concept while incorporating an MDO NATO concept, which was also being written. This parallel track was managed by merging the existing key ideas from the Capstone Concept and the emerging principles of NATO's MDO concept, removing any duplicity and driving forward to review NATO Nation's urban concepts and doctrine, gathering focused inputs from SMEs, and identifying areas requiring further research, but remaining cognizant that NATO's MDO concept was still being developed. The concept became known as Multi Domain Operations in Urban Environments (MDO in UE), and although NATO recognized four other operating environments (desert, jungle, cold weather, and mountain), the need for a specific urban environment operating concept, as outlined earlier, was critical to the future operating environment which saw conflict within urban areas as being the norm, rather than the exception.

An initial MDO concept was delivered to the Military Committee for approval in 2022 and was endorsed in 2023. Its definition of MDO was: "Orchestration of military activities, across all domains and environments, synchronized with non-military activities, to enable the Alliance to create converging effects at the speed of relevance."[7]

It had four guiding principles:[8]

- **Unity**: Allows coordinated action of all capabilities towards a common objective. Provides the basis to orchestrate military activities and synchronize non-military contributions. Requires collaboration, transparency and trust to enable the harmonized planning and execution of MDO. Benefits from a willingness to bridge diverse national perspectives.

- **Interconnectivity**: Enhances shared understanding across all Instruments of Power (IoP), Partners and stakeholders, and enables warfighting interoperability between force elements. It is challenged by differences between legacy and modern platforms, i.e., lack of technical interoperability, and by data classification. It must be resilient and requires standardized data to support user requirements.

- **Creativity**: Stimulates the development of boundless opportunities that can be tailored to offer surprise and multiple dilemmas. Relies on an ability to analyze situations from different viewpoints and turn complexity into simplicity. Enhanced by an ability to visualize context and settings. Supports a commander's aptitude to orchestrate MDO.

- **Agility**: Allows the force to take advantage of fleeting opportunities. It requires initiative, relative speed, prioritization, and flexibility of thought and action. It requires the application of mission command.

This endorsement of the overarching MDO concept enabled the MDO in UE team to adapt their concept, although the challenge of developing one concept based on a still emerging MDO concept was not insignificant. Attendees at workshops, both virtual and in-person, understandably struggled to grasp the vision of MDO while, in parallel, analyzing the impact MDO would have within the urban environment. The concept naturally developed into two parallel concepts, one describing how MDO would operate within the urban environment and a second providing urban-specific content, which ranged from strategic to tactical. This resulted in a significant volume of work covering not only current and future urban operational content but detailed future capability requirements and urban-focused adjustments to force structures, equipment, command and control processes, methods of communication, legal considerations, and future autonomous and unmanned systems.

Using NATO's Concept Development and Experimentation process, a concept is 'validated' to ensure it answers the initial problem statement.

The validation event for the MDO in UE Concept was a seminar wargame designed to enable military commanders and staff to use the concept within a future urban environment. In order to provide the essential characteristics of an urban environment at scale, a virtual model was required to depict the realities of the population, infrastructure, surface and sub-surface buildings, and a connected and partially Smart City. The virtual environment was developed by ACT in conjunction with a commercial consortium and utilized the prior work described earlier from the previous urban wargames. Four separate vignettes were designed to ensure that participants operated across the full spectrum of conflict. Limitations were necessary as NATO at that time was not prepared to wargame operations within a nonNATO Nation.

The war game's validation audience were operational commanders and their planning staff, drawn from across NATO's three Joint Force Commands and supplemented by the UK's Allied Rapid Reaction Corp, other NATO Allied Command Operations HQ staff, and members of the Hungarian Defence Force. The validation audience played the Blue Force, with domain SMEs playing the Red Force and both military and civilian staff providing a Green Force with urban-specific representation. White representatives provided NGOs and other cells including ICRC, the World Food Program, and others.

The MDO in UE concept wargame was executed in February 2023 at Joint Force Command Naples' location, with over 125 staff participating in three separate but parallel wargames conducted over eight working days. For analysis purposes Red and Green plans and policies were common across all three wargames, thereby providing three similar environments for Blue to operate within. An analytical tool, built specifically by ACT to support the wargame and linked to the model depicting the urban environment, provided objective analysis based on each Blue plan and the use of future capabilities outlined within the MDO in the UE concept. Feedback was gathered by an independent team of analysts, combined with data generated by the analytical tool and outputs from formal and informal feedback sessions, and the conduct of the war game was overseen by JFC Naples' Senior Mentor. It produced some key outputs and observations to adjust the concept. These included:

- With the Space and Cyber Domains playing such a key role commanders and staff require education and exercise opportunities to ensure the five domains are fully understood and utilized.

- The concept was too long and too detailed to be easily understood, and therefore it was a challenge to fully apply the concept for the 'first-time user'.

- The 6 principles were not critical to the success of the use of the concept but were key during the explanation and education phase prior to the wargame.

- The MDO concept, being in its infancy, was not yet fully understood or adopted, resulting in the subsequent MDO in UE concept having to include significant elements of it rather than just referring to it.

Key Content of the Multi-Domain Operations in Urban Environments Concept

After the wargame validation event, ACT concept development staff focused their efforts on reducing the length, aligning the principles of MDO and MDO in the UE, and producing a more succinct version of the concept. At the time of writing in April 2024, the concept had been reduced in length, partially by moving content to annexes, the four MDO guiding principles and the three Capstone Concepts key elements had not been aligned, and the future capability requirements to support the concept had been prioritized. Based on the draft pre-Military Committee approval version, the key content within the MDO in UE concept could be summarized as:

- Vision of MDO in the Urban Environment: an MDO force will conduct rapid and constant planning, engagement space/battle space management, and execution of operations across all five domains to seek relative advantage against an adversary within the urban environment. It will achieve this by using the four guiding principles of MDO.

- MDO, as the future doctrine for NATO, has four key guiding principles:
    - Unity
    - Interconnectivity
    - Creativity
    - Agility
- NATO's Urban Capstone Concept has three key elements:
    - Understanding the Urban Operating Environment.
    - Interaction with the Urban Environment
    - Force Agility
- NATO views the urban environment as a critical operating environment in future conflicts. NATO and NATO nations are not fully capable of operating across the spectrum of conflict in urban environments, which require operating and capability changes at scale.
- The emergence of five domains within MDO, vice three services within a Joint structure, changes the way commanders and staff plan and conduct operations and this needs to be applied to the urban environment. The two new domains, Space and Cyberspace, already have a significant role to play within modern-day operations, and their contribution will only increase as their capabilities become embedded within doctrine.
- At the operational level of warfare, operations within the urban environment will involve tactical events that could rapidly escalate and have operational and even strategic impacts due to the presence of civilians, technology, and infrastructure within any urban environment.
- Due to the scale of urban environments, the density of the population and infrastructure, and their prominence in

recent conflicts, any previous doctrine of avoiding or merely isolating cities will be impractical. Operating forces will need to be interacting and operating from within all types of urban environments at scale and duration if they are to have an effect.

- Due to scale, population, and infrastructure, providing a realistic urban environment for training purposes is not easy. If operating forces are to increase capability through training and rehearsal, significant investment and real estate, combined with effective simulation, will be required.

- Recognizing that the urban environment is unique, with its presence of dense population, physical structures and critical infrastructure, will be key to understanding that some military tactical actions within the environment could negatively impact the possibility of operational and strategic success.

Progress and Challenges

NATO's urban project has spanned some 10 years to date and is not stopping anytime soon. Its initial scoping study identified the urban environment as an emerging space for future conflict and a lack of existing doctrine within NATO beyond the Land-based tactical level. That study convinced NATO to initiate the work required to generate doctrine in the long term through the development of the NATO Capstone Concept in 2018 at the strategic level and the subsequent draft MDO in UE, which attempted to use the fledgling MDO concept as a guide and provide operational level guidance for the planning and conduct of urban operations. During a period where operations have been conducted in urban environments by other Nations and non-state actors, but not NATO, this project has maintained the interest in NATO to adapt to a unique and challenging environment. The four wargames in Rome 2015 and 2016, Shrivenham UK 2018, and Naples 2023 were focal points for urban and MDO practitioners to gather and challenge the norms of sometimes outdated and insufficient doctrine.

Their inputs and observations were critical to add validity to those within NATO who continued to bang the drum that urban was different; urban was coming and was not going away.

The MDO in UE concept, in whatever form it gains approval by the MC, will influence future doctrine, but as ever, it will need to have a greater impact on the NATO Capability Requirements process. Approved concepts are included in the NATO doctrine review cycle, which can take up to 8 years to complete. Although this appears slow, it can be faster than NATO's Common-Funded capabilities process and the NATO Nations' own individual procurement processes. However, there will be change—who had heard of MDO, autonomous systems and Artificial Intelligence only 10 years ago? NATO has a key role of being the collective forcing function and the glue to enable that change.

Conclusion

In summary, the NATO Urbanisation and Multi-Domain Operations in the Urban Environment projects covered a decade and the research resulted in a NATO conceptual study, capstone concept and operating concept. All these studies were rigorously validated through four major wargames in 2015, 2016, 2018 and 2023 and supported by the development of a modeling and simulation system of the multi-domain urban and urban littoral environments. Crucially, all these wargames included the participation of civilian international organizations who contributed directly to ensuring that the Protection of Civilians in the urban environment was considered and mitigation included in the concepts.

Early in the project development, NATO realized the importance of including the urban littorals as an integral part of the urban concept work. Subsequently, the ACT concept development team commissioned research by NATO's Maritime CoE experts, US Naval Post Graduate School, and academia to determine the future urban littoral threats and the importance of ports to NATO operations and the global supply chain. The lessons learned from these studies and the A2AD implications for NATO were built into the 3D urban littoral model which supported the concept development program and the identification of future capability requirements.

Developing an MDO in UE operating concept, at a time when NATO's primary MDO concept was still in its infancy and elevating existing and future urban content to the operational level was a challenge but an urgent and necessary one in order to equip future commanders with appropriate capabilities. A significant change to NATO's approach to urban doctrine, training, and operational capabilities needs to follow.

This significant effort and investment has nudged the needle on NATO's current lack of specialist urban doctrine and urban-specific capabilities at a time when Gaza, Mariupol, Mosul, Aleppo, Fallujah, and the Red Sea, among others, have left no one in doubt that any future conflict, whether it be within NATO's area of operations or elsewhere, will have a critical urban and urban littoral element to any operation.

Endnotes

1. Cordillera Applications Group. https://cordillera-apps.com/.
2. United Nations Department of Economic and Social Affairs, "2012 Revision of World Urbanization Prospects," United Nations News, https://www.un.org/en/development/desa/publications/world-population-prospects-the-2012-revision.html.
3. Gordon Pendleton, "Joint Urban Operations and the NATO Urbanisation Project," *The Three Swords Magazine*, 2015, https://www.jwc.nato.int/images/stories/_news_items_/2015/urbanisation_dec2015.pdf.
4. Jozsef Bodnar, "NATO Joint Military Operations in an Urban Environment," *The Three Swords Magazine*, 2019, https://www.jwc.nato.int/images/stories/_news_items_/2019/three-swords/NATOUrbanization_2035.pdf.
5. NATO Littoral definition used in the Capstone Concept: In military operations, a coastal region consisting of the seaward area from the open ocean to the shore that must be controlled to support operations ashore, and the landward area inland from the shore that can be supported and defended directly from the sea. Department of the Navy. *Littoral Operations in a Contested Environment*, 2017. https://www.mca-marines.org/wp-content/uploads/Littoral-Operations-in-a-Contested-Environment.pdf.
6. PMESII stands for Political, Military, Economic, Social, Information and Infrastructure.
7. Franklin D. Kramer, Ann Marie Dailey and Joseph Brodfuehrer, "NATO multidomain operations: Near- and medium-term priority initiatives," *Atlantic Council*, February 21, 2024, https://www.atlanticcouncil.org/in-depth-research-reports/issue-brief/nato-multidomain-operations/#:~:-

text=The%20concept%2C%20which%20was%20delivered,the%20speed%20of%20relevance."%205.

8. Jeffrey Reynolds, "NATO Multi-domain Operations Adapting Beyond Joint Operations," *The Three Swords,* 2022, https://www.jwc.nato.int/application/files/3516/7092/4186/NATO_Multi-DomainOperations2022DEC.pdf

CHAPTER 13
Subterranean Operations

Andrew Craig

Introduction

At the time of writing, the Israeli ground offensive in Gaza remains ongoing, with an assessment that there are over 500 kilometers of Hamas-prepared tunnels, over 5,000 shafts, and innumerable underground facilities (UGFs).[1] This expansive subterranean complex is a wicked problem for which there remains no perfect means of neutralization.[2] But while international headlines have highlighted the importance of subterranean operations, underground warfare has been around for as long as war itself.[3]

However extensive, the Hamas tunnels are just one facet of an operational problem that is forecast to play an ever more important part in urban operations. See, for example, Chapter 15 on "Black Shabbat" by Jacob Stoil in this text. Contemporary history documents numerous incidences of the use of subterranean space to avoid contact or observation or to offer protection. Those using such spaces range from combat forces to insurgents and terrorists, to civilians and organized criminals. The impetus, therefore, is not only for what lies beyond the horizon but also for that which lies below.

This chapter seeks to provide an overview of the problem and address some of the operational planning and capability development challenges around subterranean operations.

History

Subterranean operations have been documented for over four millennia. Ancient cities were commonly contained within protective walls and while siege tactics were the norm, the most common strategies for breaking such was to undermine the walls or to infiltrate the city via subterranean routes.[4] More advanced methods of mining drove the development of force protection design, with features such as moats and pre-prepared counter-mines adding to defenses.

In typical fashion, military technology continued to develop, often embracing industrial technology to counter the offensive and defensive use of subterranea. Large-scale mine warfare rose to prominence in the Great War (1914-1918), with large mines being used to break the entrenchment of forces both on the Western Front and the less well-recognized Hungo-Austrian-Italian Front in the Alpine Dolomites.[5] With the revolution of air power, UGFs were used more extensively to protect the government and military and to offer shelter for the more prominently at-risk civilian population. The use of the London underground was an obvious urban example of the latter during the Second World War (1939-1945).

During the Cold War (1947-1991), beyond the proliferation of enhanced UGFs designed to protect against nuclear strikes or the resulting fallout, the modernization of civilian infrastructure was often carried out with a view to offering a secondary civil resilience, e.g. the Moscow Metro or the Helsinki Underground City.[6] Large urban government UGFs were necessary for the limited notice safety and security of those who could not be evacuated to more rural UGFs such as the British Burlington Bunker, or United States Greenbriars Bunker.[7]

Contemporary Subterranea

Leading academics and military futurists appear to agree that operational environment biases attributed to the campaigns in Iraq and Afghanistan have now given way to the realization that the decisive battle will be the urban fight for peer-on-peer, or at least near-peer, conflict. If that conflict truly is to be urban-focused, then that will inevitably include some subterranean aspects.[8]

There are innumerable examples of urban subterranean environments playing a part in contemporary battles or terrorist atrocities. Examples are numerous, but notable examples include:

- United Kingdom: London terror bombings, 7 July 2005[9]
- Iraq: Mosul (16 October 2016 - 20 July 2017)[10]
- Philippines: Marawi (23 May - 23 October 2017)[11]
- Syria: Aleppo (19 July 2012 – 22 December 2016)[12]
- Ukraine: Kyiv (25 February – 2 April 2022)[13]
- Mariupol (24 February – 20 May 2022)[14]
- Soledar (3 August 2022 – 16 January 2023)[15]
- Avvdika (10 October 2023 – 17 February 2024)[16]
- Gaza: Operation Protective Edge (8 July – 26 August 2014)[17]
- Operation Swords of Iron (7 October 2023 – Present)[18]

Depending on the underlying geology and history, the urban environment may comprise a complex and interlaced system of natural, historical, and modern-day subterranean networks and features. Understanding these and classifying them is an integral step in successfully planning and operating within them. American and British military doctrine divides subterranea into three categories.[19]

Category 1 comprises natural features including tunnels and caves or chambers created via geological process and historical structures including catacombs, shelters, aqueducts, mines (material extraction) or canals. These are further subdivided by the extent to which they may have been developed:

1. **Rudimentary** structures lack basic infrastructure or even engineered support to reduce the risk of structural collapse.

2. **Sophisticated** structures will have some form of structural reinforcement to enhance the natural support of the surrounding ground to reduce the risk of collapse or damage by earthquakes or flowing groundwater. These structures will also usually be larger and have life support infrastructure such as ventilation shafts, electricity power supply, and therefore potentially lighting and powered drainage and ventilation.

Category 2 comprises modern-day urban subterranean systems, including infrastructure for power, water, transportation, and commerce, as well as shelters, storage facilities, and a great many other purposes due to restrictions on space for surface construction or the desire to avoid inhospitable weather conditions. This is likely to be the most common category in the urban environment and their location, foundation, design, and depth will be determined by the local geology. Some may be able to withstand military strikes due to their depth and/or construction materials, although they were not designed for this purpose. The subdivision of this category is as follows:

1. **Substructures.** These include basements, shelters, and car parks. These may appear to be like the sophisticated Category 1 structures but usually have explicitly designed structural features and are, therefore, more robust.

2. **Civil works.** These works include sewers, passageways, underpasses, transportation, and utility tunnels.

It is important to remember that civilians who have not been able to escape will seek protection from combat by occupying urban subterranean systems.

Category 3 are UGFs. These are sophisticated, complex, and specifically designed and built to provide maximum concealment and protection. They generally have enhanced protective engineering and design features.

UGFs usually rely on 'umbilical structures' to function, e.g. electrical power generators and supply lines; communications antennas, satellite dishes and connecting wire or fiber optic cables; life support and environmental controls such as heating, ventilation, water storage, supply, and waste disposal; means of descent such as escalators, lifts or even narrow-gauge rail. The effectiveness of UGFs can potentially be reduced if the critical umbilical structures can be made inoperable. Backup facilities may, however, have been installed to enable the facility to continue operating for extended periods. Construction standards vary, but they are subdivided into shallow and deep, based on the depth and amount of overburden (soil and rock) above them.[20]

1. **Shallow**. An underground facility with 20 meters or less overburden. Examples include silos, cut-and-cover facilities, and basement bunkers.

2. **Deep**. An underground facility with more than 20 meters of overburden. Examples include protection sites for government officials, military operations facilities, and research and production facilities.

Beyond the categorization, Figure 1 presents a range of attributes that must be reviewed during operational planning for subterranean operations.

Figure 1: Subterranean system categories and attributes.[21]

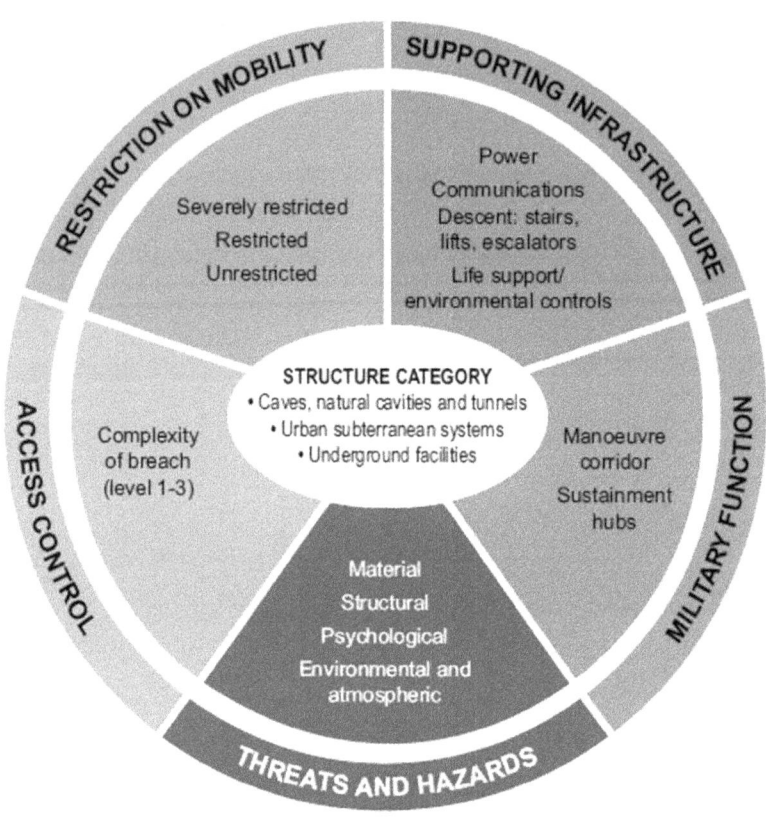

Fundamentally, no two subterranean systems are the same, and contemporary adversaries have demonstrated that they are not only capable of operating within the subterranean dimension but also highly proficient at maneuvering multidimensionally throughout the urban subterranean, surface and super-surface environment.

Engineering and construction methods and materials have steadily evolved, enabling urban underground space (UUS) to grow larger and go deeper, even in regions where there are increased risks from geohazards, such as earthquakes. UUS has become an integral component of modern cities.[22]

Beyond commercial UUS, the sale and repurposing of redundant UGFs are now commonplace for a range of purposes, including agriculture, data centers, and entertainment.[23]

Factors Affecting Subterranean Operations

That which is above is like to that which is below, and that which is below is like to that which is above.[24]

Subterranean operations will not be carried out in isolation. Indeed, it is highly likely that a tactical action might transition from the supersurface to the surface and subsurface over a matter of minutes and meters, with both super- and sub-surface elements being reliant on surface-located support.

Multi-domain actions will be required on the urban battlefield, and the need for combined and joint operational planning will be essential to securing success.

Most modern armies have developed some level of capability to contest the subterranean environment. But while many special forces (SF) may have more advanced tactics, techniques, and procedures (TTPs) and access to more sophisticated equipment and resources, few have dedicated specialists, and this is more pertinent with generalist forces.

The widely recognized exception is the Israeli Defense Forces (IDF) who, due to prescient subterranean threats, have developed a dedicated capability focused on the detection and denial of subterranea.[25] These units comprise specialists in intelligence, engineering, combat, remotely operated systems, and military working dogs (MWD). Their use has been extensively covered in the media during Operation Swords of Iron, See Chapter 15 on "Black Shabbat "by Jacob Stoil in this text.

Other armies' challenges will be to balance the draw upon a limited number of specialists against the need to operationally maneuver generalist mass through the multi-dimensional urban environment. It is logical to assume that such specialists will be used predominantly against targets such as strong points and high-value UFGs for hostage recovery.

At the tactical level, the challenge within a combined arms context will be to recognize and plan for the inflection points where an initial combat arms-led action escalates to become a specialist task requiring specialist assets, e.g. Engineers.[26]

Legality

Prior to examining military actions, it is vital to reflect upon the legality of what can and cannot be done within the scope of LOAC and IHL.[27]

Richemond-Barak's *Underground Warfare* provides the most comprehensive legal review of the use of tunnels in warfare. She concludes that a tunnel is a tunnel is a tunnel: it poses a security threat regardless of its purpose… and, underground warfare exposes the weakness of IHL at the level of theory… [and] needs to adapt and stretch beyond its primarily causative focus in order to provide answers to important tunnel related dilemmas.[28] She also highlights that the presence of subterranea within an urban battle increases the fog of war and that while there are no laws of war dedicated specifically to the use of tunnels in war, there need not be in the future.[29]

This subject is beyond the scope of this chapter, but commanders will be heavily reliant on their legal advisors, and that IHL debate, notably around distinction and proportionality, will continue around the use of subterranea and the means with which to neutralize the risk it makes to combatants and civilians.[30]

Detect & Understand

While Category 1 and 2 subterranea may be well documented via open-source intelligence (OSINT), Category 3 UGFs are likely to be clandestine in nature and may require a comprehensive suite of capabilities to detect their presence. However, one cannot escape the possibility that the media may not relinquish a well-kept secret, as was the case of the Greenbrier Bunker in 1992.³¹ A range of intelligence sources (IMINT, HUMINT, SIGINT, etc.) may offer an initial vector, as well as insight into their geometry, layout, function, and depth.³²

However, limited stand-off capabilities necessitate the need for ground forces to physically hold ground in proximity to a UGF in order to locate it and then penetrate it before follow-on actions. Ground detection methodologies include a range of geophysical systems as well as sound detection devices. Once an anomaly has been detected, physical means must be used to gain access, which may comprise heavy earth-moving plant or drilling equipment. Once penetrated, CCTV, sUAS, or MWD are commonly used to provide an initial reconnaissance of an underground space before the mission specification will dictate as to whether commanders need to order personnel underground immediately or whether more time is taken to better understand the UGF.³³

Akin to the fight against improvised explosive devices, the collation of intelligence around UGFs is an important task. This enables the international community to understand the network of resources, namely knowledgeable, skilled, and experienced personnel and funding, that have been utilized to construct the system. This may facilitate the ability to attack the network as part of a longer-term campaign.³⁴

Deny

Having located a UGF or other category of subterranea, the mission may be to deny it. Denial can be achieved via a range of actions.

- **Demolition**³⁵ (hard-kill) - may relate to the whole or part of the structure. Negating access could achieve mission success but may only be temporary if it can be re-established. Deep UGFs and advanced infrastructure may require a two-stage attack to destroy supporting engineering and then shift bulk overburden into the tunnel void. Further considerations include the type of explosive, the means, and the location of emplacement. Attack may be via ground or aerial delivery and may be explosive or thermobaric in nature.[36]

- **Disablement** (soft-kill) – may be linked to the demolition of points of access or the shutting down of supporting infrastructure. Non-destruction may facilitate re-opening and rehabilitation for future use. This may be pertinent for Category 2 urban infrastructure. Advantages: Simple and fast to disable umbilicals. Disadvantages: repair may be possible, and tunnels may still be usable at a reduced scale. Many systems will have alternative access/ventilation shafts, and these must be denied/destroyed as well, albeit they offer ingress opportunities for personnel, energy, or substances.

- **Blocking** – sophisticated blocking may entail the use of liquids, grouts, or foams to fill a tunnel void.[37] These measures may require specialist expertise, equipment, and resources and take more time to prepare and emplace but are less susceptible to clearance and reactivation. Basic blocking could be achieved by placing rubble, debris, or a large object within a portal. Clearance and reactivation might be easier, but it depends on the level of effort enemy forces are prepared to deploy. Surveillance could be used to identify and interdict enemy forces attempting to reactivate the tunnel.

- **Flooding** - Even partially flooding tunnels substantially decreases their utility. It may be able to flood with suspended solids to partially fill with solids. Water ingress is a perennial problem in underground workings and flooding may be brought about by disabling existing pumps. Alternatively, surface equipment could be used to draw water from a nearby source, but it will consume a significant amount of time and resources. Unless sufficient volume is reached, functioning umbilicals may cope with ingress, or a system may drain naturally. Environmental contamination risk is another factor that would need to be carefully considered.[38]

Due to operational constraints, denial via destructive means may not be a viable option. An example might be the presence of critical infrastructure within a Category Two structure, where collateral damage may be detrimental to the longer-term mission. This may delay post-conflict rehabilitation or indeed be vital to sustaining a civilian population that has not been displaced or may quickly return.

A subterranean network may, therefore, require to be cleared, albeit the force ratios required and operational risks increase significantly.[39] Having been cleared, a subterranean network must then be either sealed or occupied as history has demonstrated that not to do so risks re-infiltration by enemy forces, potentially with the emergence of threats behind the Forward Line of Troops, such as that might be within a Three Block War operational context.[40]

Occupation may offer protection to force elements, but lines of communication and logistics may be adversely extended. In rare circumstances, it may be desirable to isolate a particular UGF. If so, ground forces must ensure that all points of access are located and secured.[41] This action may be a temporary action ahead of a clearance or denial or to allow for an operational pause whereby specialist assets may be pulled forward or reconstituted.

Offensive and Defensive Use of Subterranea

Western military doctrine largely focuses on countering the threat posed by subterranea. We must look more proactively at how to better utilize this environment for our own means.

Protection

Recent conflict has clearly documented the need for increased levels of protection from observation and fires, whether IDW, ADW,, or sUAS.[42] While there are rare military capabilities to create new underground spaces, force protection, and infrastructure support engineers can advise on the utilization of existing subterranea to enhance survivability, albeit challenges endure around how to conduct Command and Control (C2) from within such structures.[43]

Covered/clandestine access

Subterranea may be used to provide clandestine movement and access. Trafficable systems may already be open and of immediate use. Alternatively, a significant investment of time and resources would be required to utilize a subterranean route. If used, these could provide a shock and/or surprise effect and either facilitate a raid or a break-in action to support surface maneuver.

A recent example was the Russian Forces (RUF) assault and capture of the Tsarska Okhota Ukrainian Armed Force (UAF) positions on the southern flank of Avdiivka in January 2024.[44] The RUF took several days to clear and prepare an infiltration of several kilometers via a 1.4 m diameter sewage pipe. The purported success of this action supported the subsequent capture of Avdiivka itself in mid-February 2024.[45]

Mines

The mines of the Allied Messines offensive in 1917 were designed to strike both a physical and psychological blow to the Germans. Almost a century later, Syrian rebels used mines in Aleppo to target Syrian government military facilities. The psychological effect was amplified through social media.[46] Mines have also been recorded in Afghanistan in 2019, in Ukraine in 2023, and in Turkey in 2017.[47] As with the use of subterranea to facilitate maneuver, such actions required a significant investment of time and resources, and static military elements must look to protect themselves from attack from all vectors, including underground.[48]

Others

Beyond combat operations, subterranea may be used for a variety of nefarious purposes or maybe the location of an incident requiring civil responders.

Organized Crime

Cross-border smuggling is the most obvious example of the use of subterranea by organization crime. A significant number of cross-border tunnels (CBTs) have been located across the USA-Mexico border, and the Mexican cartels have sought to use UGFs to secure operations.[49]

Further international examples include clandestine facilities for the manufacture of counterfeit goods, people trafficking, and arms supply. Tunnels have also been used to provide clandestine locations from which to tap fuel pipelines.[50]

Espionage

Notable examples of subterranean espionage include Operation Silver in Vienna

(1949-1955) and Operation Gold in Berlin (1951-1956). In both instances, British and American intelligence agencies used subterranean access to install intercept taps on critical KGB and Soviet military telecommunication lines.[51]

Counter Terrorism and Security

In 1996, the Japanese embassy siege in Lima, Peru was broken after assault tunnels were excavated to several strategic locations within the embassy complex. Local mining experts were recruited to construct the tunnels.[52]

Three major bombings were carried out by al-Qaida affiliates on the London Underground on 7 July 2005 at peak commuting time.[53] Beyond the physical and psychological impact on the population, there was significant damage to transport infrastructure that, in turn, had an economic effect.

During the Hong Kong student demonstrations of late 2019, several protesters tried to escape the besieged Hong Kong Polytechnic University via sewage and railway tunnels.[54]

Civil Responders

Civil responders may be required to conduct operations against underground infrastructure fires, natural disasters (earthquakes, floods, etc.), mine accidents, and terrorist attacks.[55]

While terrorist attacks may require armed security elements, the responders in the other scenarios may be exclusively government/civilian. Nevertheless, the physical and environmental threats and, therefore, planning and operational assumptions remain largely the same.

Planning Considerations

The UK military's Defence Lines of Development (DLODs) serve as a logical framework to follow on how to acquire and sustain generalist capability.[56]

Training

It is rare to see subterranean training integrated into major exercises.[57] This is due to the paucity of large-scale training estates which includes subterranea, but also that many commanders and planners are concerned that it will make the exercise too complex.

It is vital that other specialist capabilities are combined within exercises and that lessons are learned and shared from each other's experiences.

Western militaries often have cadres and specializations in the mountain or jungle environments, but aside from courses, there are no dedicated urban formations, let alone those with generalist capabilities for subterranea.[58]

In addition to physically conditioning soldiers for operating underground, psychological preparation is important against the potential impact of vertigo, claustrophobia, disruption of Circadian rhythm, and sensory deprivation or overload.[59] The use of caving, rock climbing, and mountaineering adventure training proxies for military subterranean training is highly recommended.

Equipment

While TTPs may not change, equipment will.[60] The most obvious requirement is for protection against the environment and, notably, air quality. Air quality can vary due to natural processes and the design and layout of a system but will also be affected by offensive and breaching actions, weapon systems, and the presence of infrastructure such as gas mains. Many subterranean spaces are essentially confined spaces that pose dangers ranging from noxious fumes and reduced oxygen levels to explosive and fire risks. They can also present flooding and drowning hazards.[61] Therefore, soldiers operating underground must have the ability to monitor the environment and then either have the means to sustain or extricate themselves.

The list of equipment that can enhance survivability and lethality within the subterranean environment is extensive, and indeed, much of it already exists, albeit within specialist areas. The challenge in the face of an urban campaign is scalability, with the burden of sustainability and the replacement of expendable or damaged items.

Key equipment includes MWD, sUAS, breaching equipment (thermal, explosive, physical), ballistic shields, SCBA, self-rescue equipment, navigation aids, communications (surface to sub-surface, sub-surface to sub-surface), lighting, NVAs, and thermal.[62] However, it is worth acknowledging that the tunnel rats of Vietnam, despite the development of exquisite pieces of equipment, largely favored the simplicity of a knife, pistol, and flashlight.[63] Aside from military-specific equipment, much can be learned from the work of industrial sectors such as mining and tunnel engineering, where research and development (R&D) often moves at a faster pace.

Personnel

Maintaining a focus on non-special forces, the simple fact is that not everyone will be suited to operating underground due to a range of physiological and psychological factors.[64]

Enabling capabilities may include chemical response, medical evacuation, bomb disposal, search, demolitions and breaching, infrastructure assessment, MWD, confided and elevated access, electric warfare, linguistics, logistics, and many others. All these capabilities must be well-versed in how to integrate, and C2 must understand the inflection points between when and where such enabling capabilities need to be brought forward or declined.

If the operation is in a homeland resilience context, beyond the primary civil responders, supporting capabilities may include government employees and technical subject matter experts (utilities, engineering, transport, etc.). Finally, it is important to recognize that Reserve specialists may be the sole source of knowledge, skills, and experience and that the C2 structures must be aware of where and how these experts can be used for operational effect, be that in person or reach-back.

Information

A wealth of OSINT information exists around the threat from the offensive use of subterranea. However, internationally, one challenge that endures is around a common understanding of what comprises the threats and opportunities. This includes such matters as a common lexicon of subterranea and, indeed, how features might be depicted on a map at various scales.

More specialist knowledge may be required to fully assess the threat in various geologies and climates. This includes understanding the purpose of Category 1 and Category 2 subterranea and the dangers that might be present while conducting operations within it, or indeed the ramifications of destroying it. It is, therefore, essential that commanders direct that subterranea is included in the Intelligence Preparation of the Environment (IPE) so that staff can process the threats and opportunities posed and integrate these into the commander's scheme of maneuver.[65]

Information may also be used offensively, with examples ranging from the threat of mines in Syria to CBTs with raids or abductions in Israel.[66]

Infrastructure

Access to subterranean training establishments is limited. While many urban training facilities have some element of subterranea, it is often limited in scale and complexity.[67] There are examples of deep and complex UGFs that can be used for training, but they, in turn, often lack the commensurate level of surface and super-surface estate.

Developments in virtual reality and the use of wargaming offer value but will never wholly negate the need for physical training.[68] The most obvious solution is to conduct exercises within real-world urban environments. While this has been done, there is a general reticence to do so.[69]

Concepts and Doctrine

The British write some of the best doctrine in the world; it is fortunate their officers do not read it.[70]

In the contemporary era, the most proactive doctrine has originated from the US Army and recognizing the need to develop the generalist capability, the Asymmetric Warfare Group declassified several guides.[71] Several specialist courses were developed, most notably around breaching.[72] In 2019, *ATP 3-21.51: Subterranean Operations* was published and remains the most comprehensive and publicly accessible doctrine on the subject.[73] British Army Doctrine Note 20/05 leans heavily on US doctrine but has evolved in synchronization with urban doctrine.[74]

Regrettably, subterranean operations are underrepresented in most military doctrine. Efforts are being made to address this, but ultimately, doctrine benefits no one if it is not consumed and thoroughly digested. In the absence of doctrine, leaders at all levels should engage with experts and voraciously consume books, papers, and podcasts that contain subterranean commentary and experience.[75]

Organization

It is unlikely that there will ever be the need or resources available to develop and sustain generalist force elements whose sole occupation is subterranean operations. Therefore, it is vital to ensure that any element that might be called upon to operate within the urban environment is trained and equipped to do so.

Organizationally and outside of the special forces community, there is a need to build and maintain groups of deep experts who can be called upon to support, be that on operations, the development of new equipment or doctrine, or the design of training estate. To sustain the depth and breadth of this capability, militaries may need to consider alternative terms and conditions of service.

Logistics

As discussed above, the amount of specialist equipment needed varies. Large amounts are required to initiate operations and then sustain against high attrition rates.[76] Time of supply becomes more pertinent when taking into consideration the time to manufacture or train, e.g. MWD.[77] Already stretched urban combat logistics will be under even greater pressure underground. Moving resources forward and casualties rearward will take more time and consume more enablers. Confined access will likely inhibit the use of larger platforms.[78]

Recent cave rescues exemplify this point. In 2018, a team of over 10,000 personnel took 18 days to rescue twelve children and one adult, and in 2021, in Wales, a team of over 300 personnel took 54 hours to extract one casualty over one mile.[79] The Thailand rescue also illustrates how weather and flooding can dynamically change logistical access. But assuming access can be secured and maintained, large scale logistics may benefit significantly from the protection offered by urban underground spaces.

The Future – Research and Development

Military research organizations are now committing more resources to R&D, e.g. the DARPA SubT Challenge, the Underminer project, and the multi-agency MoSAIC Challenge. In most cases, military and government agencies seek to leverage academic and industry knowledge, skills, and experience (KSE).[80] The Austrian Armed Forces' Project NIKE is an excellent example of a multistakeholder initiative to develop a series of thematic projects within a common operational understanding. Their multi-stage training programme is delivered at their Zentrum am Berg training facility which is hosted at an operational mine.[81] However, looking to the future, evolution must give way to revolution if the acquisition OODA loop is to truly break the asymmetric impasse that subterranea offers to a great many of our adversaries.[82]

Militaries are ultimately at the mercy of budgets, inter-service, and inter-departmental rivalries and are often remiss in appreciating the KSE that they often have within their Reserves. They may offer the modern-day parallel for 'Hellfire Jack' and his 1914 'Clay Kickers'.[83] Indeed, the technology, ranging from the mundane to the exquisite, may already be available from within the tunneling and mining sectors.

Conclusion

We learn from history only that we do not learn from history.[84]

Today, over 10,000 known UGFs exist around the world, including the layers of UUS.[85] Despite the media focus on the tunnels of Gaza, Western coalition forces and partners must ensure that objectivity is maintained when considering what is likely to present as a wicked factor in an urban fight.[86]

Over history, we have seen military technological advancements where subterranea has been used to offer an initial asymmetric advantage with a subsequent counter-advancement to reduce the aforementioned asymmetry.

That pattern endures today and will likely continue to do so for the foreseeable future.

Exquisite technology will undoubtedly have a part to play, but it will be for the sole use of SF. Even then, limited SF capabilities will need to be used as a matter of last resort or for high-value targets – an urban battle at any scale will necessitate the use of generalist capabilities.[87]

The IDF has demonstrated that specialized units can be force-generated for subterranean operations but that a considerable amount of time and resources are required to do so.

Well-known British military theoretical and historical writer Captain Sir Basil Liddell Hart eloquently captured the need to take a strategic approach towards the importance of learning from the recurring patterns, errors, and lessons of history if we are to avoid repeating mistakes from the distant and not-so-distant past.[88] Regrettably, this habit endures due to the systemic short-term memories of armies, their generals, and the politicians that ultimately control the levels of investment in defense. Looking below the horizon, a strategic, coordinated, and cooperative approach must be shaped as part of international efforts to embrace the subterranean environment. This must now happen at a rapid pace.

Endnotes

Disclaimer: *The views expressed are those of the author and do not necessarily reflect policy or position of the British Army, the Ministry of Defence, or the British Government.*

1. Toi Staff, "Gaza tunnels stretch at least 350 miles, far longer than past estimate – report," The Times of Israel, January 16, 2024, https://www.timesofisrael.com/gaza-tunnels-stretch-at-least-350-miles-far-longer-than-past-estimate-report/.
2. John Spencer, "Underground Nightmare: Hamas Tunnels and the Wicked Problem Facing the IDF," Modern Warfare Institute, West Point Military Academy, October 17, 2023, accessed April 24, 2024, https://mwi.westpoint.edu/underground-nightmarehamas-tunnels-and- the-wicked-problem-facing-the-idf/
3. The terms subterranean and underground may be used interchangeably; SubT or SbT may be used as a shortened form of subterranean; subterranea is a catch-all term for subterranean features; Daphné Richemond-Barak, *Underground Warfare* (London: Oxford University Press, 2018), 4.

4. Paul Springer, "E-Notes: Fighting Under the Earth: The History of Tunneling in Warfare," Foreign Policy Research Institute, April 23, 2015, https://www.fpri.org/article/2015/04/fighting-under-the-earth-the-history-of-tunneling-in-warfare/; John Spencer and Ze'ev Orenstein, "Discovering Jerusalem's Hidden Urban Warfare Lessons," *Urban Warfare Project Podcast*, Modern Warfare Institute, 3 September 2021, https://mwi.westpoint.edu/discovering-jerusalems-hidden-urban-warfare-lessons/

5. Simon Jones, *Underground Warfare 1914-1918* (Pen & Sword Military, 2010).

6. Wikipedia, s.v. "Military citadels under London," last modified April 7, 2024 12:09, https://en.wikipedia.org/wiki/Military_citadels_under_London; Wikipedia, s.v. "Moscow Metro," last modified April 26, 2024, 06:09, https://en.wikipedia.org/wiki/Moscow_Metro; Chris Fitch, *Subterranea* (London: Headline Publishing Group, 2020), 127, 151, 188,

7. UK Ministry of Defence (MoD), *Corsham Tunnels – A Brief History*, (MoD, undated), https://assets.publishing.service.gov.uk/media/5a7ea6cb40f0b62305b824d7/Corsham_Tunnel_version1.pdf; "Bunker Tours," The Greenbrier, accessed April 26, 2024, https://www.greenbrier.com/activities/bunker-tours/

8. School of Advanced Military Studies and John Spencer, "Urban Warfare," March 15, 2024, in *The Operational Arch,* podcast, audio, 40:07, https://podcasts.apple.com/us/podcast/the-operational-arch/id1660058003?i=1000649303775; David Johnson, "Urban Legend: is Combat in Cities Really Inevitable?," *War On the Rocks*, May 7, 2019, accessed April 26, 2024, https://warontherocks.com/2019/05/urban-legend-is-combat-in-cities-really-inevitable/

9. Wikipedia, s.v. "7 July 2005 London bombings," last modified April 25, 2024, 06:06, https://en.wikipedia.org/wiki/7_July_2005_London_bombings

10. John Spencer and Jayson Geroux, "Urban Warfare Project Case Study Series, Case Study #2 – Mosul," Modern Warfare Institute, West Point Military Academy, September 15, 2021, accessed April 26, 2024, https://mwi.westpoint.edu/urban-warfareproject-case-study-2-battle-of-mosul/

11. John Spencer and Charles Knight, "The Battle of Marawi," Mar 5, 2021, in *Urban Warfare Project*, podcast, audio, 47:10, https://mwi.westpoint.edu/the-battle-of-marawi/

12. Wikipedia, s.v. "Battle of Aleppo (2012–2016)," last modified April 24, 2024, https://en.wikipedia.org/wiki/Battle_of_Aleppo_(2012%E2%80%932016)

13. "Kyiv's Metro Is a Symbol of the City's Resilience," *Foreign Policy Magazine*, November 12, 2022, https://foreignpolicy.com/2022/11/12/ukraine-russia-war-kyiv-metro-transit-shelter-missiles/

14. "In the tunnels of Azovstal, traces of Ukraine's resistance," *France 24*, June 15, 2022, https://www.france24.com/en/livenews/20220615-in-the-tunnels-of-azovstal-traces-of-ukraine-s-resistance

15. Oleksandr Miasyshchev, "Ukraine: The Battle for Soledar's Salt Mines," *Institute for War and Peace Reporting*, March 9, 2023, https://iwpr.net/global-voices/ukraine-battle-soledars-salt-mines; Wikipedia, s.v. "Battle of Soledar," last modified April 21, 2024, https://en.wikipedia.org/wiki/Battle_of_Soledar

16. Stefan Korshak, "Russian Infantry Scores Gains in Battleground Avdiivka, Both Sides Predict More Big Attacks," *Kyiv Post*, January 26, 2024, https://www.kyivpost.com/post/27219

17. Wikipedia, s.v. "2014 Gaza War," last modified April 23, 2024, https://en.wikipedia.org/wiki/2014_Gaza_War
18. "The Hamas - Israel War", Israeli Defense Forces, accessed April 24, 2024, https://www.idf.il/en/mini-sites/hamas-israel-war-24/
19. UK Ministry of Defence, *Subterranean Operations in the Urban Environment*, Doctrine Note 20/05 (Land Warfare Centre, August 2020); United States Department of the Army, *Subterranean Operations*, ATP 3-21.51 (Washington, DC: Headquarters, Department of the Army, 2019), https://armypubs.army.mil/epubs/DR_pubs/DR_a/pdf/web/ARN19656_ATP%20321x51%20%20FINAL%20WEB.pdf.
20. The level of blast protection is related to the depth and type of overburden.
21. Adapted with permission from the UK Ministry of Defence, British Army Land Warfare Centre, Subterranean Operations in the Urban Environment, Doctrine Note 20/05, 1-4.
22. Si-Cong Liu, Fang-Le Peng, Yong-Kang Qiao, Jun-Bo Zhang, "Evaluating disaster prevention benefits of underground space from the perspective of urban resilience," *International Journal of Disaster Risk Reduction* 58, 2021,https://doi.org/10.1016/j.ijdrr.2021.102206.
23. Will Noble, "Secretive Central London Cold War Tunnels Could Open As Visitor Attraction," *Londonist*, updated January 30, 2024, https://londonist.com/london/news/kingsway-tunnels-holborn-open-public
24. From the *Emerald Tablet,* a short Hermetic text which first appeared in an Arabic source from the late eighth or early ninth century; Wikipedia, s.v. "As above, so below,", last modified March 30, 2024, https://en.wikipedia.org/wiki/As_above,_so_below
25. John Spencer and Jacob Stoil, "Israel, Gaza, and the Looming Challenge of Urban Warfare," October 13, 2023, in *Urban Warfare Project*, podcast, audio, 1:22:54, https://mwi.westpoint.edu/israel-gaza-and-the-looming-challenges-of-urban-warfare/
26. British Army military engineers (a.k.a. Sappers) include specialists in breaching, demolitions, survey, force protection, infrastructure support, civil engineering, geology, explosive ordnance disposal (EOD) & Search, and counter-chemical biological radiological and nuclear (C-CBRN); British Army, "Corps of the Royal Engineers", accessed April 26, 2024, https://www.army.mod.uk/who-we-are/corps-regiments-and-units/corps-of-royal-engineers/.
27. Law of Armed Conflict and International Humanitarian Law, respectively.
28. Richemond-Barak, *Underground Warfare*, 251-5.
29. Liam Collins and John Spencer with Daphne Richemond-Barak, "Beneath the City," *Understanding Urban Warfare* (Havant: Howgate Publishing, 2022), page 114.
30. John Spencer and Charles Dunlap, "The Law of War and the Urban Battlefield," November 24, 2023, in *Urban Warfare Project*, podcast, audio, 52:02, https://mwi.westpoint.edu/the-law-of-war-and-the-urban-battlefield/
31. Ted Gup, "The Ultimate Congressional Hideway," *Washington Post*, May 31, 1992, https://www.washingtonpost.com/wpsrv/local/daily/july/25/brier1.htm
32. IMINT – imagery intelligence; HUMINT – human intelligence; SIGINT – signal intelligence.
33. CCTV - Closed-circuit television; sUAS – small unmanned aerial systems, colloquially referred to also as drones or remotely piloted aircraft systems (RPAS).

34. Collins et al., "Beneath the City," page 118.
35. Richard Bullock, "A study of tunnel demolition by hasty methods," (master's thesis, Missouri School of Mines and Metallurgy, 1955, 92, https://scholarsmine.mst.edu/masters_theses/2589/
36. Barbara Starr and Ryan Browne, "First on CNN: US drops largest non-nuclear bomb in Afghanistan," *CNN*, April 14, 2017, https://edition.cnn.com/2017/04/13/politics/afghanistan-isis-moab-bomb/index.html
37. Toi Staff, "UNIFIL confirms tunnel filled with cement by IDF crossed border, broke UN rules ," *The Times of Israel*, December 29, 2018, https://www.timesofisrael.com/unifil-confirms-tunnel-filled-with-cement-by-idf-crossed-border-broke-un-rules/; Dominic Nicholls, "'Sponge bombs' are Israel's new secret weapon to block Hamas tunnels," The Telegraph, October 25, 2023, https://www.telegraph.co.uk/world-news/2023/10/25/sponge-bomb-new-weapon-israel-gaza-tunnels-war-hamas/
38. Tom Magnold and John Penycate, *The Tunnels of Cu Chi: A Remarkable Story of War in Vietnam* (Orion Books Ltd, 2005), 207-208; Josie Glausiusz, "As Israel Floods Gaza's Tunnels with Seawater, Scientists Worry about Aquifer Contamination," *Scientific American*, February 5, 2024, https://www.scientificamerican.com/article/as-israel-floods-gazas-tunnels-with-seawaterscientists-worry-about-aquifer-contamination/
39. United States Department of the Army, *Subterranean Operations*, ATP 3-21.51
40. Charles Krulak, "The Strategic Corporal: Leadership in the Three-Block War," Leatherneck, 82, 1, January 1999, 14 https://www.mca-marines.org/wp-content/uploads/1999-Jan-The-strategic-corporal-Leadership-in-the-three-block-war.pdf
41. United States Department of the Army, *Subterranean Operations*, ATP 3-21.51.
42. IDW - Indirect Weapons; ADW - Air Dropped Weapons.
43. "MOD states GSDF missile unit activities on Miyako might extend to civilian land," *The Ryukyu Shimpo*, May 19, 2017, http://english.ryukyushimpo.jp/2017/05/25/27041/ - the Japan Ground Self-Defense Force maintains a tunneling capability to provide shelters for equipment, notably surface-to-air and surface-to-sea missile systems ; "Communications in the Subterranean Environment," *Think Defence*, blog, August 30, 2021, https://www.thinkdefence.co.uk/2021/08/communicationsin-the-subterranean-environment/.
44. Wikipedia, s.v. "Battle of Avdiivka (2023–2024)," last modified April 22, 2024, https://en.wikipedia.org/wiki/Battle_of_Avdiivka_(2023%E2%80%932024).
45. "What to Know About the Fall of Avdiivka," *The New York Times*, February 17, 2024, https://www.nytimes.com/2024/02/17/world/europe/avdiivka-russia-ukraine-war.html
46. "Syria war: Aleppo tunnel bomb 'kills 38 government troops'," *BBC*, July 22, 2016, https://www.bbc.co.uk/news/world-middleeast-36868706
47. Ayaz Gul, "Taliban Tunnel Bomb Hits Afghan Army Base," *Voice of America*, January 2, 2019, https://www.voanews.com/a/taliban-tunnel-bomb-hits-afghan-army-base-italian-troops-survive-insider-attack/4725499.html ; Ukraine Front Line (@EuromaidanPR), "The Armed Forces of Ukraine continue to blow up pre-mined buildings in Bakhmut…," X, April 18, 2023, 10:33 a.m., https://twitter.com/EuromaidanPR/status/1648258521580941313; "Turkey militants 'used tunnel to plant explosives'," *BBC*, April 12, 2017, https://www.bbc.co.uk/news/world-europe-39576915

48. Collins et al., "Beneath the City," page 118.
49. Brenda Fiegel, "Geographic Constraints of Narco-Tunnels Along the Southwest Border," *Small Wars Journal*, September 30, 2016, https://smallwarsjournal.com/jrnl/art/geographic-constraints-of-narco-tunnels-along-the-southwest-border ;Robert Bunker and John Sullivan, "Mexican Cartel Tactical Note #44: Mexican Army (SEDENA) Re-Discovers Underground Cartel Bunker in Reynosa, Tamaulipas," *Small Wars Journal*, February 20, 2020, https://smallwarsjournal.com/jrnl/art/mexican-cartel-tacticalnote-44-mexican-army-sedena-re-discovers-underground-cartel-bunker
50. Robert Bunker and John Sullivan, "Mexican Cartel Tactical Note #40: Cártel Santa Rosa de Lima (CSRL) Tunnels in Guanajuato Highlights Tactical Considerations in Underground Operations," *Small Wars Journal*, March 22, 2019, https://smallwarsjournal.com/jrnl/art/mexican-cartel-tactical-note-40-cartel-santa-rosa-de-lima-csrl-tunnels-guanajuato
51. Steve Vogel, *Betrayal in Berlin* (London: John Murray, 2020).
52. Wikipedia, s.v. "Japanese embassy hostage crisis," last modified March 7, 2024, https://en.wikipedia.org/wiki/Japanese_embassy_hostage_crisis
53. See Note 10.
54. Tamar Lapin, "Besieged Hong Kong protesters resort to daring sewer escapes," *New York Post*, last modified November 20, 2019, 09:49 a.m. ET, https://nypost.com/2019/11/19/besieged-hong-kong-protesters-resort-to-daring-sewer-escapes/
55. Wayne Chang and Helen Regan, "Dozens trapped in tunnels after Taiwan's strongest quake in 25 years kills at least nine," *CNN*, last updated April 3, 2024, 08:00 PM EDT, https://edition.cnn.com/2024/04/02/asia/taiwan-earthquake-tsunami-warningintl-hnk/index.html; Emma Roth, "The rare NYC earthquake underscores concerns about infrastructure," *The Verge*, April 5, 2024, https://www.theverge.com/2024/4/5/24122320/nyc-earthquake-bridges-infrastructure-concerns
56. A term used by the UK MoD, particularly in the acquisition and planning for acquisition. A Defence Line of Development (DLOD) provides a way of view a programme, set of programmes or strategy from a specific perspective, and provides a means matrix management of a programme or strategy; Defence Line of Development, http://trakcommunity.org/index.php/wiki/Defence_Line_of_Development, *Trak-Community*, undated.
57. John Spencer, Jayson Geroux and Stuart Lyle, "An Urban Warfare Christmas Wish List, 2023 edition," December 22, 2023, in *Urban Warfare Project*, podcast, audio, 41:33, https://mwi.westpoint.edu/an-urban-warfare-christmas-wish-list-2023-edition/
58. John Spencer and Joe Vega, "A talk with the US Army's Underground Warfare Expert," June 26, 2020, in *Urban Warfare Project*, podcast, audio, 18:32,https://mwi.westpoint.edu/talk-us-armys-underground-warfare-expert/
59. Johnson, "Urban Legend: is Combat in Cities Really Inevitable?."
60. Spencer and Vega, "A talk with the US Army's Underground Warfare Expert."
61. Health and Safety Executive, "Introduction to working in confined spaces," accessed April 26, 2024, https://www.hse.gov.uk/confinedspace/introduction.htm
62. SCBA – self-contained breathing apparatus; NVA – night-vision aids.

63. Magnold and Penycate, *The Tunnels of Cu Chi*, 109-115; the Tunnel Rats were specialist American and Australian troops, predominantly military engineers, tasked with dealing with Viet Cong tunnels during the Vietnam War (1955-1975).
64. Ibid., 103.
65. Personal communication, Maj Geroux, Canadian Armed Forces, February 8, 2024. IPE is used to help planning teams develop an understanding of the environment within which operations will be planned and conducted. The environment may include aspects such as weather, human demographics, cultural and tribal boundaries, infrastructure, and geology.
66. Marissa Newman, "Northern residents to dig in search of cross-border tunnels," *The Times of Israel*, December 3, 2014, https://www.timesofisrael.com/northern-residents-to-dig-in-search-of-cross-border-tunnels/; Terrence McCoy, "How Hamas uses its tunnels to kill and capture Israeli soldiers," *The Washington Post*, July 21, 2014, https://www.washingtonpost.com/news/morning-mix/wp/2014/07/21/how-hamas-uses-its-tunnels-to-kill-and-capture-israelisoldiers/
67. Spencer, *et al*, "An Urban Warfare Christmas Wish List, 2023 edition."
68. 4GD Ltd, https://www.4gd.co.uk/solution
69. Personal communication, Maj Geroux, Canadian Armed Forces, February 8, 2024.
70. Attributed to Erwin Rommel and quoted in the British Army *Army Doctrine Primer* (Shrivenham: Development, Concept and Doctrine Centre (DCDC), 2011), https://assets.publishing.service.gov.uk/media/5a79b6c540f0b63d72fc7eac/20110519ADP_Army_Doctrine_Primerpdf.pdf
72. Collins et al., "Beneath the City," page 118.
73. Spencer and Vega, "A talk with the US Army's Underground Warfare Expert."
74. United States Department of the Army, *Subterranean Operations*, ATP 3-21.51.
75. UK MoD, Subterranean Operations in the Urban Environment, Doctrine Note 20/05.
76. Spencer, *et al*, "An Urban Warfare Christmas Wish List, 2023 edition."
77. Spencer, "Underground Nightmare."
78. It may take several months to train a military working dog; Ephrat Livni, "Israel Relies on Combat Dogs in Gaza," *The New York Times*, December 23, 2023, https://www.nytimes.com/2023/12/24/world/middleeast/israel-gaza-dogs.html; Yaron Doron, "A moving tribute: Commemorating the fallen canines of the Gaza war," *Israel Hayom*, February 29, 2024, https://www.israelhayom.com/2024/02/29/a-moving-tribute-commemorating-the-fallen-canines-of-the-gaza-war/.
79. Alex Sorkin, Roy Nadler, Adir Sommer, Avishai M Tsur, Jacob Chen, Tarif Bader, Avi Benov, "Medical Challenges in Underground Warfare," *Military Medicine*, 186, S1, January 25, 2021, 839–844, https://doi.org/10.1093/milmed/usaa447.
80. "The extraordinary story of how 300 volunteers rescued a stranded caver," *BBC*, November 10, 2021, https://www.bbc.co.uk/news/uk-wales-59219380; Wikipedia, s.v. "Tham Luang cave rescue," last modified April 23, 2024, https://en.wikipedia.org/wiki/Tham_Luang_cave_rescue.
81. DARPA, Subterranean (SubT) Challenge, accessed April 26, 2024, https://www.darpa.mil/program/darpa-subterraneanchallenge; DARPA, Underminer, accessed April 26, 2024, https://www.darpa.mil/program/underminer; Mobile Standoff Autonomous Indoor Capabilities Challenge, a

joint US and Israeli programme seeking cutting edge hardware and software solutions to address some of the challenging and longstanding technological gaps concerning remote autonomous indoor maneuver, accessed April 26, 2024, https://mosaichallenge.com.

82. Theresian Military Academy, Austria, "Forschungsbereich: Komplexe Einsätze unter Tage [Research Area: Complex Operations Underground]," accessed April 26, 2024, https://www.milak.at/news/detail/forschungsbereich-komplexe-einsaetzeunter-tage; Zentrum am Berg underground test and research facility, accessed April 26, 2024, https://www.zab.at/en/.

83. The OODA loop (observe, orient, decide, act) is a decision-making model developed by military strategist and United States Air Force Colonel John Boyd; Wikipedia, s.v. "OODA loop," last modified January 12, 2024, https://en.wikipedia.org/wiki/OODA_loop.

84. Wikipedia, s.v. "Tunnelling companies of the Royal Engineers," last modified December 14, 2023, https://en.wikipedia.org/wiki/Tunnelling_companies_of_the_Royal_Engineers

85. Attributed to German philosopher Georg Wilhelm Friedrich Hegel, ca. early 1800s, likely to have been derived from a series of lectures collected and published posthumously under the title "*Vorlesungen über die Philosophie der Geschichte* [Lectures on the Philosophy of History]"; Quote Investigator, "Quote Origin: We Learn From History That We Do Not Learn From History," last modified March 6, 2024, https://quoteinvestigator.com/2024/03/06/learn-history/.

86. United States Department of the Army, *Subterranean Operations*, ATP 3-21.51.

87. Spencer, "Underground Nightmare."

88. Spencer and Vega, "A talk with the US Army's Underground Warfare Expert."

89. Basil Henry Liddell Hart, *Why Don't We Learn from History*, (London: George Allen and Unwin, 1944).

CHAPTER 14
Creating Light at Tunnel's End: Ukraine's Post-war Urban Recovery

Russell W. Glenn

Introduction

Combat in Ukraine attracts world attention as does a flame a moth. Ongoing fighting merits awareness, but with it comes the danger that only belatedly do concerns turn to recovery operations. Any delay is unfortunate; history informs us that recovery planning and—to the extent possible initiation—is best fast-tracked with the disaster causing damage. The past also provides plentiful lessons regarding how to approach this recovery. Challenges trailing hostilities will differ in character from those of war but be no less imposing. It is an unfortunate truth that destruction proves far cheaper than mending.

Ukraine will justifiably blame Russia for many of its reconstruction difficulties. Others will be self-imposed. Nor will the trials be Ukraine's alone. Fortunately, the international community, United Nations agencies, nongovernmental organizations (NGOs), and others will also find history's lessons valuable when providing recovery assistance. The United States and its partners in Iraq and Afghanistan made reconstruction missteps best avoided. Though brought to their attention during operations in the former, that US aid providers nevertheless later repeated the shortcomings in Afghanistan lessens one's faith some recovery efforts will not again spawn costly inefficiencies in Ukraine.

This article draws on history both recent and more distant in the service of avoiding repetition of previous shortcomings. Its focus is primarily urban. Post-World War II (WWII) Berlin, Tokyo in the same conflict's aftermath, and cities in Iraq and Afghanistan in the opening years of this century provide helpful insights. The warnings and guidance often apply regardless of environment, rural or urban. Potentially complementing these lessons for governments willing to listen: The collective knowledge of NGOs and other other-than-governmental organizations, particularly those working in Ukraine during the years of combat. The consideration herein includes insights for addressing tasks seemingly mundane but otherwise in actuality. The rarely addressed disposal of debris is a helpful example. Other obvious tasks include effectively providing a population with food, potable water, and shelter, tasks taxing in the best of circumstances now further complex considering ongoing suffering and the need for timely, but not hasty, responses. Finally, parties aiding recovery efforts will confront unexpected tasks, challenges hard to foresee but sure to arise, the expected unexpected, if you will. What does history offer in the way of exemplars from which to adapt? The following paragraphs hopefully lend insight regarding the nature of specific remedies while also being suggestive of others.

Select Offerings from Previous Post-War Urban Recoveries

Capitalize on the Seemingly Mundane

Ukraine's suffering fortunately falls short of many WWII cities' devastation. In Japan alone, bombing destroyed an estimated 2,316,000 houses in 115 cities, killing or injuring over 758,000 residents. (The Office of the United Nations High Commissioner for Human Rights conservatively estimates 25,671 noncombatant casualties in Ukraine between February 24, 2022, and July 16, 2023, 9,287 of whom were killed.[1] Nearly 5.1 million have suffered displacement within Ukraine, while over 6.2 million have fled the country.[2]) The post-war influx of new residents in Tokyo made recovery further difficult, a 1945 population of between 2.75 and 3.5 million increasing to seven million by 1952. Estimates determined that countrywide demand would require provision of 4,200,000 living units in the years immediately following the arrival of peace.[3] Cities in Germany similarly suffered damage practically impossible to grasp: Berlin's post-war rubble constituted 55,000,000 cubic meters, Hamburg's 35,000,000, and Cologne's 24,100,000.[4] If there had been a way to stack Berlin's 1945 rubble on a US football field, the pile would have been 12.3 kilometers (7.67 miles) high.[5] A plane flying at 40,000 feet would have to climb another 500 feet to avoid colliding.

The penultimate episode in the television series *Band of Brothers* opens with Germans stacking bricks recovered from destroyed buildings, handing furniture down from atop rubble piles, and hauling debris away in wagons in a town devastated by war.[6] Much of the refuse from villages, towns, and cities had lost its original value; disposal was the only option. In Berlin, some rubble went to constructing new runways at the three airports of Tempelhof, Tegel, and Gatow.[7] Other created hills atop which appeared new parks.[8] Among Berlin's highest points today is the *Teufelsberg* (Devil's Mountain), constructed of WWII material piled atop an existing building.[9] Hamburg's Hammerbrook area literally evolved from rubble, debris raising it above former marshland to relieve residents of previous sanitation and drainage problems.[10] Canals in Hamburg, Tokyo, and elsewhere disappeared, the presumption being that the space would serve more valuably as roadways given expanding car ownership. Rubble became key material for rebuilding regardless of the city. Workers carefully cleaned and piled bricks on land adjacent to cleared land. In Germany, stacks of two hundred each formed rectangular columns topped by a single brick to mark completion. Thousands upon thousands replicated the tasks highlighted in *Band of Brothers*; Hamburg's reclamation alone recovered, cleaned, and compiled 182 million bricks for reuse.[11]

Workers moved debris from point A to point B, much done by hand, other with the help of mechanization. Property owners cleared their spaces with human labor to the extent possible, otherwise with the assistance of heavy equipment provided by city employees or private companies. Wartime authorities in Germany often used slave labor and those from concentration camps. Women made up no small number of those performing the labor, men being away in the armed forces.[12] *Trümmerfrauen* (rubble women) comprised the labor force most highlighted in Germany. Their tasks included clearing rubble but also determining what was salvageable for reuse and cleaning excess mortar and other waste from that so deemed. It could be brutal work involving loading heavy material into carts, hauling it to centralized collection points, then transferring loads to a *Trümmerbahnlokomotive* (rubble train engine) for further processing.[13]

Experience influenced cleanup efficiency. Officials in earlier bombed urban areas frequently used their cities' unfortunate precedence to improve techniques. Cities spared disaster until later found the task more burdensome. Local government and resident motivation additionally had effect, as—unsurprisingly—did the extent of devastation.[14] Select communities hastened their efforts in the service of both rebuilding and civic pride. Recovery elsewhere could lag for months, years, or even decades. One could find rubble piles as late as 1990 in the German Democratic Republic (East Germany).[15] Clearance was somewhat easier in much of Japan. Structures built of wood predominated; little but ash remained after attacks. Yet even debris in ash form had value, one author finding that in

Tokyo, "the land created through the filling in of streams and moats with the ashes of the war-damaged city provided the foundations for the rise of the business sector."[16]

Disagreements regarding what rebuilding meant could impede the speed of recovery, this in addition to funding and other constraints. Germany, with less centralized urban planning and management than Japan both before and after the war, had city officials whose approaches differed widely. Something similar is likely in Ukraine should officials take community and local government perspectives into account.[17]

Corruption, on the other hand, was a significant culprit hindering recovery's efficiency independent of time or place. Those less savory set up businesses specializing in the collection and resale of valuable debris in Berlin and elsewhere, often gathering material to which they had no right. Metal products for which scrap dealers paid well were markedly popular. Copper, brass from door and other fittings, and steel used in construction were among the products stolen.[18] Such thefts might stir unpleasant memories in veterans of recent efforts to assist Iraqi recovery where copper wire was among the items taken from public buildings, impeding the reestablishment of local governments and their services. Those same veterans would vouch that intact property records were also key to perceptions of officials' effectiveness; deliberate destruction by insurgents served the purpose of further undermining authorities who could no longer confirm ownership. Property records were as important in Germany and elsewhere in the months and years after World War II both in facilitating the legitimacy of occupying powers and confirming ownership in light of the number of, often forcibly, displaced persons returning to reclaim real estate occupied by others rendered homeless.[19] Missing property records further exposed communities to corruption in the form of illicit seizures by wealthier or otherwise more influential parties able to bribe public officials.

Seek Synergy

Given devastation fortuitously being less than was the case in post-WWII Germany and Japan, shortages of building materials, home furnishings, and other necessities should correspondingly be more manageable for Ukraine. The country's residents will likewise be fortunate if coming winters are as mild as that of 2022-2023, but neither they nor officials looking forward can rely on such providence. Berliners suffered a historically cold winter in 1946-47. They stripped wood panels from furniture and scavenged cardboard, rags, and anything else that might serve to replace shattered windows. Far from perfect in effect, any shielding from the brutal cold could be the difference between life and death given the Devil's brew of nature's chill and Soviet cutting power to the Allied-controlled western parts of the city. (The main power station was in the eastern sector.)[20] Mattresses and blankets became treasures, crucial for warmth and survival; newspapers encouraged their sharing in the interest of capitalizing on body heat.[21] Food and potable water were similarly in too short supply. *The Telegraph* estimated that some half-million Germans countrywide died of starvation or exposure that winter.[22]

Open spots amid remaining rubble, flowerboxes, or any other patch of soil became a vegetable garden when temperatures allowed, another of the seemingly minor pieces that together could keep death at bay.[23] While it appears the number lost was considerably less in Japan, hunger and starvation nevertheless stalked its urban streets as well with one report stating up to six individuals daily died of malnutrition or related causes in Tokyo's Ueno rail station alone during the autumn 1945.[24] The recipe for overcoming that Devil's brew is far more complex than dealing with its ingredients individually. Successful recovery, like war waged well, demands a systems approach to orchestration of resources brought to bear.

Resettlement is one of the challenges sure to dominate headlines in the immediate aftermath of a disaster. Those affected can remain without permanent housing or the ability to return to previous residences for months or years. Following WWII, some of Germany's camps for the displaced did not close until 1966, more than two decades after the arrival of peace.[25] No few displaced by 2005's Hurricane Katrina remained in temporary housing for over a decade. Recovery is a long-term undertaking. Sustaining external support and generating internal funding will prove both essential and difficult. How well Ukraine succeeds in maintaining external support while reenergizing domestic government income will in considerable part be a function of how well it deals with its long time corruption. Graft will take many forms. Those displaced are especially vulnerable given unfamiliarity with their surroundings and lack of established social nets.[26]

Adapt to the Expected Unexpected

This last of three urban recovery challenges consists of those unknown before their appearance or others known but with a character definable only as recovery efforts progress. Corruption again rears its head in this regard, a notable concern in a country where as recently as 2016 Transparency International reported between 38 and 42 percent of Ukrainian households having been forced to pay a bribe for access to basic public services.[27]

Corruption will prove to be Ukraine's elephant in the animal's many metaphorical forms. There is the elephant in the room: The issue all know exists but most would like to ignore given the implications of overtly recognizing its existence. Then we have the elephant as described by blind men, each grasping a different part: Tail, trunk, ear, or leg. It is an entity so complex that even several perspectives cannot reveal the nature of the whole. There is finally the elephant in its obvious, recognized, and overwhelming form, that which is the answer to the riddle "How do you know there is an elephant in the bathtub?" The response: "You can't close the shower curtain once you step in." It is this last elephant that is perhaps most apropos to the challenges officials, outside donors, and others assisting recovery confront wherever corruption exists: If the elephant cannot be ousted—or at least reduced to manageable size—those responsible will never be able to close the deal on a successful recovery.

Such was the case for the United States in Vietnam three score years ago, in Iraq more recently, and again in Afghanistan. Among the missteps in the latter two: The United States Agency for International Development's (USAID) Community Stabilization Program (CSP) in Iraq suffered significant policy shortcomings making it difficult—at times practically impossible—to inspect contractor work at building sites, inspections essential to detecting and containing fraud associated with the program. The State Department's disallowing USAID personnel to share rides in military, contractor, and other parties' vehicles meant sites went unseen by responsible US officials for months, months during which in some cases contractors completed virtually no work but payments continued to flow. Efforts to hold construction providers accountable via hiring third party inspectors fell short when the latter's contract failed to include responsibility for monitoring financial components of agreements.[28] The result of these and other planning and policy flaws was termination of the CSP tens of millions of dollars short of its allocated financing. As noted above, failure to capitalize on these identified lessons resulted in repetition of mistakes in Afghanistan.[29]

Implications for Ukraine

These few examples can only hint at the expanse of challenges and related insights history has to offer for those supporting Ukraine's recovery, to include both steps already ongoing and others to come. There will be significant similarities in conditions found in post-WWII German and Japanese urban areas much as was the case with operations in 21st-century Iraq and Afghanistan. There will be significant differences as well. Perhaps most notable in the latter case is the retention of the country's government as a sovereign entity, not the case with the above quartet of nations. The willingness of external powers to assist in funding recovery will likely be among the similarities. Another will be the desire by some to alter from their previous state the character of Ukrainian cities that suffer devastation. For all their horrors, disasters—and certainly war numbers itself as one such—offer opportunities for change. Plans for demolished cities after WWII included increasing green space, eliminating slum areas, and widening streets given the dramatic rise of the automobile. Whether such proposals merit the label improvements, history tells us, will be a matter of perspective, management of citizen expectations, substantive consideration of their input, and the nature of the changes themselves.

Most such ambitions saw implementation only in greatly condensed form, if at all. Marshall Plan and other funding went only so far, in part because many countries and needs competed for the support. Ukraine will benefit in being the primary if not sole regional focus for recovery efforts. Even where external funding was available, it was only forthcoming for so long, and the destruction suffered by countries and their cities meant reestablishment of industrial and tax bases had to precede addressing more ambitious plans. (Germany's leaders nonetheless provided tax advantages to incentivize commercial reconstruction).[30] Infrastructure surviving the war was ironically another roadblock. Subterranean infrastructure commonly survived bombings and subsequent fires. Berlin's underground infrastructure represented some twenty-two percent of the city's total capital investment. Ninety-five percent remained intact when hostilities ended.[31] Further impeding *carte blanche* changes: Bombing might have obliterated buildings, but real estate records tended to survive, remaining as definitive an obstacle to change as did remaining physical infrastructure.[32] Widening streets, creating parks, and other modifications did occur, yet achievement could be arduous even given powers such as Japan's land readjustment policy allowing officials to appropriate up to fifteen percent of an owner's property without compensation.[33] Significant change was, therefore, a task of considerable cost and difficulty, especially in cases where underground infrastructure systems were modern ones and thus only recently funded at taxpayer expense.[34]

Yet further complicating rebuilding efforts was the tension between officials desiring those substantial changes from pre-war cityscapes and others arguing for restoration of what once was. Tensions of another sort complicated recovery when conflicts involved groups with differing ethnic or other viewpoints, often the case as refugees from the east flowed into West Germany or displaced city folk mixed with more conservative rural types.[35] Though tensions existed at the personal level in Japan, conflicts with officials were less an issue as civic groups had less influence than in Europe.[36] Whether this last issue will play a role where Ukrainian and Russian ethnicities rub together is another consideration recovery planners would be well-advised to consider early in planning processes.

A further complication is the potential for an influx of individuals to larger Ukrainian urban areas like Tokyo's dramatic post-war growth. Among the factors influencing internal displacement, Russia's haphazard mining of farmlands has rendered significant agricultural land unsuitable for crops. While some adjustments are being made after repossession of such properties (such as transitioning from crops to chicken raising or other activities reducing the need for human access to mined areas), the resulting loss of income for others combined with the magnetic pull given urban areas' role as hubs of aid distribution means Ukraine should be ready for sudden urban growth and its corresponding pressures. How many of Ukraine's dislocated—both internally displaced persons and those who left the country—seek to return and settle in urban areas will also impact the pace and magnitude of this growth. Past efforts to control such movement elsewhere have tended to disappoint. Japanese official endeavors to impede internal migration by restricting ration book or coupon distribution after WWII was a mixed success.[37] Shortcomings in China's *hukou* policy of constraining residence permits and denying medical, schooling, and other benefits to those who nonetheless move to urban areas are well known.

Ukraine's recovery can also benefit from insights provided by the past suffering of others elsewhere. Impossible to predict in terms of volume, increases in both rural-to-urban and urban-to-urban migration are probable. Now is, therefore, the time to contemplate relevant options for housing, feeding, treating, and integrating new arrivals into local economies. Hardly on the scale of New York, London, or other investment-attractive urban areas where thousands of apartments stand vacant for months or years on end, Kyiv and other of Ukraine's larger cities surely have empty properties available to house the displaced on a temporary basis with compensation being made to absentee owners. Offering tax breaks or other benefits to property holders before demand presents itself could act as an incentive if accompanied by an understanding that delaying acceptance might result in later imposition of eminent domain and reduction or denial of compensation.

Wiesbaden, Germany's post-WWII mayor Georg Krücke, took a not dissimilar approach, directing the displaced to be housed in the city's abandoned apartments on a loan basis.[38] Less controversial complementary remedies might include early conversion of public or large private buildings for future use as housing or food, water, fuel, or other distribution points. Ukraine's good fortune in retaining a standing bureaucracy provides the means to begin action before cessation of hostilities despite the demands of an ongoing war. Given the country's predisposition for corruption, now is the time to create laws, regulations, and internal oversight bodies. (Pre-invasion Ukraine ranked 122 of 180 countries in terms of corruption prevention in 2021, implying that too little progress had been made since 2016 when so many were forced to pay bribes for common public services.) Donors should likewise establish their own monitoring mechanisms and firmly link continuity of funding to corruption's absence, or near absence.[39]

Ukraine can depend on the end of its shooting war not being the end of Russian intrusions. Commendable as Ukraine's rapid repair of its physical and cyber infrastructures has been, continuation of an ether war is all but assured. Economic rebuilding in light of physical destruction could simply repair and reintegrate existing power, water, waste, and other infrastructure. Past and ongoing cyberattacks, however, suggest physical infrastructure is a viable candidate for adaptation if not redesign introducing modifications to reduce cyber vulnerabilities by decentralizing critical nodes and creating redundant routing options. Design modifications might also harden select components. Wisdom suggests protecting expensive and hard-to-replace elements such as major generators from physical attack in addition to shielding them against cyberattacks. Ukraine has already instituted some of these initiatives, to include moving components of its digital infrastructure to other countries.

Making these and similar adaptations permanent seems advisable given Russia's commitment to spurning Ukrainian sovereignty.[40] Equally important considerations include:

- Identifying external supporters willing to assist Ukraine's recovery and
- Putting bodies in place to orchestrate that support.

Ukraine's bureaucracy and its talent for rebounding after attacks should prove invaluable during recovery activities to come. In this, it shares a capability that likewise facilitated Japan's dramatic recovery after WWII where select government bodies remained intact at key levels despite a nationally-governing occupying power.[41] Recovery should benefit from improved planning approaches, management procedures, and construction techniques developed since the end of WWII. Yet there are differences that will, barring counteraction, potentially introduce complications found only at lesser scales in Germany and Japan, the extent of Ukraine's corruption primary among them. Where Japan was largely bereft of natural resources, Ukraine is historically Europe's breadbasket, this in addition to benefiting from additional assets that include coal, iron ore, and other minerals.[42] Administrators must resist pressures from those seeking to gain fraudulent advantage to these resources. Recent removal of high-level officials in Kyiv notwithstanding, many remain unconvinced of the Zelensky government's commitment to purging corruption as others with questionable pasts remain.[43]

Successful approaches to addressing corruption and pandemic challenges share a Swiss cheese methodology.[44] Reducing the spread of COVID included wearing of masks, promoting vaccinations, physical spacing, effective testing, and other measures. Each approach was insufficient, having holes much as does a slice of Swiss cheese. Overlapping slices (coordinating different approaches) closes many of these holes. Corruption's many forms, ability to evolve in the face of countermeasures, the skill of practitioners in capitalizing on new opportunities, the amounts of money disbursed to encourage participation: These and other characteristics mean containment must similarly integrate multiple approaches to seal loopholes. Integration will require international and domestic cooperation as billions of aid dollars flow into Ukraine. Artificial intelligence will in future years help to identify components of, forecast evolutions in, and interdict adaptations by the corrupt. In the meantime, crowd sourcing, social media, insights from savvy NGOs, and assistance from willing technology companies will be among the keys to a relatively corruption-free recovery.

Conclusion

History will help only if its many lessons secure attention. Harry Truman, at the time a senator from Missouri heading the Senate Special Committee to Investigate the National Defense Program (commonly referred to as the Truman Commission) to investigate US WWII defense-related expenditures, observed, "I had always assumed that the War Department had paid some attention to the bitter lessons…learned during the last war."[45] Instead, an author analyzing Truman's committee wrote, "The army had had twenty years to prepare and plan and learn from the failures of the First World War, and had, spectacularly, failed to do so."[46] History's many lessons are available to assist Ukraine's recovery. Given its virtual absence in 2003 Iraq, one reinforcing lesson is the importance of an early start on recovery.[47] As Bernard M. Baruch and John M. Hancock noted in their 1944 *Report on War and Post-War Adjustment Policies*, "It is an easier task to convert from peace to war than war to peace."[48] It is likely then-Senator Harry Truman, heading the committee seeking to reduce wartime fraud and waste, had something similar in mind when he encouraged transition planners to "begin sooner rather than later."[49]

Endnotes

1. Office of the United Nations High Commissioner for Human Rights, "Ukraine Casualties from 1 to 16 July 2023," (July 17, 2023), https://www.ohchr.org/en/news/2023/07/ukraine-civilian-casualties-1-16-july-2023.
2. United Nations Refugee Agency, "Ukraine Emergency," (2023), https://www.unrefugees.org/emergencies/ukraine/.

3. Ishida Yorifusa, "Japanese Cities and Planning in the Reconstruction Period: 1945-55," in *Rebuilding Urban Japan After 1945*, ed. Carola Hein, Jeffry M. Diefendorf, and Ishida Yorifusa (NY: Palgrave MacMillan, 2003), 18, 23, https://doi.org/10.1017/s0963926804382155; Jeffry M. Diefendorf, "War and Reconstruction in Germany and Japan," in *Rebuilding Urban Japan After 1945*, 227, https://doi.org/10.1017/s0963926804382155.
4. Diefendorf, "War and Reconstruction in Germany and Japan," 214.
5. Russell W. Glenn, *Come Hell or High Fever: Readying the World's Megacities for Disaster* (Canberra, Australia: Australian National University Press, 2023), 39, http://doi.org/10.22459/CHHF.2023.
6. *Band of Brothers*, 2001, Season 1, episode 9, "Why We Fight." Directed by David Frankel, aired October 21, 2001 on HBO.
7. Jeffry M. Diefendorf, *In the Wake of War: The Reconstruction of German Cities after World War II* (NY: Oxford University Press, 1993), 27.
8. Diefendorf, "War and Reconstruction in Germany and Japan," 214; Diefendorf, *In the Wake of War*, 27.
9. Harald Jähner, *Aftermath: Life in the Fallout of the Third Reich, 1945-1955*, trans. Shaun Whiteside (NY: Vintage, 2023), 23.
10. Diefendorf, *In the Wake of War*, 27.
11. Jähner, *Aftermath*, 26.
12. Diefendorf, "War and Reconstruction in Germany and Japan," 214. Harald Jähner notes that *Trümmerfrauen* were largely a Berlin phenomenon found less elsewhere. Twenty-six thousand such women were working in the capital in comparison to only 9,000 men at the height of rubble clearance. Jähner, *Aftermath*, 20.
13. Inge E. Stanneck Gross, *Memories of World War II and Its Aftermath, 1940-1954* (Eastsound, WA: Island in the Sky Publishing, 2005), 117.
14. Diefendorf, *In the Wake of War*, 29.
15. Diefendorf, "War and Reconstruction in Germany and Japan," 214.
16. Ichikawa Hiroo, "Reconstruction Tokyo: The Attempt to Transform a Metropolis," in *Rebuilding Urban Japan After 1945*, 55, https://doi.org/10.1017/s0963926804382155.
17. Jeffry M. Diefendorf, "West Germany After World War II – Planning and the Role of Preservation Thinking," in Urban Triumph or Disaster? Dilemmas of contemporary post-war reconstruction, Report of the Symposium hosted by the Aga Khan Program at MIT, Cambridge, Massachusetts, USA, eds. Sultan Barakat, Jon Calame, and Esther Charlesworth (University of York, UK: Post-war Reconstruction & Development Unit, 1998), 8.
18. Gross, *Memories of World War II*, 118.
19. Diefendorf, "War and Reconstruction in Germany and Japan," 214.
20. Gross, *Memories of World War II*, 176.
21. Gross, *Memories of World War II*, 121, 122; Jähner, *Aftermath*, 169.
22. Daniel Johnson, "How decades of complacency have left German facing a cold, dark winter,"

The Guardian (August 28, 2022), https://www.telegraph.co.uk/business/2022/08/28/how-decades-complacency-haveleft-germany-facing-cold-dark-winter/.

23. Gross, *Memories of World War II*, 127.
24. John W. Dower, *Embracing Defeat: Japan in the Wake of World War II* (NY: W.W. Norton, 2002), 93.
25. Jähner, *Aftermath*, 75.
26. Jähner, *Aftermath*, 80.
27. Tara Law, What to Know About the Corruption Scandals Sweeping Ukraine's Government," *Time* (February 1, 2023), https://time.com/6249941/ukrainecorruption-resignation-zelensky-russia/.
28. United States Agency for International Development (USAID), *Evaluation of USAID's Community Stabilization Program (CSP) in Iraq: Effectiveness of the CSP Model as a Non-lethal Tool for Counterinsurgency* (Washington, D.C.: United States Agency for International Development, 2009), 16-17, https://pdf.usaid.gov/pdf_docs/PDACN461.pdf.
29. USAID, *Evaluation of USAID's Community Stabilization Program*, 18-19.
30. Hiroshima and other Japanese cities suffered a similar degradation of tax bases. Ishimaru Norioki, "Reconstructing Hiroshima and Preserving the Reconstructed City," in *Rebuilding Urban Japan After 1945*, 95; Leo Grebler, *Europe's Reborn Cities* (Washington, D.C.: Urban Land Institute, 1956), 92 https://doi.org/10.1017/s0963926804382155.
31. Diefendorf, "War and Reconstruction in Germany and Japan," 213.
32. Grebler, *Europe's Reborn Cities*, 83.
33. Ishida, "Japanese Cities and Planning in the Reconstruction Period: 1945-55," 20. Ishida states that Allied occupiers declared this unconstitutional, resulting in a "compensation for decreased value" alternative. Andre Sorensen, however, makes no mention of the policy's unconstitutionality in *The Making of Urban Japan: Cities and planning from Edo to the twenty-first century* (NY: Routledge, 2004).
34. Diefendorf, "West Germany After World War II," 12.
35. Claire Lagrange, "Patrimoine sans Frontières and Reconstruction of Heritage in War: Experiences in Lebanon, Croatia & Bosnia Herzegovina," in *Urban Triumph or Disaster?*, 78.
36. Carola Hein, "Rebuilding Japanese Cities After 1945," in *Rebuilding Urban Japan After 1945*, 3-4, 8.
37. Ishida, "Japanese Cities and Planning in the Reconstruction Period: 1945-55," 24.
38. Jähner, *Aftermath*, 165.
39. Transparency International, "Corruption Perception Index," 2021, https://www.transparency.org/en/cpi/2021.
40. "How Ukraine tamed Russian missile barrages and kept the lights on: Winning the electricity war," *The Economist* (March 18, 2023), https://www.economist.com/europe/2023/03/12/how-ukraine-tamed-russianmissile-barrages-and-kept-the-lights-on; David Eggers, "The Profound Defiance of Daily Life in Kyiv," *The New Yorker* (January 5, 2023), https://www.newyorker.com/news/dispatch/the-profound-defiance-of-daily-life-inkyiv.

41. John W. Dower, *Ways of Forgetting, Ways of Remembering: Japan in the Modern World* (NY: The New Press, 2014), 260.

42. Dower, *Ways of Forgetting*, 260.

43. Sources addressing Ukrainian corruption include Oleg Sukhov, "Who are officials ousted in Zelensky's largest reshuffle since start of full-scale war?" *The Kyiv Independent* (January 24, 2023), https://kyivindependent.com/explainer-why-didzelensky-launch-the-biggest-government-reshuffle-during-full-scale-invasion/; Elena Loginova, "Pandora Papers Reveal Offshore Holdings of Ukrainian President and his Inner Circle," Organized Crime and Corruption Reporting Project (OCCRP), October 3, 2021, https://www.occrp.org/en/the-pandora-papers/pandora-papersreveal-offshore-holdings-of-ukrainian-president-and-his-inner-circle; Julian Hayda, "President Zelenskyy shakes up Ukraine's Cabinet amid corruption allegations," *National Public Radio*, (January 24, 2023), https://www.npr.org/2023/01/24/1150943435/president-zelenskyy-shakes-up-ukraines-cabinet-amid-corruption-allegations; Jack Dutton, "Was Volodymyr Zelensky in the Panama Papers? Offshore Companies Revealed," *Newsweek* (January 24, 2023), https://www.newsweek.com/zelensky-panama-pandora-papers-offshore-companiesfinances-1776124.

44. "The Virologist Who Created A 'Swiss Cheese' Metaphor To Explain The Pandemic Has A Message For Educators," *Forbes* (December 10, 2020), https://www.forbes.com/sites/carminegallo/2020/12/10/the-virologist-who-createda-swiss-cheese-metaphor-to-explain-the-pandemic-has-a-message-foreducators/?sh=348eeed26335.

45. Steve Drummond, *The Watchdog: How the Truman Commission Battled Corruption and Helped Win World War Two*, (Toronto: Hanover Square Press, 2023), 78.

46. Drummond, *The Watchdog*, 80.

47. "Smart warfare: Ukraine," *The Economist* 445 (December 10, 2022): 48, https://www.economist.com/europe/2022/12/08/ukraine-is-using-foreign-tech-tomitigate-russian-destruction (accessed May 15, 2023).

48. Bernard M. Baruch and John M. Hancock, *Report on War and Post-War Adjustment Policies* (February 15, 1944), 3, https://fraser.stlouisfed.org/files/docs/historical/eccles/032_14_0003.pdf.

49. Drummond, *The Watchdog*, 317.

CHAPTER 15
Black Shabbat: Learning Lessons from the Urban Battles of October 7th

Jacob Stoil

Introduction

On the morning of October 7th, 2023, the various organizations that share the task of securing the State of Israel failed in one of the least discussed challenges in urban security—securing territory from the threat posed by a dense urban environment. As a result of this failure, Hamas and other allies came pouring out of the urban areas of Gaza to inflict carnage, atrocity, and horror in Israel. This forced the Israeli Defense Forces (IDF), Israel National Police (INP), and other arms of the state security into dozens of urban and urban-like battles over the next twenty-four hours. It highlighted all too starkly the threat posed by the Hamas government in Gaza and resulted in an Israeli counter-invasion into the dense urban terrain of Gaza that, as of the time of writing, is still ongoing. This chapter will not be an exhaustive study of the war in Gaza as it is still ongoing, and much is classified. Rather, it will focus on cases of urban fighting during the attacks of October 7th. These provide a useful case to understand modern urban security and military operations in the urban environment, especially for those interested in defending their home urban terrain against an adversary's incursions.

There is significant ambiguity about the meaning of "urban" and "rural." Scholars in a wide variety of fields have expended efforts discussing the issue.[1] The ambiguity is particularly relevant in the tight geography of southern Israel and Gaza, where agriculture zones, villages, cities, and densely populated zones are intermixed. In fact, in the classical Israeli security and military conception, the term "urban warfare" does not exist. Rather, they employ the more helpful phraseology "combat in a built-up area." This is particularly helpful as on the tactical level, the urban effect is relative to the size of the unit under consideration. Thus, what for a division may be little more than a village can function as urban terrain for a fireteam or squad.

In keeping with this more locally derived conception, this chapter will not dwell on discussions of definitions and will press ahead with considering the challenges of creating security from, conducting combat in, or securing a built-up area, which it will shorthand as "urban." The concept of a built-up area goes hand in hand with another Israeli concept that is particularly useful in understanding the nature of combat in and around Gaza—that of the "urban envelope." The urban envelope is the area which surrounds a given city, can control its approaches, and both directly affects the city and is directly affected by it. Such an area can be rural, suburban or a separate city entirely. The urban envelope of Gaza is where the attacks of October 7th began and the attempt to secure them is what has driven the IDF into the dense urban landscape of Gaza.

The creation of the Gaza Strip as a territorial unit resulted from the ceasefire lines established at the end of the 1948 War. In 1948, the Egyptian Army crossed from Sinai, overrunning the borders of the Palestine Mandate, including the territory now known as the Gaza Strip and the Strip's one Jewish town.[2] By the end of the war in 1949, Egypt was in full retreat, and the newly formed IDF captured some of Gaza only to leave as part of the armistice agreement.[3] From 1949 until 1956, Egypt controlled Gaza. The territory saw repeated clashes as Egyptian-backed irregular forces launched raids across the border into the relatively rural Israeli communities nearby, and Israel retaliated into Gaza.[4] In the 1956 War, Israel again took control of Gaza; Israel again withdrew as part of an armistice, and the cycle of violence between forces from Gaza and the IDF continued.[5]

In 1967, Israel took control of Gaza again, and this time, even with the Egyptian-Israeli. The peace treaty of 1979 kept control. During this period, the urban density of the Gaza Strip and the surrounding Israeli territories increased. As part of the Oslo Peace process, Israeli forces withdrew from most of Gaza during the late 1990s and handed over control to the Palestinian Authority, only to reinvade these dense urban areas as part of Israeli operations during the Second Intifada. Israel finally completed a full withdrawal from Gaza in 2005, handing over control to the Palestinian Authority, which a short time later was overthrown by Hamas—an organization committed to the complete destruction of Israel. By this point, the Gaza Strip had become a dense urban area. Since the Hamas takeover, there have been several major escalations where Hamas either launched bombardments at the Israeli communities across the border or, in some cases, tried limited infiltrations. Israel has most typically responded with air, naval, and artillery strikes, or in several cases, limited ground incursions into Gaza, though, until the current war, never into the densest areas of its urban terrain.

The Gaza Strip is an area of about 141 square miles (a little bit smaller than the total area of Queens in New York City and about the same as greater Chattanooga in Tennessee). It is home to about two million residents. Despite the density of the population, it has a mix of highly built-up areas and agricultural zones. It is bounded by the Mediterranean Sea to the west and the Egyptian border to the south. On its north and east, it borders Israel. There are several distinct cities in Gaza of which the largest are Gaza City, Rafah, and Khan Yunis.

Taking an expanded view of the area, there is a small border zone before the nearest Israeli communities, which are still in the urban envelope. The largest Israeli city in the Gaza Envelope is Ashkelon, a city of over 130,000 people that sits just over three miles from the nearest built-up area across the border in Gaza. At its closest point, the total distance from a neighborhood in Gaza to the small Israeli farming community of Nahal Oz is 1.12 miles and the closest distance between cities is the 1.7 miles that separates the city of Beith Hanoun in Gaza from Sderot in Israel. This is less than the distance between the Lincoln Memorial and the US Capital in Washington, DC. The area of Gaza and its surrounding envelope represents a complex operational environment of connected built-up areas separated by a border fence and intermixed with small amounts of agricultural land. From this perspective, all that occurred in the lead-up to and during October 7th are aspects of urban security.

The IDF had the primary role in protecting Israel from attacks emanating out of Gaza. It also had security responsibility at a variable depth into Israel of about five to ten kilometers back from the border, depending on location. It employed a model of intelligence-led defense. The IDF protected the border through the deployment of maneuver and patrol units, limited wire and, in some places, concrete obstacles. To enable the efficacy of the patrols, the IDF deployed significant sensing capabilities along the border and underneath the border. The concept underlying this appears to have been centered on efficiency. Rather than establishing a string of highly fortified fighting posts along the fixed frontier, which would have required a continuous deployment of forces, the observation and sensing capabilities could allow the IDF to respond quickly to a single incursion or even up to several simultaneous incursions. On October 7th, Hamas launched over 100 incursions across the border.

The urban nature of the terrain and the distances involved did not necessarily make intelligence gathering on Gaza significantly more difficult. There have been numerous reports that tactical intelligence units identified a number of indicators that attacks were imminent, and it seems that these were ignored or all but disregarded. The discussion of the intelligence failure will have to await a future study, but what is salient is that the tightly populated and built-up environment of Gaza and its surrounding envelope magnified the impact of this failure. The population density meant that when Hamas began its attacks and atrocities at 0630 on October 7th, it took a matter of minutes for its fighters to move from the relative safety of Hamas-controlled urban terrain into the heart of Israeli population centers and begin the massacre.

The Battles of Ofakim and Sderot on October 7th highlight many of the challenges of urban security against a large-scale attack. Although Israel had units such as the police counter-terror unit YASAM, which it had developed to prevent attacks similar to those in Mumbai in 2008, the scale, scope, and chaos of the attacks of the 7th quickly overwhelmed their capabilities to respond as planned. The city of Ofakim is a low-income city of about 30,000 people, which sits about 20 kilometers from the nearest built-up area of Gaza. Hamas began its attack there at 0702, approximately 30 minutes after it breached the border fence.[6] The subsequent murders and fighting in Ofakim demonstrate the confusion of operations in the urban space, the inability to assume that civilian emergency networks will be available in large-scale attacks, and the challenge of identifying hostile positions within the urban environment. Furthermore, the Battles of Ofakim and Sderot serve as important reminders that the planning of operations in the urban environment should not center on planning for offensive operations alone. The considerations for defending a friendly population in the urban environment are different and no less critical.

In the first few minutes of the attack, the Hamas commandos murdered civilians from their vehicles before dismounting and splitting into groups moving through the city. By 0712, a scratch squad consisting of a police officer, an off-duty soldier, and an armed civilian engaged the Hamas commandos but were killed. The fact that individuals and scratch squads undertook most of the initial defense of the city and that there was no clarity as to where the Hamas teams were led to a constant state of confusion. Indeed, perhaps the greatest challenge for all involved in the Battle of Ofakim was situational awareness. This applied to Hamas as well as the Israeli defenders. For example, between 0720 and 0729, the Hamas attackers entered two homes. In one case, they took hostages, and in the other, even as they operated on the rooftops and in the area of the house, they never found the surviving residents of the house who hid for hours mere meters away.

This points to another challenge of urban warfare apparent throughout the battle. The complex terrain and verticality of an urban environment mean that it is supremely difficult to have situational awareness, which in turn complicates the ability to organize a response. At Ofakim, this also led to a number of engagements where individual defenders took cover to engage Hamas, only to be outflanked and killed moments later by other Hamas teams coming from alternative directions. Hamas was not immune from this particular challenge created by the urban terrain. For example, in one instance at approximately 0730, two trained members of the Israeli security forces engaged two Hamas commandos. The Hamas fighters took cover and returned fire but, as a result, did not see an armed civilian security guard outflank their position. The guard neutralized them at close range. Such engagements continued throughout the day. The same factors that lead to the need for establishing three-hundred and sixty-degree, three-dimensional situational awareness in urban terrains also result in spontaneous and unplanned encounters. In one such instance, a Hamas commando and a well-trained armed Israeli civilian discovered each other alone at the entrance to a garage and engaged each other simultaneously. Forces in close proximity to each other rarely saw one another until they were engaged. Throughout the day, members of the INP and other responders arrived in the area and ran towards the sound of fighting but could not find the attackers before being ambushed.

The presence of friendly civilians and civilian infrastructure on the battlefield had an impact on the fighting of the day, but perhaps in ways other than those that planners could have anticipated in advance. When defending your own or a friendly city, it might be possible to assume that civilian systems could help support the situational awareness of the defending force. In a normal situation, security planners can rely on civilian systems in urban areas to limit the confusion of the battle space. For example, in Ukraine, tools like Google Maps allowed for evidence of Russian movements.[7] It is also possible that emergency call centers can provide information as to the location of commandos and other infiltrators.

Unfortunately, in the case of October 7th in general and the Battle of Ofakim in particular, the vulnerabilities of such systems became apparent. For example, given the urban density of the Gaza Envelope and the scale of the attacks, the emergency call centers were almost immediately overwhelmed by around twenty-five thousand calls in the first hour alone. This led to calls being rerouted to other districts with no understanding of the local geography and no ability to dispatch response forces. However, civilians also provided an important source of intelligence. In one important case during the battle, security forces were initially unable to pinpoint where the Hamas commandos had concealed themselves as they were observed on a set of civilian security cameras to which the security forces did not have access. However, the owner of the building was the mother of a police officer and was able to call her son on his personal phone to provide real-time intelligence.

Another of the problems with establishing situational awareness during defensive urban operations that the attacks of October 7th highlight is that of determining the identities of individuals in the densely populated terrain. In the Battle of Ofakim, the first known incidence of this was at 0720 when a police officer approached the attackers, thinking they were IDF soldiers, and were killed, but this was far from the only instance of this throughout the day. The presence of large numbers of friendly civilians and the confusion of the urban terrain in the Gaza Envelope also prevented Israel from using its preferred assets for countering large-scale enemy formations – air power. Although air power, should it have been available, could quickly have neutralized the attackers, the confusion as to the location of friendly civilians, friendly forces, and enemies prevented or significantly delayed its employment.[8] Yet the heavily populated nature of the terrain also provided advantages to the defenders. The presence of armed civilians and security guards was a critical force multiplier, especially during the first chaotic hour of the Battle of Ofakim. Such individuals became part of scratch units that combined professional and conscript combat personnel with security guards and armed civilians.

The fighting in Ofakim spanned two neighborhoods. Fighting in the southern neighborhood ended by 0742 as a result of a series of meeting engagements between Hamas and members of the Israeli security forces and civilians moving towards the sound of the guns. In the northern neighborhood, Hamas forces had barricaded themselves in two fortified positions – one in a house without hostages and one in a house with hostages. The latter house is best known as "Rachel's house" after Rachel Edri, one of the hostages.[9] In the first position, the police knew Hamas's position because of the above-mentioned phone calls from an officer's mother who provided details from her security cameras. At 0732, more police units arrived piecemeal into the northern neighborhood to begin to try to find the attackers and were ambushed from Rachel's house, but could not identify where the fire was coming from. Shortly thereafter, an organized and intact police counter-terror unit arrived in the area and switched approaches. They began to take a slow, deliberate approach to clearing each building and rapidly discovered the situation at Rachel's house. By 0745, the mobile phase of the battle was over, but the Israeli security forces did not yet know this and endeavored to continue to clear the city.

Around two and half hours after the battle of Ofakim began, organized military units began to arrive on the scene, and other than at Rachel's house, the fighting came to a rapid conclusion. At Rachel's House, the hostage rescue operation would continue for hours. The critical decision by the counter-terrorism unit to conduct a deliberate house-to-house search proved integral to ending the battle but highlights one of the other challenges that defending a friendly civilian population creates – the question of operational approach. The measured approach to maneuver was one that could eventually, in time, secure the entire city, but its slow tempo meant that had there been other Hamas teams in action throughout the city, more of the population would have been killed. Both the strengths and weaknesses of an aggressive approach to attempt to neutralize the enemy were on display throughout the first thirty minutes of the battle. This highlights the challenge of prioritization when defending friendly urban terrain and begs the question of whether, ultimately, the point of the defense of an urban area is the protection of the population, the defeat of the enemy forces, or securing the territory. In the case of Ofakim, the decision to move slowly and deliberately paid off for all concerned, but while the challenge of prioritization might be universal, the solution will always be case-dependent.

Even as the Battle of Ofakim unfolded, another urban fight occurred a mere thirty-minute drive away in the city of Sderot. Before October 7th, Sderot had a population of over thirty thousand located just over five thousand feet from the border with Gaza.[10] Across the highway from the Sderot train station and even closer to the Gaza border sits the kibbutz (semi-communal town) of Nir Am. Although it is a separate community, it forms part of the broader Sderot metropolitan area. Hamas also attacked Nir Am on the 7th, but there, the local civilian militia were able to draw weapons from their armory and set up ambushes to hold back the onslaught. They were eventually assisted by the police and, finally, in the afternoon, the IDF. The successful defense of Nir Am stands in stark contrast to the battles being fought elsewhere, but the tactical compression of urban warfare is such that the Israeli victory at Nir Am had little to no bearing on what was happening just several hundred meters away.

For Hamas, Sderot and its environs were a more important target than Ofakim.[11] They sent as many as fifty commandos to attack Sderot itself. The Hamas forces split into three groups. One set up an ambush at a major highway junction at the entrance to the city; one group began to move through the city, murdering civilians, while the final group advanced to take the police station, killing as they went.[12] It appears the purpose of the third group was to eliminate the ability of the security forces to respond and to create a base in the station from which they could continue their battle in the city. Sderot police station is not just a station from which the police operate in the city. It is a fortress built by the British to hold out against sustained attacks by insurgents during the Arab Revolt of the 1930s. While the mobile battles and the battle against Hamas's ambush highlight many of the same lessons as Ofakim, the Battle of Sderot police station demonstrates the power of an urban stronghold to become a battle by itself.[13]

Early in the day, Major General (MG) Amir Cohen, the Police Commander for the Southern District, received an alert that Hamas might be heading to the city of Ashkelon from his intelligence officer, who lived on Kibbutz Ziqim and witnessed the battle between Hamas and the INS. Minutes later, MG Cohen headed towards Ashkelon and ordered the activation of the police Gaza Envelope defense plan, which helped prevent Hamas from reaching other nearby metropolitan areas.[14] However, by 0705, multiple Hamas squads mounted in trucks converged on and stormed the police station. There they killed a number of police officers and drove the survivors to the roof.[15] At this point, the battle at the police station became two fights at different levels. On the roof, Israeli defenders attempted to hold against a Hamas assault, whereas in front of the station, an ad hoc team of Israelis attempted to drive Hamas back and assault the station. Even as they did so, the question of prioritization again became relevant. Here, the question became whether to attempt to rescue any officers that might be left in the station or wounded civilians out front or to concentrate on establishing containment and defeating Hamas by assaulting in strength.

This choice came into stark relief in a number of instances. In one case just outside of the station, Hamas had murdered a woman in a car but missed her six-year-old and toddler in the back of the car. As a scratch force of various Israeli security forces began to push Hamas back, the six-year-old called out to an NCO from the Israel prison service for help. Rather than continuing the counter-offensive, the NCO called for support as he evacuated the two children. This again highlights the challenge of prioritization that friendly civilians pose on the battlefield during an urban defense. In this case, the NCO was clear that the priority was protecting civilian lives over retaking terrain or eliminating the Hamas commandos.[16]

This same line of thinking led MG Cohen (who had heard of the fighting in Sderot from an off-duty counterterrorism officer he met on the way to Ashkelon) to lead a scratch team of police and soldiers into the station to try to effect a rescue of any trapped police. Hamas was able to use the fortified nature of the position to repel MG Cohen's effort and wound him and a number of officers. At around 0900, the police began another assault with more reinforcements. This time, they were able to break through the ground floor but were caught on the staircase heading up and took fire from both above and below. Because of the station's large, fortified, and multilevel nature, it proved difficult for a small number of attackers to clear any given area of the Hamas forces.

The fire from the station was such that the Israelis could no longer evacuate the wounded from in front of the station. As a result, MG Cohen ordered an armored vehicle to come and provide cover. By 1100, YAMAM, an elite counterterrorism unit, began to establish a secure perimeter around the station. Just over two hours later, YAMAM was able to use a civilian fire truck to access the roof and rescue the wounded police from it. In the meantime, they also began to attack the station with anti-tank rockets. By 1830, although the building was heavily damaged, Hamas was still able to mount a defense as YAMAM attempted to breach from the upper floors to the ground floor and was driven back. Finally, at 1900, the Israeli commanders made the decision to cease attempting to breach the station and instead to destroy it. They employed multiple types of air support, including a helicopter gunship, but the eventual end only came after a D9 bulldozer (a piece of equipment that would prove critical to Israeli operations in Gaza) arrived and demolished the outer walls of the station. Many of the Hamas members who took the station died trying to escape after the D9 began its work, but even so, the battle only ended at 0200 with the final liberation of the station. The fortification of the station was such that despite the forces surrounding it, it held for hours, manned only by around twenty-seven Hamas commandos.

Many of the challenges typical of all urban operations are present even when defending one's own territory. As the case of Sderot police station shows, well-built strong points can dominate and become a fight of their own. Both the battles of Ofakim and Sderot demonstrate that verticality and the three-hundred-and-sixty-degree nature of fighting test all sides equally. Furthermore, the terrain can lead to disjointed and chaotic battles with extreme tactical compression. Engagements in neighborhoods only a few hundred meters apart can rapidly develop into completely separate battles. When defending home territory, the presence of friendly civilians provides additional challenges and benefits. The presence of friendly civilians and wounded security forces forced the Israelis to decide among operational priorities and added to the chaos of the battlefield. At the same time, on October 7th, the INP, off-duty security forces, and armed civilians proved critical in preventing what could have been a worse massacre. This perhaps provides the greatest lesson on defense for those whose cities may someday be under attack—the need to create robust layers of response and coordination. Israel lost valuable time because the scratch teams of defenders lacked a mechanism for situational awareness or sharing their knowledge with the military or higher levels of command. Mitigating the possibility for the failure of the first line of defense begins with establishing robust mechanisms for civilians and emergency services to play an active role in the defense of their homes and cities.

Endnotes

The author would like to thank Chief-Superintendent Shlomi Shitrit and the officers and staff of the Israel national Police History and Heritage Units without whom the research for this chapter would not have been possible.

1. See for example, John R. Weeks, "Defining Urban Areas," in eds. Tarek Rashid and Carsten Jürgens, *Remote Sensing of Urban and Suburban Areas.* (Dordrecht: Springer, 2019), 33–45; Ayala Wineman, Dider Yélognissé Alia, C Leigh Anderson, "Definitions of "rural' and 'urban' and understandings of economic transformation: Evidence from Tanzania," *Journal of Rural Studies* 29. (October 2020): 254– 268.
2. Benny Morris, *1948: The First Arab-Israeli War* (New Haven: Yale University Press), 2009, 409.
3. Morris, *1948*, 369.
4. Michael Oren, Six Days of War: June 1967 and the Making of the Modern Middle East (New York: Ballantine Books, 2003), 9.
5. Oren, Six Days of War, 12
6. Much of the chronology for the Battle of Ofakim comes from an Israeli National Police digital reconstruction of the battle, drawing on their investigations and forensics. I was able to corroborate, at least in principle, any of its key findings from other sources, but this remains the main source for the events of Ofakim.
7. Rachel Lerman, "On Google Maps, tracking the invasion of Ukraine, *Washington Post*, February 27, 2022, https://www.washingtonpost.com/technology/2022/02/25/google-maps-ukraine-invasion/; Natalie Musumeci, *Business Insider*, February 25, 2022, https://www.businessinsider.com/professor-says-hesaw-russia-ukraine-invasion-on-google-maps-2022-2.

15: BLACK SHABBAT: LEARNING LESSONS FROM THE URBAN BATTLES OF OCTOBER 7

8. Yehuda Dov, "Footage Of Israeli Drone Crews On Oct. 7th As They Find Hundreds Of Terrorists In Israel," *VINnews*, May 1, 2024, https://vinnews.com/2024/05/01/footage-of-israeli-drone-crews-on-oct-7thas-they-find-hundreds-of-terrorists-in-israel/.

9. The house became known for the 65-year-old hostage Rachel Edri after she became famous in the aftermath of the October 7th attacks for the composure she showed during her ordeal. She or her husband warned Israeli forces of the Hamas ambush, keeping her attackers from killing her by dialogue, singing Arabic songs, and feeding them (most famously cookies). At the same time, she provided critical tactical information to the Israeli counter-terror teams.

10. Carrie Keller-Lynn, "As exodus turns Sderot into a ghost town, some stay as a reminder of what's at stake," Times of Israel, October 16, 2023, https://www.timesofisrael.com/as-exodus-turns-sderot-into-aghost-town-some-stay-as-a-reminder-of-whats-at-stake/.

11. Much of the information on the Battle of Sderot comes from Israel National Police sources and documents which I was able to cross-corroborate.

12. Ilana Curiel, "October 7: Hour-after-Hour Diary of IDF commando Squad," *Yedioth Ahronoth*, October 23, 2023 https://www.ynetnews.com/magazine/article/s12as5fz6.

13. One of the tactics in Hamas's ambushes, including by Sderot, was to use wounded Israeli civilians as bait to draw in rescuers who themselves could be killed or wounded, setting up a repeating trap.

14. "Major General Amir Cohen: The order that rescued lives," *IDSF*, October 7, 2023, https://idsf.org.il/en/stories-of-valor/rescued-lives/.

15. "The policewoman fought the terrorists to the last bullet," *IDSF*, October 7, 2023, https://idsf.org.il/en/stories-of-valor/policewoman-fought-the-terrorists/

16. *13 חדשות*/News 13, "תיעוד הסוהר שחילץ את רומי וליה באירוע השבת השחורה (Documentation of the prisoner who rescued Romi and Lia at Black Saturday events)," *YouTube*, November 9, 2023, 5:22minutes, https://www.youtube.com/watch?v=2feaVs57fqo.

CHAPTER 16
Civilian Protection in Urban Operations: Legal and Policy Approaches

Sahr Muhammedally

Introduction

Any analysis of urban operations must begin with the acknowledgment of the human cost of war. Daily headlines chronicle displacement, death, injuries, destroyed lives, homes, schools, medical facilities, and essential services with impacts felt for generations. International humanitarian law (IHL) or the law of armed conflict (LOAC)[1] was created to alleviate human suffering. It embodies the basic principle that war must be waged within certain limits to preserve the lives and dignity of human beings and protect those not, or no longer, taking part in hostilities.

The co-mingling of military objectives with civilians and civilian objects in urban environments creates significant challenges for belligerents striving to adhere to IHL. It's, however, essential that IHL rules, supplemented by policies and operational practices, are adapted to the unique challenges of the urban setting with its terrain, population, interconnectedness of essential services, communications, and infrastructure. Given the high risk of civilian harm in urban settings, belligerents must prioritize civilian protection and adapt operational and tactical approaches to warfighting, including doctrine, policies, practices, training, and tools. This chapter provides an overview of core IHL rules and cites new strategic and policy approaches to civilian protection undertaken by some militaries.

Legal Framework

IHL reflects an attempt to balance military necessity with the principle of humanity and sets out rules for conducting warfare. These rules were developed to protect the civilian population and those not, or no longer, taking a direct part in hostilities, protect combatants from unnecessary suffering, and limit the means and methods of warfare.

IHL applies in both international and non-international armed conflict and is equally binding on all parties to an armed conflict, irrespective of the reasons for fighting.[2] A State exercising its right to self-defense or restoring law and order within its territory or a non-State armed group resorting to force are bound by IHL (*equality of belligerents*), irrespective of the scale, intensity, and speed of operations. Moreover, belligerents must respect IHL even if it is violated by their adversary (*non-reciprocity of humanitarian obligations*).[3]

The four 1949 Geneva Conventions ratified following World War II, the 1977 Additional Protocols I and II, as well as in customary international law, are the bedrock of IHL.[4] The main IHL principles that apply to the conduct of hostilities are distinction, proportionality, and precautions and apply in international and non-international armed conflicts. Additional Protocol I and customary international law require that parties to a conflict must always distinguish between civilians, civilian objects, and military objectives.[5] Attacks against military objectives are not prohibited but attacks against the civilian population, individual civilians, and civilian objects are prohibited. Civilians are protected from attack "unless and for such time as they take a direct part in hostilities."[6]

AP I instructs that "in case of doubt whether a person is a civilian, that person shall be considered to be a civilian" and that "an object normally dedicated to civilian purposes, such as a place of worship, a house or other dwelling or a school" is presumed to be a civilian object.[7] An examination of urban conflicts highlights that many civilians do not leave due to disability, age, uncertainty of being able to return, or concerns about safety and access to basic services in the area of displacement. In urban war, given the proximity of military objectives and civilians, the presumption of civilian presence and objects heightens the need to comprehensively analyze the civilian environment to support targeting decisions.[8]

The rule on proportionality prohibits attacks that may cause incidental loss of civilian life, injury to civilians, or damage to civilian objects that would be excessive to the concrete and direct military advantage anticipated.[9] Identifying incidental civilian harm and ensuring that it's not excessive to the military advantage gained presents a challenge to commanders, especially in urban combat. What is foreseeable at the time of the attack is to be assessed from the perspective of the "reasonable commander."[10] What is reasonably foreseeable by a commander can be informed by past experiences and lessons learned from their country's armed forces, including drawing on analysis from other urban conflicts and allocating resources to understanding the civilian environment during the planning process to identify risks and inform mitigation options.

In all military operations, constant care must be taken to spare the civilian population, civilians, and civilian objects.[11] The term "military operations" encompasses "any movements, maneuver, and other activities whatsoever carried out by the armed forces with a view to combat" or "related to hostilities" and not just attacks.[12] Thus, measures to protect civilians must be factored into operational planning and mission execution not only as a matter of policy but also to adhere to legal obligations, not only during war but in preparation for war.[13] This can include ground operations, establishment of bases, defensive preparations, and search operations.[14]

IHL imposes additional obligations to take feasible precautions in planning an attack and requires parties to the conflict to protect civilians and civilian objects under their control against the effects of attacks.[15] Precautionary measures available to an attacking party may include assessing risks to civilians, providing advance effective warnings where feasible, adjusting the timing of an attack, canceling attacks altogether, and weaponeering—i.e., adjusting the type, size, timing, and delivery of ordnance to minimize damage to anything other than legitimate military targets.

Advance warnings must be effective, for instance, to be received and understood by civilians and not just issued without any practicality of the actions they advise. The warning, whose paramount objective is to maximize civilian protection, should be provided with sufficient notice and clarity as to where to move to safer areas, including where basic needs for survival will be available, especially in besieged areas. There is no one-size-fits-all approach to effective warnings, but they must be tailored to different situations to maximize civilian safety.

A defending party is also obligated to undertake precautionary measures from the effects of an attack, which may include giving sufficient warnings of incoming attacks, building shelters for civilians, creating safe routes for civilians to leave the area of hostilities, proactively removing civilians from places from where defenders will be firing, knowing that these locations are subject to legitimate counterfire and attack, and avoid locating military objectives within or near densely populated areas.[16]

IHL prohibits the use of human shields and the starvation of civilians.[17] Encirclement and siege tactics are lawful only when directly against enemy forces, and the besieging party may not deprive civilians of essential supplies for survival.[18] Several rules from the principle of precautions also require both parties to conflict to allow civilians to leave the besieged area where feasible. Temporary evacuations may be necessary, but sieges must not be used to compel civilians to leave an area permanently and not allowed to return.

Civilians who live in besieged areas continue to be protected as civilians. Those who undertake encirclement tactics must ensure that sufficient food, water, and medicine necessary for survival will either be provided for by the attacking party or to allow neutral humanitarian access by international or local organizations. Review of recent operations indicates challenges in providing life-saving basic needs for civilians with onerous restrictions limiting humanitarian access resulting in United Nations Security Council Resolutions urging parties to conflict to allow for timely and unfettered humanitarian access.[19] If civilians become displaced (they flee or are evacuated from besieged areas), all measures must be taken to ensure that people have adequate food, water, sanitation facilities, health care provisions, and are safe from violence, and that family members are not separated.[20]

Other IHL rules relevant to include: specific protections for medical personnel, sick and wounded) and objects (hospitals, objects indispensable to survival of civilian population and cultural property); protection of persons under control of party to conflict (those deprived of liberty, living in occupied territory or besieged areas); require the wounded and sick (civilians and members of adversary force) to be treated with respect and protected against ill-treatment; to allow for collection and evacuation of dead and protect them from ill-treatment and mutilation; allow for impartial humanitarian activities; and regulate the protection of natural environment.

Examination of recent urban operations indicates a weakening of the rules applicable to protected places such as medical facilities, personnel, and medical transport, which should remain functioning during an armed conflict to care for the sick and wounded and must not be used for military purposes. Medical facilities can lose their protection if they are used outside their humanitarian function to "commit acts harmful to the enemy."[21] Prior to conducting an attack, a warning must be given to deter military usage and to allow for the safe evacuation of sick and wounded not responsible for military conduct. The attacking party must adhere to the rule on proportionality to assess military advantage gained from attacking medical units that have lost their protected status to be weighed against the humanitarian consequences from the damage or destruction caused to those facilities on the delivery of health care both direct but longer-term second and third order effects.[22]

The rule on indiscriminate attacks prohibits attacks that are not directed at specific military objectives, which employ means and methods of combat that cannot be directed at a specific military objective, or whose effects cannot be limited as required by IHL.[23]

Finally, in future wars, the accelerated pace of operations may result in delegated decision-making authority with respect to subordinates and the use of automated decision-making tools.[24] It is, therefore, vital to ensure that emerging technologies used in warfare sufficiently assess the foreseeable humanitarian impact and are in adherence with IHL.[25]

Strategic Reasons

In addition to legal obligations, armed forces have strategic reasons to take measures to minimize civilian harm. Extensive civilian harm may undermine the legitimacy of the military mission.[26] It can result in a decline in political, military, or financial support (both local and international), including intelligence collection from sources,[27] and can become a divisive issue between multinational partners.[28] Extensive civilian harm also might eliminate avenues for reconciliation, trigger more violence, and, as recognized by the 2022 US Army Urban Operations doctrine, turn initially neutral or positive sentiment to hostility towards the US and its partners, thereby prolonging the conflict.[29] Damage to civilian objects, including critical infrastructure,[30] which civilians depend on for their survival, such as electricity, water, sanitation, and health care, generates reverberating effects on lives and livelihoods and increases post-conflict reconstruction costs[31] and risks alienating the population if services are not rebuilt and civilians remain in protracted displacement.[32] Extensive destruction also impacts military operations' ability to maneuver in an urban terrain.[33]

Militaries have cited strategic reasons to enact additional measures to minimize civilian harm. For example, the North Atlantic Treaty

Organization's (NATO) International Security Assistance Force (ISAF) policy measures in Afghanistan were imposed to "avoid the trap of winning tactical victories—but suffering strategic defeats—by causing civilian casualties or excessive damage and thus alienating the people."[34] African Union Mission in Somalia's (AMISOM) indirect fire policy was enacted due to the failure to protect civilians in the fight against al-Shabab, which was undermining AMISOM's strategic and operational success.[35] NATO's Protection of Civilians Handbook notes, "lack of consideration for [civilian harm mitigation] will have a negative impact on the overall mission" because such "failures will generate negative strategic effects and their consequences will reverberate at all levels of command. [Protection of Civilians] is therefore key for mission success and legitimacy."[36] Similarly, in August 2022, the US Department of Defense acknowledged that the protection of civilians is a strategic priority as well as a moral imperative.[37]

Policies

In recent conflicts, some militaries have enacted mission-specific policies tailored to minimizing civilian harm. ISAF enacted several tactical directives to reduce civilian deaths, injuries, and property damage[38,] and AMISOM similarly introduced an indirect fire policy in 2011.[39]

In 2016, NATO adopted its Protection of Civilians (PoC) to not only "minimize and mitigate the negative effects that might arise from its operations, but also to 'protect civilians from conflict-related physical violence or threats of physical violence by other actors, including through the establishment of a safe and secure environment.'"[40]

The previous Afghan government, in 2017, enacted a Civilian Casualties Mitigation and Prevention Policy, which committed its forces to mitigate and respond to civilian harm through training, policies, and financial assistance to conflict victims.[41] The Dutch Ministry of Defense enacted a civilian protection policy in 2023.

The US DoD, in response to reports of civilian harm attributed to the US in Iraq and Syria and an internal review of incidents[42] in 2023, issued Department of Defense Instruction (DoDI) on Civilian Harm Mitigation and Response applicable to the full spectrum of conflict, including counterterrorism operations and high-intensity conflict.[43] The DoDI reinforces commitments made in the 2022 Civilian Harm Mitigation Action and Response Plan to improve how the US military prevents and responds to civilian harm, created a center of excellence on civilian protection, and directed the military to overhaul doctrine, policies, training and response plans to mitigate civilian harm and integrate civilian harm mitigation in security cooperation and with partners and allies.

At the international level, in November 2022, over eighty states, including all NATO countries, as well as Canada, the US, France, and the U.K., signed a *Political Declaration to Limit Humanitarian Suffering from the Use of Explosive Weapons in Populated Areas*.[44]

Finally, the United Nations Security Council (UNSC) has explicitly included language on civilian harm mitigation in the mandates of peacekeeping missions in the Central African Republic (MINUSCA), Democratic Republic of the Congo (MONUSCO), and Mali (MINUSMA), and the U.N. Department of Peace Operations (DPO) has included a focus on CHM in its PoC policy and handbook.

These efforts reflect the growing concerns at the national, regional, and international levels on the need for the prioritization of civilian protection, for practical approaches to identify risks to civilians and undertake appropriate mitigation measures.

Conclusion

The humanitarian consequences of urban warfare, as seen in Aleppo, Gaza, Kyiv, Khartoum, Marawi, Mosul, and Raqqa, demand an improved approach to warfighting. The complexity of the urban battle, creates unique problems for commanders to select appropriate means and methods of warfare, enable mission success, protect its forces, operate within the rules of IHL, and integrate civilian protection as a strategic requirement. It also entails more demanding analysis during the planning phase, including learning from past operations, tailored training for the operational environment and policies, and identifying best practices on civilian protection to better enable commanders to reduce human suffering in urban warfare.

Endnotes

The views expressed herein are those of the author and do not necessarily reflect the views of the US Department of Defense.

1. The "laws of armed conflict" is the preferred term used by some militaries, but it is also referred to as "international humanitarian law." The Hague Regulations noted, "The right of belligerents to adopt means of injuring the enemy is not unlimited." Convention with Respect to the Laws and Customs of War on Land, Article 22, October 18, 1907, https://ihldatabases.icrc.org/applic/ihl/ihl.nsf/Article.xsp?action=openDocument&documentId=56AA246EA8CFF07AC1256 3CD0051675A.

2. Protocol Additional to the Geneva Conventions of 12 August 1949, and Relating to the Protection of Victims of International Armed Conflicts (Protocol I), 8 June 1977 (hereafter AP I), Preamble, para. 5. The United States has ratified the Geneva Conventions. It's a signatory to AP I and AP II but has not ratified these treaties. Many provisions of AP I are considered as customary international law. The DoD Law of War Manual is the DoD' position on the law of war, including on conduct of hostilities, weapons, treatment of prisoners of war, military occupation, neutrality, and cyber rules. The Manual relies on treaties and customary international law and is the DoD's legal guidance to US personnel and reflects the DoD's view and not of the whole US government. This article generally cites AP I and customary international law applicable in armed conflicts and does not analyze from the lens of the US Department of Defense.

3. Geneva Conventions I-IV. Common Art. 1, ICRC Customary International Law Study, Rule 10.

4. The Statute of the International Court of Justice (ICJ) describes customary international law as "a general practice accepted as law" and is generally agreed that requires state practice (usus) and a belief that such practice is required, prohibited or allowed, depending on the nature of the rule, as a matter of law (opinio juris). ICJ Statute, Article 38(1)(b). Jean-Marie Henckaerts and Louise Doswald-Beck, Customary International Humanitarian Law, Vol 1: Rules, Cambridge University Press, 2005, (hereinafter "ICRC Customary International Law Study"), https://www.icrc.org/en/doc/assets/files/other/customary-international-humanitarian-law-i-icrc-eng.pdf (see pp. xxxvii-xxxviii).

5. While nearly all States have ratified the four Geneva Conventions of 1949, Additional Protocol I applicable in international armed conflict, and which contains extensive regulations on conduct of hostilities, has been ratified by 174 states. Additional Protocol II, ratified by 164 states, is only applicable in armed conflicts taking place in the territory of a State that has ratified it and has limited regulations on the conduct of hostilities. A majority of today's armed conflicts are

non-international armed conflicts. The ICRC Customary International Law study shows that the gaps in the regulation of the conduct of hostilities in Additional Protocol II have largely been filled through State practice, which has led to the creation of rules parallel to those in Additional Protocol I, but applicable as customary law to non-international armed conflicts. See ICRC, Customary International Law Study, pp. xxxiv-xxxvi. Common Article 3 to the four Geneva Conventions also establishes fundamental rules from which no derogations are permitted and make this applicable to international and non-international armed conflict. It requires humane treatment for all persons in enemy hands, without discrimination. It specifically prohibits murder, mutilation, torture, the taking of hostages, unfair trial, and cruel, humiliating and degrading treatment. It requires that the wounded, sick and shipwrecked be collected and cared for. It grants the ICRC the right to offer its services to the parties to the conflict. It calls on the parties to the conflict to bring all or parts of the Geneva Conventions into force through "special agreements."

6. AP I, Articles 48(1), 51(2), 51(3), https://ihldatabases.icrc.org/applic/ihl/ihl.nsf/4e473c7b-c8854f2ec12563f60039c738/50fb5579fb098faac12563cd0051dd7c.

7. AP I, Arts. 51(1), 52(3). See e.g. US DoD Law of War Manual 2023 Updates, (updates on presumption of civilian presence and civilian objects), https://media.defense.gov/2023/Jul/31/2003271432/-1/-1/0/DOD-LAW-OF-WAR-MANUAL-JUNE-2015-UPDATED-JULY%202023.PDF

8. See, e.g. the 2023 US Department of Defense Instruction 3000.17, Civilian Harm Mitigation and Response, and 2022 DoD Civilian Harm Mitigation Action Plan identifies understanding the civilian environment with dedicated resources as key enablers to minimize civilian harm.

9. AP I, Articles 47 and 57.

10. P. Benvenuti, "The ICTY prosecutor and the review of the NATO bombing campaign against the Federal Republic of Yugoslavia", European Journal of International Law, Vol. 12, No. 3, 2001, p. 517.

11. AP I, Articles 57(1). Non-state parties to the AP I, including the US, do not view this as customary international law.

12. AP I, Article 57, Commentary of 1987, https://ihldatabases.icrc.org/applic/ihl/ihl.nsf/Comment.xsp?action=openDocument&documentId=D80D14D84BF36B92C125 63CD00434FBD.

13. International Law Association Study Group on the Conduct of Hostilities in the 21st Century, "The conduct of hostilities and international humanitarian law: Challenges of 21st century warfare", International Law Studies, US Naval War College, Vol. 93, No. 322, 2017, (hereafter "ILA Study Group Report"), p. 381.

14. ICRC, Reducing Civilian Harm in Urban Warfare: A Commanders Handbook, 2022 (ICRC "Urban War Commanders Handbook"), https://www.icrc.org/en/document/reducing-civilian-harm-urban-warfare-commandershandbook, (the author was one of the subject matter experts consulted for the handbook).

15. AP I, Articles 57 and 58.

16. Sahr Muhammedally, "Primer on CHM in Urban Operations," Center for Civilians in Conflict, 2022, https://civiliansinconflict.org/wpcontent/uploads/2022/06/CIVIC_Primer_Civilian_Harm_Mitigation_in_Urban_Operations.pdf.

17. AP I, Article 54 (1) and AP II, Article 14 (prohibition on starvation); Third Geneva Convention, Article 23; Fourth Geneva Convention, Article 28; AP I, Article 51(7) (prohibition on human shields).

18. See Emanuela-Chiara Gillard, "Sieges, the Law and Protecting Civilians," Chatham House, June 2019, https://www.chathamhouse.org/sites/default/files/publications/research/2019-06-27-Sieges-ProtectingCivilians_0.pdf.
19. See generally UNSC Resolutions applicable to different conflicts and UNSC Resolutions 2462, 2482, 2642 (support for humanitarian access), https://www.un.org/securitycouncil/content/resolutions-0.
20. Fourth Geneva Convention, Article 23, AP I, Article 70(2), CIL, Rule 55 (parties to conflict must allow and facilitate rapid and unimpeded passage of humanitarian relief for civilians in need, which is impartial in nature and conducted without any adverse distinction). Many state military manuals recognize this rule and has been emphasized in numerous United Nations Security Council Resolutions. See, e.g. ICRC, Customary International Law Study, https://ihl-databases.icrc.org/en/customary-ihl/v1/rule55#refFn_E763511D_0000; See generally, ICRC, Humanitarian Access: What the Law Says, https://www.icrc.org/en/document/humanitarian-access-what-law-says%20%E2%80%8B
21. Act harmful to the enemy" is not defined under IHL. This body of law merely singles out a few acts expressly recognized as not being harmful to the enemy, such as the carrying or using of individual light weapons in self-defense or defense of wounded and sick, armed guarding of a medical facility, or the presence in a medical facility of sick or wounded combatants no longer taking part in hostilities. See, ICRC, CIL, Rule 28, https://ihldatabases.icrc.org/en/customary-ihl/v1/rule28#Fn_2E87616B_00040
22. See generally, ICRC, Health Care in Danger, https://www.icrc.org/en/publication/4072-health-care-dangermaking-case.
23. AP I, Art. 51(4).
24. Robert Lawless and Sean Watts, The Law and Character of War in 2035, Lieber Institute West Point, March 25, 2022, https://lieber.westpoint.edu/law-character-war-2035/. There is robust debate on the levels of human control and human judgment in the conduct of hostilities, which this article does not discuss. The US maintains a policy of appropriate use of human judgment in use of autonomous or semi-autonomous weapons. US DoD Directive, Autonomy in Weapons Systems, January 23, 2023, https://www.esd.whs.mil/portals/54/documents/dd/issuances/dodd/300009p.pdf.
25. See generally, ICRC, New Technologies and IHL, https://www.icrc.org/en/war-and-law/weapons/ihl-and-newtechnologies.
26. Christopher Kolenda, Rachel Reid et al, "The Strategic Costs of Civilian Harm," Open Society Foundations, 2016, https://www.opensocietyfoundations.org/publications/strategic-costs-civilian-harm.
27. Andrew Shaver and Jacob Shapiro, "The Effect of Civilian Casualties on Wartime Informing: Evidence from the Iraq War," Journal of Conflict Resolution, March 10, 2021, https://journals.sagepub.com/doi/10.1177/0022002721991627
28. L.N. Condra et al, "The Effect of Civilian Casualties in Afghanistan and Iraq," National Bureau of Economic Research Working paper No. 16152, July 2010, https://www.nber.org/system/files/working_papers/w16152/w16152.pdf
29. See US Army, ATP 3-06, "Urban Operations," para 1-64, https://armypubs.army.mil/epubs/DR_pubs/DR_a/ARN35826-ATP_3-06-000-WEB-1.pdf; US Army, Protection of Civilians, ATP

30. ICRC, Explosive Weapons with Wide Area Effects: A Deadly Choice, January 2022, (hereafter "ICRC EWIPA Report"), https://www.icrc.org/en/document/civilians-protected-against-explosive-weapons, pp. 42-48.

31. See, e.g., World Bank, Ukraine Recovery and Reconstruction Estimated at 348 billion, September 9, 2022, https://www.worldbank.org/en/news/press-release/2022/09/09/ukraine-recovery-and-reconstruction-needsestimated-349-billion. CNBC, "88.2 Billion US Dollar Price Tag for Rebuilding After Islamic State War," February 12, 2018, https://www.cnbc.com/2018/02/12/88-point-2-billion-us-dollar-price-tag-for-rebuilding-iraq-after-islamicstate-war.html

32. See Michael McNerney et al, "Understanding Civilian Harm in Raqqa," March 2022, https://www.rand.org/pubs/research_reports/RRA753-1.html#:~:text=Key%20Findings&text=Civilian%20casualties%20in%20Raqqa%20were,and%20long%2Dterm%20US%20interests.

33. See US Army, "Urban Operations."

34. Gen. Stanley McChrystal, Commander of NATO's ISAF, Tactical Directive, July 2, 2009.

35. Paul D. Williams, "The African Union Mission in Somalia and Civilian Protection Challenges," Stability International Journal of Security & Development, 2(2), p.Art. 39, https://www.stability-journal.org/articles/10.5334/sta.bz/

36. NATO, Protection of Civilians ACO Handbook, 2021, p. 9, https://shape.nato.int/resources/3/website/ACOProtection-of-Civilians-Handbook.pdf (author contributed to the Handbook).

37. US Department of Defense, Civilian Harm Mitigation Action and Response Plan, August 25, 2022, https://media.defense.gov/2022/Aug/25/2003064740/-1/-1/1/CIVILIAN-HARM-MITIGATION-AND-RESPONSEACTION-PLAN.PDF.

38. Sahr Muhammedally, "Minimizing Civilian Harm in Populated Areas: Lessons from Examining ISAF and AMISOM Policies," International Review of the Red Cross, no. 901 (April 2016) (hereafter "Minimizing Civilian Harm in Populated Areas"), https://international-review.icrc.org/articles/minimizing-civilian-harm-populated-areaslessons-examining-isaf-and-amisom-policies.

39. Ibid.

40. NATO, NATO Policy for the Protection of Civilians Endorsed by the Heads of State and Government Participating in the Meeting of the North Atlantic Council in Warsaw', July 9, 2016, http://www.nato.int/cps/en/natohq/official_texts_133945.htm

41. See Sahr Muhammedally and Marc Garlasco, https://www.justsecurity.org/68810/reduction-of-civilian-harm-inafghanistan-a-wayforward/#:~:text=The%20guidance%20directs%20RS%20forces,casualties%20that%20the%20US%20investigated %2C.

42. "The Civilian Casualty Files," *New York Times*, https://www.nytimes.com/spotlight/the-civilian-casualty-filespentagon-reports.

43. Department of Defense Instruction 3000.17, Civilian Harm Mitigation and Response, 2023, https://www.esd.whs.mil/Portals/54/Documents/DD/issuances/dodi/300017p.pdf

44. Ireland Department of Foreign Affairs, Political Declaration on EWIPA, https://www.dfa.ie/our-rolepolicies/international-priorities/peace-and-security/ewipa-consultations/ (formal consultations between states, UN, ICRC, civil society began in November 2019).

POSTSCRIPT
The Future of Urban Operations in Context

David Kilcullen

> "The future is already here—it's just not evenly distributed."
>
> William Gibson[1]

The sci-fi novelist William Gibson makes a crucial point for anyone attempting to predict the future, perhaps especially in the field of urban conflict. Gibson may never have said exactly this, in these words—the attribution of the quotation is uncertain— but the general observation seems intuitively correct. Patterns of conflict in cities arise from underlying demographic and economic shifts, changes in settlement patterns and the built environment, emerging and disruptive technologies, and the evolution of state and non-state armed actors within that environment. All of these represent current conditions that it is possible to study and understand, provided one knows where to look and how to make sense of them. Hence, it should be possible to predict the general characteristics of future urban conflict by studying the state of the environment as it exists today. Since urban warfare forms part of a complex adaptive system, its behavior is non-linear by definition. Specific events are, therefore, not predictable in detail. Still, general trends are evident in the aggregate, allowing us to develop testable hypotheses about where such conflict might be heading.

This book has already examined, at varying levels of detail, the current state of urban conflict—from organized crime and urban criminality to urban irregular and guerrilla warfare, to terrorist and resistance activity in cities, to urban high-intensity large-scale combat operations. Based on that analysis, this postscript suggests some hypotheses about urban operations and how they may develop over the next ten to fifteen years. These are described in detail below, but in outline, they are as follows:

- The return of large-scale, state-on-state, high-intensity conflict in urban environments will accelerate, and will increasingly invalidate legacy tactics, weapon systems, and organizational structures;
- Interior spaces—including subterranean and interior airspace—will become increasingly important as an urban maneuver environment for both state and non-state armed actors;
- The emergence of space as a warfighting domain, combined with Ubiquitous Technical Surveillance (UTS), will increase the legibility of urban environments, limiting the freedom of action for combatants attempting to maneuver at scale;
- Info-kinetic operations will increasingly become the norm in connected urban spaces, with combatants using information as a means to inflict lethal kinetic effects on an adversary and kinetic means to achieve information effects;
- Actors of all kinds will increasingly attempt to weaponize the city, turning the urban environment and its subsystems into tools for combat;
- Robotics and Autonomous Systems (RAS), enabled by Artificial Intelligence (AI), will continue to replace humans in high-risk tasks across all domains; and

- Remote and Collaborative engagement, by distributed small teams, will be an increasingly common response to the dispersion dilemma in urban environments.

The Urban Conflict Fitness landscape

In order to establish which elements of today's environment are likely to become more prevalent in the future—in effect, to establish which aspects of the future are already here though not evenly distributed—it is necessary to determine which of today's observable traits and behaviors are likely spread and proliferate. One way to do this is through the conceptual framework of a combat fitness landscape.

I have written elsewhere in detail about the notion of a fitness landscape, a metaphor in which all possible combinations of traits are mapped for a given organism, organization, or fighting force, then assigned a positive or negative height value to reflect the degree to which they are "adaptive" (conducive to better performance and survival) or "maladaptive" (likely to harm performance and decrease survivability). The result looks like a landscape with a series of peaks and valleys, where peaks indicate trait combinations that are adaptive, and valleys are metaphors for maladaptive traits. Over time, under conditions of natural and artificial selection, trait combinations that make an actor more survivable tend to proliferate, and actors with those characteristics become more common in a given combat ecosystem. Conversely, trait combinations that are maladaptive, decreasing success and survivability for a given environment, will become less prevalent, and actors with those combinations will tend to die out.

In the operating environment, as it existed after the end of the Cold War, US dominance of a certain style of high-tech conventional combat forced all other actors to adapt, either copying the US "system-of-systems" model that enabled conventional warfighting or engaging in avoidance behavior to avoid defeat. Hiding in cities within the complex and cluttered human, physical, infrastructural, and informational terrain that defines urban areas became one key way for US adversaries—states or nonstate actors—to improve their chances of survival and success. As a consequence, since the end of the Cold War, multiple actors (with differing ideologies, points of origin, and strategic objectives) have converged, adopting remarkably similar styles of combat in complex terrain, including cities.

One way to summarize the influence of a fitness landscape on combat adaptation is to identify the characteristics that a given environment tends to reward (with better combat performance or enhanced survivability) versus those it tends to punish. Understanding this underlying fitness landscape can help predict which characteristics are likely to become more prevalent over time and which are likely to die out. These characteristics are depicted below for today's operating environment.

The Combat Fitness Landscape

A fitness landscape maps all potential combinations of characteristics for a given organism in a specific environment, indentifying combinations that are more adaptive (i.e. more conductive to survival and success) in that environment. [Kilcullen, 2020]

The environment _rewards_ systems, applications and platforms that are:	The environment _punishes_ platforms, organizations and technologies that are
• Small	• Large
• Cheap	• Expensive
• Stealthy	• Overt
• Modular	• Complex
• Composite	• Single-role
• Multi-role / swing-role	• Few
• Many	• Ponderous
• Agile	• Slow
• Mobile	• Proprietary
• Open-architecture	• Closed-source
• Easily maintainable	• Difficult to maintain
• Transferable to 3rd parties	• Non-transferable

In effect, this reading of the current environment suggests certain styles of organization or operation that are likely to proliferate in the future environment. In today's environment, these include acting across the full breadth and depth of an urban/peri-urban/rural nodal matrix that includes an urban center, "belts" of settlement around that center, suburbs, exurbs, and satellite cities. The fitness landscape described here favors a style of fighting based on leaderless resistance, without any "brain" or targetable headquarters, involving acephalous swarms, the use of remote or stand-off control nodes, or a one-way broadcast of operational guidance to autonomous actors who self-organize and self-synchronize to achieve objectives. It would favor the "infestation" of urban environments, with combat elements embedded in physical structures, hollow and interior spaces, and hiding within urban population groups. Combat formations might include large numbers of small multi-role platforms, operating in a dynamic swarm, with modular organizations down to the lowest possible level (perhaps combat pairs) and the ability to rapidly re-task and re-organize on the fly as a situation changes.

Actors seeking to fight this way employ cooperative and remote engagement, with sensors and shooters (or effectors) offset from each other in time and space, repurposing consumer electronics and the industrial capacity inherent in urban environments to improvise precision-strike capabilities with minimum detectable signature. They make use of cyber-kinetic or info-kinetic operations—with cyberspace becoming an integrated adjunct maneuver space alongside the physical domains of air, land, sea, and the electromagnetic spectrum.

Today's urban combat fitness landscape tends to favor rapidly-improvise capabilities (using advanced on-site manufacturing capabilities such as 3D printing) and technological "hugging," in which combatants seek to use systems on which an enemy relies and hence cannot target or disrupt. They use the high latent technological capacity inherent in urban populations familiar with modern consumer and industrial technologies. They exploit diaspora linkages and retaliation options, weaponizing friendly overseas populations located in an adversary's home territory, and seek to manipulate political and social movements, strikes and public protests, and global media environments to further their own objectives and limit an enemy's options. In the urban area itself, their goal is to create no-go and no-see areas that an adversary can neither observe nor control as a means to establish safe havens. They seek to control routes, choke points, and critical infrastructure by interdiction rather than occupation, and under certain circumstances, they may make tactical use of terrorism to limit and shape an adversary's deployment, creating openings for maneuver elsewhere.

In the urban defense, groups that fight in this manner tend to be less focused on the positional or area defense of urban centers, instead placing more emphasis on actively defending surrounding peri-urban and rural zones (belts). An urban center itself may be treated as an economy-of-force zone, with the defending force's main effort withheld and strong counterattack and quick-reaction forces operating in the belts or along covered access routes. Such combatants have little tendency to fight "last stand" defensive actions. Instead, they prioritize area denial and active, mobile mesh or network defense, and tend to fade away in the face of strong attacks, then mount rapid counterattacks using stay-behind groups or multi-planar re-infiltration (using covered routes across surface, subterranean, rooftop, and interior spaces) into areas that have previously been cleared but not secured by an adversary. Between major combat engagements, they conduct active mobile patrolling—employing fighting patrols, reconnaissance patrols, raids, and using many small actions as cover or to desensitize and shape defenders ahead of major strikes. They attempt to employ airborne, aerial, river-borne, and seaborne attacks, typically by night and in bad weather, wherever possible.

In the attack, combatants that fight in this manner tend to make extensive use of military deception, seeking to wrong-foot an enemy ahead of any offensive action. As noted, they make tactical use of terror to manipulate a defender's deployment, fixing the defender in place through the need to protect multiple vulnerable points. Assaults are carried out by multiple small modular fighting groups, each with a mix of hard- and soft-skinned vehicles, heavy and light weapons, drones, and specialized anti-armor, area-denial, and engineering capabilities. They seek to establish a network of urban, peri-urban, and rural support cells to enable a conventional main force which may then conduct urban siege ("raid and hold") operations, mount baited ambushes against relief forces, sabotage sea/air points of entry and critical supply routes, and make extensive use of improvised explosive devices (IEDs) of all kinds.

Under conditions of urban insurgency, today's fitness landscape seems to favor combatants who engage in multi-path re-infiltration of previously cleared areas, use loitering munitions or FPV drones as mobile IEDs that can be rapidly repositioned, conduct anti-aircraft ambushes against helicopters, surveillance and strike aircraft (whether crewed or uncrewed) and airborne forces, and emphasize runway and harbor denial operations to prevent an adversary from building up logistics or establishing secure points of entry into a theater of operations. They make extensive use of snipers, both for direct engagement of high-value targets and to direct the fire of mortars, artillery, and rockets firing from positions in depth. Observers positioned forward or located out of the combat area altogether may improvise precision engagements using Google Earth and GPS or similar systems to geolocate targets, spot the fall of shots, adjust fire, and coordinate engagements using reports from remote observers.

Extensive tunneling and placement of IEDs under buildings, with the tunnel serving as a network of covered maneuver corridors, house bombs, suicide vehicle-borne IEDS, and the placement of IEDs in thick defensive clusters protecting key locations are all characteristics of today's adaptive urban insurgent forces.

Terrorist activity in today's urban combat environment tends to make extensive use of sabotage, sometimes using internet-connected urban control systems and "smart city" internet-of-things infrastructure to enhance the effects of such sabotage. Terrorists attempt to subvert or co-opt local security forces and police, then focus their attacks on soft targets, employing a mix of low-tech and high-tech means. Terrorist attacks on infrastructure and population clusters often seek to manipulate the reaction to an initial incident or series of incidents (including riots, flash mobs, and strikes) to create targets for a secondary or tertiary attack or cluster of attacks. Collaboration and competition with criminal groups is an inherent feature of terrorist activity, and terrorist actors may seek to hide within the clutter of a broader pattern of criminal behavior or urban unrest. Deception efforts may be enhanced through the use of online or cyber tools, including false flag attacks, disinformation, or fake news to shape the reaction of a population or an adversary.

Weaponizing the city—turning key features of the urban environment and its physical, informational, infrastructural, and human terrain against an adversary—is also an increasingly common approach adopted by combatants across all these categories. The ability to engage in the manipulation of industrial systems, manufacturing plants, energy storage and distribution networks, transportation systems, and urban smart-city infrastructure is increasingly open to both state and non-state actors, turning the urban area itself into an opponent. The mass movement of civilians and the resulting requirement to protect non-combatants from harm and apply principles of proportionality, the distinction between combatants and non-combatants, and precautions in the attack are both important and onerous for all actors seeking to uphold international humanitarian law. Failure to uphold such legal requirements—in an environment of ubiquitous technical surveillance, citizen journalism, and social media—is likely to have extremely serious negative impacts on the moral and political legitimacy of combatants, undermining their strategic goals and limiting their freedom of action.

These then, are key features of current combatants that tend to be favored by today's combat fitness landscape. To the extent that such adaptive traits and behaviors are likely to proliferate while maladaptive ones become less prevalent, these indicate the likely direction of travel for urban conflict, even though (as noted) it is by definition impossible to predict specific future events. To paraphrase Gibson, then, these are the elements of a likely future that can currently be observed in today's environment, representing the future that is "already here, but not evenly distributed." If these features proliferate into the future, as the trends inherent in the fitness landscape suggest they are likely to do, then it is possible to advance several testable hypotheses about what we might see in a future urban combat environment.

Seven Hypotheses on Future Urban Conflict

As noted earlier, this analysis suggests seven such testable hypotheses.

The first is that the already-observable return of large-scale, state-on-state, high-intensity conflict in urbanized environments—currently seen in

Ukraine and Gaza—will accelerate and that this will increasingly invalidate legacy tactics, weapon systems, and organizational structures. Ukraine, in this regard, represents an injection of reality into what has been a largely theoretical debate over issues such as armored vehicle survivability, the large-scale use of UAVs as loitering munitions, the role of long-range offensive fires in conjunction with distributed, stealthy networks of intelligence, surveillance, and reconnaissance (ISR) assets including both forward field teams and air- and space-based targeting. Legacy tactics and organizations—in particular, the use of massed armored forces maneuvering on an open battlefield and seeking to defeat an adversary by dislocating and disrupting command systems and bypassing physical defenses—are not performing well under these circumstances. Assaults into urban areas have been slow, costly in lives, extremely destructive to the built environment and local inhabitants, and extraordinarily expensive in ammunition expenditure. We might hypothesize that the prevalence of extremely dense ISR coverage, extending well into rear areas, will make massed conventional maneuver increasingly unlikely in future urban combat. Instead, we may see small, stealthy distributed combat teams of the kind described in the previous section, becoming the main maneuver element for both conventional militaries and irregular forces alike.

The second testable hypothesis is that interior spaces—including subterranean areas such as tunnels, sewers, basements, interior airspace within buildings, and covered avenues of approach—will become increasingly important as urban maneuver corridors for both state and non-state armed actors. As the war in Gaza has shown, tunnel fighting at a large scale and high intensity is exhausting, slow, and costly. The ability to make use of tunnels as maneuver spaces allows combatants to reinfiltrate areas that an adversary believes have been cleared, mounting attacks on the flanks and rear of combat forces and targeting headquarters, logistics assets, and base installations. At the same time, as seen in Gaza, Ukraine, and previously in Nagorno-Karabakh and Mosul, UAVs and control systems have advanced to the point that reconnaissance drones, loitering munitions, and FPV drones can be employed within buildings, along tunnels and corridors, and within constricted urban airspace such as alleyways and covered walkways. Maneuver within such interior airspace is likely to become increasingly prevalent in future urban combat as today's combatants adapt to the challenges demonstrated by such forms of maneuver in the current environment.

The third hypothesis is that the emergence of space as a warfighting domain, with multiple state actors fielding space and counter-space systems capable of jamming, disrupting or physically destroying rival systems in orbit, combined with Ubiquitous Technical Surveillance (UTS), will increase the legibility of urban environments, making it easier for space-capable adversaries to penetrate the clutter, making sense of complex, contested urban environments, even when these are densely built-up and heavily populated. As a consequence of increased legibility, freedom of action for combatants maneuvering at scale in urban environments is likely to decline in the future. As a result—and as noted earlier for large-scale combat operations—maneuver is likely to rely increasingly on networks of small combat teams collaborating with each other, within an overall ISR and long-range fires umbrella. At the same time, efforts by combatants to knock out adversary space systems may have far-reaching impacts on urban infrastructure, particularly cellphone systems, internet access, and any system that relies on Positioning, Navigation, and Timing (PNT) satellite systems such as the US GPS, Russian GLONASS, European Galileo or Chinese Beidou system.

A fourth hypothesis, building on the last two, is that info-kinetic operations will increasingly become the norm in connected urban spaces, with combatants using information systems as a means to inflict lethal kinetic effects on an adversary, and kinetic means to achieve information effects. This may involve direct destruction of control systems and connected infrastructure using cyber tools, the use of kinetic means to disrupt information systems, and the combination of both information systems and kinetic tools to generate a combined arms effect whereby adversaries seeking to protect themselves from cyberattack expose themselves to kinetic attack, and vice versa. We can, therefore, expect that cyber and the information space will continue to evolve as adjunct maneuver spaces alongside and integrated with maneuver in physical domains rather than as a separate stand-alone domain. While the rise of info-kinetic maneuver affects both urban and non-urban environments, the fact that electronic connectivity and access to information systems remains significantly greater in cities than in rural areas will continue to make this a key feature of urban conflict.

A fifth hypothesis is that actors of all kinds—including both state and non-state actors and both armed and unarmed entities—will increasingly attempt to weaponize the city, turning urban environments and their subsystems into tools for combat. This may be seen in the use of large-scale protest action to block bridges, tunnels, and highways or to blockade critical urban infrastructure as a means of provoking a defensive reaction that can then be exploited as a baited attack. Alternatively, sabotage of critical urban control systems may be used to black out an area, disrupt transportation and traffic flow, or manipulate urban systems to deny an area, channel an adversary into particular locations or forms of maneuver, and/or support a deception plan. The increasing use of AI, more extensive penetration of cellphones and the internet, and the wider prevalence of connected smart-city infrastructure across much of the world will increase the scope for such action in the future.

Sixth, we can hypothesize that Robotics and Autonomous Systems (RAS), enabled by AI, will continue to replace humans in high-risk tasks across all domains. RAS is already replacing humans for critical tasks in underwater, subterranean, contaminated, or constricted spaces as a means of reducing the danger to human life. As AI continues to develop, we are likely to see wider application of RAS, including UAVs in the air domain, Uncrewed Surface Vessels (USVs) and Uncrewed Underwater Vehicles (UUVs) in the maritime domain and riverine environments, and Uncrewed Ground Vehicles (UGVs) and Unattended Ground Sensors (UGS). Already in 2024, we have seen—in both the Black Sea and Red Sea—the use of RAS to disrupt naval activity, close or isolate ports and transportation chokepoints, and conduct high-risk tasks in constricted spaces. All of this is likely to accelerate into the future, driven by technological developments and ongoing personnel shortages in advanced militaries, and by easy access to commercial RAS for non-state actors and irregular forces.

Finally, we can hypothesize that remote and collaborative engagement, by distributed small teams, where sensors and controllers are offset in time and/or space from shooters/effectors, will be increasingly common in the future. This can be seen as an adaptive response to the "dispersion dilemma" in which attempts to mass forces physically can expose a combatant to a kinetic strike, but dispersing the force in order to avoid such a strike creates a need for communications, which generates emissions that expose the force to electronic and kinetic strikes as a result. Combatants will continue to seek ways to achieve the benefits of massed effect without the vulnerabilities of concentration; this suggests that the style of fighting discussed above—a network of small, semi-autonomous combat teams operating cooperatively, connected using low-power or no-power mesh-based communications, and sitting under the umbrella of long-range fires that can be directed by remote observers and ISR networks—is likely to continue proliferating in the future.

All of these are hypotheses rather than predictions. They suggest things we might see in the future operating environment if these guesses turn out to be correct. In order to validate these hypotheses going forward, analysts may want to create a series of observable indicators that we would expect to see if these guesses are accurate, versus a set of indicators that might suggest a different evolutionary pathway for urban conflict. These can then be monitored on an ongoing basis to help continuously test the hypotheses outlined here.

Conclusion

Urban warfare and conflict in cities below the threshold of war have been an enduring feature of the environment ever since cities have existed. The analyses presented in this book have examined, in detail, the current state of urban conflict and the best practice thinking that today's analysts and analytical tools can bring to bear on it. In the future, we can expect the fitness landscape outlined in this chapter to continue influencing the adaptive behavior of all actors in this combat ecosystem, in non-linear ways. While specific events are impossible to predict, the fitness landscape for urban warfare today suggests a number of likely pathways for urban warfare into the future. In this sense, an analysis of today's environment suggests those parts of the future that are already here, while the trends inherent in the fitness landscape suggest how and where those elements may become more widespread (even if still not evenly distributed) in the future.

Endnotes

1. "'The future is already here – it's just not evenly distributed' William Gibson, *The Economist*, December 4, 2003", cited in *Cities & Health*, Vol. 4, No. 2, (2020), 152.

Appendices

Appendix One: Book Reviews

Come Hell or High Fever: Readying the World's Megacities for Disaster.

By Russell W. Glenn.

Canberra, Australia: Australian University Press,

2023. ISBN 978-1-760-46553-7. Abbreviations,

Bibliography, Index. Pp. ix-461. $39.95

Review by Dr. Magdalena A. Denham, Sam Houston State University

Dr. Russell W. Glenn draws on his 25 years of strategic military, disaster studies, urban warfare field, and think tank research experience to offer a systems perspective on the challenges and opportunities of disasters in the world's megacities. This excellently researched book frames the discourse on megacities in the *all-hazards* perspective, namely exploring disasters along the natural, technological, and man-made (to include war conflict) continuum. It maintains perfect balance in straddling topics and cases across emergency management, national defense, and civil defense/civil protection and, as such, is unique as an offering to Homeland Security and Emergency Management (HSEM) scholarship.

A vast array of authoritative voices collected by the author from interviews with military strategists, commanders, soldiers, emergency management professionals, elected officials, or individuals affected by disasters, to name a few, imbue the publication with depth and credibility. The originality of the work stems from the author's selection of the world's megacities—geographically widespread, densely populated, diverse, and of global resonance—as the primary unit of analysis. The selection itself offers a rich global canvass for the inclusiveness of cases across various continents, economies, and governance systems and allows for extensive comparative analyses beyond US or Western contexts. This sets it apart from books like Kelly McKinney's *Moment of Truth: The Nature of Catastrophes and How to Prepare for Them,* which at a much smaller scale explores some of the similar range of topics in localized New York City urban environment and from a uniquely US, emergency management perspective.

Glenn's main purpose and the overarching theme of the book is the portrayal of world megacities as perfect examples of complex systems in which risks from hazards and threats and their ensuing consequences are also the most complex. Notably, world megacities house the deepest pockets of social vulnerabilities to be exploited by disasters, such as the favelas of Rio de Janeiro or the slums of Lagos, Dhaka, New York, or ungoverned sections of Karachi while offering opportunities for the talent pool, learning, creativity, innovation, and collaboration in addressing calamities—Glenn refers to this as the megacity *yin of challenge and the yang of opportunity.*

Megacities are also inherently connected to other external systems, which in turn amplify potential global impacts and second and third-order effects of disasters they would face. While not explicitly stated in the book, its design mirrors a journey through the emergency management cycle from prevention, planning, and preparedness to response, to recovery, and to some extent, mitigation. For each of those phases in subsequent chapters, Glenn navigates across a range of critical focusing events to draw lessons for megacities' disaster readiness.

However, unlike HSEM publications, including systematic case studies and lessons learned to inform practice (e.g., *Critical Issues in Homeland Security:*

A Casebook by James Ramsay and Linda Kiltz), the author did not take a linear approach. Instead, his lens reflects the systems' thinking for which the book advocates. This puts topics generally amply discussed in the literature, such as urban planning for medical capacity, into a masterful web of multi-faceted comparative analyses.

Reflection on Sheri Fink's *Five Days at Memorial* depicting catastrophic events in one of New Orleans hospitals during hurricane Karina weaves into the post-mortem of medical capacity in Mumbai during 2008 Complex Coordinated Terror Attacks (CCTA), then shifts to an assessment of Paris 2015 medical surge capacities, while intersecting with reflections on Lagos hospital expertise in critical case identification during the Ebola crisis. This high level of synthesis permeates the entire book extracting rich clusters from illustrative cases across impeccably researched historical disaster events with differing anatomies to drive home- at times universal and at times nuanced-points on preparedness, capacity building, collaboration, disaster technologies, risk, and crisis communications, intelligence gathering and sharing, command, and control, centralization vs decentralization, or leveraging of lessons learned in post-disaster contexts.

In tandem with systems' perspective, the author focuses on Complex Adaptive Systems (CAS) and resiliency. While he contends megacities will be increasingly more exposed and vulnerable to disasters, most likely unprecedented in scope, he underscores the ability of megacities to self-repair and to sustain themselves as some of the largest world cities have done successfully in the past. For instance, one of the compelling arguments omnipresent in *Come Hell or High Fever* is the perennial emergence and spontaneity displayed by individuals, communities, and grassroot movements in the aftermath of a critical event. As *first* first responders time and again constitute powerful human capital in response and recovery from catastrophes, government planning, and preparedness processes need to account for emergence phenomena, sustain them, and support them. Likewise, adaptability and inclusivity should become the *sine qua non* hallmarks of the *rehearsal*—the author's operational term for a wide range of activities related to megacity planning and preparedness processes.

Dr. Russell W. Glenn identified the audiences for his book as city administrators; police, fire, and medical personnel; commercial interests; soldiers; members of local and international nongovernmental organizations (NGOs); intergovernmental organizations (IGOs) as well as individuals who might act as *first* first responders. Inarguably, the expanse of the book might make it a challenging read as a *go-to blueprint* on urban preparedness for many in the suggested readership. However, despite the publication's interlinked, scaffolded structure, chapters can standalone, allowing the reader to enter the text at random without the loss of thread. Moreover, the rich repertoire of quotes as springboards for reflection in each of the book sub-parts makes it an excellent iterative read for anyone interested in pondering the challenges of current and future crisis leadership. Finally, because of its research depth, topic integration, and saturation, as well as sophisticated comparative focus, *Come Hell or High Water: Readying the World's Megacities for Disaster* is a publication that would be of extreme value as an accompanying text incorporated into graduate curriculum for students in any of the protective disciplines.

Blood and Concrete: 21ˢᵗ Century Conflict in Urban Centers and Megacities.

Edited by Dave Dilegge, Robert J. Bunker, John P. Sullivan, and Alma Keshavarz. Bloomington, IN: Xlibris, 2019.

ISBN 978-1-9845-7375-9. Notes. Sources Cited. Acronyms.

Photographs. Notes on Contributors. Pp. xi-705. $22.99

Review by Michael L. Burgoyne, MA and Ph.D. Student

At the outset of the post 9/11 US military interventions, the only knowledge gap among military leaders more pronounced than insurgency/counterinsurgency was in urban operations. In the aftermath of the Vietnam War, generations of officers and non-commissioned officers focused on defeating conventional forces across European rural landscapes and later the deserts of Southwest Asia. At Combat Training Centers, the player unit and the opposing force (OPFOR) faced off on a pristine simulated battlefield—not a town, non-combatant, or piece of infrastructure in sight. The recommended procedure for dealing with a built-up area was bypass. When US forces found themselves in tough fights in Baghdad and Fallujah, bypass was no longer an option. In fact, it never truly was an option, and today, more than ever, understanding how to fight in urban areas is an inescapable necessity. That is why *Blood and Concrete: A Small Wars Journal Anthology* is essential reading for practitioners and scholars of modern war and security.

From its inception, *the Small Wars Journal* has filled gaps in traditional professional military education. *Small Wars Journal* has been an invaluable hub for knowledge of often neglected complex threats and operations. Urban operations hold a special place at *Small Wars Journal* as the journal began as the Military Operations in Urban Terrain homepage and later the *Urban Operations Journal*. Published in 2019, *Blood and Concrete* captures nearly a decade and a half of articles and observations into a single volume. The work is edited by three experts in terrorism and non-state actors: Robert Bunker, John P. Sullivan, and Alma Keshaverz. Importantly, the anthology represents another example of the legacy of knowledge and debate left by its fourth editor, Dave Dilegge, a founder of *Small Wars Journal*.

Blood and Concrete is an expansive work with 49 chapters, by an array of academic researchers, military officers, and law enforcement professionals. The preface, provided by insurgency expert David Kilcullen, sets the tone of the book, "we ignore or forget urban operations at our peril" (p. xxxvii). His admonishment is reinforced by John Spencer, whose *Mini Manual for the Urban Defender* informed Ukrainians resisting the Russian invasion, "Let not another needless drop of blood be spilt on concrete for the wanting of a lesson already learned or a question already asked" (p. xliv). Although many new chapters based on the war on Ukraine are being written, *Blood and Concrete* still provide a broad collection of lessons and answers across a spectrum of conflicts and threats, both unconventional and conventional.

As with counterinsurgency, ground (conventional) forces of developed nations would rather not deal with urban operations and dread the combination of insurgency and urban operations, which can negate technological overmatch. Urban insurgents and terrorists, following the guidance of thinkers like Abraham Guillen and Carlos Marighella, attempt to take advantage of this complex terrain. In chapter one, Russell Glenn notes that "cities are the richest terrorist targets." In his contribution, Luke Allison provides a frightening assessment of mass hostage taking as a serious vulnerability. In his contribution, Alex Calvo's "London Riots: Decentralized Intelligence Collection and Analysis" points to the use of technology to identify criminals and insurgents in an urban environment.

Since publication, the expansion of artificial intelligence, computing power, and ubiquitous technical surveillance have only reinforced Calvo's conclusions. Other chapters by Jeffrey Demarest, John Sullivan, and Adam Elkus examine powerful criminal organizations and their use of urban spaces. Criminal groups continue to challenge nation states. In 2019, the Sinaloa Cartel rose in the city of Culiacan in response to the arrest of Ovidio Guzman Lopez. The militarized criminal group was powerful enough to cause the Mexican government to release Guzman and back down. Insurgents, terrorists, and criminal organizations all seek to take advantage of urban terrain, the analysis in *Blood and Concrete* provides valuable insights into how to address these actors in cities.

Conventional warfare in cities is also inherently challenging. Sun Tzu cautioned that the "tactic of attacking fortified cities is adopted only when unavoidable." Attacking or laying siege to cities was a recipe for exhaustion and high casualties. The increasing density of modern cities makes the scale of fighting unfathomable for military planners. A few blocks of high rises can swallow a brigade and, at the operational level, generating sufficient force to seize a megacity of over 20 million people is a seemingly insurmountable challenge. However, as growing urbanization makes avoiding cities unlikely, *Blood and Concrete* provides useful counsel. With Jomini like efficiency, Geoff Demarest lays out a seven-point template to "hold or take a big city" (p. 370). While some argue for units specialized in urban operations, Adam Scher points to the need for urban tactics and training for general purpose forces. Armed with information from the book, a practitioner has a better chance of achieving success in the modern urban battlespace.

If *Blood and Concrete* has a weakness, it is that the world has moved quickly in the four years since its publication. Communications technology, cyberwarfare, drone technology, artificial intelligence and simulations have made significant advances which impact operations in the urban space. Most importantly, heavy urban fighting in Ukraine has provided a wealth of information on modern warfare in cities. Integrating new *Small Wars Journal* articles like Amos Fox's "The Russo-Ukrainian War and the Principles of Urban Operations," will be a must for the next addition of the anthology. Yet, the core message of the anthology, as expressed by Margarita Konaev, remains as true today as in 2019: "the future of global security will be determined by what happens in cities" (p. 651). *Blood and Concrete* are a critical resource for those focused on urban operations, but understanding this complex terrain is essential for everyone interested in war and security.

Understanding Urban Warfare.

By John Spencer and Liam Collins. Hampshire, England: Howgate Publishing Limited, 2022. ISBN 978-1912440351.

Maps. Photographs. Glossary. Notes. Sources cited. Index. Pp. vi, 392. $29.95.

Review by Amos C. Fox, Ph.D. Candidate, University of Reading

The bloody and destructive war in Ukraine, resulting from Russia's unprovoked invasion in February 2022, sparked renewed interest in urban warfare. To be sure, blistering battles outside of Kyiv, Kharkiv, and in cities like Kherson, Mykolaiv, and Mariupol brought attention to the longoverlooked aspect of urban warfare. Many militaries, to include the United States and Russia, possess doctrine built on the assumption that cities can be bypassed, or 'taken on the march.' Nevertheless, despite efforts to brush it aside, or demote its importance through institutional omission, urban warfare is one of the most prevalent and important facets of modern war. Local populations, densely packed civilian infrastructure, international humanitarian law considerations, and the ability to hide are just a few features that make urban environments challenging and make urban warfare one of the most complicated locations in which militaries can face one another or irregular fighters.

A niche topic for many years, John Spencer and his co-author, Liam Collins, relentlessly spent the better part of a decade chipping away at educating the defense studies community and militaries on the importance of urban warfare. Urban battles raged in many post-Cold War armed conflicts, like those within the 1990s Bosnian War, but those battles garnered little attention from militaries and politicians. One may assume that this inattention resulted from militaries and politicians who hoped that urban battles resulted from bad strategy, poor tactics, or destructionobsessed combatants, and not a truism in warfare.

Nonetheless, Spencer and Collins wrote relentlessly, publishing a torrent of articles over the intervening years with the United States Military Academy's

Modern War Institute (MWI), seeking to educate their audience on the perils and rigors of urban warfare. More recently, Spencer launched, and hosted, a podcast—the *Urban Warfare Project*—in which hetalked with experts from across the defense and security studies community on urban warfare and related tangential elements. This podcast, coupled with Spencer and Collins' previous publications on urban warfare, forms the backbone upon which their book, *Understanding Urban Warfare*, is built.

Summary

Understanding Urban Warfare is organized into three sections— *Understanding the Complex Operational Environment, Operational Case Studies*, and the *Conclusion*. In the book's opening section, Spencer, and Collins revisit several of the conversations from Spencer's podcast. In doing so, Spencer and Collins illustrate the nuance of cities and the impact that cities have on tactical combat operations.

The book's second section helps contextualize the first section with more theoretical musings through the use of real-world case studies. Further, the case study section relies on several first-person accounts from modern combat, to include conversations with individuals that participated in the Battle of Mogadishu, Operation Iraqi Freedom's (OIF) Battle of Fallujah, and OIF's Battle of Sadr City. The case studies provide detailed accounts of urban combat at the tactical level, in most cases, focusing on the insights and decisions of leaders and individuals at the battalion level and below. Each case study provides a riveting account of the challenges and dangers faced by individual soldiers and small units on the urban battlefield, providing useful tactical-level considerations for the practitioners of armed conflict.

In addition to first-person accounts, this section also contains supplementary case studies that provide further supporting evidence of the complexity of urban operating environments. Notable case studies include reflections from Operation Inherent Resolve's Battle of Mosul, The Philippines' Battle of Marawi, and the Battle of Shusha from the 2020 Nagorno-Karabakh conflict.

Understanding Urban Warfare's conclusion provides a series of useful recommendations for policymakers and military leaders regarding urban warfare. Spencer and Collins' recommendations parallel the narrative from the book's opening two sections. The most powerful recommendations Spencer and Collins offer are calling for the establishment of urban warfare centers, and an update to US Army urban warfare doctrine. These recommendations, according to Spencer and Collins, will help the US Army, and its partners, stay ahead of the challenges and traps of urban warfare by creating urban warfare experts that are thoroughly prepared to plan, lead, and operate on future urban battlefields.

Limitations

Despite all its goodness, *Understanding Urban Warfare* comes with a few limitations. First, the United States' post-9/11 wars in the Middle East dominate Spencer and Collins' analysis and reflections. To be sure, five of the book's nine case studies are from Iraq. This approach, largely focused on counterinsurgencies against non-state actors, does not account for the breadth of modern urban warfare. Russia's 2014-2015 Donbas campaign in eastern Ukraine, for example, provides a bevy of significant urban warfare examples. Battles at Luhansk Airport, Ilovaisk, Donetsk Airport, and Debal'tseve all proved decisive to the campaign, each contributing to the two Minsk ceasefire agreements, but none of those battles are covered in any detail within the book. The benefits in expanding the discussion beyond non-state actors and also analyzing state actor-on-state actor urban combat is that it paints a slightly different picture than does a nonstate actor/counterinsurgency focus. The battles from Ukraine in 20142015, for instance, provide clear foreshadowing of the brutal combat preference and techniques of Russia's army, which appeared to surprise onlookers during the early stages of Russia's February 2022 re-invasion of Ukraine.

Second, *Understanding Urban Warfare* is told predominately from the American perspective, and generally does not give a broader account of urban warfare. The book does not necessarily take the position of a non-US combatant, for example, and flesh out the purpose behind the benefits and limitations of operating in the urban space. Taking the position of ISIS in Mosul, the Russians in Ilovaisk, or the Ukrainians at Donetsk Airport, and telling the story from their perspective could provide additional insights into understanding urban warfare that are missed by the American counterinsurgency perspective. By the same token, much of the language used to describe urban warfare is that of the US military, which comes with its own shortcomings when analyzing and articulating events and tactics that are not found in US doctrine.

Third, *Understanding Urban Warfare* is heavily focused at the tactical level, with the storyteller rarely raising their head above the brigade-level. This focus is great for the tactical level practitioner and the student of warfare who is interested in the movement and actions of battalions, platoons, and individual soldiers. However, the book's excellent description of tactical action and tactical considerations limits its impact on the operational, strategic, and policy levels of war.

Recommendation

John Spencer and Liam Collins' *Understanding Urban Warfare* is an excellent addition to the emerging field of urban warfare studies. Spencer and Collins provide a useful handbook for practitioners looking to account for tactical battlefield considerations. The book provides rich accounts of tactical action and considerations for those attempting to navigate the perils of urban combat. Further, *Understanding Urban Warfare*'s reliance on security studies experts allows Spencer and Collins to do a good job of explaining the nuanced challenges of operating on urban battlefields. In short, *Understanding Urban Warfare* is an excellent starting point for anyone looking to get their feet wet in the field of urban warfare studies or for those looking to expand their understanding of modern armed conflict. Considering the character of the ongoing war in Ukraine, and the dominant position that urban battles have played within that conflict, scholars, practitioners, and policymakers alike would benefit from picking up a copy of Spencer and Collins' *Understanding Urban Warfare*.

Appendix Two: Book Review Essay

Megacities and Urban Warfare in the 21st Century: The City as the Cemetery of Revolutionaries and Resources

José de Arimatéia da Cruz Ph.D./MPH

Blood and Concrete: 21st Century Conflict in Urban Centers and Megacities. By Dave Dilegge, Robert J. Bunker, John P. Sullivan, and Alma Keshavarz (Editors). Bloomington, IN: Xlibris, 2019. ISBN 978-19845-7375-9. Acronyms, Photos, Figures, Tables, Recommended Reading, Selected References, Notes. Pp. Lx, 705. $22.99

Cities at War: Global Insecurity and Urban Resistance. By Mary Kaldor and Saskia Sassen (eds.). New York, NY: Columbia University Press, 2020. ISBN 978-0-231-18539-4. Maps. Figures. Notes. Sources cited. Index. Pp.250. $ 30.00

Urban Warfare in the Twenty-First Century. By Anthony King. Melford, MA: Polity Press, 2021. ISBN 978-1-5095-4365-6. Preface. Figures. Maps. Tables. Notes. Sources cited. Index. Pp. x. 270. $ 26.95.

Introduction

The world of the twenty-first century and beyond will be more complex, globalized, and interdependent, and it will also be more dangerous. There will be more conflicts in cities than in any other place. As Lt. Col. Craig A. Broyles and Charlotte Richter argued, "there is a greater likelihood that most of the battlefields US forces will face in the future will be urban fights."[1] Conflicts in different parts of the world will not be an isolated event. It will have repercussions worldwide, especially as megacities become the focus point of those conflicts.

Scholars define megacity as a world city with more than ten million or more inhabitants.[2] Today, more than half of the world's population lives in cities. Over the next 30 years, that figure will likely increase to 66 percent.[3] Those large population concentrations will be the new urban jungles where military forces will be deployed to fight the subsequent future wars. Those large population concentrations will be deeply interconnected globally, especially given the technological revolution and the Revolution in Military Affairs (RMA) underway worldwide. Urban security is the new national security. Yet, despite the call to action by the four books here under review, we are still far from fully understanding the intricacies and nuances of major global cities as the new battlefields of the future. As Michael Evans succinctly points out, "the art of war must seek closer interaction with the science of cities."[4]

The books under review offer a seminal set for urban security researchers and practitioners to understand how megacities are in the rural jungles in the future. The first book reviewed is David Kilcullen's *Out of the Mountain*, which sets a paradigm shift in urban warfare studies. Kilcullen's book set the stage for the next decade and called out a missing link of conflicts in the post-9/11 world—the importance of cities as the new battleground.

After reviewing Kilcullen's *Out of the Mountain*, we continue our study of megacities with an eye-opening anthology edited by colleagues Dave Dilegge, Robert J. Bunker, John P. Sullivan, and Alma Keshavarz in their fascinating book *Blood and Concrete: 21st Century Conflict in Urban Centers and Megacities*. As conflicts proliferate in megacities, the US military, due to its lack of training or understanding regarding megacities, will pay a heavy price in terms of "blood" as they fight in the "concrete" jungles of the Global South.

Next, we review Mary Kaldor and Saskia Sassen's book *Cities at War: Global Insecurity and Urban Resistance*. Kaldor and Sassen argue that "the urban built environment has become the equivalent of jungles and mountains—both as a way to hide and evade fighting and as a source of succor and support."[5] We conclude our review essay with Anthony King's *Urban Warfare in the Twenty-First Century*. King is a Professor of War Studies at the University of Warwick and a leading authority in warfare. King argues that rebels have long left the mountains and are integral to the megacities' social fabric. All four books reviewed point to a single concern regarding urban warfare: the "continuing weaknesses of Western strategic studies is the paucity of serious research on the city's role in armed conflict."[6] Let us begin our review.

Out of the Mountains, Into the City

A decade ago, David Kilcullen's *Out of the Mountains* offered military practitioners and scholars a new perspective on the nature of future conflicts, given four powerful tectonic forces impacting the twenty-first-century world: population, urbanization, coastal settlement, and connectedness. Fast forward to the 2020s, and Kilcullen's concepts have proven true as battles in Iraq and Afghanistan have shown the importance of a clear understanding of urban warfare.

Kilcullen's thesis is that the cities of the future—primarily coastal, highly urbanized, and heavily populated—will be the central focus of tomorrow's conflicts, which will be heavily impacted by the four megatrends of population growth, urbanization, littoralization, and connectedness. He emphasizes that "more people than ever before in history will be competing for scarcer and scarcer resources in poorly governed areas that lack adequate infrastructure, and these areas will be more and more closely connected to the global system so that local conflict will have far wider effects."[7]

Within this heavily populated, highly urbanized, littoralized, and connected world, adversaries are likely to be non-state armed groups, whether criminal or military, or to adopt asymmetric methods of fighting, and even the most conventional hypothetical war scenarios turn out, when closely examined, to involve very significant irregular aspects.[8]

Kilcullen defines nonstate armed groups as "any group that includes armed individuals who apply violence but who aren't members of the regular forces of a nation-state."[9] Kilcullen's nonstate armed groups include

urban street gangs, communitarian or sectarian militias, insurgents, bandits, pirates, armed smugglers or drug traffickers, violent organized criminal organizations, warlord armies, and certain paramilitary forces. The term encompasses both combatants and individuals who don't personally carry arms or use violence but who belong to groups that do.[10]

In Kilcullen's analysis, as the four megatrends impact the world, some cities in the developing world will become a breeding ground for conflict. Those cities will become "urban no-go areas," where government presence and authority are minimal, if not nonexistent at all. Those so-called "urban no-go areas" of megacities have become

safe havens for criminal networks or non-state armed groups, creating a vacuum that is filled by local youth who have no shortage of grievances, whether arising from their new urban circumstances or imported from their home villages.[11]

Kilcullen explains, rapid urban growth in coastal, underdeveloped areas is overloading economic, social, and governance systems, straining city infrastructure, and overburdening the carrying capacity of cities designed for much smaller populations … the implications for future conflict are profound with more people competing for scarcer resources in crowded, under-serviced, and under governed urban areas.[12]

One essential contribution by Kilcullen is his theory of competitive control. Kilcullen defines the theory of competitive control as follows: In regular conflicts (that is, in conflicts where at least one combatant is a nonstate armed group), the local armed actor that a given population perceives as best able to establish a predictable, consistent, wide-spectrum normative system of control is most likely to dominate that population and its residential area.[13]

Kilcullen's theory of competitive control holds that nonstate armed groups, of many kinds, draw their strength and freedom of action primarily from their ability to manipulate and mobilize populations.

Furthermore, Kilcullen argues nonstate armed groups use a spectrum of methods from coercion to persuasion, by creating a normative system that makes people feel safe through the predictability and order that it generates.[14]

The theory also suggests a behavioral explanation for how armed groups of all kinds control populations …. It also suggests that group behaviors may be an emergent phenomenon at the level of the population group, implying that traditional counterinsurgency notions, including "hearts and minds," may need a rethink.[15]

In the following review, we move out of the mountains and into the new century's concrete jungles called the city. The twenty-first-century cities are unique places where an island composed of the wealthy and well-to-do is surrounded by a sea of poverty, despair, and hopelessness coexist side-by-side.

The Urban Jungle of the Twenty-First Century: Long Live the City

Blood and Concrete: 21st Century Conflict in Urban Centers and Megacities, edited by Dave Dilegge, Robert J. Bunker, John P. Sullivan, and Alma Keshavarz, provides a foundation for understanding urban operations and sustaining urban warfare research—this *Small Wars Journal* (SWJ) Anthology documents over a decade of writings on urban conflict.

In addition to essays originally published at SWJ, it adds new content, including an introduction by the editors, a preface on "Blood and Concrete" by David Kilcullen, a foreword "Urban Warfare Studies" by John Spencer, a postscript "Cities in the Crossfire: The Rise of Urban Violence" by Margarita Konaev, and an afterword "Urban Operations: Meeting Challenges, Seizing Opportunities, Improving the Approach" by Russell W. Glenn. These essays frame the discussion found in the collection's forty-nine chapters.

This anthology also addresses various issues faced by military forces worldwide when "fighting in built-up areas (FIBUA) or policing urban communities."[16] As the editors point out, "urban conflict is dominated by blood in terms of casualties and concrete in terms of the built environment," which is where future conflicts will occur.[17] While some military leaders still romanticize conflicts in remote jungles worldwide, the reality of future military conflict is quite different.

Future conflicts, or so-called mega-urban operations, will occur in a megacity. A megacity is any large urban center, common in the twenty-first century, with a population of ten million or more. Megacities are present in the developing world. Those major urban centers are often loosely integrated, and many parts of its sovereign territory may be ungoverned areas or "no-go zones" controlled by transnational organized crime (TOCs), criminal factions, militias, or cartels. An ungoverned area is a sector where the government has lost control and capacity to manage the population. Security is challenged by non-state actors such as terrorists, insurgents, criminals, and extremist organizations.[18]

The provision of essential services, usually a traditional function of the government, is relegated to militia that prey on the poor and marginalized members of society.

Several characteristics of megacities make them a suitable environment for conflict in the future. For instance, most megacities have the following attributes: potential for massive poverty and social unrest, possible for environmental concerns; the likelihood of ungoverned spaces; quick mobilization of the population by social media during times of social unrest, and demographic indications of higher birth rates, city migration, and young unemployed masses.[19]

Furthermore, due to urbanization, littoralization, and connectedness, megacities will be the new "bazaar of violence" in the future.[20] According to this idea, urban insurgents will attempt to destabilize governments through strategies of sheer violence indiscriminately applied to government officials and civilian populations. Those heinous acts of violence aim to demonstrate to the people that the authorities cannot help them and that they are helpless against the power of the gun.[21]

After reading this anthology, an important lesson is that, in many instances, government response to the challenges in megacities may exacerbate the problem. As John P. Sullivan and Adam Elkus pointed out in their essay "Postcard from Mumbai: Modern Urban Siege,"

Government responses to urban terrorism, however well-intentioned, have exacerbated the problem through the usage of urban military special operations and the construction of militarized space.[22]

In many instances, the community, rather than partnering with the authorities to identify criminals and drug dealers, resents the police for how they treat members of the shantytowns. Rather than becoming an asset in warfighting against criminal elements in the megacities, the citizens become abettors. For the police forces operating within those megacities' shanties, "there is little distinction made between residents of the favela [shantytown] and drug traffickers."[23]

The megacities of the twenty-first century also resemble Richard J. Norton's idea of the "feral city." According to Norton's seminal essay "Feral Cities," a feral city is a metropolis … of more than a million people in a state the government of which has lost the ability to maintain the rule of law within the city's boundaries yet remains a functioning actor in the greater international system.[24]

In the megacities or feral cities of the developing world, militants can easily blend into the local civilian population and use the city's complex and dense terrain for cover and concealment. Furthermore, the unwillingness, or perhaps the inability of governments in megacities or feral cities, to address issues such as urban poverty, youth unemployment, and social and economic marginalization allows criminal networks to gain ground, enabling the flow of illicit drugs, arms, and money into those already relatively deprived communities.

While some military leaders may believe that future conflicts will be open terrain, the reality of most present-day conflicts is quite different. In 2014, then Chief of Staff of the Army General Raymond T. Odierno convened a strategic studies group to research a new reality facing the US Army. In the foreword of the group's report, *Megacities and the United States Army: Preparing for a Complex and Uncertain Future,* Odierno wrote:

Our Army has [had] experience throughout its history of operating in urban environments, from Aachen to Seoul to Baghdad. We have not, however, operated in urban areas with populations of over 10 million people— the megacity.[25]

As the strategic studies group concluded, "the Army is currently unprepared" for conflicts in megacities, and "…although the Army has a long history of urban fighting, it has never dealt with an environment so complex and beyond the scope of its resources."[26] Margarita Konaev succinctly states, "As the world's urban population continues to grow, the future of global security will be determined by what happens in the cities."[27]

Any responsible military force understands that the megacities of the twenty-first century and beyond can no longer be ignored as part of its strategic planning. To ignore the centrality of megacities in conflicts is to ignore the future of combat. In their book *Cities at War: Global Insecurity and Urban Resistance*, Mary Kaldor and Saskia Sassen follows, clearly illustrate the centrality of cities given that "cities are the strategic ground for armed conflict because it is mostly in cities that irregular combatants are safest."[28]

Negotiation of Space in the City

The next book in this review essay is Mary Kaldor's and Saskia Sassen's *Cities at War: Global Insecurity and Urban Resistance* (2020). Mary Kaldor is a professor of global governance and director of the Civil Society and Human Security Research Unit in the Department of International Development at the London School of Economics. At the same time, Saskia Sassen is the Robert S. Lynd Professor of Sociology and a member of the Committee for Global Thought at Columbia University.

As the book title implies, Kaldor and Sassen's primary focus is on the city as the new milieu for future conflicts, whether the conflict is between nation-states, irregular warfare, criminal organizations fighting for fiefdom control, or terrorist attacks. Cities have become the "equivalent of jungles and mountains," according to Kaldor and Sassen.[29] The authors further state that as cities become the equivalent of jungles and mountains in the new battlefields of the 21st Century, they provide "a way to hide and evade fighting" and become a "source of succor and support."[30]

Kaldor and Sassen's primary contribution to the literature with their book is the fact that while the literature on cities and war focuses almost exclusively on the militarization and securitization of cities, the authors treat the city as a lens through which to understand contemporary violence as well as contemporary peace.[31] They utilize empirical case studies of various cities worldwide and provide perspectives from the inhabitants' viewpoint, thus shedding "light on how to explain, interpret, perceive twenty-first-century war without the blinkers of geopolitical preoccupations."[32]

Another significant contribution by Kaldor and Sassen to the global insecurity in the cities is their discussion of "new wars" vis-à-vis "old wars." The "old wars," as the authors indicate, took place between the late eighteenth to the middle of the twentieth century, and it was primarily restricted to the countryside, where battles were fought in fields. During World War II, the Allies destroyed cities during the liberation process from German forces. Yet, cities were hardly the main center of gravity during the conflict. Cities "were bombed or under siege; they were not necessarily theaters of war in the way they are today."[33] For example, think about Russia's unprovoked and illegal war of annexation against Ukraine. Russian military forces and paramilitary forces, composed of the Wagner Group, have continuously bombed significant city centers in Ukraine, disregarding the rules of military engagement and protecting civilian populations as non-combatants. Furthermore, the "old wars" were caused by deep-seated political contests."[34]

The "old wars" would continue targeting cities as a significant focus of conflicts until the Cold War, when a sudden shift began. This shift during the Cold War is exemplified by the Battle of Algiers (1957), Hue in Vietnam (1968), and the Northern Ireland conflicts. As Kaldor and Sassen explained, those conflicts represented

> three examples of an emergent pattern of asymmetric war: regular armies confronting insurgencies fought by so-called irregular combatants who lacked airplanes and tanks but had only guns and bombs and thus found in urban space a strategic space for their types of operations.[35]

Those conflicts represent the beginning of what Kaldor and Sassen referred to as the "new wars," where "both conventional forces and irregular combatants including militias, private security contractors, terrorists, paramilitary groups, warlords, and criminal gangs" strive and the urban space become a new tool in their arsenal for war.[36]

There are several key characteristics of the "new wars" in the post-Cold War world of the 21st Century and how its characteristics fit in with the world's megacities. First, new wars are fought by networks of state and non-state actors that are both global and local.[37] Recruits for the "new wars" can be village residents with unresolved issues with the local authorities or the newly arrived rural-urban migrants searching for a job and a better life in the city. However, since those individuals do not have the same safety network as they would in rural areas, they cannot find decent jobs. Therefore, a life of crime as a mercenary may be the only hope of survival in the new urban concrete jungle. The second characteristic of the "new wars" is that new identity politics are being nurtured in cities.[38] While the "old wars" conflicts were primarily ideological, identity politics fueled today's "new wars."

Identity politics has a tremendous impact on the lives of ordinary citizens and has recently been the primary source of political polarization worldwide, especially in the United States.[39] Identity politics creates a division between "Us" and "Them." "Them" are the undesirable members of society. They are replaceable and discarded. They are the residents of shantytowns worldwide. They are often uneducated and easily convinced that their interests are better advanced by a particular segment of the population, traditionally the elite and well-educated. Identity politics within the context of "new wars" can have a devasting impact on the nation-state. It can destroy the social fabric of society. Turn friends into foes. Neighbors into enemies.[40]

The third characteristic of the "new wars," perhaps one of the most consequential, is that military-style battles are avoided, and most violence is directed against civilians.[41] Kaldor and Sassen explained, "In such wars, the aim is political control of territory, which is achieved through expelling or terrorizing those who might challenge political control."[42] Again, Russia's unprovoked war against Ukraine is the best current example.

Russian forces have wreaked havoc on the cities of Schastia and Volnovakha in Ukraine in retaliation for its citizens standing up against Russian aggression.[43] As one resident testified: In the city, there is not any building that has not suffered from direct or collateral damage. So, some buildings have major, minor destruction; some are destroyed to the ground.[44]

Kaldor and Sassen also argue that the "new wars" suit cities due to their lack of infrastructure and disorganized architectural design. This disorganized environment, which lacks police protection and basic living conditions, has created an environment where *urbicide*[45] is the norm. As Kaldor and Sassen explained, *urbicide* is used to describe how new wars deliberately target the very fabric of society—the notion of publicness and the idea of a civic community on which cities are based.[46]

The cities of the twenty-first century and the "new wars" have developed a security culture among their population. The authors define a security culture a style or a pattern of doing security that brings together a range of interlinked components (narratives, rules, tools, practices, etc.) and that are embedded in a specific set of power relations.[47]

From this perspective, an issue becomes a problem depending on where we stand. For example, Mary Martin argues in her essay "A Tale of Two Cities," in Kaldor and Sassen's *Cities at War*, that Ciudad Juarez has a border security culture, a public and citizen security problem, and a neoliberal security problem. Each seeks to describe the city's predicament differently, articulate a particular set of threats and risks, identify distinct referent objects as requiring protection, and prescribe responses to the violence."[48]

In addition to developing a security culture, the "news wars" in megacities are also developing a process called "*enclavization*." The process of *enclavization*, according to Sobia Ahmad Kaker in her essay "Responding to, or Perpetuating, Urban Insecurity," denotes the process of enclave-making. Processes of *enclavization* are therefore the ongoing means—material and/or discursive—through which enclaves are created and upheld.[49]

Enclavization further delineates the separation between those in and those outside the city limits. Again, as Kaker argued, the primary purpose of *enclavization* "is to ensure collective security and create distance between those living inside and the wilder city outside."[50] *Enclavization* creates by its very nature a group of second-class citizens as it highlights the differences between the haves and have-nots of society and further alienates some segments of society. Kaker states that the

processes of *enclavization* generate extreme marginality and vulnerability for the urban poor, who are forced to return to their forms of community protection and preservation in the face of eliteled violence and state terror.[51]

Rio de Janeiro, Brazil, the "marvelous city," is an excellent example of this extreme marginalization and vulnerability to residents of Rio's *favelas* or shantytowns. According to a recent study conducted by the *Instituto Fogo Cruzado*, in partnership with *the Grupo de Estudos de Novos Ilegalismos at the Universidade Federal Fluminense (GENI/UFF)*, militias are the fastest-growing criminal enterprise in Rio de Janeiro. The study asserts that militia-controlled areas grew 387.3 percent over the past 16 years. As a result, militias control essentially half of Rio's areas dominated by criminal armed groups (CAGs).[52]

During the COVID-19 pandemic in Rio de Janeiro, gangs played a significant role in preventing the spread of the virus among poor communities by imposing curfews in areas dominated by criminal armed groups. These vulnerable populations often lack essential lifelines like adequate potable water supply, sewage, and public services like policing.

When the police intervene in those communities, their abuse of authority and use of force is displayed once they exist in those communities. For example, in São Paulo and Rio de Janeiro, a police raid has left forty-five dead. In Rio de Janeiro, ten people were killed on Wednesday, including two suspected drug-trafficking kingpins, according to Brazil's state news agency. Officials say 19 suspects were killed over the weekend in the northeast state of Bahia. An additional 16 died at the hands of the police during a five-day raid this week in São Paulo, Brazil's most populous state, after a police officer on patrol was shot dead.[53] Yet, the gangs and CAGs often fill the void in governance and, in collusion with corrupt public officials, provide access to services.[54] In the final analysis, Kaldor and Sassen argued that "cities become the key strategic ground for armed conflict because it is mostly in cities that irregular combatants are safest."[55]

Another important issue discussed regarding the future megacities under "new wars" will rely heavily on digitization. Today, cities, from London to São Paulo, are under the watchful eyes of government officials as the aesthetics of cities are transformed from planted trees to installed cameras monitoring every movement of every single citizen. We are witnessing what *The Economist* has called "a civilianisation of the digital battlefield."[56] Wars in the future megacities show that "connectivity is increasingly a vital military resource."[57] Ordinary citizens armed with the latest iPhone or a laptop will be a force multiplier as they become part of a crowd-sourced "civilian sensor network," providing enemy troops' location and movement.[58]

The final book in this review essay answers the following question: What are the defining characteristics of urban warfare today? Anthony King argues that not all urban warfare operations are novel. What is novel is how cities have transformed the nature of warfare, given the shrinking of military forces worldwide. As former Secretary of Defense Donald Rumsfeld once stated, "You go to war with the Army you have, not the Army you might want or wish to have a later time."[59]

The Rise of Urban Warfare: A Complicated History

Anthony King's *Urban Warfare in the Twenty-First Century* emphasizes the dynamics of urban warfare. It uses examples to show that while the rise of urban warfare is deeply troubling, urban warfare is as old as civilizations. As King succinctly states, "It would be wrong to suggest that urban warfare itself is new. Urban warfare was a regular occurrence in antiquity."[60]

Using historical and Biblical examples, King highlights that urban warfare is as old as cities. He argues that warfare has always been and always will be integral to city life, stating that "from the moment humans, as aggressive, intelligent and highly social primates, began to live in urban settlements, they also began to fight each other for them and to kill each other in them."[61] Since urban warfare seems to be an ingrained and innate part of humanity, urban warfare, according to King, will continue to increase in the coming decades. It will remain a global issue, affecting the lives of millions, threatening major political, economic, and cultural centers.[62]

King's central argument in *Urban Warfare* is that while scholars and practitioners of urban warfare have attributed its rise to the explosion in the global population of megacities to understand urban warfare in the twenty-first century, a better focus would be the tremendous decrease in the size of armed forces themselves.[63]

This is a direct challenge to David Kilcullen's *Out of the Mountains* assertion that demography and asymmetry have been the main forces driving the increased incidence of urban warfare. Instead, King argues that smaller and more precise weapons are the key drivers of the carnage and violence in places such as Sarajevo, Mogadishu, and Grozny, to name a few. As King points out, the operational significance of urban warfare in the early modern period is directly correlated with the size of armies: "In any historical era, the smaller the armies," according to King's observation: the more important cities become, urban warfare attains priority as military forces contract. By contrast, the larger the armies, the more likely open warfare will predominate over siegecraft. As forces expand, cities become less operationally significant. The frequency and importance of urban warfare is, therefore, substantially a function of the size of military forces.[64]

King also disagrees with Kilcullen's argument that insurgents have come out of the mountains in recent decades. Instead, King argues that urban insurgency was already a constant feature of the twentieth-century battlefields.[65] This more significant presence of urban insurgency directly correlates with the size of armed forces worldwide. As King points out, The reduction of combat densities on the battlefield should be expected in and of itself to increase the frequency of urban fighting. Reduced state forces necessarily converge on cities and towns.[66]

King also argues that combat density—the sheer number of military personnel deployed into a theater—is likely to play an increasingly important role in the modernization of warfare over the twenty-first century.[67]

According to King, there are two schools of thought regarding urban warfare in megacities. One school of thought argues that urban warfare is a novelty and an unprecedented phenomenon in the history of revolution in military affairs (RMA). Proponents contend that "a profound military transformation –even an urban revolution- has occurred, altering the characteristics of contemporary military operations in cities."[68] The other school of thought rejects the novelty and the revolution in military affairs arguments. Instead, they argue that "nothing fundamental has changed."[69] King rejects both schools of thought. Instead, he contends that "it is insufficient to focus on specific weapons or individual techniques; it is, rather, necessary to consider the urban battlefield as a whole."[70]

Using an interdisciplinary or "transcend disciplinary boundaries" approach, King argues that urban warfare consists of three fundamental elements: cities, weaponry, and forces: Urban warfare is defined by the scale and geography of the urban settlements in which fighting occurs, the weaponry available to the combatants, and the size of the military forces...These three factors constitute the atomic elements of urban warfare...The interplay of these three factors is key to understanding urban warfare.[71]

Furthermore, the topographies of urban warfare are also being transformed by the forces of fortification, airpower, firepower, armor, partnering with local forces, and information operations.

The Debates and Concurrence

One theme discussed by all four books is Brazil's gang proliferation and how those gangs manifest failed policy by the federal government and remnants of early urban guerrilla activists such as Abraham Guillén in Uruguay or Carlos Marighella in Brazil. King states, "Urban super-gangs have replaced Marighella's urban guerrillas."[72] Armed criminal organizations (ACOs) such as *Comando Vermelho* (Red Command/CV), *Primeiro Comando da Capital* (First Command of the Capital/PCC), and *Amigos dos Amigos* (Friends of Friends) dominate cities and *barrios* in Brazil today. They are influential transnational criminal organizations (TCOs) and fully integrated into the interdependent economy of the twenty-first century. Another important characteristic of Brazil's gangs is controlling and dominating territories. As King points out, Brazil's super-gangs are intimately attached to specific *favelas,* in which their leadership and organization are based. The *favelas* are crucial to the super-gangs because they allow the gang members to operate away from government interference.[73]

As King once again highlights, the urban guerrilla is not new, nor have they recently come out of the mountains in the twenty-first century. The urban guerrilla has always been in the city. One important point mentioned by the four books under review is that "insurgents now typically situate their enclaves inside cities; they dominate neighborhoods, which they transform into no-go-areas."[74] In this process of *enclavization,* King, Kaldor, and Sassen respectively argued that modern cities typically contained poor areas and ethnic minorities, often segregated into ghettos.[75]

In King's conclusion, he examines the future of megacities in 2040. According to King, four essential elements define global cities: size, height, polarization, and globalization.[76] Furthermore, three interrelated factors explain why megacities will be the future battles' center of gravity in the twenty-first century. According to King, "cities have grown so big that it is difficult for forces to avoid them, especially since they are political, economic, and social hubs." Second, King further argues, "weapons are more accurate; as the field has become more lethal, state and nonstate forces have sought refuge in cities." Finally, "military forces are much smaller. Consequently, standing state armies can no longer envelop or inundate cities."[77] Therefore, according to King, there are three possible trajectories or "Armageddon" in 2040: megacity war, autonomized urban warfare,[78] and nuclear holocaust.[79]

Conclusion

The greatest Chinese military strategist, Sun Tzu, in *The Art of War,* argues that military strategists should avoid urban warfare unless necessary.[80] In other words, attack cities only when there is no alternative (TINA). There is no alternative in future wars. Warfare is an urban phenomenon. As King states, megacities are rapidly becoming the epicenters of human activity on the planet and, as such, they will generate most of the friction which compels future military intervention.[81]

Conflicts, political violence, and war will most likely occur in urban megacities as those cities become a conurbation of complexities "interconnected globally by many different mediums, including economics, culture, modern communication technology, and social media."[82]

As King points out, The war of fronts, defined by large engagements in the field, has been replaced by more dispersed operations, which converge on urban areas, where the decisive tactical and operations objective have been located. As fronts disappear, towns and cities, having become the focus of military operations, are where the major battles now occur.[83]

The megacities of the twenty-first century, as pointed out by Dave Dilegge, Robert J. Bunker, John P. Sullivan, and Alma Keshavarz, due to urbanization, littoralization, and connectedness, megacities will be the new "bazaar of violence" in the future. This "bazaar of violence" represents one of the most complex operational environments "due to the coalescence of various domains and scales"[84] in which the urban guerrillas want to "win without fighting."[85]

Any responsible military force understands that the megacities of the twenty-first century and beyond can no longer be ignored as part of its strategic planning and operations. To ignore the centrality of megacities in conflicts is to ignore the future of combat. The megacities' conflicts occur not only between conventional armed forces but also among non-state actors. As the White House's National Security Strategy, released in October 2022, makes clear, nefarious actors—some state-sponsored, some not—are exploiting the digital economy to raise and move funds to support illicit weapons programs, terrorist attacks, fuel conflict, and to extort everyday citizens targeted by ransomware or cyber-attacks on national health systems, financial institutions, and critical infrastructure.[86]

Military leaders ignore megacities at their perils. The proliferation of emerging destructive technologies (EDTs) and new players in the international system is creating a "world adrift." According to the National Intelligence Council (NIC) *Global Trends 2040: A More Contested World,* "in a world adrift the international system is directionless, chaotic, and volatile as international rules and institutions are largely ignored by major powers like China, regional players, and nonstate actors.[87]

I highly recommend those four books seminal books on urban security. They should be on the bookshelves of military strategy and history students and provide a solid foundation for any course on urban security operations, insurgency-counterinsurgency, and urban warfare.

Endnotes

1. Lt. Col. Craig A. Broyles and Charlotte Richer, "Concrete Command: Why Combat Training Centers Should Prioritize Training on Urban Command Posts," Military Review (July-August 2023): 12-19.
2. United Nations Department of Economics and Social Affairs, Population Dynamics, "World Urbanization Prospects—2018, Infographic," 2018, https://www.un.org/development/desa/publications/graphic/world-urbanizationprospects-2018-more-megacities-in-the-future.
3. Raymond Odierno and Michael O'Hanlon. "Securing Global Cities: Best Practices, Innovation, and the Path Ahead," Brookings Institution, March 2017, https://www.brookings.edu/wpcontent/uploads/2017/03/fp_201703_securing_global_cities.pdf.
4. Michael Evans, "Future War in Cities: Urbanization's Challenge to Strategic Studies in the 21st Century," International Review of the Red Cross 98, no. 1, (2016): 37–5, https://international-review.icrc.org/sites/default/files/irc_97_901-5.pdf.
5. Mary Kaldor and Saskia Sassen (Eds). Cities at War: Global Insecurity and Urban Resistance. (New York: Columbia University Press, 2020), 2.
6. Evans, "Future War in Cities," 35
7. David Kilcullen, Out of the Mountains: The Coming Age of Urban Guerrilla. (New York: Oxford University Press, 2015), 50.
8. Kilcullen, Out of the Mountains, 170.
9. Kilcullen, Out of the Mountains, 126.
10. Kilcullen, Out of the Mountains, 126.
11. Kilcullen, Out of the Mountains, 40.
12. Kilcullen, Out of the Mountains, 35-36.
13. Kilcullen, Out of the Mountains, 126.
14. Kilcullen, Out of the Mountains, 114.
15. Kilcullen, Out of the Mountains, 127.
16. Dave Dilegge, Robert J. Bunker, John P. Sullivan, and Alma Keshavarz (Eds.). Blood and Concrete: 21st Century Conflict in Urban Centers and Megacities. (Bloomington: Xlibris, 2019), 1.
17. Dilegge, Bunker, Sullivan, and Keshavarz (Eds.), i.
18. Dilegge, Bunker, Sullivan, and Keshavarz (Eds.), 177.
19. Dilegge, Bunker, Sullivan, and Keshavarz (Eds.), 174-175.
20. Dilegge, Bunker, Sullivan, and Keshavarz (Eds.), 35, 176.

21. Dilegge, Bunker, Sullivan, and Keshavarz (Eds.), 6.
22. Dilegge, Bunker, Sullivan, and Keshavarz (Eds.), 8.
23. Dilegge, Bunker, Sullivan, and Keshavarz (Eds.), 9.
24. Richard J. Norton, "Feral Cities," Naval War College Review 56, no. 4, (2003): 2, https://digital-commons.usnwc.edu/nwc-review/vol56/iss4/8/. Colonel Marc Harris, Lieutenant Colonel Robert Dixon, Major Nicholas Melin, Command Sergeant Major Daniel Hendrex, Sergeant Major Richard Russo and Michael Bailey, "Megacities and the United States Army: Preparing for a Complex and Uncertain Future," Chief of Staff of the Army, Strategic Studies Group, June 2014, https://api.army.mil/e2/c/downloads/351235.pdf.
26. "Megacities and the United States Army," 21.
27. Dilegge, Bunker, Sullivan, and Keshavarz (Eds.), 651.
28. Mary Kaldor and Saskia Sassen (Eds). Cities at War: Global Insecurity and Urban Resistance. (New York: Columbia University Press, 2020), 230.
29. Kaldor and Sassen (Eds), Cities at War, 2.
30. Kaldor and Sassen (Eds), Cities at War, 2.
31. Kaldor and Sassen (Eds), Cities at War, 3.
32. Kaldor and Sassen (Eds), Cities at War, 3.
33. Kaldor and Sassen (Eds), Cities at War, 8.
34. Kaldor and Sassen (Eds), Cities at War, 11.
35. Kaldor and Sassen (Eds), Cities at War, 7.
36. Kaldor and Sassen (Eds), Cities at War, 5.
37. Kaldor and Sassen (Eds), Cities at War, 7.
38. Kaldor and Sassen (Eds), Cities at War, 7.
39. Amy Chua, "How America's Identity Politics Went From Inclusion to Division," The Guardian, March 1, 2018, https://www.theguardian.com/society/2018/mar/01/howamericas-identity-politics-went-from-inclusion-to-division
40. For an excellent reading on identity politics and its consequences, read Philip Gourevitch, I Wish to Inform You That Tomorrow We Will be Killed with Our Families: Stories from Rwanda. (New York: Farrar, Straus, and Giroux, 1998).
41. Kaldor and Sassen (Eds), Cities at War, 8.
42. Kaldor and Sassen (Eds), Cities at War, 8.
43. Emma Graham Harrison, and Isobel Koshiw, "90% of Houses Are Damaged": Russia's Syria-Honed Tactics by Lay Waste Ukraine Towns," The Guardian, March 4, 2022, https://www.theguardian.com/world/2022/mar/04/ninety-per-cent-of-houses-aredamaged-thousands-trapped-in-ukraines-small-towns.
44. Harrison and Koshiw, "90% of houses are damaged."
45. Kaldor and Sassen (Eds), Cities at War, 9.

46. Kaldor and Sassen (Eds), Cities at War, 9.
47. Kaldor and Sassen (Eds), Cities at War, 105.
48. Kaldor and Sassen (Eds), Cities at War, 105.
49. Kaldor and Sassen (Eds), Cities at War.
50. Kaldor and Sassen (Eds), Cities at War, 137.
51. Kaldor and Sassen (Eds), Cities at War.
52. John P. Sullivan, José de Arimatéia da Cruz, and Robert J. Bunker, "Third Generation Gangs Strategic Note No. 51: Milícias (Militias) Continue to Surpass Gangues (Gangs) in Dominating Criminal Territory in Rio de Janeiro," Small Wars Journal, September 27, 2022, https://smallwarsjournal.com/jrnl/art/third-generation-gangs-strategicnote-no-51-milicias-militias-continue-surpass-gangues.
53. Lyric Li, "Concerns Over Police Violence in Brazil as Raids Kill at Least 45 in a Week," Washington Post, August 3, 2023, https://www.washingtonpost.com/world/2023/08/03/brazil-police-raids.
54. Vanda Felbab-Brown and Paul Wise, "Commentary: When Pandemics Come to Slums," Brookings. April 6, 2020, https://www.brookings.edu/articles/whenpandemics-cometoslums/#:~:text=Slums%20provide%20uniquely%20challenging%20conditions,No%20tests.
55. Kaldor and Sassen (Eds), 230.
56. Special Report, "Special Report: Warfare after Ukraine," The Economist, July 8, 2023, https://www.economist.com/special-report/2023-07-08.
57. The Economist, 9.
58. Jose de Arimatéia da Cruz, and Stephanie Padron, "Cyber Mercenaries: A New Threat to National Security," International Social Science Review 96, no. 2 (2020): 1–33.
59. Anna Mulrine, "In His Memoir, Donald Rumsfeld Admits Five Mistakes, Sort Of," Christian Science Monitor, February 9, 2011, https://www.csmonitor.com/USA/Military/2011/0209/In-his-memoir-DonaldRumsfeld-admits-five-mistakes-sort-of/Treatment-of-detainees.
60. Anthony King. Urban Warfare in the Twenty-First Century. (Medford: Polity, 2021), 9.
61. King, Urban Warfare, 12.
62. King, Urban Warfare, 12.
63. King, Urban Warfare, 16, 24.
64. King, Urban Warfare, 27.
65. King, Urban Warfare, 42.
66. King, Urban Warfare, 28.
67. King, Urban Warfare, 40.
68. King, Urban Warfare, 13.
69. King, Urban Warfare, 14.
70. King, Urban Warfare, 15.

71. King, Urban Warfare, 15.
72. King, Urban Warfare, 61.
73. King, Urban Warfare, 62.
74. King, Urban Warfare, 64.
75. King, Urban Warfare, 69.
76. King, Urban Warfare, 66.
77. King, Urban Warfare, 203.
78. Stephanie M. Pedron and Jose de A. da Cruz, "The Future of Wars: Artificial Intelligence (AI) and Lethal Autonomous Weapon Systems (LAWS)," International Journal of Security Studies 2, no. 1 (2020): 3 https://digitalcommons.northgeorgia.edu/ijoss/vol2/iss1/2.
79. Pedron and da Cruz, "The Future of Wars," 205.
80. Sun Tzu, Art of War (transl. Ralph D. Sawyer). (New York: Basic Books, 1994).
81. King, Urban Warfare. 205.
82. Richard L. Wolfel, Amy Richmond, and Lt. Col. Jason Ridgeway, "Dense Urban Environments: The Crucible of Multi-Domain Operations," Military Review (JanuaryFebruary 2021), 30.
83. Wolfel, Richmond, and Ridgeway, "Dense Urban Environments," 40.
84. Wolfel, Richmond, and Ridgeway, "Dense Urban Environments," 22-32.
85. US Army Training and Doctrine Command (TRADOC) Pamphlet (TP) 525-3-1, The US Army in Multi-Domain Operations 2028 (Fort Eustis, VA: TRADOC, (December 6, 2018), viii–x.
86. "National Security Strategy," The Whitehouse, October 2022, https://www.whitehouse.gov/wp-content/uploads/2022/10/Biden-HarrisAdministrations-National-Security-Strategy-10.2022.pdf.
87. "Global Trends 2040: A More Contested World," Office of the Director of National Intelligence, March 2021, https://www.dni.gov/index.php/gt2040-home/introduction.

Appendix Three: Acronyms

(A2AD) Anti-Access and Area Denial

(ACOs) Armed criminal Organizations

(ACT) Allied Command Transformation

(AI) Artificial Intelligence

(AMISOM) African Union Mission in Somalia

(AMLO) Andres Manuel Lopes Obrador

(APC) Armored Personnel Carrier

(ARGUS-IS) Autonomous Real-Time Ground Ubiquitous Surveillance-Imaging System

(BPD) Boston Police Department

(BLO) Beltran-Leyva Organization

(C2) Command and Control

(CAGs) Criminal Armed Groups

$(CAS)_1$ Close Air Support

$(CAS)_2$ Complex Adaptive Systems

(CBT) Cross-Border Tunnels

(CCTA) Complex Coordinated Terror Attacks

(CDS) Cártel de Sinaloa

(CJNG) Cártel de Jalisco Nueva Generación

(CIA) Central Intelligence Agency

(COE) Centers or Centres of Excellence

(COIN) Counterinsurgency

(CSP) Community Stabilization Program

(DARPA) Defense Advanced Research Project Agency

(DCA) Directorate of Civil Affairs

(DHS) Department of Homeland Security

(DLOD) Defence Lines of Development

(DOD) Department of Defense

(DoDI) Department of Defense Instruction

(DOTMLPFI) Doctrine, Organisation, Training, Material, Leadership, Personnel, Facilities and Interoperability

(DPO) Department of Peace Operations

(EDT) Emerging Destructive Technologies

(FCC) Federal Communications Commission

(FFAO) Framework for Future Alliance Operations

(FIBUA) Fighting in Built-Up Areas

(FPV) First-Person View

(GDP) Gross Domestic Product

(GOFAI) Good Old-Fashioned AI

(HIC) High Intensity Conflict

(HSEM) Homeland Security and Emergency Management

(HUMINT) Human Intelligence

(HVT) High-Value Targeting

(ICP) Incident Command Post

(ICS) Incident Command System

(IDF) Israel Defense Forces

(IED) Improvised Explosive Devices

(IGOs) Intergovernmental Organizations

(IHL) International Humanitarian Law

(IMINT) Imagery Intelligence

(INP) Israel National Police

(IoP) Instruments of Power

(IPB) Intelligence Preparation of the Battlefield

(IPE) Intelligence Preparation of the Environment

(ISAF) International Security Assistance Force

(ISR) Intelligence, Surveillance, and Reconnaissance

(ISIS) Islamic State of Iraq and Syria

(JIC) Joint Information Center

(JSOC) Joint Special Operations Command

(JTTF) Division Joint Terrorism Task Force

(KSE) Knowledge, Skills and Experience

(M&S COE) Modelling & Simulation COE

(MACV) Military Assistance Command, Vietnam

(MC) Military Committee

(MCIs) Mass Casualty Incidents

(MDO) Multi-Domain Operations

(MDO in UE) Multi Domain Operations in Urban Environments

(MEMA) Massachusetts Emergency Management Agency

(MG) Major General

(MINUSCA) Mandates of Peacekeeping Missions in the Central African Republic

(MINUSMA) Mandates of Peacekeeping Missions in Mali

(MIT) Massachusetts Institute of Technology

(MJDDH) Ministry of Justice and Human Rights and Cults

(MONUSCO) Mandates of Peacekeeping Missions in Democratic Republic of the Congo

(MSP) Massachusetts State Police

(MWD) Military Working Dogs

(MWI) Modern War Institute

(NATO) North Atlantic Treaty Organization's

(NATO HQ SACT) Headquarters Supreme Allied Command Transformation

(NGO) Nongovernmental Organizations

(NGS) Naval Gunfire Support

(NIC) National Intelligence Council

(NIMS) National Incident Management System

(NVA) North Vietnamese Army

(NWCC) NATO's Warfighting Capstone Concept

(LIC) Low-Intensity Conflict

(LOAC) Law of Armed Conflict

(LSCO) Large-Scale Combat Operations

(OCGs) Organized Crime Groups

(OIF) Operation Iraqi Freedom's

(OPFOR) Opposing Force

(OPSEC) Operational Security

(OSINT) Open-Source Intelligence

(OWS) Operational Wargame Series

(PAN) National Action Party

(PATRIOT Act) The Uniting and Strengthening America by Providing

Appropriate Tools Required to Intercept and Obstruct Terrorism Act

(PIO) Public Information Officer

(PLB) *Passive Lucht Beschering*

(PLO) Palestine Liberation Organization

(PNT) Positioning, Navigation and Timing

(POC) Protection of Civilians

(PRD) Democratic Revolution Party

(PRI) Institutional Revolutionary Party

(PTUV) Political Trajectory of Urban Violence

(R&D) Research and Development

(RAS) Robotics and Autonomous Systems

(RMA) Revolution in Military Affairs

(*ROE*) Rules of Engagement

(RUF) Russian Forces

(SCBA) Self-Contained Breathing Apparatus

(SEDENA) *Secretaría de la Defensa Nacional* or Secretariat of National Defense

(SEMAR) *Secretaría de la Marina* or Naval Secretariat

(SF) Special Forces

(SFA) Strategic Foresight Analysis

(SHAEF) Supreme Headquarters Allied Expeditionary Force

(SIGINT) Signals Intelligence

(TCO) Transnational Criminal Organizations

(TINA) There is No Alternative

(TOC) Transnational Organized Crime

(TTP) Tactics, Techniques, and Procedures

(UAF) Ukrainian Armed Force

(UAS) Unmanned Aerial Systems

(UAV) Unmanned Aerial Vehicles

(UCAV) Uncrewed Aerial Combat Vehicle

(UCC) Unified Command Center

(UGF) Underground Facilities

(UGS) Unattended Ground Sensors

(UGV) Uncrewed Ground Vehicle

(UNSC) United Nations Security Council

(USAID) United States Agency for International Development

(USECT) Understand-Shape-Engage-Consolidate-Transition

(USV) Uncrewed Surface Vehicles

(UTS) Ubiquitous Technical Surveillance

(UUS) Urban Underground Space

(UUV) Uncrewed Underwater Vehicles

(VC) Vietcong

(VNSA) Violent Non-State Actors

(VPs) Victory Points

(WAMI) Wide Area Motion Imagery

(WPS) Wireless Priority Service

Biographies

Editors:

Dr. Nathan P. Jones is an Associate Professor of Security Studies in the College of Criminal Justice at Sam Houston State University. He is the author *of Mexico's Illicit Drug Networks and the State Reaction* (2016) with Georgetown University Press. His areas of interest include organized crime violence in Mexico, social network analysis, border security, and the political economy of homeland security. Dr. Jones is also a Senior Fellow with the Small Wars Journal–El Centro, a Rice University Baker Institute Drug Policy and US-Mexico Center non-resident scholar, and the book review editor for *the Journal of Strategic Security*.

Dr. John P. Sullivan retired as a lieutenant with the Los Angeles Sheriff's Department. He is an Instructor in the Safe Communities Institute, University of Southern California. He has a PhD from the Open University of Catalonia, an MA from the New School for Social Research, and a BA from the College of William and Mary. He received a lifetime achievement award from the National Fusion Center Association in November 2018 for his contributions to the national network of fusion centers. He is an instructor in the 40th Infantry Division Urban Warfare Planners Course and a Member of the Urban Violence Research Network (UVRN) and the Network of Experts at the Global Initiative against Transnational Organized Crime (GI-TOC).

Dr. Daniel Weisz Argomedo earned his PhD in Political Science at the University of California Irvine with a focus on International Relations and Comparative Studies. His dissertation focused on the war on drugs and its impact on women's security in Mexico. He holds an M.A. in Political Science from San Diego State University where he wrote a dissertation on 'Hacktivism and social movements; and earned a B.A. in Political Science from the University of Alberta where he wrote a thesis on the Mexican war on drugs. He wrote "Climate Change, Drug Traffickers and La Sierra Tarahumara" for the special issue on climate change and global security at the *Journal of Strategic Security*. He is fluent in Spanish and his research interests include cyberwarfare, the environment, the war on drugs, women's security and contemporary Latin American politics and history.

Contributors:

David J.H. Burden has been a wargamer and wargame designer for around 50 years—although ironically not for the 10 years he spent in the British Army. David founded his software & consultancy company Daden in 2004. Working with MOD to automatically generate social media to support urban wargames David developed a wider interest in the issues of urban conflict and how they could best be war-gamed. David started his part-time PhD on wargaming urban conflict at Bath Spa University under Dr John Curry in early 2022, and is currently researching the unique features of urban warfare and how it has been war-gamed in the past. Alongside the research David is also designing new urban wargames looking at different aspects of the challenge. David is an ex-Royal Signals officer, a Chartered European Engineer, a TEDx presenter, and is currently also series co-editor for Taylor & Francis on their Metaverse Series of books.

Michael L. Burgoyne is a former US Army Foreign Area Officer, he served in various policy and security cooperation positions in the Americas including assignments as the Army Attaché in Mexico, the Andean Ridge Desk Officer at US Army South, and the Senior Defense Official in Guatemala. He deployed twice in support of Operation Iraqi Freedom in command and staff positions and served as the Defense Attaché in Kabul, Afghanistan. He is the co-author of *The Defense of Jisr al-Doreaa*, a tactical primer on counterinsurgency. He holds an M.A. in Strategic Studies from the US Army War College and an M.A. in Security Studies from Georgetown University. He is a professor of Practice at the University of Arizona.

Fausto Carbajal-Glass is a researcher and consultant on political risk and security. He holds a BA in International Relations from *Universidad Iberoamericana*, Mexico City, a Master degree in War Studies from King's College London, and graduated from the Strategy and Defense Policy course from the National Defense University, Washington D.C. He has worked for the Mexican government, particularly for the Ministries of the Interior and Foreign Affairs. He is member of the Urban Violence Research Network (UVRN), the Strategic Hub for Organized Crime Research (SHOC-RUSI), the European Consortium for Political Research—Standing Group on Organized Crime (ECPR-SGOC), the World Futures Studies Federation (WFSF), the Mexican Council on Foreign Relations (COMEXI), and Mexico Research Centre for Peace (CIPMEX). He has also served as a non-resident fellow of the Mexican Navy Institute for Strategic Research (ININVESTAM). He is lecturer of the BA in Strategic Intelligence at Universidad Anáhuac Mexico, where he teaches the module "Trends in Organized Crime." His analyses on the crime-conflict compound, the conflict-security-development nexus and the evolution of organized crime have appeared in newspapers as well as academic and policy publications.

Andrew Craig graduated with Honours in Geology from the University of St Andrews in 1997 and worked in the UK oil industry before completing a master's degree in Mineral Exploration at the Royal School of Mines, Imperial College London. He started his own independent geological consultancy in 2002 focusing on exploration and development in the minerals sector. Having worked with a range of mining companies Drew has developed strong management and communication skills at both corporate and operational levels. He commands a wide range of practical field skills with specializations in remote exploration, target generation and early-stage project development. Drew has served as a reservist in the British Army for over 30 years, currently as a Lieutenant Colonel in the Royal Engineers. He has served in a range of roles, including defense and geospatial intelligence, infrastructure support, explosive ordnance disposal and search, and civil-military cooperation. He has deployed on operations in Iraq and supported capacity development in several African states. Whilst serving as the British Army's principal geologist, he managed a team of specialists, supporting homebase and overseas taskings, notably around subterranean operations, infrastructure assessments, HADR, resilience, and natural resources. He maintains a keen interest in the military geosciences and is the secretary for the International Association for Military Geosciences. Drew is a Fellow of the Geological Society of London and a Chartered Engineer registered with the Institute of Materials, Minerals and Mining.

Alex Case is a former UK Royal Marine and now COO of Cordillera Applications Group, a diversified consulting company providing services in the US and Europe for defense and commercial clients. He has provided support as both a serving NATO staff officer and a consultant to NATO since 2008.

Dr. José de Arimatéia da Cruz is Currently Visiting Research Professor at the Center for Strategic Leadership, Homeland Defense and Security Studies, Strategic Landpower Futures Group at the United States Army War College in Carlisle, PA. and Professor of International Relations and Comparative Politics at Georgia Southern University, Savannah Campus, Savannah, GA. Dr. da Cruz received his Ph.D. from Miami University, Oxford, Ohio, in Comparative Politics and International Relations. His publications have appeared in the *Journal of Advanced Military Studies, International Journal of Security Studies & Practice, International Social Science Review*, and Journal of Global South Studies. He is the editor of *Xenophobia and Nativism in Africa, Latin America, and the Caribbean* 2023 (Routledge Studies in the Modern History of Africa).

Dr. Magdalena Denham is a Professor of Practice at Sam Houston State University, College of Criminal Justice, Department of Security Studies. Her research on homeland security and emergency management (HSEM) focuses on social and organizational impacts of disasters and on emergency response. She has worked with vulnerable populations in pre-disaster and post-disaster contexts and conducted extensive post-hurricane field research. She has published mixed methods and qualitative studies in school policing, emergency management and response, homeland security policy, homeland security education, community engagement, leadership, and HSEM policy. Her recent focus has been on public health within disaster response to include the role of healthcare coalitions in health preparedness and response, crisis communications, and state and regional public health disaster response capabilities during the COVID-19 pandemic. Her prior professional experiences in federal law enforcement and in higher education support her teaching philosophy, grounded in social aspects of learning and collaborative practice.

Dr. James M. Duggan is an Assistant Professor of Criminal Justice at Anna Maria College in Paxton, MA. Dr. Duggan honorably retired from the Massachusetts State Police (MSP) in 2018 after 25 years of service. He retired as a Detective Lieutenant, commanding the MSP's Anti-Terrorism Unit. Dr. Duggan was a member of FBI Boston's Joint Terrorism Task Force for five years before his retirement. He completed his Ph.D. at the University of Massachusetts Lowell. Academic and professional awards bestowed upon Dr. Duggan include UMass Lowell's Outstanding PhD Student (2022) and Amy Finn Human Spirit Award (2022), an Academy of Criminal Justice Sciences Doctoral Summit fellowship (2019), FBI Boston's Award of Excellence for contributions to the Marathon bombing response and investigation (2013), the New England Narcotic Enforcement Officers' Association Enrique Camarena Memorial Award (2010), and the Latham–Moynihan Award for contributions to the Middlesex District Attorney's Office Detective Unit.

Amos Fox is a PhD candidate at the University of Reading and a freelance writer and conflict scholar writing for the Association of the United States Army. His research and writing focus on the theory of war and warfare, proxy war, future armed conflict, urban warfare, armored warfare and the Russo-Ukrainian War. Amos has published in *Comparative Strategy, RUSI Journal*, and *Small Wars and Insurgencies* among many other publications. He has also been a guest on numerous podcasts, including Royal United Services Institute's *Western Way of War, This Means War*, the *Dead Prussian Podcast, Voices of War*, and History Hit's Warfare.

Major Jayson Geroux is an infantry officer with The Royal Canadian Regiment within the Canadian Armed Forces. He has been a fervent student of urban warfare and an urban operations instructor for over two decades, having participated in, planned, executed and intensively conducted lectures and training exercises on the subject internationally, and was involved in urban operations events while overseas in the Former Yugoslavia (Bosnia-Herzegovina) and Afghanistan. He is an equally passionate military historian and has discussed and written about various urban warfare historical case studies, both online and in-person around the world for a majority of his military career. He holds his Masters Degree from the University of New Brunswick, in which his thesis focused on the urban battle of Ortona, Italy (20-27 December 1943) during the Second World War (1939-1945).

Dr. Russell W. Glenn spent sixteen years in the think tank community as a senior defense analyst after retiring from the US Army, later joining the faculty of Strategic and Defence Studies Centre at The Australian National University. His education includes a Bachelor of Science degree from the United States Military Academy and master's degrees from the University of Southern California, Stanford University, and the US Army's School of Advanced Military Studies. He earned his PhD in American history from the University of Kansas. He is the author of over fifty books or book-length reports on urban operations and other security-related topics. His most recent book, *Come Hell or High Fever: Readying the World's Megacities* *for Disaster*, is available for free download at http://doi.org/10.22459/CHHF.2023 or purchasable on Amazon.

Dr. Anthony King is the Chair of War Studies at the University of Warwick, UK. He has published widely on the armed forces. His most recent book, Urban Warfare in the Twenty-First Century, was published by Polity in 2021. A second edition will appear next year. He is currently writing a book on AI and military transformation.

Dr. David Kilcullen is President and CEO of the multinational research and analysis firm Cordillera Applications Group, headquartered in Denver Colorado, with branches in the US, UK, Australia, and Singapore. Cordillera works with defence research and development agencies such as DARPA in the United States, Dstl in the UK, the NATO Science and Technology organisation, and several leading technology companies, along with global banks and agencies of the US and allied governments. David is a theorist and practitioner of irregular and unconventional warfare, with over 25 years of operational experience with the Australian Army, and service with Australia's Office of National Intelligence and with the US State Department. He served in Iraq as senior counterinsurgency advisor to General David Petraeus, then as senior counterterrorism advisor to Secretary of State Condoleezza Rice, deploying to Afghanistan, Pakistan, Somalia, Libya, and Colombia. He is the author of eight books and numerous scholarly papers on terrorism, insurgency, urbanization, advanced military technology, special operations, and future warfare. He was named as one of *Foreign Policy*'s top 100 global thinkers in 2009, and was awarded the 2015 Walkley Award (Australia's equivalent of the Pulitzer Prize) for his war reporting on the rise of Islamic State. He also serves as Professor of International and Political Studies and Head of the Future Operations Research Group at the University of New South Wales, Australia's leading STEM university.

Dr. Jorge Mantilla is a political scientist, who holds PhD in Criminology Law and Justice from UIC Chicago. He has worked as a practitioner and analyst with public agencies and international organizations on topics related to armed conflict, public safety, and drug policy. His current interests are criminal governance, proxy wars, and organized violence.

Dr. Nadav Morag is Professor of Security Studies and Chair of the Department of Security Studies at Sam Houston State University. He is the author of *Comparative Homeland Security: Global Lessons*, Wiley, 2018, and previously served as a Senior Director at Israel's National Security Council, where he developed recommendations for national security policy for the Prime Minister and Cabinet.

Sahr Muhammedally is Senior Faculty Associate at the US Defense Security Cooperation University, Defense Security Cooperation Agency, where she teaches, trains, and advises on civilian protection, urban warfare, and emerging technologies. The views expressed herein are those of the author and do not necessarily reflect the views of the US Department of Defense. Prior to joining the DoD, Sahr was the inaugural MENA regional director at the Center for Civilians in Conflict where she led a team of 45, engaged with governments and militaries on civilian protection, and oversaw research and training with militaries on civilian harm mitigation. Sahr is a Fellow at the 40th Infantry Division Urban Warfare Center and has worked at Human Rights Watch and Human Rights First and practiced law in New York.

Dinesh Napal is a SJD candidate at American University Washington College of Law. His doctoral research seeks to explore the relevance of Hannah Arendt's theorisations on the 'banality of evil' and Michel Foucault's work on thanatopolitics to international law concerning remote weapons. He is particularly interested in the interaction between national security, the proliferation of drone technologies in the military-industrial complex, and power's relationship to legal subjectivity. Mr. Napal received his LLM in Law, Development and Globalisation from SOAS University of London, and his BA in Law and Sociology from the University of Warwick.

Carolina Andrade Quevedo holds a Master's Degree in Political Science, with a concentration in Public Affairs from the Panthéon-Sorbonne University. She has more than twelve years of leadership experience in Public and State Security, as well as Strategic Intelligence. Between 2018-2020, she served as a regional adviser to the United Nations on peace and security, climate action, women in power, and global governance. In this framework, Carolina conducted field research in Africa and the Middle East and accompanied diplomatic negotiations in the Americas. Recently, she acted as a regional advisor for the Climate and Security Program of the Igarapé Institute. Currently, Carolina is Secretary of Security of Quito.

Gordon Pendleton is a former Royal Air Force Officer and is now the Managing Director of Cordillera Applications Group, UK Limited. He led the NATO HQ SACT Urbanization Program from 2013 to 2017 and participated in all the NATO urban and urban littoral wargames. For the NATO MDO in UE 2023 wargame he designed and delivered the wargame scenario and vignettes and was a key member of the modeling and simulation development team. He continues to deliver urban training, capability development and urban wargaming to military and commercial clients.

John Spencer is Chair of Urban Warfare Studies at the Modern War Institute, co-director of MWI's Urban Warfare Project, and host of the Urban Warfare Project Podcast. He served twenty-five years as an infantry soldier, which included two combat tours in Iraq. He is the author of *Connected Soldiers: Life, Leadership, and Social Connections in Modern War,* the author of the *Mini-Manual for the Urban Defender* and co-author of *Understanding Urban Warfare.*

Dr. Jacob Stoil is the Chair of Applied History at West Point Modern War Institute, an Associate Professor of Military History at the US Army School of Advanced Military Studies (SAMS), Senior Fellow of 40th ID Urban Warfare Center, Assistant Director of the Second World War Research Group (North

America), and Trustee of the US Commission on Military History, and a founding member of the International Working Group on Subterranean Warfare. Dr. Stoil received his doctorate in History from the University of Oxford. He holds a BA in War Studies and an MA in History of Warfare from the Department of War Studies at King's College London. Dr. Stoil's doctoral work focused on irregular warfare in the Middle East and Horn of Africa during the Second World War. He regularly publishes award winning articles on topics related to military history, irregular warfare, contemporary warfare, as well as Middle Eastern security and has presented his scholarly work at academic conferences around the world. He has given lectures on military history in universities across three continents including University of Haifa, Johns Hopkins, Cornell, Georgetown, and Oxford. Dr. Stoil's career focuses on developing deep academic expertise and applying rigorous historical research to help inform contemporary operational, strategic, and policy discussions. In addition to his more traditional academic work, Dr. Stoil specializes in applying history to contemporary operational and policy challenges. Dr. Stoil helped to establish the curriculum for the US Army's Urban Warfare Planner's Course. He has served as an expert advisor to a number of US military organizations, units, and commands. Since October 7th, 2023, Dr. Stoil has studied Israel's war against Hamas and worked to help develop and disseminate its lessons to US military and security practitioners.

Dr. Louise Tumchewics is a visiting fellow in the Department of War Studies, King's College London. She is the editor and contributing author of *Small Armies, Big Cities: Rethinking Urban Warfare.*

María Fe Vallejo holds a double major in Political Science and International Relations from Universidad San Francisco de Quito. She has conducted research at the Climate and Security Program at Igarapé Institute. Currently, she is a Research Assistant at FARO, an Ecuadorian research center, in the Democracy, Transparency and Active Citizenship Area.

www.ingramcontent.com/pod-product-compliance
Lightning Source LLC
Chambersburg PA
CBHW052027030426
42337CB00027B/4891